The Academic Library in the United States

The Academic Library in the United States

Historical Perspectives

Edited by MARK L. MCCALLON
and JOHN MARK TUCKER

Foreword by John M. Budd

McFarland & Company, Inc., Publishers
Jefferson, North Carolina

Library of Congress Cataloguing-in-Publication Data

Names: McCallon, Mark L., 1967– editor. | Tucker, John Mark, editor. | Budd, John, 1953– writer of foreword.
Title: The academic library in the United States : historical perspectives / edited by Mark L. McCallon and John Mark Tucker ; foreword by John M. Budd.
Description: Jefferson, North Carolina : McFarland & Company, Inc., Publishers, 2022 | Includes bibliographical references and index.
Identifiers: LCCN 2022017882 | ISBN 9780786495870 (paperback : acid free paper) ∞ ISBN 9781476645704 (ebook)
Subjects: LCSH: Academic libraries—United States—History. | BISAC: LANGUAGE ARTS & DISCIPLINES / Library & Information Science / General | LCGFT: Essays.
Classification: LCC Z675.U5 A347 2022 | DDC 027.70973—dc23/eng/20220521
LC record available at https://lccn.loc.gov/2022017882

British Library cataloguing data are available

ISBN (print) 978-0-7864-9587-0
ISBN (ebook) 978-1-4766-4570-4

© 2022 Mark L. McCallon and John Mark Tucker. All rights reserved

No part of this book may be reproduced or transmitted in any form or by any means, electronic or mechanical, including photocopying or recording, or by any information storage and retrieval system, without permission in writing from the publisher.

Front cover: Cravath Hall, Fisk University, was opened in 1930 and served as the university library until 1969. The interior features floor-to-ceiling frescoes by Aaron Douglas, leading artist of the Harlem Renaissance and founder of the Fisk University Art Department. Architect was Henry Hibbs of Nashville. Named for Fisk co-founder and president Erastus Milo Cravath, the neo-Gothic structure currently serves as the university administration building. Cravath Hall is listed on the National Register of Historic Places as part of the Fisk University Historic District (John Mark Tucker).

Printed in the United States of America

McFarland & Company, Inc., Publishers
Box 611, Jefferson, North Carolina 28640
www.mcfarlandpub.com

To Marsha W. Harper
Who hired Mark L. McCallon into
this great profession

and to

Donald W. Krummel
Who welcomed John Mark Tucker into
the history of books and libraries

The past is never dead. It's not even past.
—William Faulkner
Requiem for a Nun

Table of Contents

Acknowledgments ... ix

Foreword
    John M. Budd ... 1

From the Bequest of John Harvard to the Dream of Alexandria: Historiography of the Academic Library in the United States, 1638–2015
    Mark L. McCallon *and* John Mark Tucker ... 3

Introductory Essays ... 43

The Development of the Academic Library in American Higher Education and the Role of the Academic Librarian
    Beverly P. Lynch ... 45

Perceptions of the Academic Library: Midwestern College Libraries as They Have Been Depicted in College Histories
    John Caldwell ... 60

Book Collections and Classical Training, 1638–1799 ... 69

Books Across the Atlantic
    Eric Glasgow ... 73

Libraries in America to 1850: College Libraries
    Elmer D. Johnson *and* Michael H. Harris ... 78

Liberal Arts Colleges and Professional Education, 1800–1875 ... 81

The American College Library, 1800–1860
    Howard Clayton ... 85

Formation of the University, 1876–1919 ... 99

The Transformation of American Scholarship, 1875–1917
    Arthur E. Bestor, Jr. ... 103

Research Libraries, the Ideology of Reading, and Scholarly Communication, 1876–1900
    Wayne A. Wiegand ... 118

Experimentation and Redefinition, 1920–1945 — 131

Private Dominance in Black Academic Libraries, 1916–1938
   James E. Hooper — 135

Toward a New Cultural Design: The American Council of Learned Societies, the Social Science Research Council, and Libraries in the 1930s
   Kenneth Carpenter — 147

Expansion, Science, and Technology, 1946–1988, Part I — 167

The Influence of Computer Technology on Academic Library Buildings: A Slice of Recent History
   Philip D. Leighton *and* David C. Weber — 171

Diversity and Retrenchment, 1946–1988, Part II — 187

In the Eye of the Storm: Academic Libraries in the Sixties
   Fay M. Blake — 191

ACRL's Fiftieth Anniversary: For Reflection, for Celebration, and for Anticipation
   Edward G. Holley — 201

Digital Expansion, 1989–2015 — 217

Context and Background [on the Transformation of Scholarly Communication]
   Rikk Mulligan — 223

Historiographical Futures — 229

Historiographical Futures for Library History: Conceptual Observations for Future Historians
   Jean-Pierre V.M. Hérubel — 233

Further Reading — 261

The Academic Library in the United States: Selected Historical Readings
   Jean-Pierre V.M. Hérubel, Mark L. McCallon, *and* John Mark Tucker — 263

About the Contributors — 271

Index — 275

Acknowledgments

The privilege of collecting these essays and introducing them stems from our life-long fascination with academic librarianship. We have learned much from personal interaction with hundreds of librarians—thoughtful, highly skilled professionals devoted to serving college and university communities. Foremost among this group are those connected with institutions where we have studied or where we have served as librarians, administrators, faculty, lecturers, or staff. These include Abilene Christian University, Baylor University, LeTourneau University, Lipscomb University, Middle Tennessee State University, Purdue University, Texas Woman's University, University of Hawai'i, University of Illinois, Vanderbilt University, and Wabash College. We are grateful to these institutions, and we admire the individuals who model resourceful and innovative practices and who go to work every day committed to serving the intellectual interests of others. We have likewise benefited from contacts with on-campus collaborators: professors, IT specialists, students, staff, and administrators; colleagues who partner with librarians on behalf of teaching and learning are highly prized.

We are equally thankful for hundreds of other librarians and professors of library and information science with whom we interact at state, regional, and national conferences, at meetings of consortia, at conventions devoted to education and technology, and at colleges and universities. Gathering with colleagues to discuss the purposes and methods of librarianship has become the "bread and butter" of professional development. Though we tend increasingly to do this virtually, rather than face to face, we regard informal communication as something that, for exposure to ideas and expertise, should never be underestimated.

These same scholars write about history and libraries and librarianship, continuing to challenge our preconceptions, and they enlarge our thinking about the nature and the narratives of the library story. We have interacted with many of these individuals at meetings of the Library History Round Table (LHRT) of the American Library Association and the co-sponsored library history seminars conducted every five years. Incidentally, we have both served as chair of the LHRT, a vitally important venue for expanding formal and informal connections. Most of the books, articles, and reviews we have read acknowledge, tacitly or explicitly, the countless hours required for painstaking research in archives and libraries across the country. Those pursuing this task do so with no apparent concern for remuneration but rather out of a deep desire to ensure that the great wide narrative of the library is gathered and preserved, documented and shared, respected and appreciated. It is this complex of motives that we hope to emulate.

We are thankful for McFarland, which shares our enthusiasm for this book, having signed on early in the process of development, and having expressed faith

x   Acknowledgments

in our ability to bring it to a meaningful conclusion. Layla Milholen and her associates at McFarland are the souls of patience, professionalism, and discernment. We are grateful for their commitment to produce a high-quality product, as we hold ourselves accountable for errors and inconsistencies in these pages. We are likewise thankful for our families who waited patiently and inquired gently while we devoted ourselves to immersion in and analysis of the literature of academic librarianship. The gracious support of Beverly McCallon and Barbara Tucker is warmly celebrated. We are likewise indebted to other family members as well as friends and colleagues for their respective roles in sharpening our ideas through inquiry and dialogue. These include: Carisse Berryhill, Jim Bracken, James V. Carmichael, Jr., Evelyn Curry, Donald G. Davis, Jr., Edward A. Goedeken, Mark and Samjung Hamilton, Larry Hardesty, Joe Johnson, Emily R. Mobley, Jack Reese, Jessie Carney Smith, Paavo and Miika Tucker, Joan VanRheenen, Jeanine Varner, John B. Weaver, Andrew B. Wertheimer, John Willis, James Wiser, and to those who have gone before: Evan Ira Farber, Edwin S. Gleaves, Edward G. Holley, David Kaser, Kenneth J. Potts, Gaines B. Stanley, Sr., Tim Tucker, and Dwayne VanRheenen.

—M.L.M. and J.M.T.

Print Credits

Beverly P. Lynch. "Development of the Academic Library in American Higher Education and the Role of the Academic Librarian." Republished with permission of ABC-CLIO, LLC, from *Leadership and Academic Librarians*, edited by Terrence Mech and Gerard B. McCabe, 3–21. Westport, CT: Greenwood Press, 1997; permission conveyed through Copyright Clearance Center, Inc.

John Caldwell. "Perceptions of the Academic Library: Midwestern College Libraries as They Have Been Depicted in College Histories." In *Academic Libraries: Myths and Realities: Proceedings of the Third National Conference of the Association of College and Research Libraries, Seattle, April 4–7, 1984*, edited by Suzanne C. Dodson and Gary L. Menges, 301–07. Chicago, Illinois: Association of College and Research Libraries, 1984.

Eric Glasgow. "Books Across the Atlantic." Republished with permission of Emerald Publishing Limited from *Library Review* 49:3 (2000): 135–38; permission conveyed through Copyright Clearance Center, Inc.

Elmer D. Johnson and Michael H. Harris. "Libraries in America to 1850: College Libraries." In *History of Libraries in the Western World*, 3d. ed, completely revised, 189–92. Metuchen, NJ: Scarecrow Press, 1976. Reproduced with permission of Rowman and Littlefield International Limited through PLSclear.

Howard Clayton. Originally published as the article "The American College Library, 1800–1860." *Journal of Library History* April 3:2 (1968): 120–37. Copyright © by the University of Texas Press. All rights reserved.

Arthur E. Bestor, Jr. "The Transformation of American Scholarship, 1875–1917." Republished with permission of University of Chicago Press—Journals from *Library Quarterly* 23:3 (July 1953): 164–179; permission conveyed through Copyright Clearance Center, Inc.

Wayne A. Wiegand. "Research Libraries, the Ideology of Reading, and Scholarly Communication, 1876–1900." Republished with permission of ABC-CLIO, LLC, from *Libraries and Scholarly Communication in the United States: The Historical Dimension*, edited by Phyllis Dain and John Y. Cole, 71–87. New York: Greenwood Press, 1989; permission conveyed through Copyright Clearance Center, Inc.

James E. Hooper. "Private Dominance in Black Academic Libraries, 1916–1938." In *Untold Stories: Civil Rights, Libraries, and Black Librarianship*, edited by John Mark Tucker, 47–61. Champaign: Graduate School of Library and Information Science, University of Illinois, 1998. Reprint provided courtesy of the Board of Trustees of the University of Illinois through the University of Illinois Urbana–Champaign School of Information Sciences.

Kenneth Carpenter. "Toward a New Cultural Design: The American Council of Learned Societies, the Social Science Research Council, and Libraries in the 1930s." Reprinted from *Institutions of Reading: The Social Life of Libraries in the United States*, edited by Thomas Augst and Kenneth Carpenter, 283–309. Copyright © 2007 by the University of Massachusetts Press.

Philip D. Leighton and David C. Weber. "The Influence of Computer Technology on Academic Library Buildings: A Slice of Recent History." In *Academic Librarianship, Past, Present, and Future: A Festschrift in Honor of David Kaser*, edited by John Richardson, Jr., and Jinnie Y. Davis, 13–30. Englewood, CO: Libraries Unlimited, 1989.

Fay M. Blake. "In the Eye of the Storm: Academic Libraries in the Sixties." Republished with permission of ABC-CLIO, LLC. In *Activism in American Librarianship, 1962–1973*, edited by Mary Lee Bundy and Frederick J. Stielow, 61–72. Westport, CT: Greenwood Press, 1987; permission conveyed through Copyright Clearance Center, Inc.

Edward G. Holley. "ACRL's Fiftieth Anniversary: For Reflection, for Celebration, and for Anticipation." *College & Research Libraries* 50:1 (January 1989): 11–24.

Rikk Mulligan. "Context and Background [on the Transformation of Scholarly Communication]." In "Issue on the Transformation of Scholarly Communications," edited by M. Sue Baughman. *Research Library Issues: A Report from ARL, CNI, and SPARC*, no. 287 (2015): 2–6. https://doi.org/10.29242/rli.287.2. http://publications.arl.org/rli287/2-6. Creative Commons Attribution 4.0 license: https://creativecommons.org/licenses/by/4.0/.

Jean-Pierre V.M. Hérubel. "Historiographical Futures for Library History: Conceptual Observations for Future Historians." History of Librarianship (Lyon, France 25–26 August 2014). International Federation of Library Associations and Institutions. Université de Lyon, ENNSIB.

Foreword

John M. Budd

I feel compelled to begin with George Santayana's maxim, stated in 1905: "Those who cannot remember the past are condemned to repeat it." These words certainly apply to academic librarians, but they apply equally forcefully to colleagues in all colleges and universities. Arguments are frequently made that the present is so different from the past, and that we must concentrate on progress, that the past is not so relevant. This sentiment could not be more erroneous; human nature and human action are components of phenomena that do not change nearly so rapidly. The workings of colleges and universities, and their libraries, depend for success upon a clear understanding of what has gone before. For one thing, mistakes regarding organization, management, service, and other activities have histories that all should be aware of going forward in time. All this is a preface to the realization that we sorely need the collection that Mark L. McCallon and John Mark Tucker have compiled. Perhaps more importantly, we need the introductory essay that these editors have written. It provides an excellent introduction to the essays included and it is, in itself, an extremely astute summary of the importance of a knowledge and an application of that knowledge in contemporary academic librarianship.

McCallon and Tucker state early in their introduction, "The relative paucity of historical scholarship about the academic library is, we believe, a matter of grave concern, contributing in a major way to professional myopia, a failure to grasp the large conceptual issues of our high calling and a failure to facilitate wide dialogue about the meaning and value of what we do." This both sets the tone for the introduction and offers a promise of the critique that is to come. [N.B.: I use the word "critique" deliberately here; the introduction presents a clear analysis of the state of historical scholarship from the early years of publishing to the present.] The data they present about publication on historical topics are genuinely informing and are cause for concern. I can attest that, when I was teaching, I began every course with a portrait of the past, not merely to depict how things have changed, but to instill in students what we can learn from those who came before us. Of course, a historical picture necessarily has the errors that may have been made in the past, but it also portrays the innovation and creativity that have gone before. Students can be asked to examine the past so as to compel the awareness of those innovations and creative actions that have been vital components of our history. This may be the most valuable contribution of the McCallon and Tucker volume; they clearly comprehend and depict what can be learned from the accomplishments of the past, drawing from the masters of historical research.

2 Foreword

This volume offers works by some of the luminaries in the field of the history of academic libraries and librarianship. To name just a few of the scholars, essays are included by Beverly P. Lynch, Michael H. Harris, Arthur E. Bestor, Jr., Wayne A. Wiegand, David C. Weber, Fay M. Blake, Edward G. Holley, and Jean-Pierre V.M. Hérubel. The essays are arranged, by and large, chronologically, so that the reader can comprehend the zeitgeist of the times in which the libraries existed. Moreover, the essays demonstrate the place of libraries within their parent colleges and universities and in higher education at large. I must end with a paean: this collection is long overdue, is blessed by the addition of a thorough and critical introduction and represents some of the best historical work of the past many decades. All academic librarians—and most charged with administering colleges and universities—should read and discuss the contents of this volume. Yes, it is that valuable.

From the Bequest of John Harvard to the Dream of Alexandria

Historiography of the Academic Library in the United States, 1638–2015

MARK L. MCCALLON
and JOHN MARK TUCKER

This book arose out of our concern over the lack of scholarship on the history of college and university libraries. We came to this topic having examined the literature and compared the volume of historical publications about academic libraries with that of other types of libraries. The Davis-Tucker bibliography on American library history, for example, identifies 750 entries for the academic library and 1,443 for the public library and its predecessors.[1] Edward A. Goedeken of Iowa State University further confirmed the trend identified by Davis and Tucker when he examined the topics of seminars sponsored by the Library History Round Table (LHRT) of the American Library Association (ALA). Goedeken reported that only three of 129 papers in the first nine seminars (1961–1995) treated academic libraries, although other contributions may have mentioned pertinent content (for example, papers on print culture, reading, or women in librarianship that might have incorporated significant information on academic libraries).[2] The relative paucity of historical scholarship about the academic library is, we believe, a matter of grave concern, contributing in a major way to professional myopia, a failure to grasp the large conceptual issues of our high calling and a failure to facilitate wide dialogue about the meaning and value of what we do.

Our profession, for the most part, has been overtaken by a narrow, short-range perspective. Librarians of the twenty-first century are quite effective at early adoption of educational and technological innovation, and our service commitments match or exceed those of other helping professions. We are marked by numerous other excellent qualities including commitments to intellectual freedom, a deep appreciation for ethnic and lifestyle diversity and inclusion, the intellectual dexterity that embraces multiple styles of teaching and learning, the creativity to reenvision physical space, and the ability to design and develop digital repositories and to curate massive amounts of data—to name recurring examples. These and other achievements and attributes make ours an attractive undertaking, fueling our capacity to engage in the information-intensive tasks of modern society.

But our purpose in this collection is to address what seems to us a glaring weakness.

4   Historiography of the Academic Library

We are concerned about the librarian's distinct disadvantage at the task of interacting with members of the academy, specifically with professors, administrators, and other specialists on our home campuses. Graduates of library and information science (LIS) programs begin careers ill-equipped to engage colleagues in the large dialogue about college and university mission and culture, continuing advances in teaching and learning, or the task of defining the library's role in campus intellectual and operational affairs. We do not propose to know all the reasons for this circumstance, but we have come to regard the absence of a strong historical consciousness as a vital contributing factor. We raise this issue out of our deep, lifelong devotion to academic librarianship, a profession in which we have invested more than seventy-five years combined of professional labor, and in which we continue to practice, read, study, and write.

Of the academy specifically, Edward G. Holley (1927–2010), who served as Dean of Libraries at the University of Houston and of the School of Information and Library Science at the University of North Carolina at Chapel Hill, noted that "widespread ignorance about the nature of colleges and universities—their history, mission, and politics [including presumably academic libraries], often leads to counterproductive action."[3] Holley's assertion, while itself a definitional concern, symbolizes larger issues. The limitations of the librarian's perspective reflect the limitations of the larger academic environment and, indeed, of the great wide national ethos of contemporary culture. Writing in *The History Manifesto*, David Armitage (Harvard University) and Jo Guldi (Brown University) claim that the entire society has been plagued by a paucity of long-term thinking. The phrase they adopt—in the language of a syndrome or even a disease—is "short-termism," the notion that what has come to matter most in the public arena or even in academe is a model, a theory of what is likely to happen in the future based on projections of human behavior under specific circumstances. In an admittedly simplified, abbreviated manner, we suggest that social science disciplines tend to conduct research with the intent of anticipating the future constructed on such projections.

Alternatively, the study of history, both as a discipline and as a methodology, offers the long-term perspective, the opportunity for fact and analysis and synthesis to provide the "guide of life" envisioned by Cicero, the ancient Roman philosopher and rhetorician. Historians commit to approaching the future on the basis of things that actually occurred in real time and space rather than on the basis of an experimental design or a theoretical projection. And the urgent pathology of short-termism cries out for remedial action, a cogent, well-considered response from the community of trained historians. Universities (accompanied by religious institutions and, we might add, research libraries) are remarkably durable. Universities are positioned to offer remedies as the "carriers of traditions, the guardians of deep knowledge ... [as locations] where research takes place without regard to profit or immediate application ... [with the capacity] to ponder long-term questions using long-term resources."[4] The university has cultivated a longitudinal ethos, one with the resilience to endure and to create and to preserve the human narrative across time periods, political borders, and cultural frontiers. As Armitage and Guldi observe, the "average half-life of a twentieth-century business corporation" is seventy-five years; universities, by comparison, date from the eleventh century and, in North America, the eighteenth and nineteenth centuries.[5]

Much more than we realize, our understanding of the past shapes how we think about the future, and even as the humanities—history included—are declining in the academy, historians receive and process the past, and explain the traditions that define who we are as a people and what attributes are instructive as we face the challenges that lie ahead. To remedy the marginalization of history, Armitage and Guldi propose to enlarge the task of historians, moving us beyond the confines of academe and into the arena of a "public future," developing a deeply researched narrative at the same time cultivating public support with brief, popularized accounts—a sort of "bridge" form of writing that expands the readership for historical findings, claiming their relevance as richly informative to contemporary problems. Armitage and Guldi endorse the ideology of historian and archivist J. Franklin Jameson (1859–1937) who argued that history should not be the preserve of an academic guild alone but rather it is something that belongs to everyone, an inheritance that is rightly passed from generation to generation throughout society and the nation.[6]

Our goal is similar in one important way. We seek to enlarge the conversation about the academic library beyond immediately professional circles, promoting the library as an essential resource in academe, and arguing that it is not the preserve of the librarian alone but rather of the whole campus. Our dream is that every university constituency becomes invested in the life and health of the library. We thus target a specialized readership, not the general reader necessarily (though with vocabulary readily accessible to the general reader) but the core constituents of the academy: professors, administrators, colleagues, students, alumni, development officers and, in fact, any other stakeholder.

Too often, the librarian's on-campus clientele evidences both a minimal understanding of and a limited expectation about what librarians do, thus thwarting the library's potential to impact the educational enterprise. The development of a professional historical consciousness is, we propose, one vitally important competence that should equip us to participate in dialogue on the social, political, and intellectual significance of the academic library. Such capacity embraces knowledge of the history of higher education and the history of individual libraries, also larger syntheses of libraries collectively and over selected periods. It would include individual and collective biography. Librarians should also be acquainted with the history and development of knowledge within and among disciplines, and understand how disciplines function internally, and how they might interact when brought together for interdisciplinary work or among resources in a library setting.[7] These perspectives should enliven collaborative efforts between librarians and the campus communities we serve.

Our hope for librarians is that we emerge fully engaged and completely unfettered in our work as academics, able to contribute in meaningful ways to our home institutions. The librarian's task may be viewed, in the language of Pierce Butler (1884–1953), as either "the administration of a sacred trust" or the "correct supervision of a routine procedure."[8] Unfortunately, our own accumulated personal, research, and vicarious experience suggests that our colleagues in the academy too frequently perceive it as the latter. In seeking to address this concern, we have gathered these essays. As we discuss in further detail, scholars have often called for a one-volume history of the academic library. And, indeed, we have two important monographs—by Arthur Hamlin (1913–99) and Lee Shiflett (1947–2016) whose works are now four decades old—to help us inculcate historical perspectives. While not prepared to write a book for a new generation in the vein of Hamlin or Shiflett, we offer rather a sourcebook, a group of readings, a guide for an academic readership. We have sought to provide an essential building block both for the interested contemporary reader and for the future scholar who will write the history of the academic library in the United States.

Synthesizing Life Itself

Knowing the traditions and history of librarianship has been a high priority for some of the most influential leaders in our profession. Pierce Butler was one of the earliest of the modern era to address this concern. In 1933 he wrote that the librarian without a "clear historical consciousness" is "quite certain to serve his [or her] community badly."[9] He thus suggested for librarianship the classic argument that those unfamiliar with history are condemned to repeat mistakes of the past. This is the practical point of view, not the only one to be made on behalf of the "historical perspective" but perhaps, for a profession devoted to the urgent demands of high-quality service, the most insistently important. Trained as a theologian, Butler directed the John M. Wing Foundation on the History of Printing at the Newberry Library, and he transformed it into a major collection with international distinction. He later taught at the University of Chicago, in his day the nation's leading school of librarianship and habitat of the profession's first doctoral program. And Butler's well-respected classic, *Introduction to Library Science* (published by the University of Chicago Press in 1933 and reprinted in 1961, 1967, and 1992) stands as one of the most durable theoretical statements about the mission and purpose of the library. Butler had cast a wide net methodologically, and he embraced the social sciences as well as the humanities, but his statement on history paved the way for later scholars whose own contributions would constitute foundational studies, further facilitate synthesis and interpretation, and make compelling arguments for the historical method.

Military historian Stanley Pargellis (1898–1968) directed the Newberry Library (though not contemporaneously with Butler's tenure), and he complained sardonically of the librarian's focus on the temporary. In 1948 he described the library world as busily discussing an "often trivial agenda in terms of the fleeting present only, occasionally with a pious hope for the future, but seldom with any sense of the past from which both present and future spring. Creatures of a day we deliberately allow ourselves to be, like those butterflies whose whole span of existence is compressed into the hours between sunup and sunset."[10]

Few library leaders have spoken more persuasively on behalf of historical study than Jesse Hauk Shera (1903–1982). Writing in 1952, Shera complained that the librarians' rush to apply social scientific methods to contemporary problems resulted in "means [having] been mistaken for ends, techniques [having] been employed without thought of their appropriateness, results [that] have been hastily interpreted, and the historical method that [has] been all but trampled underfoot"; Shera contended that the "writing of history is one of the oldest major forms of human literary activity, if not the oldest. This very fact of survival for so many centuries is in itself eloquent testimony of its social importance."[11] Shera's emphasis, not coincidentally, may be taken broadly enough to incorporate history written for the millions, thus intoning J. Franklin Jameson's argument for history as a matter of public interest, a common good. While the library community's social science methods have improved in the more than sixty years since Shera voiced his alarm, his concern about the role of history in library science research was most prescient. Researchers in librarianship have come to marginalize historical methods even though, as Shera observed, history has demonstrated amazing durability across cultures and over much of the human experience. Still, Shera's caution has proven prophetic in the face of our profession's growing expertise in social science research.

Shera was a brilliant interdisciplinary scholar and leader. He was a doctoral graduate of the University of Chicago GLS (Graduate Library School), who served in various capacities at Miami University, the Library of Congress, the United States Office of Strategic Services, and Case Western Reserve University where he was dean of the library school. His groundbreaking study, *Foundations of the Public Library: The Origins of the Public Library Movement in New England 1629–1855*, was published by the University of Chicago Press in 1949 and stood for decades as a model interpretation for neophytes and experienced historians alike. But Shera ranged far beyond the methods of the historian's craft; he was an innovator in the application of electronic methods of storing and retrieving information. He was instrumental in founding the American Documentation Institute, organizational ancestor of the American Society for Information Science. He also established the Center for Documentation and Communications Research on his home campus, a repository of social science data to serve the practical and research interests of librarianship, higher education, industry, business, and government.

Cognate to these activities, Shera urged that history not be neglected, and he posited three reasons for librarianship's indifference to historical methods. The first of these was the maturation and success of the social sciences in general with their vast capacity to isolate, investigate, and analyze social phenomena thus transforming disciplines such as economics, education, political science, psychology, and sociology and, as a byproduct, undermining the stature and presumed value of history especially as a method for research in librarianship. The second reason is that the social sciences, which identify multiple factors, may seem at first instance (by their nature) to overwhelm or even deny the predictive power of history. And the third reason, he believed, was embedded in contemporary practices of historians themselves who too often yielded to the temptation to follow unduly a simple restatement of fact, evidencing deep affection for detail with minimal regard for the significance or meaning of the narratives they had created.[12] Although historians have long since moved into wider and more complex terrain with regard both to theory and subject matter, Shera's admonition has remained relevant both for his own era and for many of us who came after him.

Throughout his career, Jesse Shera continued to honor and to promote the historical method. In 1972 he wrote in *The Foundations of Education for Librarianship* that an understanding of the library as a "social agency" and the roles it has undertaken should be sought in the "theories of the functions of the library in society" and in "analysis of the historical development of the library and the roles the library has assumed during the centuries of its existence."[13] Four years later, in *Introduction to Library Science*, he urged readers to remember the "humanistic values that for so many centuries shaped the library, gave it a sense of direction, and built the great collections that we know today."[14] Both books feature lengthy sections of historical narrative describing earliest occasions of writing and collecting to the present, citing the role of the library in materials conservation, self-education, the promotion of reading, the information needs of research, and the origins of information services. The opening chapter of *Introduction to Library Science* is something of a classic, tracing the library story from Egyptian temples to the work of the Council on Library Resources (now Council on Library and Information Resources) in the 1970s. And four years before his death, Shera joined George S. Bobinski and Bohdan S. Wynar in compiling the *Dictionary of American Library Biography* "dedicated to the idea that the history of librarianship is important to the profession. [The] historical study of library leaders and their accomplishments makes it possible to gain a proper historical perspective and to interpret and appreciate the profession's present resources and ... origins."[15]

Since its inception in 1952, *Library Trends*, a quarterly journal issued by the Graduate School of Library and Information Science (now School of Information Sciences) at the University of Illinois at Urbana-Champaign, has published contributed essays organized thematically by issue. The quarterlies devoted to research in librarianship appear at intervals of several years, and typically include the contribution of a scholar who has regarded historical methods as important tools in understanding our profession. Collectively, the *Library Trends* articles provide a convenient snapshot (though hardly the only such source) of evolving ideas on the function and purpose of library historical narratives. In 1957 in "Research in Backgrounds in Librarianship" Haynes McMullen (1915–2005) wrote the first of these, reviewing contemporary scholarship on the philosophy of librarianship and the comparatively more popular topics of the history of libraries and biographies of librarians. Identifying key sources from Germany, the United Kingdom, and the United States, he described a small but rising tide of books, theses, and articles. McMullen's research agenda called for large synthesizing studies that, in the future, would reflect fully the cultural and social environment of their institutions.[16] Like Shera, McMullen was a product of the University of Chicago doctoral program. His work reflected careful inquiry, precise reasoning, and close editing, and he influenced generations of students at Indiana University and the University of North Carolina at Chapel Hill. His own major contributions stand well the test of time: *Libraries in American Periodicals before 1876: A Bibliography with Abstracts and an Index*, with Larry J. Barr and Steven G. Leach (Jefferson, North Carolina: McFarland, 1983) and *American Libraries before 1876* (Westport, Connecticut: Greenwood Press, 2000). McMullen collected information for both books over a period of many years, and his influence has been extended through the Davies Project at Princeton University which maintains a web accessible database with supporting statistics on the topic of American libraries before 1876.

The *Library Trends* research volume published in 1964 featured "Historical Research and Library Science" by Felix Reichmann (1899–1987). He suggested that, twelve years after Shera's warning in *Library Quarterly*, a certain cynicism, some of it healthy and some of it less so, had taken hold in library history. Reichmann quoted Mark Twain to the effect that "history is the best investment; one gets a wholesale return of conjecture out of a small number of facts."[17] Reichmann chronicled a few factual errors made by historians and then took a decidedly interdisciplinary approach illustrating how historians rely on the findings of other disciplines and, in turn, cited history's impact on law, medicine, and other professions. He wrote that the historian collects "primary data with care and precision. The vestiges of the past must be examined and authenticated and classified by systematic methods and scrupulously weighed. All the techniques of modern science as far as applicable are put to the use of the historian."[18]

Reichmann offered a counterbalance to the utilitarian view, that one must know history to avoid repeating mistakes of the past. He noted that many historians took pains not to overemphasize the utilitarian view, and adopted instead an approach of more inherent value, one that chronicled the growth of our understanding. The proper objectives of the historian's craft would be intellectual maturity and individual and collective fulfillment, springing from an increasingly nuanced grasp of historical developments and transitions. Reichmann also noted American ambivalence toward historical matters, observing a common misgiving about history that it amounts to a dry, unengaging recitation of dates and events. Ironically, he added, Americans also like to identify pioneers, honor their achievements, and thus cultivate optimism and hope in the face of an uncertain future. Reichmann elaborated the idea that history and librarianship must embrace habits of the heart as well as the head, that one must be motivated by the artistic as well as the scientific if one seeks to construct a compelling narrative (or to engage in the challenging professional task of building a scrupulously designed library collection). He quoted Shera's classic essay to the effect that "library history is the concern of every librarian, for history is not an esoteric or special branch of knowledge but a synthesis of life itself."[19]

Reichmann served for many years as assistant director of the Cornell University libraries, and he brought to the task of collection development a rich international perspective. He had earned a doctorate in Art History at the University of Vienna and was pursuing work as an antiquarian book dealer. He had been mentored by publishers and booksellers in the great cities of Europe including Florence, Frankfurt, London, Paris, and Vienna. Following Germany's invasion of Austria, he was imprisoned at Dachau and Buchenwald until an aggressive campaign secured his release in 1939. He migrated to the United States where he studied under Douglas Waples and completed a library science degree at the University of Chicago. In 1947 Stephen McCarthy recruited Reichmann to Cornell to oversee collection building during postwar expansion, and he remained in that capacity until 1970.

The next *Library Trends* issue devoted to research topics appeared in 1976, the year commonly regarded as the centenary for professional librarianship. The dramatic events of 1876 had featured the establishment of the American Library Association and the appearance of major publications: Melvil Dewey's classification scheme, the inaugural issue of *Library Journal*, and the massive government report, *Public Libraries in the United States of America, Their History, Condition, & Management*, which collectively constituted the beginnings of a professional literature. Parenthetically, the government report—1358 oversized pages in three volumes—featured several retrospective accounts, thus affording wider and deeper perspectives than would have been available with a volume devoted exclusively to contemporary practice. Another signal event from 1876 changed forever the trajectory of higher education: The Johns Hopkins University was established expressly to promote graduate research and learning, representing a movement that made original research an ultimate priority for the university. A natural byproduct of this new research ethos became the urgent need to redefine the college library, transforming it into a powerful, active instrument supporting faculty inquiry and the creation of new knowledge, accompanied by fresh levels of professional consciousness about library practice. The organizational features of the new library professionalism, combined with the redefinition of higher education, made 1876 a landmark year, and yielded—one hundred years later—a "cottage industry," a strategic outpouring of books and essays recounting the major events, trends, institutions, and people of a transformational age. A memorable contribution to this literature was the *Library Trends* issue of July 1976, a special issue on "American Library History: 1876–1976."

For this collection, John Calvin Colson (1926–2007) penned the essay, "The Writing of American Library History, 1876–1976." He wrote that history was neither a "humanity" nor a social science but rather a way of studying something by analyzing its record. He proposed that history could borrow from the methods and practices of both the humanities and the social sciences but that, in effect, it transcended both. It could emerge as its own way of knowing. In this manner, history holds the capacity to liberate, to open opportunities to expand one's understanding of any subject. Colson adopted Fritz Stern's definition that history "springs from a live concern, deals with life, serves life."[20] Historians search not only for patterns but also deviations from patterns; the historian could enlarge the vision of scholars of many disciplines, taking us beyond "a discipline, profession, or institution" into uncharted terrain, and making new connections among disciplines, providing fresh ideas and, in effect, breathing life into the whole project of intellectual inquiry.[21]

Colson challenged the thinking that seemed to him implicit in courses offered by graduate library schools, that history held secondary status, that it was employed to inculcate an ethos of professionalism, convincing students of the wisdom of their choice of librarianship—his concern was that history was being expected to serve these limited, programmatic functions rather than to realize its full potential as intellectual engagement. He worried over the practical ideology of history as essential to administrative success, and he expressed concern that the "didacticism of such beliefs … created an intellectual attitude about the values of history that makes it easy for the certitudes of social science to prevail."[22] Despite notes of caution, he expressed optimism about the progress of doctoral study in graduate library schools. He examined 140 dissertations in preparing his essay, finding that sixty-six treated the history of libraries and librarianship in the United States and concluding that regular academic departments of history were, comparatively, hardly as productive as the graduate library schools which, he asserted, "accounted for nearly all the significant histories of American libraries and librarianship."[23]

Colson held a master's and a doctorate from the University of Chicago GLS; he worked at the Milwaukee Public Library and the State Historical Society of Wisconsin. He also taught in several library schools including Northern Illinois University and the University of Maryland; and he consulted for several organizations including the Environmental Sciences Service Administration, the National Education Association, the U.S. Civil Service Commission, and the U.S. Superintendent of Documents.

In 1979 Phyllis Dain (1929–2018) and Margaret Stieg (1942–2022) edited the *Library Trends* issue on *Libraries and Society: Research and Thought*, challenging contributors to address their ideas and personal experiences in the context of a search for theory. They wrote that the "changing technology and the different theories of library management and operations seem to be largely the history of the adaptation of ideas and techniques first developed for nonlibrary uses."[24] They established the tone for their collection in appealing to the interdisciplinary and multiple points of view acknowledged by no less a literary giant than Samuel Johnson (1709–1784). They quoted W. Jackson Bate's biography of Johnson, inserting the great author's own comments.

> Difference of opinion is inevitable simply because so many different considerations have to be taken into account, and that "as a question becomes more complicated and involved, and extends to a greater number of relations, disagreement of opinion will always be multiplied, not because we are irrational but because we are finite beings, furnished with different kinds of knowledge, exerting different degrees of attention, one discovering consequences which escape another, none taking in the whole concatenation of causes and effects … each comparing … with a different criterion, and each referring it to a different purpose."[25]

Dain and Stieg thus solicited a wide range of views, in effect concurring with Colson that complex, multifaceted research—precisely the sort of research that marks the joy and unpredictability and messiness of the historian's craft—could enliven the whole of intellectual inquiry. Dain and Stieg had served together as professors in the Columbia University School of Library Service, Stieg (later Margaret Stieg Dalton) having also taught at the University of Alabama. Although Columbia's School of Library Service closed in 1992, it was the nation's oldest (having begun when Melvil Dewey began instruction in 1887), educating thousands of library professionals. Dain and Stieg, thus, have mentored numerous practitioners and scholars, influencing the profession for decades to come.

In 1984 *Library Trends*, returning to the topic of research, published an article by Lee Shiflett (1947–2016) on the role of history in library and information science. By the early 1980s, schools of library science had begun enlarging curricula, transitioning into disciplines that incorporated information science. But in introducing her collection, Mary Jo Lynch preferred not to use the phrase "library and information science" but rather a term she considered more comprehensive, "librarianship," a clear effort to acknowledge multiple influences including information science among other social sciences such as economics, education, psychology, and sociology. She sought to strike a unifying chord, acknowledging both variations and similarities in the ideas and terminology of the professional literature.[26]

Shiflett described history as more effective than most research methods at incorporating findings and interpretations from a variety of disciplinary sources. He argued that techniques commonly in use, such as experimental designs and survey research, possess historical features that require exploration if a topic is to be thoroughly examined. He classified history not as a discipline but rather as a methodology, and he argued that it possesses the rare capacity to consider a topic from any number of perspectives, an approach simply not available among the social science projects of isolated factors and controlled variables. The downside of history was that its open-ended nature and its accommodation of multiple variables made it appear, especially to outsiders, to lack intellectual rigor. He claimed that history could never expect to be the dominant model for LIS research, describing a rift between those favoring the social sciences and those favoring history. In the end, he charged both camps with focusing unduly on methodology to the neglect of the importance of conclusions and outcomes.[27]

Shiflett held a master's and a doctorate from Florida State University. He gained academic library experience in various capacities at the University of Wisconsin at La Crosse before moving into library education as a professor at Louisiana State University and, later, as chair of the Library and Information Studies Department at the University of North Carolina at Greensboro. Shiflett produced two of the more significant monographs in academic librarianship, *Origins of American Academic Librarianship* (1981) and *Louis Shores: Defining Educational Librarianship* (1996). In *Origins*, he analyzed the context for the librarian's on-campus status and contributions to higher education during the period of the dramatic growth and redefinition of the American university and the transformation of the college library into the research university library. In *Louis Shores*, he examined the life and career of one of our profession's most idiosyncratic minds, an important college librarian, library educator, and founder of the *Journal of Library History*.[28]

The next major *Library Trends* declaration favoring the historical enterprise appeared in 2004 in an issue on "Pioneers in Library and Information Science." W. Boyd Rayward, editor for this special issue, has provided one of the more cogent and compelling arguments on behalf of historical studies. He sees in history a dialectic, a back-and-forth conversation that probes the past, seeing things anew and then revising our points of view in light of fresh insight, perspectives gained from both current and historical events. Rayward writes that

> we are nothing without a past.... Not only how we think but what we think and when we are able to think it depend to some degree on historical circumstance. Each time we seek from historians an account of something important to us as a group—a profession, the lay public, a cadre of scholars—the past changes because of what the group as consumers of history, and historians as its producers, bring to it and seek from it. What is brought to it are different frames of references and knowledge of the current status of the cumulating record of earlier historical studies. These [references and knowledge] help determine what will be recognized now as important both as historical evidence and as explanation.[29]

Rayward thus describes history as continual dialogue and revision, with the present interrogating the past and the past informing the present, and both influencing how people interpret events. History thus emerges as a lively, dynamic, and never-ending process; Rayward confirms Lee Shiflett's claim, that history is open-ended and flexible enough to examine and critique numerous topics and interrelationships.

The Rise and Fall of Academic Library History in the United States

The core of the literature of academic library history, in particular that portion of it devoted to more than one library, resides in no more than a dozen major monographs. These works, providing historical synthesis by examining several colleges and universities, appear only after disturbingly long intervals. Nineteen years elapsed between the contributions of Louis Shores and Kenneth J. Brough (1934 to 1953), ten years between those of Brough and J. Periam Danton (1953 to 1963), and another eight between those of Danton and Thomas Harding (1971). Although several monographs appeared in the late 1970s and early 80s, nothing major has appeared since Ralph Wagner's history of the Farmington Plan (2002).[30] When thorough accounts do appear, they sometimes address current topics and policy proposals in ways that overshadow the more lasting concerns of historiography.

Historians, moreover, have yet to write the compelling one-volume narrative introducing readers to the academic library in much the same way that Frederick Rudolph has introduced generations of readers to American higher education.[31] We see the need for a Rudolph-like work, a synthesis gracefully integrating the library and the university with the larger contexts of social, economic, educational, and political forces. In the absence of this kind of monograph, we offer these essays as a starting point, a sourcebook for students and professors interested in library origins and traditions as well as the wider environment that frames present-day library-related conversation. We also seek to introduce librarians to the wisdom inherent in good historical writing, and thus to encourage those of us confronting multiple challenges in workplaces marked by ambiguity, rapid change, and overlapping technologies. We view our collection as a reader's companion, a guide for raising historical consciousness, perhaps to foster fresh interest in both the small stories and the large narrative of our profession. It has become possible to assemble this book from a steady, if narrow, stream of historical literature that includes an occasional monograph but, much more frequently, journal articles, conference proceedings, and essays in collected works. From this stream, we chose sources that are durable, representative, or especially insightful and that were issued in the years from the mid-twentieth century into the twenty-first.

The relative paucity of academic library history has long been acknowledged by scholars evaluating the literature. Michael H. Harris called attention to this concern in 1972, noting that "most of the substantive histories of American academic libraries were written by graduate students pursuing degrees. Unfortunately, unlike dissertations [about other] areas of librarianship, these dissertations rarely find their way into print."[32] Harris struck a chord that has reverberated through succeeding decades, and the limited output on this topic emerged as a recurring theme. Harris and Donald G. Davis, Jr., together repeated this concern in 1974 and 1976. They wrote of the period, 1974–1975, that academic library history was "both less extensive and of less consequence" than that for public libraries.[33]

By the mid–1970s the appearance of a review essay on key historical publications had become routine, and readers of the *Journal of Library History* (*JLH*) grew to anticipate consistent overviews. These reviews have not appeared precisely on schedule but, even when occasionally late, they were always "in the works" and have continued to inform, evaluate, and guide. Soon after his appointment as *JLH* editor, Donald G. Davis, Jr., reviewed the publications issued in 1976, noting that uncommonly strong historical consciousness had yielded unprecedented retrospective scholarship in honor of the Centennial. Davis complimented *Libraries for Teaching, Libraries for Research: Essays for a Century*, edited by Richard D. Johnson who had invited seasoned scholars, initially publishing their contributions, along with several others, in *College & Research Libraries*.[34] The Johnson collection featured notables such as Edward G. Holley (University of North Carolina) on the state of the library in 1876, Helen W. Tuttle (Princeton University) on technical services, Connie R. Dunlap (Duke University) on library organizational patterns, Robert B. Downs (University of Illinois) on the role of the librarian, Robert Vosper (UCLA) on international relations, and David Kaser (Indiana University) on library literature. Both the original journal essays and the selected reprints featured black and white drawings, portraits, and photographs, enlivening the retelling of our stories during the formative years of the research library. Though the occasion was celebratory, the scholarship that resulted was richly analytical rather than merely honorific—it was well-researched and well-written, examining challenges, key events, and persistent issues against the backdrop of institutional and professional cultures.

And yet the volume and quality of scholarship appearing in 1976 proved to be the exception rather than the rule. If scholarly output since 1976 is indicative, we may be forced to wait until the year 2076 for enthusiasm equivalent to that of our centennial year. While academic librarians were fully onboard with the ALA Centennial, of which *Libraries for Teaching, Libraries for Research* remains a shining example, we have not been able to marshal much historical interest in the years since, even as anniversary opportunities have come and gone. Academic librarians, for example, assembled in Cincinnati to honor the 100th anniversary of the founding of the American Library Association's College Library Section, organizational predecessor of the Association of College and Research Libraries (ACRL). Conference planners had solicited presentations with the theme "Building on the First Century" and, though several presenters mentioned the past as a building block, few presented historical papers. Of seventy-seven presentations, categorized as twenty-one research papers and fifty-six position papers, only six seem to us authentically historical. These were Greg Anderson (Georgia) on the Library of Congress MARC records, Sallie H. Barringer (Trinity in San Antonio) on budget allocations, Barbra Buckner Higginbotham (Brooklyn College) on preservation, Donald G. Davis, Jr. (Texas) and John Mark Tucker (Purdue) on historiography, Gemma DeVinney (SUNY at Buffalo) and Mary L. Reichel (Arizona) on faculty status, and Anne F. Roberts (SUNY at Albany) on enduring values amidst technological change.[35]

Another opportunity presented itself at the seventy-fifth anniversary of ACRL. A committee, co-chaired by Nancy Allen and Betsy Wilson, solicited three of our most talented bloggers on the current academic library scene who then provided twenty incisive statements scanning the environment and projecting fresh ways to think about the future. The resulting publication appeared in 2015 as *New Roles for the Road Ahead: Essays Commissioned for ACRL's 75th Anniversary* by Steven Bell, Lorcan Dempsey, and Barbara Fister. Provocative and challenging, this brief tome is well worth the attention of those who care about our profession, but what strikes us as historians is the absence of historical interpretation in a publication occasioned by a historically significant moment. Nancy Allen described the work of the ACRL 75th Anniversary Task Force Commissioned Report Working Group as seeking to "recognize the outstanding history" of the ACRL, and to "honor the impact of our association on the lives of librarians and the legacy of libraries in academic and research settings." Ironically, the Working Group then pursued these goals with a publication that focused "on the future [only], not on the past,"[36] making a reference to history but failing to incorporate it as an analytical tool or a source for contextualized insight.

Returning to the literature reviews, Wayne A. Wiegand prepared six of them for *JLH* and its successor, *Libraries & Culture*. In 1979 he wrote that "the history of academic libraries continues to receive scant attention from the profession."[37] In successive articles he did not revise this assessment even while citing new publications. In 1992 Joanne Passet succeeded Wiegand as literature reviewer and did not mention the paucity of academic topics, but rather a decline in the number of overall entries from the previous essay—from 171 to 156.[38] Edward A. Goedeken wrote the reviews following Passet, and he continues to the present in *Information & Culture: A Journal of History*, successor to *Libraries & the Cultural Record*, itself earlier renamed from *Libraries & Culture*. In 2000 Goedeken confirmed the dismay already expressed, that relatively few academic topics had appeared in previous years. Goedeken also issued a call for someone to write the definitive book length history of academic librarianship, and he repeated both concerns in 2002, 2004, 2009, 2013 and 2018.[39]

Goedeken's observation—that the entire *corpus* of historical scholarship on academic libraries is significantly smaller than for other types of libraries—concurs with our own assessment and, naturally, we are compelled to ask why. Not expecting a definitive answer, we hope simply to advance the conversation. Kenneth E. Carpenter, for thirty-five years a librarian at Harvard, suggests that potential historians are dissuaded from pursuing the academic library as a subject because they attach little value to a seemingly inevitable outcome. Historians of the public library, by comparison, may explore the large themes of democracy, an informed citizenry, or the freedom to read.[40] More troubling is James V. Carmichael, Jr.'s claim that the library profession harbors an absence of concern, but also a lack of knowledge of history and biography and their capacity to inform (from a theoretical perspective) especially given the ready availability of methods seemingly more pertinent to current practice or, at least, to short-term marketability.[41] Joanne Passet addressed the culture in which LIS scholars operate, that history is among the most time consuming of research methods and that some scholars must respond to the pressure to conduct other types of research that presumably yield more tangible, discernibly immediate results.[42] Carmichael and Passet, each writing within a year of the other, thus warned about trends that have been accelerating since the 1970s, that the grant supported social sciences increasingly displace the humanities among LIS faculty, and thus the optimism expressed by John Colson as recently as 1976 has not been sustainable. The inevitable result of these trends is the decline of historical methods in LIS research and publication. Lee Shiflett reported that historical methods accounted for 33.2% of library science dissertations from 1925 to 1972 and for only 15.6% from 1973 to 1981.[43] Five years later, Carmichael indicated, this figure stood at 13%, and studies of the literature from 2001 to 2010 indicate a continuing decline in history to the extent that its frequency barely registers among a list of sixteen research strategies.[44] Fewer students and fewer professors (than in the 1950s, 60s, and 70s) conduct historical research in pursuit of the origins and meaning of librarianship and its purpose in culture and society. Incoming students in graduate library schools express minimal interest in history, and few curricular options are available to them given that professors from earlier generations, who were skilled in historical methods, have now entered retirement.

Sharon G. Weiner hypothesized a circumstance known as "transparency" in which an entity, taken for granted and not well understood, is relatively invisible. This, she posits, is precisely the position of the academic library, a dilemma confirmed by the fact that professional historians have produced little scholarship about university libraries. Using different vocabulary, Lee Shiflett had been saying the same thing; he traced the marginalized status of the library to managerial assumptions in higher education, noting that librarians have won top positions for their ability to manage large masses of information rather than for their stature as scholars in librarianship.[45] Thus administrative and professorial perceptions of the library as an academic department influence negatively its potential as a subject for scholarly inquiry. If we accept these assertions, we would concur that, at best, academic library history occupies a place on the periphery, a position that mirrors, though differently from one university to another, the position of the library on its home campus.

Writing History from the Inside Out and the Outside In

Sharon Weiner makes a telling point about who writes the histories of the college and university library.

> The contexts and institutional structures of libraries are for the most part explored only in the library literature by librarian-historians. It is a disturbing indicator of the relative invisibility of libraries in higher education that there are few articles or books about them in the literature of that discipline. Their role in acquiring and producing knowledge within intellectual, institutional, and social contexts needs to be developed with a research base and disseminated in the literature of disciplines that are related to and affected by them.[46]

Weiner claims that academic library history in general is produced by the "librarian-historian." We verified the accuracy of this statement and, while she suggested what this means for the library historian, we decided to add some analysis of our own.

Presumably, librarian-historians have come to their subjects, in part, because they have served as practicing librarians. Extending this notion further, the librarian-historian is both—practicing librarian and practicing historian—and the implication is that such scholars, while skilled at creating historical narrative, are also library insiders. They (or, in our cases, we) produce a narrative qualitatively different, bearing a distinctly different tone with differing parameters and perspectives, from the author acculturated only as a professional historian. By different we mean that the librarian-historian tends to employ a vocabulary and tell a story premised on professional values and practices not uniformly understood or readily appreciated by a wide readership. The extent to which this assessment is accurate is also the extent to which library historical literature retains characteristics of insularity. Ironically, the relative strength of an insular literature indicates something quite favorable, a high degree of professional development. On the other hand, an insular literature is inherently less accessible to the general professoriate and the educated reader than literature written by someone on the outside looking in. So presumably the library narrative written by a professional historian (one who teaches and researches history for a living) would use a vocabulary with fewer references to library professional terminology and with descriptive language more readily appreciated beyond a library professional audience.

Weiner's assertion is easily enough confirmed in that the core monographic literature has been produced by individuals with experience as academic librarians. Leading authors, whose works we consider, and the libraries they served are Louis Shores (Fisk University, Peabody College [since merged into Vanderbilt University]), Kenneth J. Brough (Eastern New Mexico, Stanford, San Francisco State), J. Periam Danton (Colby College, Temple University, Williams College), Thomas S. Harding (University of Evansville, Missouri Valley College, Northwestern, Washburn), Jessie Carney Smith (Fisk), Charles Osburn (Alabama, Cincinnati, North Carolina, Northwestern, SUNY at Buffalo), O. Lee Shiflett (Wisconsin at La Crosse), Arthur T. Hamlin (Cincinnati, Columbia, Harvard, Pennsylvania, Temple), Wayne A. Wiegand (Urbana College in Ohio), Neil A. Radford (University of Sydney), Roland C. Person (Southern Illinois), Stephen E. Atkins (Illinois, Iowa, Texas A & M), David Kaser (Ball State, Cornell, Vanderbilt, Washington University in St. Louis), and Ralph D. Wagner (Eureka College, Northern Illinois, Western Illinois, Westfield State University). Some of these scholars did not remain in library practice throughout their careers but rather transitioned full-time into professional library education: Shores at Peabody and Florida State; Danton at California; Shiflett at LSU and North Carolina at Greensboro; Wiegand at Kentucky, Wisconsin, and Florida State; and Kaser at Indiana. Shores, Brough, and Person had earned doctorates in education; Danton, Smith, Osburn, Shiflett, Radford, Kaser, and Wagner in LIS; and Harding, Wiegand, and Atkins in history. Hamlin did not hold a doctorate.

We are more concerned about Weiner's statement which seems to imply that little or no research base exists for these monographs written by the librarian-historian, and that such a research base exists within a discipline related to and affected by the library. We confess that we could misrepresent her observation or misunderstand it, but it seems to us like she views history (to take an example we have chosen, or some other discipline impacted by the library) as offering theoretical constructs essential for solid historical work on academic libraries in ways, perhaps, that the discipline of LIS cannot. History does, indeed, offer much interpretive potential, but some argue that history alone is inadequate absent meaningful interaction with other disciplines and habits of knowing.

While library historiography may seem insular due to its dependence on those who have served as librarians, the practice of librarianship itself is far from insular—it is rooted deeply in interdisciplinary ideas and modes of operating, and the stories that make up the large library narrative must be based in meaningful connections between history and other disciplines. The field of history is open-ended enough to accommodate and make effective use of theory, data, and results from any number of disciplines. History may be regarded as a humanistic or a social scientific subject depending on institutional settings, faculty expertise, and related factors, although Shiflett saw history as a methodology rather than a discipline. Though not especially concurring with this perspective, we find Shiflett's explanatory comments filled with insight. He wrote that "each of the subjects under investigation by survey research, case study, experimental design or other methods have historical aspects that need to be thoroughly understood ... for a topic to be completely researched."[47] Shiflett urged that these other methods, commonly used in LIS, should be contextualized historically. Thus, a richly informative library historiography is one that integrates content from multiple disciplines and research perspectives (where appropriate, within the parameters of a topic), and we regard the librarian-historian, no less than the non-librarian historian, as fully capable of this sort of intellectual labor.

As library practice is interdisciplinary and as history is open-ended, so also LIS bears the marks of both. It is interdisciplinary and open-ended, and the historical narratives that would prove most fruitful for conceptual development would be rich with interdisciplinarity. That LIS presents an open-ended project is confirmed by Anne Buchanan and J.-P. Hérubel. After distinguishing professional practice from the discipline of LIS, they write of the latter that it uses various domains of knowledge "from economics, management, computer science, and sociology to education and other humanities and social sciences," and that "it can be intrinsically open and receptive to continual importation of ideas, perspectives, and techniques."[48] They believe in the fluidity of LIS, specifically its inherent capacity to integrate research and theory from a variety of intellectual threads. They thus confirm, from a broad perspective, the validity of Wayne Wiegand's proposal of the field of American Studies as potentially fruitful for LIS. He has endorsed historical approaches that incorporate concepts of the "library as space" and the "history of reading," both topics that have been evolving and informing scholarship about civic space, intellectual tastes, and cultural studies.[49] It is noteworthy that Wiegand has long promoted a library historical scholarship richly informed by the broad intellectual and social forces impacting American cultural life.

Returning to the observations of Sharon Weiner, she might assume that writing by the librarian-historian lacks intellectual rigor, an implication that, however valid, may apply equally to history written by the professional historian or research conducted by social scientists. Her claim that, for the most part, the librarian-historian writes academic library history does, indeed, bear the ring of truth. If our analysis is on target, this distinction applies more to the character and the vocabulary of the narrative than to the quality of historical research, writing, or interpretation. The task of LIS remains the same; it requires continuous effort at theory creation regardless of progress or lack thereof both when writing from within and when importing ideas from beyond LIS.[50] At the end of the day, the successful historian must craft a readable tale, an intellectually rigorous narrative that integrates ideas from various disciplines—where appropriate—whether written from the perspective of a librarian-historian or a historian of some other stripe.

Early Dissertations and Their Authors

In examining the literature, we begin with *Origins of the American College Library 1636–1800* (1934) by Louis Shores (1904–1981) who thus launched a method of inquiry frequently emulated. He revised *Origins* from his dissertation, written at George Peabody College for Teachers, where he was directing the library and the school of library science. He constructed generalizations by examining a selected core of colleges with similar characteristics, taking note of common values and practices as well as important differences. He had visited Brown, Columbia, Dartmouth, Harvard, Pennsylvania, Princeton, Rutgers, William and Mary, and Yale, reading college publications, minutes of meetings, letters, and memoranda, and placing his account in the collegiate practices of the Colonial Era.[51] Before his Peabody sojourn, the peripatetic Shores had attended the University of Chicago where he studied under educational psychologist Douglas Waples. Shores was thus exposed to concepts that were remapping librarianship into a social service informed by rigorous research, although his own contributions would tend toward humanistic study or popularized reporting. Though the significance of *Origins* had less to do with findings than with methodology, it was acknowledged by Harry Clemons (University of Virginia) and Louis Round Wilson (Chicago, North Carolina) as solid scholarship and a foundational source in the history of the library profession.[52] Similarly Benjamin Powell (1905–1981), studying at the University of Chicago, analyzed "The Development of Libraries in Southern State Universities to 1920," an examination of Alabama, Georgia, LSU, Mississippi, North and South Carolina, Tennessee, and Virginia (1946). Powell compared these schools with the state universities of California, Illinois, Michigan, Minnesota, and Wisconsin. He noted that in 1860 the Southern schools held an average of twice as many books as the comparators (not counting Illinois and California, established in 1867 and 1868 respectively). By 1920 the library holdings of state universities outside the South were an average of eight times larger than their Southern counterparts, the chaos of Civil War, Reconstruction, and poverty having taken their toll.[53]

Kenneth Brough's dissertation at Stanford resulted in a monograph issued by the University of Illinois, *Scholar's Workshop: Evolving Conceptions of Library Service* (1953), a study of Columbia, Harvard, the University of Chicago, and Yale from 1876 to 1946. Brough examined the rhetoric of practice, evaluating the words, phrases, and ideas that administrators, professors, and librarians had employed to describe the transformation of the liberal arts college library into the university research library. Well-written and conceptually strong, *Scholar's Workshop* continues to inform academic library historiography. When Yale historian Jaroslav Pelikan asserted that "it would be possible to write the history of university scholarship on the basis of the history of libraries," he chose *Scholar's Workshop* as primary evidence.[54]

Following Shores and Brough, several scholars analyzed carefully selected groups of institutions and produced fresh insight, perspectives on how the academic library came to be—its purposes, values, practices, campus settings, and persistent challenges. One influential example is that of Joe Kraus whose dissertation at Illinois featured studies of collection development at Brown, Harvard, Princeton, William and Mary, and Yale. He excerpted his findings for *Library Quarterly*.[55]

The rising tide of American higher education in the 1950s and '60s brought within its wake unprecedented growth in graduate library education and, subsequently, in dissertations on academic libraries. The principal factor in judging library excellence was the size of printed collections, and even those scholars examining other phases of librarianship seldom strayed far from collection size as a defining characteristic. Although doctoral students adopted a wide range of methodologies, the dominant historical model tended to involve a selected group of colleges with key characteristics in common. Jessie Carney Smith, for example, analyzed library growth patterns for the period, 1870–1960. She compared the major state universities of Illinois, Indiana, Iowa, and Michigan with land-grant universities Ohio State, Purdue, Iowa State, and Michigan State, concluding that expanded curricula in science and technology did not result in expanding library resources.[56] Richard E. Miller, Jr., examined the evolution of reference services at Amherst, Bowdoin, Carleton, Mount Holyoke, Smith, Trinity (Connecticut), and Williams. He found that the reserved book system favored by the professoriate undermined the emergence of reference work but that a closed stack arrangement tended to stimulate growth in organized reference services. Miller posited that earliest iterations of reference were not reference services as we know them but rather instruction in library organization, bibliographical tools, and other reference sources.[57] Michael Waldo examined the libraries of colleges and literary societies on twelve Midwestern campuses. He compared subject coverage, publication dates, and other variables, finding that the scope of the college library was broader and the currency of its collection more contemporary than previously thought. He claimed that earlier scholarship tended to highlight differences between the two types of libraries while undervaluing similarities.[58] J. Michael Rothacker analyzed the growth of collections in non–Western studies (defined broadly in the 1960s and 70s as publications from Africa, Asia, Eastern Europe, and Latin America) collections at three liberal arts colleges in the state of Indiana: Earlham, Marian, and Wabash.[59] Willie Hardin examined growth patterns in five black land-grant colleges—Alcorn State University, Arkansas at Pine Bluff, Prairie View A&M in Texas, Southern University in Louisiana, and Tennessee State University. Hardin considered a range of factors including federal funding, enrollment, and civil rights activism, concluding that the emergence of graduate programs was the most effective stimulant for library growth and support.[60] Additional examples include Robert Brundin on junior colleges in California. He examined Fullerton Junior College, Long Beach City College, Los Angeles City College, Modesto Junior College, and Pasadena City College, covering a sixty-year period. Norma N. Yueh studied six New Jersey state colleges that had evolved from normal schools and, more recently, Ramirose Attebury and Michael Kroth examined libraries at teacher training colleges from the 1890s to the 1970s.[61]

Ernst Erickson investigated the historical significance of a popular assessment tool in the mid-twentieth century, the library survey, analyzing twelve universities that had conducted them in the period 1938 to 1952.[62] He concluded that surveys stimulated positive change and raised library consciousness among on-campus stakeholders. John Boll studied nineteenth century library architecture. He focused on Amherst, Brown, Harvard, Mount Holyoke, Wesleyan, Williams, and Yale, finding that, in the era prior to the rise of the research university, the overriding principle of contemporary planners was to protect resources and facilities, only secondarily providing services, instruction, or ease of access.[63]

The appeal of a core of selected institutions as a structure for historical inquiry has continued into present day scholarship. Noteworthy essays following this model include

Lowell Simpson on literary society libraries at Columbia, Dartmouth, Princeton, and Yale from 1783 to 1830. William Olbrich, Jr., discussed nine historically black college libraries in Texas; Michael Stuart Freeman studied library cooperation at Bryn Mawr, Haverford, and Swarthmore; and Marjorie Hassen examined the development of music libraries at Chicago, Cornell, Indiana, North Carolina, and Vassar.[64]

The Heroic Ideal in Research Librarianship

In the latter half of the twentieth century, more book length studies appeared, complementing the kind of work modeled by Louis Shores and his academic progeny. J. Periam Danton (1908–2002) addressed contemporary policy in a narrative deeply grounded in historical context. Danton compared book selection and collection growth in Germany and the U.S.A., having traced the birth of the modern university to forces impacting Göttingen as early as the 1730s. By the end of the nineteenth century, the first generation of American university scholars had drawn deeply from German ideas about universality, and graduate seminar instruction and the seminar library had been imported enthusiastically from Germany. At the same time, new disciplines and professional societies were emerging and the pursuit of knowledge was becoming equivalent to undergraduate education, surpassing it on many campuses as a motivating impulse.[65] Especially where graduate research was the defining characteristic, as at Johns Hopkins and the University of Chicago (founded in 1892), the seminar library (known in some circles as the subject departmental library) became the primary venue for collection growth. In Germany the seminar libraries retained much independence, and their subject specialties, dependent on faculty input, grew richer and deeper. In the U.S.A., the seminar libraries were less independent operationally but enjoyed greater overall growth through collaboration with librarian selectors and robust central administrations. Throughout his extended argument, laced with practical knowledge and a nuanced grasp of academic culture, Danton clarified the meaning of the library for the academy and for society at large, and historians of this genre have rarely matched his combination of historical perspective, erudition, and lofty purpose.

Danton proposed, on behalf of post-war generations, the motivating ideal for the research university library

> more than any other institution whatsoever, [as] the custodian of the world's actual knowledge and the reservoir of its potential knowledge. More than any other institution it preserves and makes available the results of previous human thinking; more than any other institution it makes possible the fruitful continuation of that search.[66]

Danton thus promoted the concept of completeness in building collections, and he claimed that the library, responding to the creation of new knowledge, should be open ended—a finite limit should never be placed on its ultimate size.[67] Edward G. Holley recalled that the University of Illinois Libraries, deeply committed to the interests of the future researcher, was attempting to be as comprehensive as possible, not throwing anything away, keeping things "no matter how esoteric or apparently valueless."[68] Robert Vosper (1914–1994), also with an eye to the future, argued that the robust ambitions of university research libraries embrace "an omnibus intellectual style that hardly exists" outside the U.S.A. and Canada.[69] This statement, many years removed, reflects the view of one who had directed libraries at Kansas and UCLA. Vosper wrote that outside observers often take note of the number of American universities whose research libraries have achieved distinction in the relatively brief time of about one hundred years. He cited, as examples, California at Berkeley, Cornell, Illinois, Indiana, Michigan, Minnesota, UCLA, and Wisconsin. More specifically, he added:

> Berkeley's East Asiatic Library is one of the greatest of its kind in the world. The collections of original works in the history of science at Wisconsin and Cornell are exceeded no doubt by those at Harvard but hardly matched elsewhere. Perhaps nowhere else, not even in Great Britain, would a scholar find in one place so rich a Milton collection as at Illinois or so extensive a collection of nineteenth century English fiction as at UCLA. Indiana's Lilly Library, Berkeley's Bancroft, Michigan's Clements, and UCLA's Clark are all in their fields of concentration, probably *non pariel*.[70]

Vosper apparently intoned a version of American exceptionalism, a not uncommon perspective for one whose life was forged in the Great Depression and World War II. But the lesson of history is not to view our topic through an ethnocentric lens or to over emphasize persistent issues in administration and technology, it is rather to consider the power of the motivating ideal—that the university research library virtually alone among cultural institutions seeks to preserve and disseminate the great wide and deep narrative of humankind. Danton thus redirected historical dialogue about the library, confirming our sense of high calling. Although economic constraints have limited the library's range of possibility, the ideal itself continues to exhibit remarkable power and resilience.

Breon Mitchell, formerly director of the Lilly Library at Indiana University, confirmed Danton's vision in longitudinal terms.

> [The] concept of looking backward needs to be redefined, at least on an institutional level, to incorporate works whose impact remains unproven, especially when the mission of these institutions is charged with gathering materials that will be of historical and cultural significance generations from now.[71]

To redefine looking backward is a task of sweeping proportions, and an elite band of libraries continues to pursue the holy grail of the creation and preservation of knowledge in all its forms, even as this task requires that librarians pursue resources of unproven value. Mitchell also anticipated collecting digital media, as he recalled his conversations with leading authors.

> "We have many authors now who say to me, 'You want my papers, does that mean you want the disks also?' Or 'You want my electronic files? You want my emails?' Right now, I'm saying yes, send us your disks, copy out your emails, send them by attachment, whatever. That's the correspondence we have, and we have to figure out how to preserve it ..."[72]

Visionaries like Mitchell, along with Danton and Vosper from an earlier generation, have earned for their universities international distinction by building collections as an act of faith, committing themselves to unbounded growth. They reflect the ethos of their age, convinced of the social necessity of assembling the richest and deepest collections that time and resources and circumstances allow.

Historically, the high-water mark of the heroic ideal in the print culture era may have been the Farmington Plan, a powerful expression of faith in the nation's ability to accomplish great things in the decades immediately following World War II. Research librarians pursued unfettered growth with a program of acquisition that committed the participants to obtain at least one copy of every book published anywhere in the world that might be of interest to American researchers. This project attracted support from the likes of the American Council of Learned Societies, the American Library Association, the Council on Library Resources, the Carnegie Corporation, and the Rockefeller Foundation. The Farmington Plan was more than a matter of post-war hubris; it began as if its initial goals were genuinely achievable, and it marshaled the tools of international cooperation and resource sharing. The materials thus acquired would serve the participant group and, indeed, an entire nation of scholars and scientists.

The large context that made this idea seem viable was that the U.S.A. had emerged from World War II with new responsibilities as an international power. And the nation thus allocated unprecedented financial support for education amidst a combination of Cold War tension and renewed interest in area studies and international affairs, impacting not only education but business and government at multiple levels. The Farmington Plan, despite problems of coordination and implementation, brought many previously unavailable resources within the range of American researchers, further underscoring the library's desire to serve the interests of rapidly expanding scholarly and scientific communities.[73]

Modern leaders who have promoted concepts of unbounded growth intone, of course, the voice of ages past. One rather illustrious forerunner, sometimes overlooked due, perhaps, to an occasionally contentious relationship with his colleagues, was John Langdon Sibley (1804–1885) who served Harvard University in various capacities, directing the library from 1856 to 1877. As the U.S.A. descended into Civil War, Sibley took note of an armed Confederacy and its role in shaping the course of American history. Presciently, he sought to gather the documents and artifacts that would preserve the stories of the war for future generations. In July 1861 he wrote that

> one of the greatest favors to the future historian and philosopher would be to collect all the books, pamphlets, maps, files, newspapers, engravings, photographs, caricatures, ephemeral publications of every kind, even in printed notices, circulars, handbills, posters, letter envelopes, and place them beyond the reach of destruction, that as a collection they may reflect the sentiments and feelings, which otherwise will in a great measure pass into oblivion with the occasions which gave them birth. If I could, I would appeal to every inhabitant of the continent to send me everything which could be obtained in order that every phase of mind, in every section of the country, North, South, East, West, for the Union and against the Union, for secession and against secession, might be represented on our shelves, in all the variety of reasoning and imagination, virtue and vice, justice and injustice, fiction and fact, freedom and oppression, kindness and cruelty, that can be found. I would say, send me collections, if possible; but, if not, send to me a single pamphlet, book, or picture …[74]

Sibley's appeal, an early argument for unbounded growth, promoted the research library as collector of every kind of publication or related artifact as a matter of obligation to future generations. Sibley thus anticipated the rise of the graduate research library as an essential partner in expanding original research and nurturing emerging disciplines in the great transformational task the university would later assume as discoverer, creator, preserver, and disseminator of knowledge.

Words About Vocabulary

The vocabulary of higher education as it applies both to parent institutions and to libraries is often confusing, making it difficult for stakeholders to keep track of the central and unique role of the academic library. We use the terms "college" and "university" interchangeably with "academic" and, less frequently, have given them equivalent value for stylistic purposes. It is instructive to acknowledge the work of academic authorities seeking definitional clarity. As early as 1921 James I. Wyer, Jr. (1869–1955, New York State Library, University of Nebraska) differentiated the terms in his brief classic, *The College and University Library*. He indicated that the "college library" should serve undergraduates. The "university library" should support graduate and professional programs, and he promoted these terms as an effective way to think about libraries serving academe. He also noted the easy mutability of terms, reflecting the fluid state of parent institutions, and he proposed separate libraries for undergraduates.[75] Wyer wrote at precisely the moment when the broad outlines of higher education had solidified, when the modern research university had become uniquely positioned to begin providing cultural and scientific leadership.

By 1976 Jean Key Gates in her classic, *Introduction to Librarianship*, had offered, among numerous other interpretations, a centennial appraisal of college and university terminology. She confirmed the influence of German higher education and its impact on institutional structure and accreditation practice, also noting the American expressions of that influence. To be designated a "university," she said, an institution would organize into two or more professional schools or faculties and it would offer multiple degrees at the graduate level.[76] While such structure may have described a common pattern, many observers, including academics, may be forgiven for seeming confused by a "university" with 2,000 students—though it might be primarily a teaching institution organized into two colleges—or a "college" which may enroll 20,000 students. Institutions by both designations, moreover, display an infinite variety of the relative strengths of research and teaching, graduate and undergraduate curricula. Several writers have subsequently spoken to the complexities of graduate and undergraduate classifications and their impact on library terminology and structure.[77]

While the US federal government has not specified a preferred terminology, the regional accrediting agencies have impacted terminology in the context of evaluating program offerings. It is well to remember that, historically, "college" was the dominant term, rooted in English antecedents, but that "university" has begun to prevail in the contemporary environment of competition and marketability. Our purpose here is not to explore fully the dilemmas of vocabulary but simply to acknowledge their existence, and to provide entrée into writers who address the topic.

The Enduring Dream of the Liberal Arts

In 1971, eight years after Danton's *Book Selection and Collections*, Thomas S. Harding issued his massive *College Literary Societies*, analyzing the origins and development of a foundational predecessor of the modern research library. Harding studied the libraries operated by literary societies in colleges in sections of the nation where they had developed significantly, in the Northeast, South, and West (the region of the Old Northwest, now regarded as the Midwest), for the period 1815–1876. He described literary societies as focusing on student debates and other modes of expression that necessitated access to current materials, and thus building library facilities better equipped and collections richer with contemporary publications than their college counterparts.

The college libraries of this period relied primarily on gift collections and part-time or retired faculty for staffing while the societies charged membership fees, purchased contemporary books and journals, and staffed facilities with student employees. Harding's thesis confirmed the dominant paradigm and remained unchallenged, with respect to the intellectual contents of libraries, until Michael Waldo's dissertation in 1985. Even with careful analysis on Waldo's part, the weight of historical opinion remains with Thomas Harding. Further research is surely warranted, raising questions about the availability of documentary evidence, and it may be possible that present-day programs to digitize institutional records will facilitate further inquiry.

Harding found that the vitality of the literary societies could not be sustained through the final quarter of the nineteenth century. The societies had flourished when they served as the principal extracurricular venue for undergraduates but, by the 1880s, student options had begun to expand. And although the societies rose and fell at different times by region, students eventually left them in favor of music and theater, fraternities and sororities, and intramural and intercollegiate sports. Meanwhile the rapidly growing elective system rendered the societies less important intellectually, in effect, co-opting their pedagogical features into the regular curriculum. Simultaneously, the college libraries grew at unprecedented rates, responding to seminar teaching and graduate research, reinvigorated humanities and science disciplines, and the increasingly specialized social sciences. A rising generation of full-time library directors focused increasingly on helping students locate and use resources strategically. As the college library transitioned into the university research library, it absorbed the society library—a change occurring over several decades and that was largely completed by the 1920s.

Studying the literary society library, Harding considered schools that would later emerge as distinctly different types of institutions, the college that would become the major research university and the college that would remain committed primarily to liberal arts for undergraduates throughout the twentieth century. Among research universities he examined Brown, Cornell, Dartmouth, Harvard, Pennsylvania, Rutgers, Syracuse, and Yale. Beyond the Northeast, he studied Georgia, North and South Carolina, and Wake Forest, also Miami University, Ohio University, Michigan, Western Reserve (now Case Western), Wisconsin, and Oregon. Among liberal arts colleges, he studied Amherst, Colby, Davidson, Dickinson, Earlham, Hamilton, Illinois College, Knox, Muhlenberg, Oberlin, Randolph-Macon, Trinity (North Carolina), and Wabash.[78]

Another type of smaller institution, also benchmarked with quantitative data, was that of historically black colleges and universities (HBCUs). In 1977 Jessie Carney Smith examined the history, condition, and prospects for eighty-nine such schools in *Black Academic Libraries and Research Collections*. She told a story of instability: colleges arose, sometimes merged, sometimes did not survive, or were unable to maintain a dominant black presence. As they matured, a few emphasized graduate and professional education but most focused on arts and sciences and pre-professional curricula for undergraduates. Smith laid some important markers, noting that twenty institutions were founded before 1900, seventeen of those twenty were private, and that private colleges tended to fare better financially than public colleges. She identified libraries that had received Carnegie construction grants: Alabama A & M, Atlanta (now Clark Atlanta), Cheyney, Fisk, Howard, Knoxville College, Tuskegee, and Wilberforce. She also identified those libraries with significant black studies resources including manuscript collections: Atlanta, Dillard, Fisk, Hampton, Howard, Lincoln in Pennsylvania, Texas Southern, and Tuskegee.[79]

Not surprisingly, Smith found that black academic libraries had not been able to support the educational programs of the schools they served. She reviewed the training programs for professional librarians, establishing claims for their continuation and urging new funds to help the libraries achieve higher levels of relevance and functionality with better prepared staff. Several such interrelated programs, with a series of internships as a founding component, were active in the 1970s, '80s, and early '90s but have not been continued.[80] In Smith's historical overview, she observed that most of the HBCUs were in the Southeast, and that they had been established to provide education for blacks in a rigidly segregated society, where stronger libraries in white colleges were offering no hope for black access. Smith concluded that even though many of the HBCUs were products of nineteenth-century philanthropic efforts, their libraries, even those begun simultaneously with the birth of parent institutions, were essentially products of the twentieth century.

Scholarly Communication, Library History, and Philanthropy

In 1979 Charles Osburn issued *Academic and Research Libraries*, an overview of national educational policy, trends in disciplinary and interdisciplinary research, and their impact on the aims and practices of collection development in university libraries. Though occasionally addressing the pre–1940s, he concentrated on the period 1940–1975, years of unprecedented expansion during and following World War II. He provided rich context, a macro-level view of what some regard as the golden years of academic librarianship. In fact, Osburn described collection development in the 1950s as "proceeding with great, unharnessed energy."[81] He explored disciplinary transitions, tracing the incremental development of humanities research, the more expansive growth in the social sciences, and the dramatic explosion of research in science and technology. He distinguished the spirit of inquiry and experimentation of the sciences and social sciences from the authority and tradition of the humanities, and he analyzed the remarkable growth in publishing, especially in scholarly and scientific journals. He examined the shift from faculty book selection to librarian selection and the library's internal transition from acquisitions to collection development, featuring the rise of the chief bibliographer accompanied by a corps of subject specialists.

Osburn outlined the role of the U.S. federal government in research and development (R. & D.) as it impacted university priorities. He showed that, even though research expanded at a greater pace than library collections, it succeeded in stimulating library growth in unprecedented ways, and that the research libraries continued to grow until the economic contractions of the late 1960s and early 1970s. Especially illuminating, among Osburn's many tabular reports, was one that identified U.S. Federal R. & D. commitments compared to library collection holdings and expenditures. At a glance we can see a short list of institutions that have emerged as premier research universities with robust patterns of library acquisition: California at Berkeley, California at San Diego, Chicago, Columbia, Cornell, Harvard, Illinois, Johns Hopkins, MIT, Michigan, Minnesota, Penn State, Stanford, UCLA, University of Southern California, Washington, Washington in St. Louis, and Yale.[82] Osburn acknowledged the meaning and value of Danton's appeal for unbounded growth while favoring principles of selectivity given the harsh economic realities of his era.[83] Due to his deep knowledge of the interwoven roles of federal support, the publishing industry, disciplinary trends, and the university cultures of faculty labor and library collection growth, Osburn matches Danton for having produced a durable, nuanced, well-researched, broadly conceived interpretation.

By any definition, 1981 was an unusual year. It featured two one-volume histories of the academic library, each as vastly different from the other as it was improbable that they appeared almost simultaneously. In *The University Library in the United States*, Arthur T. Hamlin divided his narrative into two sections, a chronology of five chapters tracing Colonial origins to post–World War II expansion. A second section, "aspects" of librarianship, treated differing facets of practice: collection development, leadership and governance, finance, services, buildings, departmental libraries, cooperation, classification and cataloging, and technology. With a cogent, readable text, Hamlin sought an audience of non-library academics as well as neophyte librarians, and in the chronology section he largely succeeded.

Although in introductory remarks he decried library jargon, Hamlin organized the second section, the bulk of his narrative, around terms and concepts best understood by library practitioners. He produced the ultimate insider's story, using professional language, based on his career in six major research libraries—by any measure a rare personal achievement. But while *The University Library* represented the insightful views of a seasoned "pro," it also demonstrated the weaknesses of a narrative constructed from the inside out. With Hamlin's contribution as one piece of evidence, Sharon Weiner could logically conclude that the history of the academic library was often the product of the librarian-historian. Fortunately, Hamlin had given the reader qualifiers; he claimed no intent to provide the one-volume definitive history but rather a personalized account, one that wove into his narrative the details of personal experience.[84] So the reader is presented with an amalgamation of research and memoir at once both savvy and idiosyncratic.

In *Origins of American Academic Librarianship*, Lee Shiflett produced a much different book, one that addressed not the whole of research librarianship but one central defining facet—that of the role and status of the practicing librarian. He focused on the formative period in American academic libraries, 1876–1920. These years encompassed the confluence of the forces that established librarianship as a profession and higher education as an agency for specialized research. The rise of the university ideal did not displace undergraduate education but rather overwhelmed it as an encompassing, motivating force, thus transforming the labor of the professoriate from an emphasis on broad training for civic life into a focus on tightly defined but original inquiry resulting in peer-evaluated publication.

Preparation for such work became the Ph.D., the scientific and scholarly rite of passage, essential for entrée into academic life. But Shiflett discerned, in this circumstance, a serious disconnect for the academic librarian—that formal preparation did not involve the doctorate as a union card but rather the MLS or its equivalent, which had deep roots in public library standardization and practice as promoted initially by the nation's founding library educator, Melvil Dewey. Moreover, the higher-level scholarly curriculum needed for academic librarianship had failed to obtain the support sufficient to evolve into a full program of study—from rudimentary elements in Europe and America—even after formal library education had transitioned from the urban public library into the university in the 1920s and 30s. While academic librarians sought to create a place for themselves in the academy, one that was rooted in faculty partnerships and in expertise in research and user instruction, they did so at great disadvantage, without the tools of socialization, acculturation, and vocabulary possessed by holders of the earned doctorate. Thus, in the early and middle years of the twentieth century, librarians functioned *de facto* at an intellectual disadvantage. This problem would find partial remediation in the fresh opportunities offered by information science (sometimes incorporated into education for librarianship), or computer sciences, or in the new curricular options that provided, in a single integrated program, two masters' degrees, one in librarianship and one in another discipline (for example archival studies, education, history, literature, management, music, or theology). By the latter part of the twentieth century, many library leaders held, in addition to a master's degree in LIS, a Ph.D. in LIS or in a discipline commonly regarded as among the humanities or social sciences. Thus, several newly minted practitioners had accumulated both professional and disciplinary expertise, the acculturative and rhetorical tools necessary to secure a place in the academy.

Shiflett revised his book from his doctoral dissertation written in the School of Library Science (now School of Library and Information Studies) at Florida State. The final product is a thoughtful synthesis, and we concur that Shiflett aptly pinpointed the sources of present-day ambivalence about the position of the librarian in academe. When grouped with his later contributions, this work marks Shiflett as perhaps the premier authority on the history of American academic librarianship.[85]

Two years after Hamlin and Shiflett, Wayne A. Wiegand issued *Leaders in American Academic Librarianship: 1925–1975* (Pittsburgh, Pennsylvania: Beta Phi Mu, 1983), though not a monograph, in the sense of a continuously written narrative, *Leaders* is a collection of biographical essays based on interviews, correspondence, and other primary sources. The idea was the brainchild of Richard Dougherty, formerly director of libraries at California and Michigan, founding editor of *Journal of Academic Librarianship* and later co-editor of *Library Issues: Briefings for Faculty and Administrators*. An advisory board (constituted of Dougherty, Arthur T. Hamlin, Michael H. Harris, Edward G. Holley, David Kaser, and Jesse Hauk Shera) selected the subjects. Wiegand edited the papers written by various authors on the careers of fifteen individuals. The subjects, their universities, and periods of service are as follows: Charles Harvey Brown (Iowa State, 1922–46), William S. Dix (Princeton, 1953–75), Robert B. Downs (Illinois, 1943–71), Ralph E. Ellsworth (Colorado, 1937–43 and 1958–72; and Iowa, 1943–58), Lillian Baker Griggs (Duke University Women's College, 1930–49), Guy R. Lyle (LSU, 1944–54; Emory, 1954–72), Stephen McCarthy (Cornell, 1946–67), Blanche McCrum (Washington and Lee, 1922–37; Wellesley, 1937–47), Keyes D. Metcalf (Harvard, 1937–55), Jerrold Orne (Knox College, 1941–43; Washington in St. Louis, 1945–51; North Carolina, 1957–73), Lawrence Clark Powell (UCLA, 1944–61), Ralph Shaw (professor at Rutgers, 1954–64), Maurice F. Tauber (librarian and professor at Columbia, 1944–76), Robert Vosper (Kansas, 1951–61; UCLA, 1961–73), and Louis Round Wilson (North Carolina, 1901–32; and library school dean, University of Chicago, 1932–42).

These leaders reached beyond home campuses to impact librarianship at large. Brown's diplomacy helped to keep the Association of College and Reference Libraries (now Association of College and Research Libraries) under its parent organization, the American Library Association. Downs published more than 400 articles and books, championing the freedom to read and faculty status for librarians. Ellsworth led the movements to establish the Midwest Inter-Library Center (now Center for Research Libraries) and to microfilm doctoral dissertations through University Microfilms. Lyle issued several editions of his classic, *The Administration of the College Library*. Metcalf became an authority on library building design and construction. Ralph Shaw established Scarecrow Press, which grew into what may be the most prolific publisher of books about American library history and practice (among other subjects). Wilson modeled a highly successful librarian-president partnership at North Carolina and led the Graduate Library School at Chicago. These achievements indicate something of the sweeping change underway at mid-century. With *Leaders in American Academic Librarianship*, Wiegand and his contributors had recalled key individuals and compelling ideas against the backdrop of an expansive age.

One year later Neil Radford, University Librarian at the University of Sydney in New South Wales in Australia, issued *The Carnegie Corporation and the Development of American College Libraries, 1928–1941*. He analyzed the interplay between philanthropic support and library beneficiaries with a rare tome on the small college library. Radford recounted the shift in the Carnegie Corporation from the leadership of Andrew Carnegie and his assistant, James Bertram, to that of Frederick Keppel and Keppel's assistant, Robert M. Lester. This transition coincided with growing Corporation engagement with higher education, and it resulted in new support for book collections for college libraries. The Carnegie grants strengthened library holdings for undergraduate reading in individual colleges and raised administrative and professorial awareness of the educational potential of libraries, both for grant recipients and for numerous other colleges across the country.

The Corporation had operated through a series of advisory committees to provide funds to liberal arts colleges, teachers' colleges and normal schools, junior colleges, and HBCUs. The chief library consultant for this program was William Warner Bishop (1871–1955). As library director at the University of Michigan (1915–41), Bishop was arguably the leading academic librarian of his era as author, ALA president, founding director of Michigan's graduate library school, international leader, and frequent advisor to the Vatican library and archives. The Corporation eventually gave $1,636,800 to 248 libraries to acquire books, complementing several hundred thousand for endowments and the more than $4 million allocated to 108 colleges for library building construction.

By funding college libraries, the Corporation had raised awareness of the library as a pedagogical instrument, placed hundreds of libraries on sounder footing, and stimulated the need for various publications, the most urgently needed being book lists for evaluating collections and guiding acquisitions. Thus, were published three reference sources, *A List of Books for College Libraries* and *A List of Books for College Libraries, 1931–1938* (ALA, 1931 and 1940) by Charles B. Shaw, and *A List of Books for Junior College Libraries* (ALA, 1937) by Foster E. Mohrhardt. These books became conceptual, though not lineal, ancestors of the periodical that appeared in the 1960s, *Choice: Books for College Libraries* (complemented by several editions of *Books for College Libraries* and *Resources for College Libraries*, widely used multivolume standards). Similarly, Francis L.D. Goodrich and William M. Randall issued *Principles of College Library Administration* (ALA and University of Chicago Press, 1936 and 1941), authoritative sources that became foundational for the college library management texts later written by Guy R. Lyle and his successors.

Radford had revised *The Carnegie Corporation and the Development of American College Libraries* from his doctoral dissertation at the University of Chicago and, though with prose less fluid than that of Danton and Osburn, Radford has produced something equally important, a well-conceived, well-researched account that covers a critical period of the college library story. This book also stands as an essential companion to George S. Bobinski's *Carnegie Libraries: Their History and Impact on American Public Library Development* (ALA, 1969). Taken together, Radford and Bobinski are "must reads" for those interested in philanthropic support and undaunted by the insider perspectives of the librarian-historian.[86]

In 1988 Roland C. Person issued a brief historical and descriptive account of the undergraduate library. He surveyed libraries designed for undergraduates that were part of graduate research universities and housed in a separate library building or in a self-contained section of a general library building. He began with the nation's first undergraduate library, the Lamont Library at Harvard, examining memoranda, reports, and mission statements, and detailing the transition in emphasis from collections and facilities to instruction and services. A revised dissertation written at Sothern Illinois University, *A New Path* underscored definitional clarity as the essential attribute for compelling undergraduate library practice and, in fact, examined twenty-four universities that once had undergraduate libraries but later disbanded them. The characteristic that the twenty-four lacked was a precisely defined rationale, something persuasive enough for stakeholders to regard the undergraduate library as an essential pedagogical instrument. Indeed, successful undergraduate libraries held in common the ability to elicit professorial engagement and library administrative support due to their unique role in higher education.[87] Person complemented well the earlier work of Harding, Smith, and Radford by focusing on services and instruction for undergraduates, thus offering a foundational source that explores the potential of the undergraduate library in teaching and learning.

Serving the Campus and Serving the Nation

In 1991 Stephen E. Atkins (1941–2010) published *The Academic Library in the American University* as one of those rare ALA imprints that treats topics historically. His first two chapters are exclusively historical, covering 1638 to about 1990. He analyzed historical events for their impact on the relationship of the academic library to professors, administrators, and budget officers. He tracked the growth of college and literary society libraries against the backdrop of growth in numbers of institutions, earned degrees, and expenditures for research.

Atkins posed penetrating questions drawn from personal experience. He had begun library work at the University of Iowa as a member of the cataloging staff while completing his doctorate in French history. He asked colleagues about librarians' rapport with professors and administrators, questions he raised again as a student in Iowa's School of Library and Information Science. In courses on university management, he learned that even highly talented administrators appeared to be puzzled about the role of the academic librarian and that, for their part, experienced librarians often misunderstood faculty and university cultures. He worried that the academic community at all levels gave too little consideration to the purpose and stature of the library on the local campus.

He concluded that libraries, though having been early responders to trends in higher education and early adopters of information technology, were receiving proportionally less of the university's resources at a time when demands for materials and services had never seemed greater. Reasons for this dilemma lay with the limited appreciation of the library on the part of administrators and a culture of higher education that offered minimal incentive to learn about the library. Atkins also concluded that faculty status and requirements for librarians, although drawing a wide range of opinions from the professoriate, offered the most effective, forward-looking strategy for librarian-faculty interaction.[88] Atkins complemented well the work of Lee Shiflett although the latter is more comprehensive and more gracefully written. Together, Shiflett and Atkins thoughtfully evaluate the principal functions of the librarian and locate them in the sociopolitical system of the university.

In 1997 David Kaser (1924–2017) released *The Evolution of the American Academic Library Building*. He focused on structures intended primarily or exclusively as central libraries on four-year college and university campuses. He compiled a list of 1,526 buildings constructed from 1840 through 1994, claiming that his list was at least eighty-five percent complete, and inviting readers to send information about buildings he might have omitted.[89] He excluded remodeling projects, additions, and separate departmental and professional school libraries.

Kaser marked 1840, the year when the University of South Carolina erected the first building in the nation designed exclusively for academic library purposes, as the time and place to begin the main points of his narrative. While noting antecedents in Europe and the UK as well as the multiuse building in the U.S.A., he focused on four general periods, each of them characterized by a dominant principle of design and informed by his intimate knowledge of how libraries work. The first was the single function hall intended to store books, 1840–75, when libraries simply housed materials, when collections were built with gifts almost exclusively, and when inhospitable, unheated buildings were generally opened for twenty hours per week or less. The second period, 1875–1910, was one of exponential growth featuring multipartitioned structures with separate areas for collections, administration, and services. In the age of the behemoths, 1910–1945, the designated function spaces were combined with multitiered stacks to accommodate rapid growth. The final period, 1945—mid-1990s, has been dominated by modular construction, allowing librarians to shift and integrate collections, reader services, and staff functions. Contextually, Kaser explained that architecture and librarianship as specialized professions came of age almost simultaneously, and that the timing of library building construction was, in the main, concurrent with the transitions underway in higher education during each given era.[90]

The Evolution of the American Academic Library Building was a labor of love. Kaser had visited at least 600 campuses, conducting interviews, researching institutional records, and scanning images. His narrative is deeply researched and carefully written, complemented by tables, diagrams, and photographs, most of which the author made himself. He was uniquely qualified to write this book—it appeared in the final phases of his career when he was seventy-three years of age—and it was his last major work prior to his memoir. He had served as a consultant for more than 220 library buildings in North America, Asia, Africa, and the Middle East. A career that spanned many years of library practice, scholarship, and LIS teaching ranks David Kaser with virtually any other American leader as an expert in academic librarianship.

In 200 freelance writer and sometime librarian Ralph D. Wagner published *A History of the Farmington Plan* as a revision of his doctoral dissertation written at the University of Illinois. With the outbreak of World War II, research librarians expressed a growing interest in access to foreign books and periodicals. The catalyst to launch the plan was an appeal by Librarian of Congress Archibald MacLeish (1892–1982) for a gathering of library leaders and association officers, a conference that took place in 1942 in Farmington, Connecticut. Under the direction of the Association of Research Libraries (ARL), librarians established headquarters at Harvard with Farmington agents, located throughout the world, purchasing, classifying, and shipping materials to participating libraries. At its inception, the Plan focused on Western European materials; by the mid–1950s it had expanded into other parts of the world, especially Asia. The Program eventually foundered due to mundane problems of implementation but also due to the magnitude of its ambitions—it was simply too large an undertaking to be effectively maintained given the financial constraints and institutional priorities of participants. It had called forth the likes of Julian Boyd (Princeton), Robert B. Downs (Illinois), and Keyes D. Metcalf (Harvard) but it could not be sustained as designed given the financial contractions of the 1970s.[91] Wagner's retelling is grounded in sources at Harvard, Illinois, the Library of Congress, and the New York Public Library and in Herrington Bryce's concepts of strategic management for non-profits. The resulting narrative is the definitive word for the foreseeable future; Ralph Wagner's work is essential reading for those in pursuit of our highest ideals of unbounded growth and resource sharing. Collectively, the major monographs from Shores to Wagner (1934 to 2002) constitute the essential perspective on the large picture, providing the lens through which to view academic library historiography.

More recently, two important textbooks stand out, not only for analyzing contemporary issues and best practices, but also for their grounding in academic library history. These volumes inherit a tradition of college library management guides that began in the 1930s, and they outline the trends that characterize librarianship in the twenty-first century. They also consider the value of historical sensibilities in the process of managing an academic library. The first of these, by Camila A. Alire and G. Edward Evans, makes a strong case for history, stating that academe "owes much more to the past than many people outside and inside higher education realize," specifically that the "structure, culture, basic purposes, and ceremonies" are rooted in the earliest days of collegiate life in Europe.[92] They identify Italy, France, England, and Germany as especially influential for American development. They organize their narrative into the periods of 1636 to 1770, the post-revolutionary war to 1860, and the 1860s to World War II, adding sections on more recent developments labeled as "wars and higher education" and "retrenchment and realignment."

Though they offered historically useful insight, they mitigated somewhat their stated perspective on history. They noted, for example, that a pre-publication reviewer for their book had urged omission of a historical section as unnecessary for managing an academic library. Remarkably, Alire and Evans agreed, stating that "one can operate an academic library without any thought to how we arrived at where we are."[93] Fortunately, they disagreed with this sentiment sufficiently enough to insert their own thoughtful, well-crafted overview.

In another textbook, the second edition of *The Changing Academic Library: Operations, Culture, Environments*, John M. Budd traces the university from Medieval origins, also noting that the library as an institution is at least two millennia older than the university. He recounts the transitions from Medieval college curricula in Europe to rudimentary beginnings fueled by Enlightenment ideas in Colonial America. He identifies college founding dates and describes library growth interrupted by military conflict and economic volatility.

Budd interprets the major events in a way that coincides with the overarching narratives of academic history. He notes the rapid expansion of the university in the late nineteenth and early twentieth centuries, the pause in confidence and growth during the 1930s, explosive growth after World War II, and the subsequent transitions wrought by social and economic change and technological innovation. He concurs with historians of higher education in identifying key presidential leaders from the era of transformative growth: James B. Angell (1829–1916) at the University of Michigan, Nicholas Murray Butler (1862–1947) at Columbia, Charles W. Eliot (1834–1926) at Harvard, Daniel Coit Gilman (1831–1908) at Johns Hopkins, and William Rainey Harper (1856–1906) at the University of Chicago. Budd recounts the emergence of professional scholarship as a way of life in the twentieth century amidst growing scientific prowess and the impact on the academy of business operations and bureaucratic structures. He identifies the criticisms leveled against higher education by its detractors some of whom are only minimally inclined to appreciate the contributions of higher education to the commonweal. Along the way, Budd speaks unequivocally for history. He writes that

> as each one of us is a product of all that has happened to us, of the experiences, events, and thoughts of an individual past, so too are colleges and universities (and their libraries) shaped by all that has gone before … the history of higher education was not a journey taken in isolation. Higher education has been the product of many of the aims and ambitions of humans, and it has not been separat[ed] from the religious, political, social, and economic lives of the people who have helped to shape it and those who themselves have been shaped by it.[94]

To Alire-Evans and to Budd, we mention a third text, one that had preceded theirs by several decades. Hundreds or, perhaps, even thousands of academic librarians have been exposed to the classic by Guy R. Lyle, *The Administration of the College Library*. Lyle was, by any definition, a rare academic librarian, as director for two leading research university libraries, LSU and Emory University. But he began his career in liberal arts colleges, Antioch College in Ohio and the Women's College of the University of North Carolina at Greensboro. With pertinent administrative experience and writing skills, Lyle was uniquely suited as textbook author; he published four editions (1944, 1949, 1961, 1974), instantly and continuously well-received for clarity, common sense, and a thorough understanding of the needs of students and of the library's potential to educate. Carolyn M. Coughlin and Alice Gertzog issued two editions under the title, *Lyle's Administration of the College Library* (1992, 1997).

In examining the text edition, 1997, we note happily that Coughlin and Gertzog retained a sense of history in their chapter, "Evolution of Higher Education in the United States." They began with the curriculum of the colonial college and identified key leaders from the nineteenth and twentieth centuries. They noted the rise of the research university and the origins of HBCUs; they described the expansion of programs and the birth of new universities with the return of veterans after World War II, and the surging emphasis on student and faculty diversity in the latter part of the twentieth century. They closed their chapter with a quotation by Vartan Gregorian, former president of the New York Public Library and of Brown University, on the inadequacies of undergraduate education, specifically that it includes national amnesia toward our heritage.[95] Thus, Coughlin and Gertzog exhibited great respect for history, for how the academic library in the U.S.A. came to be, and for the potential of historical knowledge in collegiate education and library practice. That *Lyle's Administration*—the text edition—incorporates a strong historical treatment suggests that perhaps academic librarians have been exposed to some small amount of historical perspective. One caveat might be that, if *Lyle* had been an assigned reading in a school of librarianship, the professor might have encouraged the student to simply omit reading the historical section. The hope is that readers discovering *Lyle's Administration of the College Library*, or other contributions to this genre, might on their own possibly draw a connection between library history and library practice.

A Future Historiography

The motivating ideal of the research library—unbounded growth—still holds the capacity to inspire. Alberto Manguel writes that

> the Library of Alexandria rose when stories took on the shape of books, and strove to find a syntax that would lend each word, each tablet, each scroll its illuminating and necessary place.... Nothing like it has ever again been achieved, though other libraries (the Web included) have tried to copy its astonishing ambition. It stands unique in the history of the world as the only place which, having set itself up to record everything, past and future, might also have foreseen and stored the chronicle of its own destruction and resurrection.[96]

Visions of Alexandria continue to beckon more as metaphor than fact, despite the Egyptian government's construction of a new Alexandrian Library with a capacity of 8,000,000 printed volumes.

The Alexandrian dream appears in modern iterations outlined by Wayne Bivens-Tatum. He describes the research library as rooted in the Enlightenment, a powerful movement that defines, motivates, and energizes. He writes that the librarian's roles of collecting, organizing, and providing information are constructed on professional commitments to the "intellectual virtues of reason, discovery, invention, classification, understanding, and experiment [and the] political virtues of intellectual freedom, democracy, liberty, equality, and emancipation."[97] He traces concepts of unbounded growth, which he terms "the universal library," from the Library of Alexandria to Gabriel Naude's *Advice on Establishing a Library*, through the contributions of Diderot and H.G. Wells and Vannevar Bush all the way to Google Books and the *Digital Public Library of America*. Like Manguel, Bivens-Tatum draws a direct line from Alexandria to Google. Almost as if to illustrate what this sort of limitless horizon might look like in library practice, Matthew Battles, in *Library: An Unquiet History*, points the way to the next logical short-term step for digital collections. He writes that as present-day librarians digitize texts, future librarians will seek to preserve the metadata, searching for "beauty and truth in the code our programmers" have traditionally rendered invisible. "These digital texts, these 'objects,' will be classified, described, and annotated. Undoubtedly this will be a labor of love. The digital objects of today are the incunabula of a not-too-distant tomorrow."[98] This seems like the next logical step in a pattern of practice, that librarians will forever envision a limitless future, dreaming dreams that will never die.

Three landmark essays, in addition to that of Sharon Weiner, may be said to mark the progress of academic library historiography. In "The Literature of American Library History," published in 1945, Jesse Shera cited Shores's book on the colonial college library as the single tome worthy of note on academic libraries. More than fifty years later in "American Library History Literature, 1947–1997: A Theoretical Perspective?" Wayne Wiegand devoted two paragraphs to academic topics. He mentioned Brough, Harding, Johnson, Smith, Osburn, Hamlin, Shiflett, Radford, Person, and Kaser plus his own collection on academic library leaders. To inform further research, he proposed analyses of the academy's connections with corporate and governmental agencies. He cited *Cloak & Gown: Scholars in the Secret War, 1939–1961* and *No Ivory Tower: McCarthyism and the Universities* as holding interpretive possibilities. Reflective of his wider research agenda, Wiegand also proposed studies of circulation records to aid our understanding of how students and faculty used books and journals at their disposal.[99]

A third landmark essay is that of M. Connor Sullivan. In 2015 he re-examined the metaphors commonly used in our understanding of research libraries. The library as "warehouse" or "storehouse" offered contemporary practitioners and subsequent historians concepts of the mid-nineteenth century college library as a place where printed materials were stored, preserved, kept for posterity, and only occasionally and perhaps grudgingly made available for use. The phrases "age of accumulation" and "age of use" offer instructive categories, allowing us to grasp something of the magnitude of the transition occurring in the late nineteenth century from the college library, focused on materials for undergraduates, into the research university library supporting graduate education and the search for new knowledge. Likewise, the term "workshop" connotes a major transformation in how students and faculty were beginning to regard the library and to integrate its effective use into their academic pursuits.

In similar fashion, historians have tended to regard John Langdon Sibley as symbolizing the era of accumulation, emphasizing the preservation and protection of materials. His successor, Justin Winsor (1831–1897), who directed the Harvard library the last twenty years of his life, came to symbolize the age of use which, ironically, also coincided with unprecedented collection growth. Sullivan reviews these interpretations and revises them, urging something more nuanced—that we consider a continuum of practice, that Sibley was hardly as reactionary as we might have supposed, and that Winsor may not have been as successfully progressive as recent generations have thought. Sullivan has mined the scholarship of library historians as well as key players in the Harvard community, among them Clifford K. Shipton (1902–1973), Harvard University archivist and later director of the library of the American Antiquarian Society, and Keyes Metcalf (1889–1983) who directed the Harvard University library from the latter part of the Great Depression into the years following World War II. Sullivan has an innate grasp of Harvard's potential to shed light on academic librarianship since the beginnings of our nation; he urges that we do not devalue the processes of gathering, storing, and organizing; and he redirects academic library historiography in ways that honor long-supported core values.[100] Sullivan would quite likely echo Princeton historian Robert Darnton who wrote

> long live Google, but don't count on it living long enough to replace that venerable building with the Corinthian columns. As a citadel for learning and as a platform for adventure on the Internet, the research library still deserves to stand at the center of the campus, preserving the past and accumulating energy for the future.[101]

We understand that the essays we have gathered may present organizational dilemmas and that our inclusions and interpretations are debatable. For practical reasons, we reprinted a highly selected core. We also cite several pertinent books and articles in "The Academic Library in the United States: Selected Historical Readings." On these and related matters, we invite reader input, hoping to enlarge the conversation among those who agree or disagree about our choices. Responses, whatever the venue, will enrich our understandings about the large narrative of the academic library and its capacity to nurture intellectual life in the academy. We embrace wholeheartedly argument, dissent, and fully engaged, well informed input. Free and open respectful conversation marks the best traditions of our profession and of the academy, paying homage to the historical significance and virtually unbounded potential of the academic library.

Notes

1. Donald G. Davis, Jr., and John Mark Tucker, eds. *American Library History: A Comprehensive Guide to the Literature* (Santa Barbara, California: ABC-Clio, 1989), 55–163.
2. Edward A. Goedeken, "The Library Historian's Field of Dreams: A Profile of the First Nine Seminars," in *Library History Research in America: Essays Commemorating the Fiftieth Anniversary of the Library History Round Table*, eds. Andrew B. Wertheimer and Donald G. Davis, Jr. (Washington, D.C.: Library of Congress, Center for the Book, 2000), 168. *Library History Research in America* was also published as an issue of *Libraries & Culture* 35:1 (Winter 2000).
3. Edward G. Holley, "Defining the Academic Librarian," *College & Research Libraries* 46:6 (November 1985), 462.
4. David Armitage and Jo Guldi, *The History Manifesto* (New York: Cambridge University Press, 2014), 5.
5. Armitage and Guldi, 5.
6. Armitage and Guldi, 125. See also Victor Gondos, *J. Franklin Jameson and the National Archives* (Philadelphia, Pennsylvania: University of Pennsylvania Press, 1981).
7. See Len Clark, "Library Instruction from the Philosopher's Point of View," in *Faculty Involvement in Library Instruction*, ed. Hannelore B. Rader (Ann Arbor, Michigan: Pierian Press, 1976), 33–34; and Jesse H. Shera, "What the Librarian Needs to Know," in *The Foundations of Education for Librarianship* (New York: Becker and Hayes, 1972), 195–226. The Shera chapter stands out as a compelling challenge to those who pursue librarianship as a career, placing the profession within larger social contexts and outlining the intellectual, educational, and managerial attributes of effective practice. See also Holley, "Defining the Academic Librarian," 462–68. The wise counsel of Shera and Holley could benefit practitioners of any culture or any era.
8. Pierce Butler, *An Introduction to Library Science* (Chicago, Illinois: University of Chicago Press, 1933, Phoenix Edition, 1961), 104.
9. Butler, 101.
10. Stanley Pargellis, "Long Life to the Library History Round Table," in *An American Library History Reader: Contributions to Library Literature*, ed. John David Marshall (Hamden, Connecticut: Shoe String, 1961), 9. Reprinted from *Wilson Library Bulletin* 22:8 (April 1948), 601–03, 607. See also Donald W. Krummel, "Stanley Pargellis (1898–1968)," in *Dictionary of American Library Biography*, eds. George S. Bobinski, Jesse Hauk Shera, and Bohdan S. Wynar (Littleton, Colorado: Libraries Unlimited, 1978), 389–91.
11. Jesse H. Shera, "On the Value of Library History," in *Reader in American Library History*, ed. Michael H. Harris (Washington, D.C.: NCR Microcard Editions, 1971), 5. Essay reprinted from *Library Quarterly* 22:3 (July 1952), 240–51.
12. Shera, "Value of Library History," 10–11.
13. Shera, *Foundations*, 136.
14. Jesse H. Shera, *Introduction to Library Science: Basic Elements of Library Service* (Littleton, Colorado: Libraries Unlimited, 1976), 10.
15. Bobinski, Shera, and Wynar (1978), xxx.
16. Haynes McMullen, "Research in Backgrounds in Librarianship," *Library Trends* 6:2 (October 1957), 107.
17. Felix Reichmann, "Historical Research and Library Science," *Library Trends* 13:1 (Summer 1964), 31.
18. Reichmann, 33.
19. Shera, "Value of Library History," 13; also quoted in Reichmann, 36.

20. Fritz Stern, *The Varieties of History*, 2nd Ed. (New York: Vintage Books, 1973), 24; also quoted in John Calvin Colson, "The Writing of American Library History, 1876–1976," *Library Trends* 25:1 (July 1976), 11.
21. Colson, "The Writing of American Library History," 11.
22. Colson, 13.
23. Colson, 15.
24. Phyllis Dain and Margaret F. Stieg, "Introduction," *Library Trends* 27:3 (Winter 1979), 221.
25. Dain and Stieg, 223; and quoted from W. Jackson Bate, *Samuel Johnson* (New York: Harcourt Brace Jovanovich, 1977), 532.
26. Mary Jo Lynch, "Introduction," *Library Trends* 32:4 (Spring 1984), 361–62.
27. Orvin Lee Shiflett, "Clio's Claim: The Role of Historical Research in Library and Information Science," *Library Trends* 32:4 (Spring 1984), 385–88.
28. Shiflett, *Origins of American Academic Librarianship* (Norwood, New Jersey: Ablex, 1981); and *Louis Shores: Defining Educational Librarianship* (Lanham, Maryland: Scarecrow Press, 1996).
29. W. Boyd Rayward, "When and Why Is a Pioneer: History and Heritage in Library and Information Science," *Library Trends* 52:4 (Spring 2004), 672.
30. Louis Shores, *Origins of the American College Library 1638-1800* (Nashville, Tennessee: George Peabody College for Teachers, 1934 and New York: Barnes & Noble, 1934); Kenneth J. Brough, *Scholar's Workshop: Evolving Conceptions of Library Service* (Urbana, Illinois: University of Illinois Press, 1953); J. Periam Danton, *Book Selection and Collections: A Comparison of German and American University Libraries* (New York: Columbia University Press, 1963); Thomas S. Harding, *College Literary Societies: Their Contribution to Higher Education in the United States, 1815–1876* (Brooklyn, New York: Pageant-Poseidon, 1971); and Ralph D. Wagner, *A History of the Farmington Plan* (Lanham, Maryland: Scarecrow Press, 2002). The Shores book was reprinted by Shoe String (1966); Brough was reprinted by the University of Illinois Press (1966) and by University Microfilms (1966,1970); both were reprinted by Gregg Press (1972).
31. Frederick Rudolph, *The American College and University* (New York: Vintage Books, 1962); reissued with introductory essay and supplemental bibliography by John R. Thelin (Athens, Georgia: University of Georgia Press, 1990). Other examples in this genre include James Axtell, *Wisdom's Workshop: The Rise of the Modern University* (Princeton, New Jersey: Princeton University Press, 2016); John S. Brubacher and Willis Rudy, *Higher Education in Transition: A History of American Colleges and Universities*, 4th Ed. (New Brunswick, New Jersey: Transaction Publishers, 1997); David F. Labaree, *A Perfect Mess: The Unlikely Ascendancy of American Higher Education* (Chicago, Illinois: University of Chicago Press, 2017); John R. Thelin, *A History of American Higher Education*, 3rd Ed. (Baltimore, Maryland: The Johns Hopkins University Press, 2019); and Laurence R. Veysey, *The Emergence of the American University* (Chicago, Illinois: University of Chicago Press, 1965).
32. Michael H. Harris, "Two Years Work in American Library History, 1969–1970," *Journal of Library History* 7:1 (January 1972), 40. Sources of academic library historiography include Kenneth E. Carpenter, Preface to *The Harvard University Library: A Documentary History: Bibliographic Guide* (Bethesda, Maryland: Congressional Information Service, University Publications of America, 1989), viii—xiv; Davis and Tucker (1989); Michael H. Harris and Donald G. Davis, Jr., eds. *American Library History: A Bibliography* (Austin, Texas: University of Texas Press, 1978); Ned Fielden, "Academic Library History Bibliography," http://online.sfsu.edu/~fielden/ulib07a.html, accessed 3 March 2017; Nathaniel Stewart, "Sources for the Study of American College Library History, 1800–1876," *Library Quarterly* 13:3 (July 1943), 227–31; and Arthur P. Young, *American Library History: A Bibliography of Dissertations and Theses* (Metuchen, New Jersey: Scarecrow Press, 1988). Young built on the earlier work of Michael H. Harris, *A Guide to Research in American Library History* (Metuchen, New Jersey: Scarecrow Press, 1968 and 2nd Ed., 1974). See also Sharon Gray Weiner, "The History of Academic Libraries in the United States: A Review of the Literature," *Library Philosophy and Practice* 7:2 (Spring 2005), e-journal accessed 3 March 2017. Weiner's analysis of the historiography covers books, articles, and dissertations published from 1980 to 2003. See also M. Connor Sullivan, "From Warehouses to Workshops, from Libraries to Labs: Investigating the History of Academic Libraries to Imagine Their Future" (paper presented at Library History Seminar XIII, Boston, Massachusetts, Simmons College Graduate School of Library and Information Science, July 31—August 2, 2015).
33. Donald G. Davis, Jr., and Michael H. Harris, "Two Years Work in American Library History, 1974–1975," *Journal of Library History* 11:4 (October 1976), 282. See also Davis and Harris, "Three Years Work in American Library History, 1971–1973," *Journal of Library History* 9:4 (October 1974), 296–317.
34. Donald G. Davis, Jr., "The Year's Work in American Library History—1976," *Journal of Library History* 13:2 (Spring 1978), 187–203; and Richard D. Johnson, ed., *Libraries for Teaching, Libraries for Research: Essays for a Century*, ACRL Publications in Librarianship no. 39 (Chicago, Illinois: American Library Association, 1977). Davis also cited Howard W. Winger, ed., *American Library History 1876-1976* (Urbana, Illinois: University of Illinois, Graduate School of Library Science, 1976); and Sidney L. Jackson, Eleanor B. Herling, and E.J. Josey, eds., *A Century of Service: Librarianship in the United States and Canada* (Chicago, Illinois: American Library Association, 1976).

35. Janice C. Fennell, ed., *Building on the First Century: Proceedings of the Fifth National Conference of the Association of College and Research Libraries Cincinnati, Ohio, April 5–8, 1989* (Chicago, Illinois: Association of College and Research Libraries, A Division of the American Library Association, 1989). The preface to *Proceedings* cited Michael Hawley as keynote speaker on the historic transformation of academic librarianship through the inventions of paper, the printing press, the computer, and digital texts, yet did not print Hawley's paper or explain why it was not included. See Fennell, *Building on the First Century*, xvii.

36. Stephen Bell, Lorcan Dempsey, and Barbara Fister, *New Roles for the Road Ahead: Essays Commissioned for ACRL's 75th Anniversary*, ed. Nancy Allen with an Afterword by Betsy Wilson (Chicago, Illinois: Association of College and Research Libraries, 2015), 7.

37. Wayne A. Wiegand, "The Literature of American Library History, 1977–1978," *Journal of Library History* 14:3 (Summer 1979), 328.

38. Joanne E. Passet, "The Literature of American Library History, 1989–1990," *Libraries & Culture* 27:4 (Fall 1992), 405–29. See also "The Literature of American Library History, 1991–1992," *Libraries & Culture* 29:4 (Fall 1994), 415–39.

39. Edward A. Goedeken, "The Literature of American Library History, 1997–1998," *Libraries & Culture* 35:2 (Spring 2000), 319–20; "The Literature of American Library History, 1999–2000," *Libraries & Culture* 37:2 (Spring 2002), 146–48; "The Literature of American Library History, 2001–2002," *Libraries & Culture* 39:2 (Spring 2004), 183–85; "The Literature of American Library History, 2006–2007," *Libraries & the Cultural Record* 44:4 (Fall 2009), 442–44; "The Literature of American Library History, 2010–2011," *Information & Culture: A Journal of History* 48:4 (2013), 514; and "The Literature of American Library History, 2014–2015," *Information and Culture: A Journal of History* 53:1 (2018), 93.

40. Carpenter (1989), ix—xi.

41. James V. Carmichael, Jr., "Ahistoricity and the Library Profession: Perceptions of Biographical Researchers in LIS Concerning Research Problems, Practices, and Barriers," *Journal of Education for Library and Information Science* 31:4 (Spring 1991), 329–56.

42. Passet (1992), 405.

43. Shiflett, "Clio's Claim," (1984), 385–87.

44. Carmichael (1991), 332. See Heting Chu, "Research Methods in Library and Information Science: A Content Analysis," *Library & Information Science Research* 37:1 (January 2015), 36–41; and Philip Hider and Bob Pymm, "Empirical Research Methods Reported in High-Profile LIS Journal Literature," *Library & Information Science Research* 30:2 (June 2008), 108–14. Christine Pawley surveys the current environment in "Still Breathing: History in Education for Librarianship," *Information & Culture: A Journal of History* 54:1 (2019), 44–52.

45. Weiner (2005); and O. Lee Shiflett, "Academic Libraries," in *Encyclopedia of Library History*, eds. Wayne A. Wiegand and Donald G. Davis, Jr. (New York: Garland, 1994), 13. Shiflett also critiqued formal education for librarianship, explaining that historically it had followed Dewey's emphasis on standardization in public librarianship while neglecting the interests of the emerging universities and their research libraries (1994), 11.

46. Weiner (2005).

47. Shiflett (1984), 385–87.

48. Anne L. Buchanan and Jean-Pierre V.M. Hérubel, "Subject and Bibliographic Characteristics of Library History," *Journal of Scholarly Publishing* 42:4 (July 2011), 516.

49. Wayne A. Wiegand, "To Reposition a Research Agenda: What American Studies Can Teach the LIS Community about the Library in the Life of the User," *Library Quarterly* 73:4 (October 2003), 369–82. To enrich the context for the concepts of library as space, Wiegand proposed Jürgen Habermas, *The Structural Transformation of the Public Sphere: An Inquiry into a Category of Bourgeois Society* (Cambridge, Massachusetts: Harvard University Press, 1989); and David Henkin, *City Reading: Written Words and Public Spaces in Antebellum New York* (New York: Columbia University Press, 1998). Background on the history of reading could be provided by Janice Radway, *Reading the Romance: Women, Patriarchy, and Popular Literature*, 2nd Ed. (Chapel Hill, North Carolina: University of North Carolina Press, 1991), or Elizabeth Long, *Book Clubs: Women and the Uses of Reading* (Chicago, Illinois: University of Chicago, 2003).

50. Several scholars have contributed to the theoretical foundations for LIS. See Pierce Butler, *An Introduction to Library Science* (Chicago, Illinois: University of Chicago Press, 1933). Butler was reprinted by the University of Chicago Press (1961, 1964, and 1967) and by John V. Richardson, Jr., in *The Gospel of Scholarship: Pierce Butler and a Critique of American Librarianship* (Metuchen, New Jersey: Scarecrow Press, 1992). See also Jesse Hauk Shera, *Sociological Foundations of Librarianship* (New York: Asia House, 1970) and *The Foundations of Education for Librarianship* (New York: Becker and Hayes, 1972); Conrad Rawski, ed., *Toward a Theory of Librarianship: Papers in Honor of Jesse Hauk Shera* (Metuchen, New Jersey: Scarecrow Press, 1973); Barbara McCrimmon, ed., *American Library Philosophy: An Anthology* (Hamden, Connecticut: Shoe String Press, 1975); Lloyd J. Houser and Alvin Schrader, *The Search for a Scientific Profession: Library Science Education in the U.S. and Canada* (Metuchen, New Jersey: Scarecrow, 1978); Michael H. Harris, "The Dialectic of Defeat: Antimonies in Research in Library and Information Science," *Library Trends* 34:3 (Winter 1986), 515–31; Michael F. Winter, *The Culture and Control of Expertise: Toward*

a Sociological Understanding of Librarianship (New York: Greenwood Press, 1988); Wayne Wiegand, "Tunnel Vision and Blind Spots: What the Past Tells Us about the Present: Reflections on the Twentieth-Century History of American Librarianship," *Library Quarterly* 69:1 (January 1999), 1–32.; John M. Budd, *Knowledge and Knowing in Library and Information Science: A Philosophical Framework* (Lanham, Maryland: Scarecrow Press, 2001); André Crosette, *Humanism and Libraries: An Essay on the Philosophy of Librarianship*, translated and edited by Rory Litwin (Duluth, Minnesota: Library Juice Press, 2009), originally published in 1976; Stephen Bates, *The Dialectic of Academic Librarianship: A Critical Approach* (Sacramento, California: Library Juice Press, 2015); and Alice Crawford, ed., *The Meaning of the Library* (Princeton, New Jersey: Princeton University Press, 2015).

51. Harvard, Dartmouth, and the College of William and Mary have retained original designations. Other institutions changed from previous names as follows: Brown (College of Rhode Island); Columbia (King's College); Princeton (College of New Jersey); Rutgers (Queen's College); University of Pennsylvania (College of Philadelphia); and Yale (Collegiate School of Connecticut). Rutgers and William and Mary are public; the other seven are private.

52. Clemons reviewed for *Library Journal* and Wilson for *Library Quarterly*. Lee Shiflett contextualized the reviews in *Louis Shores* (1996), 42. Harvard historian Samuel Eliot Morison, unlike Clemons and Wilson, was not complimentary. Although Morison attacked Shores for factual errors in documentation pertaining to Harvard, he failed to engage the functions of the overall narrative or to consider references to any college other than Harvard. A point well stated was Morison's view that Shores seemed to care little for the intellectual contents of the Harvard College Library. See *New England Quarterly* 8:3 (September 1935), 430–31. Ten years later Jesse Shera, echoing Morison, questioned the quality of the Shores dissertation in "The Literature of American Library History," *Library Quarterly* 15:1 (January 1945), 21.

53. See Benjamin E. Powell, "Southern University Libraries during the Civil War," *Wilson Library Bulletin* 31:3 (November 1956), 250–54, 259; reprinted in Marshall (1961), 73–82.

54. Jaroslav Pelikan, *The Idea of the University: A Reexamination* (New Haven, Connecticut: Yale University Press, 1992), 196; and Brough (1953).

55. Joe W. Kraus, "The Book Collections of Early American College Libraries," *Library Quarterly* 43:2 (April 1973), 142–59 and "Book Collections of Five Colonial College Libraries: A Subject Analysis," (Ph.D. Dissertation, University of Illinois, 1960).

56. Jessie Carney Smith, "Patterns of Growth in Library Resources in Certain Land-Grant Universities," (Ph.D. Dissertation, University of Illinois, 1964).

57. Richard Earl Miller, Jr. "The Development of Reference Services in the American Liberal Arts College, 1876–1976," (Ph.D. Dissertation, University of Minnesota, 1984).

58. Michael J. Waldo, "A Comparative Analysis of Nineteenth-Century Academic and Literary Society Libraries in the Midwest," (Ph.D. Dissertation, Indiana University, 1985). Waldo's findings vary from the conventional wisdom on this topic and merit further inquiry. See Catherine P. Storie, "The American College Society Library and the College Library," *College & Research Libraries* 6:3 (June 1945), 240–48; Rudolph (1962), 143–44; Roscoe Rouse, "The Libraries of Nineteenth Century College Societies," in *Books in America's Past: Essays Honoring Rudolph H. Gjelness*, ed. David Kaser (Charlottesville, Virginia: University Press of Virginia, 1966), 26–42; and Harding (1971).

59. John Michael Rothacker, "The Role of the Library in the Non-Western Studies Programs of Three Liberal Arts Colleges," (Ph.D. Dissertation, Indiana University, 1975).

60. Willie Hardin, "An Analysis of the Growth Patterns in Select Black Land-Grant Colleges and Universities: Five Case Studies," (Ph.D. Dissertation, Simmons College, 1979).

61. Robert E. Brundin, "Changing Patterns of Library Service in Five California Junior Colleges, 1907–1967," (Ph.D. Dissertation, Stanford University, 1970); Norma N. Yueh, "The Development of Library Collections at Former State Teacher Education Institutions: 1920–1970, with Special Consideration of Six New Jersey State Colleges," (Ph.D. Dissertation, Columbia University, 1974), and Ramirose Attebury and Michael Kroth, "From Pedagogical Museum to Instructional Materials Center: Education Libraries at Teacher Training Institutions, 1890–1970s," *Education Libraries* 35:1-2 (Summer-Winter 2012), 48–58.

62. Ernst W. Erickson, "College and University Library Surveys, 1932–1958," (Ph.D. Dissertation, University of Illinois, 1958) and (Chicago, Illinois: American Library Association, 1961).

63. John J. Boll, "Library Architecture 1800–1975: A Comparison of Theory and Buildings with Emphasis on New England College Libraries," (Ph.D. Dissertation, University of Illinois, 1961).

64. Lowell Simpson, "The Development and Scope of Undergraduate Literary Society Libraries at Columbia, Dartmouth, Princeton, and Yale," *Journal of Library History* 12:3 (Summer 1977), 209–21; William Olbrich, Jr., "'An Adjunct, Necessary and Proper…': The Black Academic Library in Texas, 1876–1986," *Texas Library Journal* 62 (Spring 1986), 94–103; Michael Stuart Freeman, "Almost a Unified Library: Bryn Mawr, Haverford, and Swarthmore College Library Cooperation during the 1940s," *Libraries & Culture* 32:1 (Winter 1997), 1–37; and Marjorie Hassen, "The Early Development of American Music Libraries Serving Academic Departments of Music," *Fontes Artis Musicae* 48:4 (October-December 2001), 342–52. In general, we have not considered specialized subject libraries in research universities such as those devoted to art, law, medicine, theology, or other subjects.

65. Arthur E. Bestor, Jr., "The Transformation of American Scholarship, 1875–1917," *Library Quarterly* 23:3 (July 1953), 164–79; and Alexandra Oleson and John Voss, eds., *The Organization of Knowledge in Modern America, 1860–1920* (Baltimore, Maryland: Johns Hopkins University Press, 1979).

66. Ernest H. Wilkins, "The University Library and Scholarship," *Harvard Library Bulletin* 4:1 (Winter 1950), 16. Danton quoted Wilkins in *Book Selection and Collections* (1963), 1. Wilkins (1880–1966) taught Romance languages at Harvard and the University of Chicago; he later served as president of Oberlin College.

67. Danton (1963), xvii.

68. Edward G. Holley, "North American Efforts at Worldwide Acquisitions Since 1945," *Collection Management* 9:2-3 (Summer/Fall 1987), 89; and Phyllis Dain, "The Old Scholarship and the New: Reflections on the Historic Role of Libraries," in *For the Good of the Order: Essays in Honor of Edward G. Holley*, ed. Delmus E. Williams, et al. (Greenwich, Connecticut: JAI Press, 1994), 223. Holley had firsthand knowledge of Illinois, having been a member of the library staff during his years as a doctoral student.

69. Robert Vosper, "Collection Building and Rare Books," in *Research Librarianship: Essays in Honor of Robert B. Downs*, ed. Jerrold Orne (New York: R.R. Bowker, 1971), 93.

70. Vosper (1971), 92.

71. Quoted in Nicholas A. Basbanes, *Every Book Its Reader: The Power of the Printed Word to Stir the World* (New York: HarperCollins, 2005), 44.

72. Quoted in Basbanes (2005), 45.

73. Ralph Wagner is the authority on the Farmington Plan. Summaries that contextualize Farmington include Hendrick Edelman and G. Marvin Tatum, Jr., "The Development of Collections in American University Libraries," in *Libraries for Teaching*, ed. Johnson (1977), 34–57; Abner J. Gaines, "Farmington Plan," in *Encyclopedia of Library History*, eds. Wayne A. Wiegand and Donald G. Davis, Jr. (1994), 193; and Edelman, "Intelligent Design and the Evolution of American Research Library Collections," (Janus Conference on Research Library Resources, Cornell University, Ithaca, New York, October 9, 2005). Forerunners of the Farmington Plan are discussed by David S. Zubatsky, "'No Book Should Be Out of Reach': The Role of the American Library Association in the Sharing of Resources for Research, 1922–45," (Ph.D. Dissertation, University of Illinois, 1982).

74. Quoted in George Winston Smith, "Northern Libraries and the Confederacy, 1861–1865," in Marshall (1961), 69. Marshall reprinted Smith's essay from *Virginia Librarian* 3:1 (April 1956), 7–8. The ideal of unbounded growth had numerous challengers, among them Charles Osburn who argued for principles of selectivity in *Academic Research and Library Resources: Changing Patterns in America* (Westport, Connecticut: Greenwood, 1979), 104–08; and Daniel Gore who sponsored a conference on the topic published as *Farewell to Alexandria: Solutions to Space, Growth, and Performance Problems of Libraries* (Westport, Connecticut: Greenwood, 1976). M. Connor Sullivan offered a much-needed corrective to the conventional view of John Langdon Sibley as representative of a conservative, staid, bygone era in academic librarianship. See "From Warehouses to Workshops, from Libraries to Labs: Investigating the History of Academic Libraries to Imagine their Future."

75. James I. Wyer, Jr., *The College and University Library* (Chicago, Illinois: American Library Association, 1921), 2–3. James Axtell considers the American origins of the "college" and "university" terminology from the late eighteenth century into the nineteenth century in *Wisdom's Workshop: The Rise of the Modern University* (Princeton, New Jersey: Princeton University Press, 2016), 217–21.

76. Jean Key Gates, *Introduction to Librarianship* (New York: McGraw-Hill, 1976), 193–200. Sources in the Gates genre include Jesse Hauk Shera, *Introduction to Library Science* (1976) and Richard E. Rubin, *Foundations of Library and Information Science*, 4th Ed. (Chicago, Illinois: ALA Neal-Schuman, 2016). In brief historical references to the academic library, Rubin notes the importance of three trends with roots in the nineteenth century: German patterns of research and seminar instruction, the land-grant movement, and curricular expansion driven by the elective system.

77. Contributors to the management literature include Gerard B. McCabe, *The Smaller Academic Library: A Management Handbook* (New York: Greenwood, 1988); Caroline M. Coughlin and Alice Gertzog, *Lyle's Administration of the College Library*, 5th Ed. (Metuchen, New Jersey: Scarecrow, 1992 and Text Ed., 1997); John Mark Tucker, "College Library, University Library: What's the Difference?" *Library Issues* 30:6 (July 2010), 1–4; and Rachel Applegate, *Managing the Small College Library* (Santa Barbara, California: Libraries Unlimited, 2010). For further context on terminology, see Richard Harwell, "College Libraries," in *Encyclopedia of Library and Information Science*, Vol. 5, ed. Allen Kent (New York: Marcel Dekker, 1970), 269–81; and Thomas G. Kirk, Jr., "College Libraries," in *Encyclopedia of Library and Information Science*, 2nd Ed., Vol. 1, ed. Miriam Drake (New York: Marcel Dekker, 2003), 591–601. Standard texts on academic libraries include John M. Budd, *The Academic Library: Its Context, Its Purpose, and Its Operation* (Englewood, Colorado: Libraries Unlimited, 1998); *The Changing Academic Library: Operations, Culture, Environments*, ACRL Publications in Librarianship no. 56, 2nd Ed. no. 65, 3rd Ed. no. 74 (Chicago, Illinois: American Library Association, 2005, 2012, 2018); Camila A. Alire and G. Edward Evans, *Academic Librarianship* (New York: Neal-Schuman, 2010); and G. Edward Evans and Stacey Greenwell, *Academic Librarianship*, 2nd Ed. (Chicago, Illinois: American Library Association, Neal-Schuman, 2018).

78. Harding (1971), 313–19.

40   Historiography of the Academic Library

79. Jessie Carney Smith, *Black Academic Libraries and Research Collections: An Historical Survey* (Westport, Connecticut: Greenwood, 1977), 24, 158–67. See also David Kaser, "Andrew Carnegie and the Black College Libraries," in *For the Good of the Order* (1994), 119–33.

80. Casper L. Jordan and Beverly P. Lynch, "ACRL's Historically Black College & Universities Libraries Projects, 1972–1994," in *Untold Stories: Civil Rights, Libraries, and Black Librarianship*, ed. John Mark Tucker (Champaign, Illinois: University of Illinois Graduate School of Library and Information Science, 1998), 156–66.

81. Osburn (1979), 93.

82. Osburn (1979), 103.

83. For background on this discussion, see Osburn especially pp. 94–107.

84. Arthur T. Hamlin, *The University Library in the United States: Its Origins and Development* (Philadelphia, Pennsylvania: University of Pennsylvania Press, 1981), ix—xi. An excellent example of an intelligent, readable narrative employing minimal professional vocabulary (written incidentally by a librarian from Harvard), is by Matthew Battles, *Library: An Unquiet History* (New York: W.W. Norton, 2003).

85. See Shiflett (1996); and "Academic Libraries," in *Encyclopedia of Library History*, ed. Wayne A. Wiegand and Donald G. Davis, Jr. (New York: Garland, 1994), 4–14.

86. Summarized from Neil A. Radford, *The Carnegie Corporation and the Development of American College Libraries, 1928–1941*, ACRL Publications in Librarianship no. 44 (Chicago, Illinois: American Library Association, 1984). For an architectural study of Carnegie buildings, see Abigail A. Van Slyck, *Free to All: Carnegie Libraries and American Culture, 1890–1920* (Chicago, Illinois: University of Chicago Press, 1995).

87. Summarized from Roland Conrad Person, *A New Path: Undergraduate Libraries at United States and Canadian Universities, 1949–1987* (New York: Greenwood, 1988).

88. Stephen E. Atkins, *The Academic Library in the American University* (Chicago, Illinois: American Library Association, 1991, reissued with a new preface by Charles B. Lowry [Madison, Wisconsin: Parallel Press, 2003]), ix—xi, 190–97.

89. David Kaser, *The Evolution of the American Academic Library Building* (Lanham, Maryland: Scarecrow Press, 1997), xi—xii.

90. Kaser (1997), 1–11.

91. The legacy of the Farmington Plan resides in the durability of concepts and projects of unbounded growth. Wagner asserted that several large-scale projects have demonstrated conceptual, if not structural, connections to Farmington ideas: the National Cataloging and Acquisitions Program, the Latin American Cooperative Acquisitions Project, Public Law 480 passed by the Eighty-Third Congress which facilitated acquisition of area studies resources, and the establishment of the Center for Research Libraries. See Wagner (2002), 359–82. Latter day iterations constitute massive digital projects. *Wikipedia*, the online encyclopedia, is one example. It does not include full text information but rather summaries. In July 2008, it included 11 million articles in 264 languages, and its 2.5 million English language articles totaled more than all the world's printed encyclopedias combined. See James Gleick, *The Information: A History, A Theory, A Flood* (New York: Pantheon, 2011), 379. Contemporary reports identify more than 5.8 million articles attracting 18 billion page views per month. See http://en.wikipedia.org/wiki/Wikipedia, accessed 25 May 2019. Other remarkably ambitious projects include the Internet Archive, a non-profit based in San Francisco, California that contains 534 billion web pages plus nearly forty million books, texts, movies, and software programs: http://www.internetarchive.org. Similarly, the HathiTrust, a partnership of libraries and other research institutions, is committed to "collecting, organizing, preserving, communicating, and sharing the record of human knowledge": http://www.hathitrust.org/home.

92. Camilla A. Alire and G. Edward Evans, *Academic Librarianship* (New York: Neal-Schuman, 2010), 17. A revised edition is by Evans with Stacey Greenwell (Chicago, IL: ALA, Neal-Schuman, 2018).

93. Alire and Evans (2010), 17.

94. Budd (2012), 15.

95. Quoted in Caroline M. Coughlin and Alice Gertzog, *Lyle's Administration of the College Library*, 1997 Text Edition (Lanham, Maryland: Scarecrow Press, 1997), 26.

96. Alberto Manguel, *The Library at Night* (Toronto, Canada: Knopf Canada, 2006), 24.

97. Wayne Bivens-Tatum, *Libraries and the Enlightenment* (Los Angeles, California: Library Juice Press, 2012), 186. Writers like Bivens-Tatum, Manguel, and Wagner confirm the long-revered values that a librarian's first duty is to increase the stock of the library, and the highest purpose of the library is to render the "heritage of the past fully available to all the people all the time." See Elmer D. Johnson quoted in James Thompson, *A History of the Principles of Librarianship* (London: Clive Bingley, 1977), 100, 110. The values underscored by Bivens-Tatum and others have proven to be durable across cultures and time periods and through times of war, economic depression, and social upheaval. While these values, indeed, fuel the growth of the research library, they also face a rising anti–intellectualism, a congeries of impulses that undervalue knowledge and professional expertise in science, technology, education, and other areas of human endeavor.

98. Battles (2003), 212. Battles also describes the Alexandrian as "the first library with universal aspirations; with its community of scholars, it became a prototype of the university of the modern era" (2003),

30. Sidney L. Jackson has referred to the Alexandrian Library as "the nursery of philologists and humanists" and the "very heart of the humanities," in *Libraries and Librarianship in the West: A Brief History* (New York: McGraw-Hill, 1974), 11. Edith Hall regards the significance of the Alexandrian Library as an "institution where the whole resource constitutes something infinitely greater than the sum of the parts." The concept of the Alexandrian was "designed to preserve intact the memory of humankind." See "Adventures in Ancient Greek and Roman Libraries" in *The Meaning of the Library: A Cultural History*, ed. Alice Crawford (Princeton, New Jersey: Princeton University Press, 2015), 10.

99. Shera (1945), 21; Robin Winks, *Cloak & Gown: Scholars in the Secret War, 1939–1961* (New York: William Morrow, 1987); Ellen W. Schrecker, *No Ivory Tower: McCarthyism and the Universities* (New York: Oxford University Press, 1986); and Wayne A. Wiegand, "American Library History Literature, 1947–1997: Theoretical Perspectives" in Wertheimer and Davis (2000), 14–15.

100. M. Connor Sullivan, "From Warehouses to Workshops, From Libraries to Labs," (2015).

101. Robert Darnton, *The Case for Books: Past, Present and Future, with a New Chapter on Google and the Digital Future* (New York: Public Affairs, 2009), 41.

Introductory Essays

Article-length essays that treat the whole of academic library history are quite rare, as they should be, given the complexity of the subject. Still, a few authors have attempted essays of wide scope, some of them dating from the nineteenth century. While scholarly writing and historical research have advanced dramatically in the years since, something vital can be gleaned from early accounts with fragmented quotations and sketchy quantitative comparisons; we cite some of these sources in our section, "The Academic Library in the United States: Selected Historical Readings." If as readers we gain little more, we surely can learn of the limited goals and minimal resources of the early college libraries and develop, perhaps, an appreciation for their will to survive and to overcome seemingly insurmountable odds.

As historical writing about academic libraries has matured, the more prevalent form that has emerged is the article length contribution about some component of library practice. To cite several examples, historical essays have appeared that treat collections, public services, instruction, management, cataloging and classification, preservation, cooperation, computerization and other forms of technology, library buildings and spaces, special collections and archives, and fundraising and development. Overlapping topics address human relations and the labor force, treating matters such as quality of life in the workplace, equity and opportunity for women, international students and international relations, and the LGBTQ experience, as well as racial, ethnic, religious, political, pedagogical, and economic influences. Thus, relatively few articles paint with a broad enough brush to offer a single portrait of the library from rudimentary origins to a complex present.

The two essays reprinted here are among those few, appearing in the form of an introductory historical account while focusing on a signal feature of the library that holds broad interpretive potential. The essays by Beverly P. Lynch (1935–2020) and John Caldwell hold implications for the roles of the library and the librarian and their reputation on campus. They incorporate insight into the library's stature asking, in one form or another, the burning questions that undergird the narratives, "How important is an academic library to its parent institution?" "Has the library had the opportunity to impact the educational work of the college or not?" "If it has, how did that happen?" "To what extent and under what circumstances did it happen?" Beverly P. Lynch traced the library from Colonial beginnings to the 1990s and pinpointed influential leaders as well as key transitions in management, pedagogy, research, and technology. She noted, with approval and hope, the resilience and flexibility of library workers, particularly those in the mid-late twentieth century, the first generations to benefit from a combination of strong professional acculturation and graduate study. She observed, intertwined into the D.N.A. of the academic librarian, a proclivity for early adoption—especially of new technology—and a strong impulse to innovate in order to improve service or enhance efficiency.

John Caldwell examined the book-length histories of twenty-eight liberal arts colleges in Illinois, Indiana, Michigan, Ohio, and Wisconsin (the states of the Old Northwest Territory) in search of references to college libraries. He thus replicated the approach of Louis Shores and others, seeking to uncover general trends by examining historically a core group of colleges with important traits in common. Within the narratives, he identified statements historians have made about the on-campus library while telling the institutional story, thus getting to the core of how the library has been regarded on its home campus.

Caldwell joined those who challenge the received wisdom of the oft-repeated phrase, "the library is the heart of the college," a statement appearing in some histories that then, ironically, say little of importance about the library. In a way similar to that of Stephen Atkins, Caldwell observes that professors and administrators have seldom understood the role of the library or the librarian responsible for it. He found the college library to be in the throes of benign neglect: a college and its stakeholders would, indeed, claim the library as essential to their institution but they would fail, ultimately, to present a rationale for why that might be the case. Caldwell thus reflected little of the optimism expressed by Lynch, offering an alternative but equally insightful point of view. Incidentally, much of the excitement that accrued to the ideas marked by the "heart of the college" vocabulary, which at best served limited administrative purposes, emerged in universities that were building new buildings, expanding research capacity, and attracting graduate faculty in the nationwide higher education movement arising in the late nineteenth and early twentieth centuries. The small colleges that remained committed to civic education (while fostering a traditional liberal arts curriculum) tended, at the time, to experience comparatively less of the intellectual and professional ferment that was transforming the research library into an essential component of the modern university.

The Development of the Academic Library in American Higher Education and the Role of the Academic Librarian

Beverly P. Lynch

Introduction

This chapter sketches the historical development of the academic library, placed in the context of the history of American higher education. Emphasis is given to the role of the librarian in that development.

Libraries have been an integral part of American higher education ever since 1636, when the Massachusetts Bay Colony's college at Cambridge was founded and then, two years later, took the name of John Harvard in recognition of the bequest of his library (326 titles in more than 400 volumes). Today the more than 3,500 colleges and universities in the United States have collections that total many millions of volumes. Over the intervening years, the libraries have functioned in varying ways depending on the changing purposes and policies of the institutions they have served. During this time, the role of the libraries has changed from that of keeper of the books to one of broad responsibilities for sophisticated information services. The academic library director of today is a consummate professional, responsible for information services to faculty and students through the provision of information in all formats using every available technology.

The Colonial Period, 1636–1789

The nine colleges established during the Colonial period—Harvard (1636), William and Mary (1693), Yale (1701), Princeton (1746), the University of Pennsylvania (1749), Columbia (1754), Brown (1764), Rutgers (1766), and Dartmouth (1769)—though different in details, embraced the same general purpose: to train the leadership of the churches and of the colonies. Colleges were formed to provide leaders for denominations and, in the event, found themselves also supplying the leaders of the secular society. Though only a tiny fraction of the population attended college, one-half of the signers of the Declaration of Independence were college graduates.

The college curriculum was drawn from the Reformation and from the Renaissance, so the ideals of educating the learned clergy and the gentleman scholar were merged. Within a short time, the American colleges developed their own character. While educating the clergy was an important objective, by the end of the Colonial period, only about forty percent of the graduates were entering the clergy; the others followed the occupations of farming, law, medicine, teaching, and commerce. The numbers entering the clergy continued to decline.[1]

The American colleges were small. For example, in 1710, Harvard had 125 students; Yale had thirty-six. In 1770, there were 413 students at Harvard, 338 at Yale. The faculty comprised the president and a small group of itinerant young men who wanted to be preachers and who took the post of tutor until they could find a permanent appointment to the clergy. The tutors were young men about twenty years old who had just received their BA degrees and were preparing for careers in the ministry. A tutor was assigned to the twenty-four-hour care of a single class, guiding the moral and spiritual development of students as well as their intellectual development. Tutors rarely stayed long in their post, for they were seeking a position in the clergy and left as soon as one was found. In the early years, the faculty consisted of a president/professor and one or two tutors. Later, professors responsible for particular subjects were appointed.

The finances of the colleges were precarious. Most depended on donations and a little bit of public money. The president spent much of his time raising money as well as teaching and administering. In the early days, the president was [often] the librarian.

Each college president acknowledged the importance of building a library to serve the institution. Solicitations for books were made regularly, and the libraries grew as a result of donations. Funds occasionally were allocated for the purchase of books, but most colleges were strapped for money, and the demands for salary support and facilities development took most of the available moneys.

During the Colonial period, while book collections were being established and were growing, the methods of instruction remained lecture and recitation. Libraries were not important to the life of the student; they sometimes were important, however, to the life of the tutors and the emerging faculties, and they were important to the health of the American college curriculum. Kraus's study of the printed catalogs of Harvard, Yale, Princeton, William and Mary, and Brown shows that the libraries were much more than theological collections; half of the books were on other subjects, largely history, literature, and science.

Additional insight into the character of the collections is found in the gift to Yale of books sought out by Jeremiah Dummer, the Connecticut agent in England. Dummer was one of the most important donors to Yale Library in its early years, and largely through Dummer's efforts, Elihu Yale became a benefactor of the college. Included in the Dummer gift of some 800 volumes were all of the issues of the *Tattler* and *Spectator* published between 1710 and 1713; the entire collection of the works of Robert Boyle; the second edition of the *Works of Samuel Johnson*, published in 1713; John Locke's "Essay on Human Understanding"; a complete collection of the works of John Milton; and the works of Isaac Newton.[2]

Even in the early years, the books in the library began to exert an influence toward additional subject matter beyond that of the traditional classical curriculum.

> Yale's first two tutors, Samuel Johnson and Daniel Browne, both of the Class of 1714, [were so carried away by the secular books in the Yale Library that] [t]heir lectures and conversations

with their students soon made clear that the "New Learning," which had arrived in Dummer's parcels of books, could not be understood without more mathematics than the meager arithmetic with which students entered Yale. In 1718 algebra appeared in the Yale course of study, in 1720 astronomy was being studied in mathematical terms.... The growth of mathematical studies in the curriculum was unavoidable once Newtonian physics made its way into the course of natural philosophy.[3]

In 1739, Yale changed its curriculum to make way for science and mathematics. The growing library collections were of major importance to the development and change in the curriculum of the American colleges.

As the collections grew larger and more diverse, the responsibilities for managing the library also increased so that the presidents had to delegate the care of the library to one of the tutors. Thirty years after its founding, Harvard appointed its first librarian, Solomon Stoddard. A graduate of Harvard in 1662, he was made a Harvard tutor in 1666, and in 1667 he was appointed "library keeper," a position he held for about 3 years. His was one of the longer tenures in those years, when tutors left as soon as a permanent church position was found. With the appointment of James Winthrop as librarian of Harvard College in 1772, the post became more stable, Winthrop continuing for fifteen years. He was responsible for dispersing the Harvard Library collections during the Revolutionary War, and then reassembling them.

Many libraries, private as well as collegiate, were lost during the Revolution, but there were other reasons besides war that the collegiate collections remained small. Books were scarce; with little publishing in the colonies, they had to be acquired from abroad. There were problems of fire; by 1764, Harvard had a collection of over 5,000 books, but these were lost in the calamitous fire of that year. Still, by 1790, through donations and purchases, the Harvard College library had more than 12,000 volumes.

The library of William and Mary had 3,000 volumes after the Revolution, with an annual rate of accession of thirty volumes. Yale, also growing by an annual rate of thirty volumes per year, had 7,200 volumes in its collection.[4]

Early National Period, 1789–1870

During the period following the Revolutionary War, the country expanded westward, bringing new colleges to frontier towns. The emphasis on the founding of a college remained denominational. Once established, however, the colleges were open to all students, for the colleges served more a geographical clientele than a religious community. The denominational interest often came from financial backers, who would stipulate that trustees were to be of a certain denomination. The colleges, desperate for tuition-paying students and seeking faculty to teach those students, prohibited religious tests for students and faculty; they were interested more in attracting students than in proselytizing. College-founding in the nineteenth century was undertaken in the same spirit as canal-building, cotton-ginning, farming, and gold mining. In none of these activities did completely rational procedures prevail.[5] By 1860, about 250 colleges, enrolling about 25,000 students, had been founded; of these, 182 colleges have survived.[6]

The curriculum continued as it had been established in the Colonial period. The subjects were primarily Latin, Greek, and mathematics. Rote recitation was standard practice. The purpose was to strengthen and discipline the mind. There was emerging, however, a discontent with the rigidity of the curriculum, reflecting the American interest in the practical and mechanical arts. The US Military Academy, established in 1802 at West Point, and the Rensselaer Polytechnic Institute, established in 1824 at Troy, New York, were the first technical institutes in the United States. Their founding marked a beginning of a shift in the curriculum to science and engineering. Despite the attempts at reform of the curriculum by a few leaders, little change took place until after the Civil War. What did happen, the development of a thriving extracurricular activity, was led by students.

Undergraduates established debating clubs and literary societies and supported society libraries, strong in modern works, containing English literature and American fiction, current works of history, and current politics and science. These libraries not only were larger than those of the college but also reflected a wider range of content. Unlike the college libraries, which were opened perhaps only one or two hours a day and discouraged circulation, they were much more accessible. The literary societies introduced the concept of the student-centered college library. The undergraduate literary societies also introduced subjects not yet included in the college curriculum, exerting the influence that finally led to curricular changes.[7]

In 1849, the society libraries of Yale had an estimated total of 27,700 volumes; the collection of the Yale College library at the time was 20,500. Amherst College's society libraries had 8,000 volumes; the college library had 5,700. By contrast, Harvard's library had 56,000 volumes and the society libraries 12,000.[8]

During this period, productive scholarship was not associated with a career in college teaching. While professors did do some serious writing, it had little connection with the author's teaching responsibility. Scholars did not rely on the college library for their work, except for the transactions of learned societies, which the librarians did seek to acquire.[9] The college libraries were more the kind of library an educated man would expect to possess. To support their scholarship, professors sought to build their own personal collections but, while doing so, they also criticized the state of the college library. The often-quoted letter by George Ticknor, written in 1816 while in Germany, reflected the thinking of many:

> One very important and principal cause of the difference between our University [Harvard] and the one here is the different value we affix to a good library, and the different ideas we have of what a good library is.... We found new professorships and build new colleges in abundance, but we buy no books; and yet it is to me the most obvious thing in the world that it would promote the cause of learning and the reputation of the University ten times more to give six thousand dollars a year to the Library than to found three professorships, and that it would have been wiser to have spent the whole sum that the new chapel had cost on books than on a fine suite of halls.[10]

There were exceptions, of course. Thomas Jefferson, instrumental in the founding of the University of Virginia in 1824, worked diligently to select a library suitable to the purposes of the university and one that would support the work of the faculty he was appointing and the curriculum he was designing. President Tappan at Michigan solicited library funds from the citizens of Ann Arbor in the 1850s, and the first book purchased at Michigan was Audubon's birds. Francis Wayland, president of Brown in the 1830s, also worked to build the library. John Langdon Sibley, librarian at Harvard from 1856 to 1877, emphasized the building of collections to support scholarship. Primarily a collector, Sibley raised moneys and sought gifts that would be useful to the scholar. As a general rule, however, during this period, other newly established colleges were not as diligent in developing their libraries.

As the century progressed, the curriculum was changing, albeit more slowly than some would want. Professors with strong backgrounds in particular subjects were being appointed. While tutors remained, their roles began to change; a fledgling junior faculty was being established. Library collections were growing even if the collections were not appropriate or did not serve well the students and faculty. The library, while not playing much of a role in the life of the college during this period, still was regarded as one of the institution's principal assets. Elaborate codes of rules were written to govern its activity. The story is told often of Sibley, who upon meeting Harvard's president, Charles Eliot, was asked where he was going, whereupon Sibley replied with enthusiasm that all the books were in the library but two, and he was on his way to get those. (The faculty member who had these books is reported to have been Louis Agassiz.) While people reciting this story use it as an example of the custodial nature of librarianship, the truth is that the librarian was responsible and was held accountable for every item in the collection. He was expected to pay for those items not accounted for.

Harvard's library remained the premier academic collection of the country. Most college libraries were much more feeble institutions. Charles Coffin Jewett, librarian of the Smithsonian Institution, in his famous report on the libraries of the 1850s, dismissed the college libraries as "frequently the chance aggregations of gifts of charity; too many of them discarded, as well-nigh worthless, from the shelves of the donors."[11]

Although the quality of many of the collections may not have been high, libraries were continuing to grow. Those people in charge were becoming increasingly concerned about how to manage the organization of the collections and the attendant building conditions.[12] The first steps were taken in the professionalization of the librarian.

The Rise of Leadership: Charles Coffin Jewett

The meeting of 1853 called by the publisher and bookseller Charles B. Norton was a milestone in the development of American librarianship. The meeting was led by Jewett, who was the premier librarian of the day. Of the eighty-three men attending the three-day meeting, forty-five were librarians, and twelve of those were librarians of colleges and universities. In addition to his report on libraries published in 1850, Jewett had published in 1853 *On the Construction of a Catalogue for Libraries*, the first attempt in the United States to codify a standard cataloging practice. The issues addressed in the meeting ranged widely: cataloging practice at the Smithsonian, the formation of a national central library, the distribution of government documents, the problems of library classification, the international exchange of publications, and the indexing of American literature. Four major resolutions were adopted. One favored the establishment of public libraries in every town. The second approved the plan and execution of Poole's *Index*, just published in its second edition. The third proposed the compilation of a manual of standard library practice. The fourth called for the appointment of a committee to draft plans for the formation of a permanent association of librarians.[13]

For those college librarians attending the 1853 conference, there was little expectation that any special qualifications were needed to be a librarian, and the developing hierarchy in the college had no special place for the librarian. While it was obvious that care of the library was necessary, it was a minor task for a professor but one of the tasks necessary in the life of the college. During the period, appointment of a professor as librarian was the standard practice, but it was by no means universal. If it were convenient to place a student or someone else such as the janitor in charge of the library, that was done.[14] Only at the end of the century, as the university movement developed, did librarianship as a profession emerge.

Before the committee to draft plans for a professional association of librarians could be established, the fortunes of the organizers changed, and the Civil War intervened. So, it was not until 1876 that the next meeting of librarians was held. During the intervening period, though, librarians continued to reflect upon the issues relating to the growth and the development of libraries.

Civil War, Industrialization, and Expansion, 1860–1890

The Civil War and its aftermath produced a transformation of American society and its demands on higher education. The colleges, though in many cases still denominational, began to serve the secular society directly. With western expansion and the passage of the Morrill Act, the states themselves began to take responsibility for higher education. The new curriculum no longer bowed to preparation of the clergy but sought to prepare graduates for places in the new industrial society.

Following the Civil War, the country prospered. Men made fortunes, the North became industrialized, and many of the newly rich were beginning to think of philanthropy. The desire for practical, scientific knowledge as opposed to the classical education still emphasized in the colleges was beginning to change, as was the demand to introduce scientific inquiry as found in the German universities.

In 1862, the Morrill Federal Land Grant Act was passed. This led to the formation of the land-grant colleges, ultimately one in every state, doing more to change the face of American higher education than any other event. It placed responsibility for college education in state government and emphasized the importance of vocational and technical education. Morrill, a senator from Vermont, was as early as 1848 seeking ways in which students could receive an education of more practical value. He placed in his legislation the reform notions sought by others regarding technical education. The purpose of the legislation was "to promote the liberal and practical education of the industrial classes in the several pursuits and professions of life."[15]

The founding in 1869 of Cornell University, which merged the land-grant idea along with a curriculum in science and technology and the spirit of scholarship of the time, was a major innovation. President Andrew White, at the time of opening, had one new building, seventeen residents and six nonresident faculty, and 400 students. The university had the incredible luxury of turning away fifty applicants for admission. Clearly, the curriculum of Cornell in its equality of studies, its de-emphasis of the classics, and the introduction of freely elective courses appealed to the college student. Other colleges were watching.

Money remained an important concern. Many of the older colleges opposed the development of the land-grant colleges, fearing the loss of the state support that they had enjoyed and seeking federal support for their own institutions. Competition among institutions for resources characterized much of higher education. By contrast to this competitive environment among institutions, librarians had begun to seek ways to work together and to cooperate on issues of importance to their emerging service emission.

The Emergence of the University, 1890–1944

Strong leadership by presidents and boards of trustees enabled American higher education to transform itself from a college with a limited curriculum, a small amateur faculty, precarious finances, and modest facilities, to the complex system it has become. Eliot at Harvard, White at Cornell, Daniel Coit Gilman at Johns Hopkins, William Rainey Harper at Chicago, Nicholas Murray Butler at Columbia, and James B. Angell at Michigan are among the presidents who led in the development of the research university. Except for Gilman, who decided to make use of the strong libraries already in place in Baltimore and allow the building of seminar libraries in the university rather than build a strong central library, these presidents gave high priority to the development of strong libraries containing collections useful to the scholarship of their faculties.

A Strong President: A Great Library Begins

Before the University of Chicago was opened, Harper, traveling in Germany, bought an entire bookshop, overnight making Chicago, in 1892, the third or fourth largest university library in the United States, and six years later it was the second largest library behind Harvard. By the end of the 1800s, faculties had become professionalized, and the competition among universities for outstanding faculty members was intense. The availability of a strong library was a decided asset in faculty recruitment. Harper recruited professors away from Yale, took the majority of the academic staff at Clark, including fifteen professors, and hired eight former college presidents, succeeding in hiring in his first year 120 faculty members (having money to hire only 80). Harper offered the post of librarian to Melvil Dewey, but Dewey declined.

No librarian was appointed at Chicago until 1910, four years after Harper's death; the general library was managed by an assistant librarian. By the time Ernest Burton, a professor of New Testament theology, was appointed librarian, the dominance of the faculty over library acquisitions, administrative regulations, and departmental branch collections was secure. The pattern of library development at Chicago, after Harper's initial efforts, was dominated by strong academic departments less interested in a general library than in forming their own departmental libraries. While library directors debated the merits of centralized versus departmental collections at their conferences and in their publications, faculties at the University of Chicago were competing for money, resources, and recognition. Having one's own departmental collection was an indicator of success in a fiercely competitive academic environment. While Harvard placed strong emphasis on building a major library at the university yet did not appoint a university librarian, the faculty worked to build specialized collections. The faculty played the central role in library development. Librarians, interested in efficiency and in the promotion of the rational argument that a centralized collection, serving the entire campus, would enable the purchase of more books and the parsimonious use of staff, could not convince the scholar who wanted materials as close to the workplace as possible and wanted to control directly the acquisition of those materials.

The role of the faculty in library development in this period was a critical factor in many institutions. The world of scholarship was changing rapidly. Institutional support for that scholarship had emerged as an important incentive to faculty recruitment. Strong faculty members had strong views as to what should be included in the collections they and their students were using. The university librarian had to manage well the relationships with the president and influential donors and also had to work, preferably as a faculty colleague, with the faculty being served. Some of the important library collections central to research today grew out of the single-minded purpose of a faculty member who was steadfast in his demands for collections to support his work.

The Melville J. Herskovits Library of African Studies at Northwestern University is an example of the impact of the single-mindedness and strong interest of one faculty member upon university library development. The Herskovits collection now is the largest separate library for the study of Africa in existence. Neither the university's administration nor the library's administration planned or anticipated that the collection would develop into the extraordinary resource it now is. Herskovits, appointed to the faculty of sociology at Northwestern in 1927, immediately began to develop the collection. He sought out and found external money to buy materials. Not until 1942 did the institution provide support for the collection. Only in 1959 did the library appoint a curator of the collection.

The larger institutions had full-time librarians by the latter part of the 1800s, and Harvard and Yale had assistants, including several young ladies who carried out clerical tasks. But most college libraries still were one-person operations, and the librarians in these institutions had other duties and responsibilities; some were teaching several subjects.

Library Leaders Emerge

Some extraordinary library leaders emerged during this period, and they set the direction for academic librarianship. The model of the library director as faculty member became well established. As staffs grew in order to care for the growing collections and to maintain longer hours of service, formal programs of library training were established, first at Columbia in 1887. By the time of the famous Williamson report on library education in 1923, fifteen institutions were offering professional programs of training for library service. These were training programs in the techniques required to deal with the internal operations of libraries. There was no theoretical underpinning that would support scholarly inquiry.

University library collections continued to grow. By 1920, Harvard and Yale had collections over one million: Yale 1,250,000; Harvard 2,971,000. By 1940 [the following] university libraries had collections over one million volumes: University of California at Berkeley, Chicago, Harvard, Illinois, Michigan, Minnesota, and Yale. But the college libraries were not faring as well. In an analysis of about 200 four-year liberal arts colleges in the United States published in 1932, only 33 institutions had libraries with more than 60,000 volumes.[16]

William Warner Bishop

Leaders of American librarianship during the late 1920s and 1930s, led by William Warner Bishop, librarian of the University of Michigan, with the support of the

Carnegie Corporation, were seeking to improve the college libraries. Under a mandate of the college library program of the Carnegie Corporation, standards were proposed and then used in making decisions about which college libraries would receive Carnegie grants.[17] Institutions were uneven in the support they provided to their libraries. Many colleges continued to work under constrained fiscal conditions, and most college libraries suffered from lack of support. Only in the 1960s, following the publication of the American Library Association's *Standards for College Libraries* in 1959, did college libraries improve. The standards specified that a college library budget should be a minimum of five percent of the total general and educational budget of the college, that three professional librarians constituted the minimum number of professional staff, and that the minimum size of the collection should be 50,000 volumes. The impetus for improvement came from the standards, from the application of the standards in collegiate accreditation reviews, and from the infusion of moneys for libraries from the federal government through the Higher Education Act of 1965. College libraries prospered.

College librarians worked diligently to provide library service to their students, and many sought ways to inform the college presidents of the important role the library played. But many presidents were preoccupied with other issues and so ignored the library. Bishop described the role of the college librarian:

> The demands which a college makes on its librarian are really manifold and extremely difficult to fill with any success. The college requires its librarian to be a businessman, an administrator, a scholar, and an effective instructor of students, and at the same time to oversee and guide reading in many fields. It is practically impossible to produce a paragon who will succeed in all these lines of activity. The most that can be expected is that we shall develop of necessity a type of scholarly administrator who will understand the problems of instruction and will be able to deal sympathetically with the problems of students and at the same time will be sufficiently versed both in the technique of his profession and in the management of financial affairs to administer a college library with a fair degree of success.[18]

One sees in Bishop's characterization of the college librarian the antecedents in the early college president: that the president had to do everything, so did the librarian. In mastering this role, the library director in many colleges emerged as an important and powerful member of the community. The library staffs, as they grew and developed, however, did not share in the [director's] esteem, nor were they expected to be scholars or faculty members.

Justin Winsor

During this transformation period, American librarianship emerged as a profession, and academic librarianship developed. The American Library Association (ALA) founded in 1876, had as its first president, Harvard's Justin Winsor, who served as ALA's president from 1876 to 1885. Winsor was a founding member of the American Historical Association (1884) and during this period also edited the eight-volume *Narrative and Critical History of America*.

As a result of the Williamson report, the first advanced program in library science, including a program leading to the doctoral degree, was established at the University of Chicago in 1926 with the support of the Carnegie Corporation. In 1931, the Graduate Library School began publishing *The Library Quarterly*, the major research publication of the field. Many of those earning the Ph.D. at Chicago went on to direct major university libraries: Lewis Branscomb, Ohio State; John Dawson, Delaware; Andrew Eaton, Washington University; Ralph Ellsworth, Colorado; Herman Fussler, Chicago; Carl Hintz, Oregon; Richard Logsdon, Columbia; Arthur McAnally, Oklahoma; Archie McNeal, Miami; Stephen McCarthy, Cornell; Errett McDiarmid, Minnesota; Robert Miller, Indiana; Benjamin Powell, Duke.

In 1931, the Association of Research Libraries was founded as an organization separate from the American Library Association and as an organization of research libraries, not librarians. The founding group comprised library directors of institutions that held membership in the Association of American Universities, along with a few other institutions whose directors were prominent in university library circles. In 1938, the Association of College and Research Libraries (ACRL) was organized by the restructuring of the College and Reference Section in the American Library Association, and in 1939 ACRL began publication of *College & Research Libraries*. Finally, in 1947, the first executive secretary of ACRL was appointed, giving the American Library Association a full-time staff member expert in the affairs of college and university libraries.

As the staffs of the university libraries grew in size to accommodate the growing collections and the growing demands on use, the position of the library staff within the framework of the university was emerging as a concern. The position of the library director was secure, generally as a scholar/administrator and often as a member of the faculty. Library staff members, however, generally fell into the classification of clerical workers, for the administrative classification of positions had not yet emerged, and the growing size of the professional staff had not been anticipated. In 1911, Columbia University trustees voted, "The Librarian shall have the rank of Professor, and the Assistant Librarian that of Associate Professor, and the Supervisors shall rank as Assistant Professors and Bibliographers as Instructors," and in 1944, the University of Illinois granted full faculty status and rank to all professional staff. Unlike Columbia, Illinois did not tie rank to position. The nature of the appointment and rank of library staff continued to vary from institution to institution. Even in those institutions with faculty rank for the professional staff, the librarians did not organize themselves as a faculty, did little teaching, and did less research and publication. The professional body of librarians was joined by a larger group of clerical workers who, in many of the state university libraries, were organized under civil service regulations.

Much of the impetus for faculty rank at the University of Illinois was to remove librarians from the clerical/civil service categories and recognize them as professionals in the only way the university then had, the faculty rank.

Mass Education Period, 1945–1990

The expansion of higher education after World War II was driven by three major events: the adoption in 1944 of the GI Bill (the Serviceman's [actually Servicemen's] Readjustment Act), the establishment of the National Science Foundation in 1945, and the Higher Education Act of 1965. Libraries also expanded.

The GI Bill marks the agreement on the policy that higher education should be available to all who qualified and desired it, a social policy that is firmly in place. The legislation, providing direct financial assistance to returning veterans, enabled 2.25 million veterans to go to college.[19] The demand for places led to a great expansion in facilities and an expansion in faculties. By 1964, college enrollments nationwide equaled forty percent of the 18–21-year-old population. By 1970, college enrollments equaled forty-eight percent of the 18–21-year-old population.

The goal of the National Science Foundation was to harness the scientific capabilities developed during wartime for peacetime uses. Universities increased their scientific capabilities, and the federal money supplied to universities for research vital to the interests of the nation helped fuel the expansion of higher education after the war. Anyone watching the development of American higher education could have predicted that the universities would expand greatly on the side of the natural sciences and engineering and the applied social sciences such as business and public administration. Such expansion would come about not because society needed more people educated in the natural sciences and engineering but, rather, because strong and powerful social pressures would push universities that way, as they had been doing since the early years. The research dollars from the federal government were powerful persuaders.

The liberal arts colleges also shifted their curriculum to reflect student choice, adding professional programs in business, computer science, and other professional and vocational areas to match the interests of potential students. American colleges have been very resilient. Colleges that rely heavily on tuition as a source of revenue have been as likely to add professional programs as have colleges that rely on state funds for support.

Library budgets for collections began to shift toward the sciences, but the humanities and social sciences benefited as well from the great increases in the library budgets that came about in this period as a result of the Higher Education Act.

Universities, anxious to develop into major research institutions, appointed strong librarians who sought out collections, embarking upon a period of collection building that has been described as "imaginative and resourceful, often imprudent and risk-taking, and remarkably successful."[20] University libraries bought private collections, entire bookshops, every item in the catalog of an antiquarian dealer. Institutional collecting was a major force in the support universities provided to their scholars. Competition for faculty during this period was as intense as it was during the late 1800s, and the library continued to be an asset in faculty recruitment. By 1990, all members of the Association of Research Libraries (107 universities) had collections over one million volumes.[21]

The size of the library staffs grew during this period, for more professional librarians were added as the collections grew, and more nonprofessional staff members were needed as well. But salaries remained low. In 1973, fewer than ten percent of the professional librarians were in positions in which the average compensation exceeded that of assistant professors in similar institutions.[22]

In the 1950s and 1960s there was a push for faculty status for librarians, led by Robert Downs at the University of Illinois and Arthur McAnally at the University of Oklahoma and culminating in the "Standards for Faculty Status" adopted by the Association of College and Research Libraries in 1972. Faculty rank and status were achieved by librarians in many of the Midwestern land-grant universities, and librarians in the state universities and colleges in California, the State University of New York (SUNY), and the City University of New York (CUNY) also were appointed as faculty. In those institutions in which the faculty groups were organized as unions, the salaries of librarians were raised to match the salaries of other faculties.

There was resistance by other universities ("What teaching and research does a librarian do?"), by librarians who did not relish the responsibilities of the faculty ("I don't want to publish; I just want to do my job"), and by library administrators ("I can't run a library like an academic department"). There was also an attack on the faculty status of academic librarians by those faculty members teaching in schools and departments of library science. As one put it: "[a]pplying publish-or-perish to academic librarians, devalues their role as librarians. The implication is that it is better to be pseudo-faculty, than [to be] genuine librarians with their own distinct expertise and unique contribution to the university community. This is damaging to the profession's image within the university and to its self-image as well."[23]

Although librarians might not have wanted the responsibilities of faculty, they did want a share in the governance of the library. Many libraries experienced discontent, particularly among newly hired library school graduates who were eager to participate in what they saw to be the central affairs of the library, not just the issues relating to their own work.

As collections continued to grow, librarians turned to the new developments in computing for help in managing the collections. During the 1980s, libraries introduced automated circulation systems and shared copy cataloging on a regional and national basis, bringing cost-savings and improvements in library efficiencies. On-line catalogs, and electronic access to databases through on-line services or CD-ROM technology, were important additions to the improvements in quality library services. Academic libraries, by using existing staff to introduce and implement the new technologies, experimented early with the team-based approaches to library management. Library committees and task forces were formed to develop many of the automated programs in libraries. The successful adoption of new technologies lessened the tensions between the library administration and the professional staff, which might have continued had academic libraries not begun to change their methods of operations.

The absorption of computing technologies in libraries brought librarians early into the information age. For many faculty and students, the use of on-line catalogs was their first experience with computing technologies. Academic librarians at first applied computing technologies to internal operations, and then extended the new technologies to all aspects of information service. Because of the scale of the libraries' internal operation, library staff members were important players in the development of automation on the campus. Because librarians were knowledgeable and well versed in the technology of the day, they were influential in much of the planning of the campus infrastructures.

The New Era: Technological Imperatives

Academic librarianship's successful adoption of information technology to improve library services, operations, and management emphasized the administrative aspects of the profession, not the scholarly aspects. The leadership of the university library for the last twenty years or so has concentrated on its relationships to the campus administration, where the decisions on resource allocations are made. The interactions with faculty members and students were left as the responsibility of the library's professional staff. College librarians, by contrast, continued to be more closely allied to the faculty and to the teaching programs of the college campus. The integration of the college library into the academic life of the college campus has been more immediate and direct than it has been for the university library.

Those librarians who work closely with faculty and students relate to the scholarly and instructional side. A difficulty academic librarianship has is that it has become so specialized that it is difficult to keep up with what faculty members are doing or even in what direction a particular academic department is moving. Furthermore, the central role the library might have played in the work of a particular department or discipline has changed as the way the faculty member does his or her work also has changed. Big science has dominated the American university for the last forty years and has dominated the acquisitions budgets of university libraries. Now, as the move to electronic publishing of journals grows, the use that faculty and students are making of collections of scientific publications is changing. Will libraries assess the information-seeking behaviors of their users and allocate budgets accordingly? Will the library still be seen as an asset in faculty recruitment, in institutional prestige, in donor support? What indicators besides print collections might be used in deciding whether or not the library is an asset? These questions confront academic librarianship today.

As the core functions of librarianship were automated, acquisitions, cataloging, and circulation became routine tasks assigned to lower-level staff. As the same time, librarians were looking for ways to measure performance of libraries beyond just the historical input measures of size of collection, size of staff, and size of budget. During the 1980s, greater attention was being given to the information services provided by reference units and to methods of instruction in the use of libraries, formally through library-based classes or more informally through cooperative arrangements with various faculty and academic departments. Now, librarians are being asked to address the issue of what value the library adds to the educational mission of the campus. So, the role of the library in the institutional process has become an important issue and one to which librarians are responding, using their experience and knowledge with new technologies to great advantage.

The faculty's influence in the administrative life of the campus, while significant, is not strong. Strong presidents and strong boards continue to dominate the important issues of organizational change, major programmatic shifts, and budget allocations. Faculty committees can and do propose change, but if resources are needed to implement proposals, the administration determines the implementation. While some would say that the faculties are impediments to change, the history of change in American higher education belies that. Change has been embraced from the beginning, with the college adapting to social pressures and demands made upon it by students, but that change has not come quickly but more deliberately.

Significant changes in higher education are in the offing; on that everyone agrees. There are changes in student demographics, in the nature of public support for higher education, in the costs of higher education. There are changes in the scholarly disciplines that will lead to changes in teaching, research, and scholarly communication. There are changes in student expectations about higher education. The technological changes libraries made in the 1980s were guided by agreed-upon library priorities that emphasized the use of technology to improve library operations. The changes coming about in the next ten years will be guided more by academic programs, institutional priorities, and economic concerns. As Clifford Lynch so aptly stated,

> [L]ibraries will have increasingly less latitude in the coming years to pursue autonomously defined, technologically determined manifest destiny at a pace that is comfortable to the library administration and staff (and patrons), and hope that this future will conveniently and serendipitously converge with university programmatic needs. Instead, libraries will be

expected to provide leadership in supporting institutional programmatic objectives and to move more rapidly than they have in the past.[24]

The successful adaptation of the American academic library to the new technologies and the ability of library staff members, at every level, to use computer technologies in their work have been obvious to all users. Campus administrators, confronted with the budget requests from libraries for more wiring, for network improvements, for equipment upgrades, for materials in new formats, and for leasing arrangements instead of purchasing agreements, have recognized the knowledge and abilities of librarians to manage the technologies and the change. This recognition has led to a growing movement of adding responsibility for campus computing and telecommunications to the librarian's role. The director of libraries is emerging as the chief information officer in many colleges and universities.

Beginning in the early 1990s and accelerating rapidly as digital information resources become more pervasive, librarians and faculty members are assessing the impact of the networked environment on instruction and research. Resources formerly available only in print at a specific place now are accessed through the networked desktop. The role of the librarian and the nature of the library are being influenced profoundly.

Final Comment

Academic librarians have retooled themselves continuously. Upgrading their knowledge, skills, and abilities, librarians now are experts in the use of new technologies. They are developing new methods of providing support to users who do not use libraries and are adapting the digital technologies to the development of new resources and services. Librarians are being asked by faculty members and educational policy committees to help in the delivery of new information services, unfettered by time and place. Librarians are placing themselves in academic departments, being asked to assist directly in the provision of instruction using the new technologies. While the library director may have policy and program responsibilities for all forms of information, the professional staff, well-educated and well-trained, are implementing the programs.

Academic librarians do not have a monopoly on the provision of information services and the selection of resources. They never have. From the beginning, though, librarians have played a central and vital role in the development of scholarship and in the support of instruction. That rule remains, and the profession has positioned itself to continue in it. Campus administrators and faculties rely on the librarians for support for the academic enterprise—as they always have.

Note

I am indebted to Arthur M. Cohen, William L. Williamson, and the editors (Terrence F. Mech and Gerard B. McCabe) for their help with this chapter.

NOTES

1. 1. Sheldon S. Cohen, *A History of Colonial Education 1607–1776* (New York: Wiley, 1974), 101.
2. Joe W. Kraus, "The Book Collections of Early American College Libraries," *Library Quarterly* 43:2 (April 1973), 142–59.

3. Anne Stokely Pratt, "The Books Sent from England by Jeremiah Dummer to Yale College," in *Papers in Honor of Andrew Keogh*, Yale University Library Staff, ed. (New Haven, Connecticut: privately printed, 1938), 7–44; and Louise May Bryant and Mary Patterson, "The List of Books Sent by Jeremiah Dummer," in *Papers in Honor of Andrew Keogh* (New Haven, Connecticut: privately printed, 1938), 423–92.

4. Frederick Rudolph, *Curriculum: A History of the American Undergraduate Course of Study since 1636* (San Francisco, California: Jossey-Bass, 1977), 33–34.

5. Frederick Rudolph, *The American College and University: A History* (Athens, Georgia: University of Georgia Press, 1990), 48. John R. Thelin issued this version from the original, published in 1962, and added an introductory essay and supplemental bibliography.

6. Rudolph (1990), 47.

7. Rudolph (1990), 136–55; Thomas S. Harding, "College Literary Societies: Their Contribution to the Development of Academic Libraries, 1815–76 : I. The Golden Age of College Society Libraries, 1815–40," *Library Quarterly* 29:1 (January 1959), 1–26; and Thomas S. Harding, "College Literary Societies: Their Contribution to the Development of Academic Libraries, 1815–76 : II. The Decline of College Society Libraries, 1841–76," *Library Quarterly* 29:2 (April 1959), 94–112.

8. Kenneth J. Brough, *Scholar's Workshop: Evolving Conceptions of Library Service* (Urbana, Illinois: University of Illinois Press, 1953), 14–15.

9. Arthur E. Bestor, Jr., "The Transformation of American Scholarship, 1875–1917," *Library Quarterly* 23:3 (July 1953), 166.

10. Samuel Eliot Morison, *Three Centuries of Harvard, 1636–1936* (Cambridge, Massachusetts: Harvard University Press, 1936), 266.

11. C.C. Jewett, "Statistics of American Libraries," in *Fourth Annual Report ... of the Smithsonian Institution ... during the Year 1849* (Washington, D.C.: Smithsonian Institution, 1850), 39.

12ҫW.N. Chattin Carlton, "College Libraries in the Mid-Nineteenth Century," *Library Journal* 32:11 (1907), 479–86.

13. George Burwell Utley, *The Librarians' Conference of 1853, A Chapter in American Library History* (Chicago, Illinois: American Library Association, 1951).

14. Orvin Lee Shiflett, *Origins of American Academic Librarianship* (Norwood, New Jersey: Ablex, 1981), 45–48.

15. Rudolph (1990), 249.

16. William M. Randall, *The College Library: A Descriptive Study of Libraries in Four-Year Liberal Arts Colleges in the United States* (Chicago, Illinois: American Library Association, 1932).

17. William Warner Bishop, *Carnegie Corporation and College Libraries, 1929–1938* (New York: Carnegie Corporation of New York, 1938).

18. Bishop (1938), 47.

19. Arthur Levine, *Handbook on Undergraduate Curriculum* (San Francisco, California: Jossey-Bass, 1978), 510.

20. Robert Vosper, "Collection Building and Rare Books," in Jerrold Orne, ed. *Research Librarianship: Essays in Honor of Robert B. Downs* (New York: R.R. Bowker, 1971), 89.

21. Association of Research Libraries, *ARL Statistics 1900–91* (Washington, D.C.: Author, 1992), 44.

22. Donald F. Cameron and Peggy Heim, *Librarians in Higher Education: Their Compensation Structures for the Academic Year 1972–73* (Washington, D.C.: Council on Library Resources, 1974).

23. Nancy A. Van House, "Assessing the Quantity, Quality, and Impact of LIS Research," in Charles R. McClure and Peter Hernon, eds. *Library and Information Science Research: Perspectives and Strategies for Improvement* (Norwood, New Jersey: Ablex, 1991), 85–100.

24. Clifford A. Lynch, "The Technological Framework for Library Panning in the Next Decade," in Beverly P. Lynch, ed. *Information Technology and the Remaking of the University Library* (San Francisco, California: Jossey-Bass, 1995), 95.

Perceptions of the Academic Library

Midwestern College Libraries as They Have Been Depicted in College Histories

John Caldwell

That the library is the heart of the college is one of the most persistent of American academic myths. It is a metaphor frequently used by college presidents and trustees, brochures and catalogs proclaim it, faculty members subscribe to it. To measure this myth against reality, I studied the portrayal of the library in the published histories of twenty-eight Midwestern colleges. By what they say about them, the historians tell us what they believe libraries to be and how vital they seem to the life of the colleges. The importance ascribed to libraries by the colleges can be inferred from the support given to them and the resources that have been committed to their development.

I chose to study the colleges of the Old Northwest—Ohio, Indiana, Illinois, Michigan, and Wisconsin—because it was the first part of the West to be systematically settled and organized. This area attracted people from all the Atlantic seaboard states, people who brought with them the social, political, and religious opinions represented in the original states and merged into a developing Americanism. All of the colleges studied had denominational beginnings. Founded primarily to provide an educated clergy for the frontier, they were soon producing Christian laymen who became the lawyers, politicians, doctors, and business leaders of the region. To ensure a similarity of history, I studied only private liberal arts colleges that are at least one hundred years old; seven of them founded before 1840, eight in the 1840s, eight in the 1850s, and five in the 1860s. Throughout much of the nineteenth century, American college education changed very little so that all of these schools, whether founded in 1830 or 1860, had some period of similar curriculum and experienced change and innovation in their programs at about the same time.

I believe that it is legitimate to use these college histories as a measure of the importance attached to libraries by the institutions and their authors, and to some degree, by the academic community at large. The histories were all published by, or under the sponsorship of, the institutions and all but three of them were written by faculty members or administrators. Because of some joint authorship, thirty-one individuals participated in writing the twenty-eight histories. Five of these were college presidents; four were other administrators; ten were history professors; five were English professors; and four were professors in other disciplines. The three that were neither administrators nor faculty of the colleges were a local newspaper editor long acquainted with the school; a professional editor, daughter of a long-time faculty member and herself a graduate of the school; and a professional historian hired by the college to spend a year on the campus researching and writing its history. Because almost all of these authors are academicians, the references that they make to the college library should be some indication of what they understand about its place in the life of the college. At least three of these authors speak of the library as "the heart of the educational enterprise,"[1] "the heart of the university,"[2] and "at the heart of any college."[3]

In many of these histories, a library is referred to as part of the founding of the college. In conjunction with finding a site, raising money, and hiring teachers, we are told that steps were taken to acquire a library. "I have collected about three to 400 volumes of books, some very valuable works," a founder of Carthage wrote.[4] In 1834, subscriptions for Marietta included "books to the value of $150."[5] President Jacques of MacMurray College, "starting the institution on a high academic level ... organized a library and a laboratory."[6] While he traveled around Ohio looking for a site for a college, Wittenberg's first president was also "to collect books and money ... for the institution's library."[7]

The historian's first reference to a library is frequently as a space in an early building. In Davenport's history of Monmouth, the first mention of the library is as a room in a building constructed in 1875, twenty-three years after the beginning of the college.[8] In the first building at Eureka College, "the Library was about ten feet square and most of the space was occupied by vacancy."[9] The first president of McKendree College wrote, "we ... made the library and recitation rooms cheerful with paint, paper, and whitewash."[10] An 1880 report at Olivet refers to: "a new building ... in process of construction ... for a chemical laboratory, library, and other purposes."[11] Antioch's first building had "a chapel 50x90x30 feet, a lecture room, a library, laboratories, and a recitation room."[12] The first catalog of Carroll College announced a new building containing "three Recitation Rooms, an Academy Room, a Chapel, and a Library."[13]

The conception of library as space continues throughout the histories, the migration of the "library room" from one building to another is faithfully recorded. The greatest amount of space devoted to the library is sometimes the record of the raising of the money, the planning and construction of a library building—Augustana's Denkmann Library,[14] Eureka's Melick Library,[15] DePauw's Carnegie Library[16]—but in the majority of the histories only a page and some scattered references are devoted to this event. The actual move into a new building is sometimes described with admiration:

> In January of 1970 ... the temperature was -20 degrees Fahrenheit that morning of the move! Hundreds of students presented themselves for work ... two long lines stretched between the buildings.... It was truly one of the great days of Monmouth history, perhaps the greatest.[17]

In 1900, ninety-four young men with thirty-six young women to give them directions moved the Wooster College collection into the new Frick Library. "In two hours and five minutes the job was done, and almost every book was in its proper place."[18]

In the histories of Eureka, Illinois College, Rockford, Earlham, Albion, and Hope, the move into a new building is the last mention of the library. In each case the reference is from fifty-five to eighty-two pages from the end of the volume.

The single most frequently noted library information is the number of volumes held. All of the histories give this statistic, frequently exhibiting it as a measure of excellence. Wooster in 1942, "accessioned its 100,000[th] volume."[19] "A library that had 55,000 volumes in 1907 ... contained almost three times that number ... in 1937" we are told of

Ohio Wesleyan's library.[20] "Academically the college was strengthening," we are told of Rockford College in 1899, "the library contained 7,000 books."[21] At Albion there was an increase of 12,000 in twenty years, "this meant that the library possessed in 1921 almost double the number of books it contained in 1901."[22] The Wabash "library had grown from 6,000 to 30,000 volumes ... by 1892."[23]

References to rare books and special collections are also used to demonstrate the quality of library book collections. Earlham has "the best collection [of Friends publications] west of the Appalachians."[24] A 1561 Book of Hours, "five volumes of a 1793 edition of Dante owned and annotated by Shelley" and a valuable collection of papal manuscripts are in the Saint Mary's College library.[25] As early as 1836, Kenyon had some "rare and costly" volumes.[26]

Marietta has "priceless collections" of Americana both books and manuscripts.[27] The Methodist Historical Society Collection at Ohio Wesleyan "because of the rarity of some of its items [has drawn] special students from a distance ... for research purposes."[28] None of these statements are wrong or, in and of themselves, bad, but when they are given undue emphasis, they present a distorted view of the library in the life of the college. The prominence given to collection size and rare items demonstrates that, in the eye of the historian, these have a greater importance than other aspects of the library.

In some histories, except for an occasional reference to the director, there is virtually no mention of a librarian. When colleges were founded in the nineteenth century, almost anyone could be designated to look after the few books. At Wabash College in 1833–34 "the steward's recompense for acting as librarian consisted of the privilege to 'make free use of the books.'"[29] At Olivet the first librarian was a student and the library was kept in his room.[30] At Kenyon the first librarian was Mrs. Chase, the president's wife, who "kept the accounts of the institution and looked after the library."[31] At Illinois Wesleyan during the 1860s, H.C. DeMott, while doing graduate work also taught mathematics and served as librarian.[32] The arrangement at North Central was typical, "almost from the beginning ... various members of the faculty were selected as librarians, a responsibility in addition to their regular academic teaching."[33] During most of the nineteenth century the professor-librarian carried on a one-person operation with the library open only a few hours a day. As more hours were demanded, the professor remained in charge but was given a full-time assistant to keep the library open. At DePauw "Mrs. A.E. Lester was placed in immediate charge of the reading room and kept it open seven hours each day."[34] "Dr. Robert F. Cornell was appointed director of the library [at Kalamazoo] and Mrs. L.J. Hemmes, chief librarian."[35] Ohio Wesleyan, in 1943, still had a professor-librarian but since the 1870s had had a series of library attendants. Joseph R. Dickenson, whose "remarkable memory made the library catalog superfluous," and "Aunt Kate" Schock, "a familiar and beloved figure behind the library desk for several decades," seem to have been the most noteworthy.[36] Occasionally the assistant became the librarian. At Beloit in 1909:

> Miss Iva M. Butlin of the class of 1902, whose service in the library ... had been invaluable in its intelligence and fidelity, now received the appointment of Associate Librarian. Later she was promoted to the office of Librarian and Associate Professor of Library Science.[37]

The change from the part-time professor-librarian to the librarian as trained professional with a full-time appointment as library director was slow in coming and happened at different times in the various schools, often not until well into the 1930s. That many of the historians see this appointment as a significant event is demonstrated by the frequency with which they note the fact that, typically expressed as "Miss Margaret Jane Gibbs … became [Hope] College's first professional librarian in 1931."[38] In 1935, William W. Sweet exclaims in his history of DePauw:

> Perhaps nowhere has there been a greater change in the interests of better academic service than in the library. For the first time in the history of the university a trained library staff has been installed.[39]

The anomalous status of these newly arrived professionals is best expressed in the history of Wabash: "also practically a part of the faculty [have] been the librarians."[40]

Some authors become almost patronizing when they attempt to describe the hard-working librarian:

> In 1944, Miss Elizabeth Bechtel retired after forty-four years. Since 1915, she had carried responsibility as librarian, always stretching the budget as far as it would go, always looking ahead, always considerate of the various faculty—and how well she knows them and their eccentricities—always expecting and getting the best from her growing staff of assistants, always there when somebody needed her, always cheerful…. Her own little cubby-hole of an office in the northeast corner of the old Frick library was her home. She never missed a day there. Outside her window was an old and rather sprawling elm and farther off some of the venerable oaks of the old campus. These and the books around her were her world.[41]

> Through the thirty-seven years…. Mr. Wedding has missed few days at the Library…. In his early years as librarian, Mr. Wedding accomplished the huge task of rearranging … and recataloging [the books] on the system then most advanced. As this book is being written he is resolutely beginning a completely new cataloging of them. The system that was so new in 1896 has become old in 1931 … But the librarian then as now is indefatigable, patiently and capably performing each day more than one man's work, possessed of such knowledge of books as only a lifetime of managing a great collection of them can bring.[42]

"The primary function of the library, of course, was the housing of the College's treasury of books."[43] Statements like this one, written in 1982, betray a complete misunderstanding of what libraries are about. Although there are some exceptions, the historians studied exhibit a general misunderstanding of why libraries exist or how they are organized. We are told that "the library was cataloged on the Dewey system of classification,"[44] and that librarians "had been busy cataloguing the books according to the approved Dewey system."[45] One writer who treats library matters most extensively refers to the standards set by the National Library Association.[46] Most references to the growth of the collection exhibit no interest in how books are acquired. There is, however, one reference to an early approval plan at Albion, where the 1884–1885 catalog reported that they had established:

> … an arrangement with Phillips & Hunt, whereby we are to receive for examination monthly installments of the newest books in various departments, thus enabling us to keep up with the very best thought.[47]

The perennial problem of the allocation of funds among departments was discussed by one historian. Book funds had been divided equally at Wabash but it became "obvious that history and English needed more books than Greek and mathematics"; all attempts to change the system failed until a lawyer worked out a "scheme of division so equitable that it has stood ever since."[48] In the area of collection development it is noted that in 1900, Wooster was trying to complete its sets of the standard British periodicals "so that *Poole's Index* might become a useable reference book."[49] The problem of a centralized collection as opposed to departmental libraries is discussed at DePauw where, in 1912, the departmental libraries that had developed over a twenty year period were, with the active encouragement of a new president, assembled in the new library building. Endowed collections were given special shelving but "all the others were placed in the general stacks."[50] There are descriptions of this same solution being applied to problems at Valparaiso[51] and Kalamazoo.[52] Censorship is sometimes depicted as a problem in the early days of collection management. A student's recollection of an incident at MacMurray is reported, Emerson's *Representative Men* was removed from the library by the faculty who claimed "… 'its influence would be pernicious upon our young minds.'"[53] At Wooster the Reverend T.K. Davis, librarian 1877–1915, "guarded closely, on forbidden shelves, many books which he regarded as morally or intellectually dangerous."[54] There are also infrequent references to other aspects of library service. There is mention of the development of reference services at Ohio Wesleyan,[55] of bibliographic instruction at MacMurray in the 1940s[56] and at Ohio Wesleyan between 1905 and 1907,[57] and of interlibrary loan at Monmouth in the 1970s.[58]

Although there are some exceptions, some indications of an understanding of the depth and breadth of the library's place in a college, for the most part the historians studied indicate by the emphasis that they place on collection size, rare books, and buildings that they perceive the library to be a place where books are kept, where quiet and decorum preside. They see librarians not as colleagues in the educational process but rather as a breed of acolytes performing their own mysteries in the temple of learning.

I have not counted pages nor compared the number of paragraphs given to the library as contrasted to other subjects, but other matters do get a great deal more attention in these histories. Throughout the nineteenth century all of these colleges were under-financed, and much space is given to their struggles to raise enough money each year to survive. There is an emphasis on the development of the curriculum and of the faculty, sometimes with extended biographical sketches of presidents and faculty members. The development of intercollegiate competition receives considerable emphasis; during the ante-bellum period contests were usually in oratory and other forensic activities, by the 1880s they had become increasingly athletic. There are whole chapters chronicling the increasing prowess of the Little Giants, the Vikings, and the Crusaders in baseball, football, and basketball. During World War I, seventeen of these colleges had units of the Student Army Training Corps. These were organized in September 1918 and were disbanded almost immediately after the Armistice two months later, yet they always receive several pages of coverage, occasionally whole chapters. In this milieu, the library remains a refuge, a quiet retreat for the historian, not unimportant but certainly not the vital, pulsating heart that sends life throughout the campus.

When these college histories are considered as a unit, they become a history of higher education in these five Midwestern states. In this general history, we can measure the commitment to libraries exhibited by the colleges.

Libraries were established at the founding of the colleges, but they were usually made up, as was that of Olivet, of "donations from the libraries of clergymen and others, and were not the most valuable class of books,"[59] or of Beloit which had "too large a proportion" of government reports and miscellaneous gifts.[60] At Augustana the first five thousand volumes were from the library of Sweden's King Charles XV and consisted of books in French about the French revolution.[61] As the years passed many colleges made few improvements in their libraries. A faculty report at North Central College, in 1880, called the library a disgrace and said that they were ashamed to report the number of volumes to the Bureau of Education.[62] A visiting committee for the Society for the Promotion of Theological and Collegiate Education, in 1851, reported that the library at Illinois College was more like an appendage than an integral part of the institution.[63] In 1892 a State Board of Visitors advised Kalamazoo that it should give immediate attention to its meager library which contained few books of real value.[64]

These collections, poor as they were, were not made available to the students. The Carthage library, in 1884, was open only a half hour after lunch each day.[65] In the 1870s Wooster's library was open a few hours each morning,[66] that of Wabash "only a limited period each day,"[67] and the same was true of Illinois College,[68] North Central,[69] Kalamazoo,[70] and Marietta.[71] In 1895, Ohio Wesleyan built the Sturgis Library but it was open for only an "hour or two on Saturdays."[72] At Earlham in the 1860s:

> Since there was no full-time oversight, the use of the library was restricted to the girls in the morning hours and to the boys in the afternoon, while the doors to the forbidden side were locked.[73]

At DePauw, before 1880, when regular hours were set, the library was kept locked. To borrow a book a student had first to find the librarian to get the key, go get the book and then return the key.[74]

It has been suggested that, because of the classical curriculum and the text-book method of teaching, students in the mid-nineteenth century did not need a college library.[75] This is demonstrably not true. When the students did not have a satisfactory library, they created their own. All of the colleges had literary societies: the Phrenokosmian, the Periclesian, the Ionian, and many more. As the classical curriculum did not provide for instruction in modern literature or forensics, the literary society was established to provide these extracurricular activities; to support these programs the societies established libraries which supplied books for general reading.[76] At Kalamazoo, in 1868, Philolexious had nearly one thousand volumes of historical, biographical, philosophical, and general works.[77] The three societies at Marietta together had seven thousand volumes by 1860 and Psi Gamma had begun the systematic purchase of histories of the early settlements in the Ohio and Mississippi valleys.[78] In 1869 the Phi Nu at MacMurray hosted a complete set of Dickens[79] and one society reading room at Augustana received "a score of periodicals in English, Swedish, German, and Norwegian."[80] Mary Watters, writing about MacMurray College, says that because their collections were accessible "society libraries were far more extensively used than the college library."[81] This was probably true at most of the other colleges as well. The students in the nineteenth century Midwestern colleges needed library service: when the colleges did not provide it, they created it for themselves.

When the college curriculum broadened to include modern literature and as athletic fever swept through the campuses in the 1880s, the societies began to wither; some died, others changed themselves into fraternities and sororities. Athletics had caught the fancy of students and faculty; intercollegiate competition began to blossom, and physical education departments appeared. At about this time the college library collections, under the pressure of curricular change, began to grow; by the early 1900s they had absorbed the society libraries, and most campuses were in need of a library building. However, at nineteen of the twenty-eight colleges studied, including two of the three women's colleges, a gymnasium was built before a library. At Kenyon, some kind of library victory was scored when, in 1881, a cornerstone was laid for a gymnasium, but the building was completed in 1885 as a library.[82] Although many gyms had also to do duty as an auditorium, many of the libraries housed the administration of the college or gave space to one or two academic departments.

Libraries developed slowly, and buildings often were constructed only if someone could be found to donate a large sum of money. Sometimes faculty-administration pressure was effective in getting action; sometimes it took external force. When Rockford was denied a Phi Beta Kappa chapter because its library was inadequate[83] and St. Mary's was rejected by the AAUW for the same reason[84] they began to take effective steps to strengthen their libraries.

If the historians in this study, or the colleges that they wrote about, really believed that the library is the heart of the college, it cannot be said that either demonstrated it. The history of libraries and library services in these colleges is one of benign neglect on the part of the schools; the historians give only cursory attention to the library and, concentrating on the externals of collection size and buildings, rarely exhibit any real understanding of the intrinsic problems of library growth and organization for effective service; and these, of course, are the things that libraries are all about and that are at the heart of the college.

Notes

1. Charles Goodsell and Willis Frederick Dunbar, *Centennial History of Kalamazoo College* (Kalamazoo, Michigan: Kalamazoo College, 1933), 178.
2. David B. Owens, ed., *These Hundred Years: The Centennial History of Capital University* (Columbus, Ohio: Capital University, 1950), 184.
3. Lucy Lillian Notestein, *Wooster of the Midwest*, 2 vols. (Kent, Ohio: Kent State University Press, 1971), 2: 297.
4. Quoted in Harold H. Lentz, *The Miracle of Carthage: History of Carthage College, 1874-1974* (Lima, Ohio: C.S.S. Publishing Company, 1975), 10.
5. Arthur G. Beach, *A Pioneer College: The Story of Marietta* (Chicago, Illinois: John F. Cuneo, 1936), 46.
6. Mary Watters, *The First Hundred Years of MacMurray College* (Jacksonville, Illinois: MacMurray College for Women, 1947), 43-44.
7. Harold H. Lentz, *A History of Wittenberg College (1845-1945)* (Springfield, Ohio: Wittenberg Press, 1947), 27.
8. F. Garvin Davenport, *Monmouth College: The First Hundred Years* (Cedar Rapids, Iowa: Torch Press, 1953), 25.
9. Harold Adams, *History of Eureka College* (Eureka, Illinois: Board of Trustees, Eureka College, 1982), 25.
10. Quoted in William Clarence Walton, *Centennial History of McKendree College* (Lebanon, Illinois: McKendree College, 1928), 147.
11. Quoted in Wolcott B. Williams, *A History of Olivet College* (Olivet, Michigan: Olivet College, 1901), 45.
12. Harvard F. Valence, "A History of Antioch College" (Ph.D. dissertation, Ohio State University, 1936), 38.
13. Quoted in Ellen Langill, *Carroll College: The First Century, 1846-1946* (Waukesha, Wisconsin: Carroll College Press, 1980), 31.
14. Conrad Bergendoff, *Augustana, A Profession of Faith; A History of Augustana College, 1860-1935* (Rock Island, Illinois: Augustana College Library, 1969), 135-38.
15. Adams, 237-43.
16. William W. Sweet, *Indiana Asbury—DePauw University, 1837-1937; A Hundred Years of Higher Education in the Middle West* (New York: Abingdon Press, 1937), 135-38.

17. William Urban, *A History of Monmouth College Through Its Fifth Quarter Century* (Monmouth, Illinois: Monmouth College, 1979), 172.
18. Notestein, 1: 223.
19. Notestein, 2: 336.
20. Henry Clyde Hubbart, *Ohio Wesleyan's First Hundred Years* (Delaware, Ohio: Ohio Wesleyan University, 1943), 306.
21. C. Hal Nelson, ed., *Rockford College: A Retrospective Look* (Rockford, Illinois: Rockford College, 1980), 82.
22. Robert Gildart, *Albion College, 1835-1960: A History* (Albion, Michigan: The College, 1961), 188.
23. James Insley Osborne and Theodore Gregory Gronert, *Wabash College, The First Hundred Years, 1832-1932* (Crawfordsville, Indiana: R.E. Banta, 1932), 153.
24. Opal Thornburg, *Earlham: The Story of the College, 1847-1962* (Richmond, Indiana: Earlham College Press, 1963), 246.
25. Helen Creek, *A Panorama: 1844-1977: Saint Mary's College, Notre Dame, Indiana* (Notre Dame, Indiana: Saint Mary's College, 1977), 146-47.
26. George Franklin Smythe, *Kenyon College, Its First Century* (New Haven, Connecticut: Yale University Press for Kenyon College, 1924), 319.
27. Beach, 245-50.
28. Hubbart, 306.
29. Osborne and Gronert, 38.
30. Williams, 74.
31. Smythe, 39.
32. Elmo Scott Watson, *The Illinois Wesleyan Story, 1850-1950* (Bloomington, Illinois: Illinois Wesleyan University, 1950), 66.
33. Clarence N. Roberts, *North Central College, A Century of Liberal Education, 1861-1961* (Naperville, Illinois: North Central College, 1960), 132.
34. Sweet, 136.
35. Goodsell and Dunbar, 177.
36. Hubbart, 304-05.
37. Edward Dwight Eaton, with Chapters by Members of the Faculty, *Historical Sketches of Beloit College*, 2nd ed. (New York: A.S. Barnes, 1935), 166.
38. Wynand Wichers, *A Century of Hope, 1866-1966* (Grand Rapids, Michigan: Eerdmans, 1968), 210.
39. Sweet, 256.
40. Osborne and Gronert, 199.
41. Notestein, 2: 337.
42. Osborne and Gronert, 200.
43. Notestein, 2: 337.
44. Charles Henry Rammelkamp, *Illinois College, A Centennial History, 1829-1929* (New Haven, Connecticut: Yale University Press for Illinois College, 1928), 433.
45. Notestein, 1: 223.
46. Notestein, 2: 336.
47. Quoted in Gildart, 133-34.
48. Osborne and Gronert, 298-99.
49. Notestein, 1: 223.
50. Sweet, 129.
51. John Strietelmeier, *Valparaiso's First Century; A Centennial History of Valparaiso University* (Valparaiso, Indiana: The University, 1959), 100.
52. Goodsell and Dunbar, 129.
53. Quoted in Watters, 98.
54. Notestein, 1: 86.
55. Hubbart, 307.
56. Watters, 511.
57. Hubbart, 305.
58. Urban, 172.
59. Williams, 74.
60. Eaton, 153.
61. Bergendoff, 23.
62. Roberts, 104.
63. Rammelkamp, 171.
64. Goodsell and Dunbar, 99.
65. Lentz, 92.
66. Notestein, 1: 86.
67. Osborne and Gronert, 72.

68 Introductory Essays

68. Rammelkamp, 55.
69. Roberts, 132.
70. Goodsell and Dunbar, 99.
71. Beach, 101.
72. Hubbart, 302.
73. Thornburg, 143.
74. Sweet, 134.
75. Orvin Lee Shiflett, *Origins of American Academic Librarianship* (Norwood, New Jersey: Ablex, 1981), 272.
76. Thornburg, 104.
77. Goodsell and Dunbar, 102.
78. Beach, 101, 110.
79. Watters, 286.
80. Bergendoff, 75.
81. Watters, 175.
82. Smythe, 226.
83. Nelson, 104.
84. Creek, 75.

Book Collections and Classical Training, 1638–1799

American colleges during the seventeenth and eighteenth centuries were derived from British and, to a lesser extent, continental antecedents while bearing distinctively American characteristics. The nine colleges of the Colonial Era, established by British charter, did not benefit thereby in any discernible way. They lacked public and state support, relying heavily on church denominational and individual resources, and they created their own structure, becoming stand-alone colleges rather than smaller entities clustered around a central university as at Oxford and Cambridge. People of influence and wealth sent their white, Anglo-Saxon, Protestant sons to college which served as a kind of finishing school, preparing youth for participation in public life. Graduates would then become understudies for careers in business, law, medicine, and the ministry. The colleges were small operations, usually with little more than a hundred students and a handful of professors. Since the colleges attracted only the tiniest of populations, women and ethnic minorities and the laboring classes (farmers, artisans, and shopkeepers, for example) were not part of the collegiate scene. The college libraries were small: Harvard led the way with about 5,000 volumes, destroyed by fire in 1764 but replenished over the next decade. The other eight college library collections were substantially smaller throughout the later years of the eighteenth century.

College curricula and pedagogical methods stressed memorizing and reciting texts, relied on subjects rooted in the Greek and Roman classics, and did not constitute settings essential for library use or library growth. Colleges had evolved from European models; curricula had been informed by Medieval and Renaissance thought and subsequently revised in the Enlightenment. Much of what the Colonial college offered was at least remotely traceable to the *trivium* and *quadrivium* of the Medieval university. The college drew from these traditions and focused on training for mental acuity and character-building with a mid-nineteenth century curriculum constituted of Latin, Greek, logic, rhetoric, mathematics, and natural philosophy, and the capstone course—moral philosophy—frequently offered to seniors by the college president. Students had limited opportunity for inquiry, comparison, and experimentation as modes of learning. Although certain colonial elites pursued scholarly and scientific investigation, they did so without any direct relationship to the limited functions of the colonial college.

Amidst the impulse to establish institutions of higher learning, cultural leadership lay beyond the colleges. Colonial leaders, some of them landed gentry, nurtured intellectual life, and they constituted the professional classes as physicians, lawyers, judges, ministers, and businessmen, individuals who followed well-established pathways to social status and public service. People of influence sometimes established libraries and supported colleges but almost never focused on strengthening the library on a college campus. They created personal libraries heavily dependent on books and journals imported from Europe, given the nascent printing and publishing trades in North America. The collections themselves were specialized, reflecting multiple obsessions, and while collectors sometimes opened their libraries to friends, family, and guest scholars, their practices of use varied widely so that the interested reader could not necessarily expect admission to a given private library.

Among leading collectors was John Winthrop, Jr. (1606–1676), a member of one of New England's most distinguished families, who promoted scientific research and by 1640 had accumulated about a thousand volumes plus manuscripts and medical notebooks. Minister and author Cotton Mather (1662–1727) likewise represented a prominent family, inheriting a private collection later expanded by his heirs to more than 8,000 volumes. Quaker jurist James Logan (1674–1751) collected 3,000 volumes on humanities and scientific subjects. Benjamin Franklin (1706–1790), one of the premier minds of the eighteenth century, explored numerous subjects, founded the colonies' first subscription library, and left a personal collection of about 4,000 volumes. We cite Winthrop, Mather, Logan, and Franklin to illustrate what an individual collector could accomplish in support of ravenous intellectual pursuits, also offering a glimpse of the larger scene of books and libraries in the colonies.

John Winthrop, Jr., a physician and scientist, was appointed the first American fellow of The Royal Society. Though extracting minerals and overseeing an iron factory for a living, he pursued scientific interests as an avocation but with characteristic enthusiasm. Library historians Elmer D. Johnson and Michael H. Harris described his library as one of the more prominent of its period and region; collection strengths included science, medicine, alchemy, Greek and Latin, Dutch, English, French, Italian, and Spanish. Winthrop bought collections in history, law, literature, philosophy, and religion, and made them available to his friends and colleagues.[1] His descendants preserved and expanded his library, modeling the trajectory often sought for a significant collection—that it would eventually find a home in an established research institution with the capacity to serve scholars and researchers for decades and centuries into the future. Thus, a number of volumes originally collected by Winthrop, Jr., are housed in the New York Society Library; in similar fashion, hundreds of books collected by Benjamin Franklin subsequently landed at Harvard and Yale.

The academic library becomes a part of this story as eventual beneficiary of collectors like these whose libraries influenced culture in the colonies, were preserved through generations, and eventually found permanent homes in research universities. Colonial scholars and scientists were frequently avid collectors, their private libraries essential to vocational and recreational interests and, subsequently, to scholars of today. Historians have cited the college library's dependence on gifts as a sign of its relative insignificance, with the lack of consistent funding a defining feature. And yet the gifts of individual collectors came, albeit generations later, to constitute valuable and durable assets for academe in general, so much so that as libraries grew aggressively, they did so, in part, by acquiring entire collections either through gift or purchase. In fact, the founding contribution to Harvard University, established by charter in 1636, was made as part of a bequest by Puritan minister John Harvard (1607–1638), and it included a sum of money plus a library of almost 400 volumes. Individual collectors, typically immigrants themselves like Mr. Harvard, relied on travel to England and the Continent in order to prowl book stalls, and establish connections with booksellers, publishers, and other bibliophiles. The vast majority of colonists, bent on pushing back the frontier, had minimal leisure for cultural pursuits but a tiny corps—those well-endowed intellectually and financially—traveled far and wide in search of elusive titles.

Harvard was the only college in the colonies until William and Mary was established in 1693 but it was Yale, established in 1701, that attracted some of the most remarkable gifts, modeling an early method of collection building. Colonists subsequently founded Princeton (1746), Columbia (1754), Pennsylvania (1755), Brown (1765), Rutgers (1766), and Dartmouth (1769). The compelling tale of their libraries is intertwined with their durability as institutions and in their intellectual stature today.

Historians have rightly decried the text-based recitations of the eighteenth-century classroom as too rigid to ensure for the colleges a formative role in American life. The small liberal arts college is often portrayed negatively in contrast to the emerging university of the late nineteenth century with its expansive research prowess, imported from Germany and elsewhere, and that eventually transformed higher education. And yet the importance of the small college must not be overlooked. The colleges schooled revolutionaries, citizens who established villages, states, and a nation by fighting a war, writing laws, and creating the political infrastructure for representative government. College graduates typically represented colonial elites, and they succeeded in bringing to life the new United States of America, assuming the mantle of public service, and creating an environment that nurtured the slow but inexorable growth of colleges and their libraries.

The essays we included offer insight into the colonial scene. In "Books Across the Atlantic," Eric Glasgow (1925–2005) outlined the practical challenges of transporting a library across the ocean into the New World where the struggle for survival dominated daily affairs to the virtual exclusion of cultural interests. Still, the prescient vision of John Harvard beamed brightly, highlighting forever his role in establishing the nation's most revered academic institution and, simultaneously, his pioneering work as a library benefactor. Glasgow contextualized John Harvard's collection, launched in the New World but wholly dependent on the Old World, a library with theology at the center, surrounded by literature, philosophy, and science, both ancient and modern. To accompany Glasgow, we excerpted "Libraries in America to 1850: College Libraries," reprinting the seventeenth and eighteenth-century section from *History of Libraries in the Western World* (3rd edition, 1976) by Elmer D. Johnson (1915–2009) and Michael H. Harris (1941–2017), a survey timed for centennial celebrations. Johnson, a college librarian with a doctorate in history from the University of North Carolina, had issued the first two editions (1965, 1970), and Harris followed with updates (1984, 1995, 1999). Together and separately, they have provided historical insight and inspiration for the library community for half a century. Reviewing the Colonial Era, they identified dates and events of origin, and considered methods of collection organization and growth, management, and patterns of use.

Note

1. Elmer D. Johnson and Michael H. Harris, *History of Libraries in the Western World*, 3d ed. (Metuchen, New Jersey: Scarecrow Press, 1976), 183; and Louis B. Wright, "Books, Libraries, and Learning," in Michael H. Harris, ed. (Washington, D.C.: NCR Microcard Editions, 1971), 21. Harris reprinted Wright's essay from *Cultural Life of the American Colonies* (New York: Harper and Row, 1957), 126–33. Elmer D. Johnson discussed book collectors in *History of Libraries in the Western World*, 2nd Ed. (Metuchen, New Jersey: Scarecrow Press, 1970), 307–08, 318, 322, as did Donald C. Dickinson in *Dictionary of American Book Collectors* (New York: Greenwood Press, 1986), selected entries.

Books Across the Atlantic

Eric Glasgow

Abstract

The name of John Harvard is widely known through the university that bears his name, yet relatively little is known of the man himself. One of the Puritan Fathers of New England, he was not the founder of Harvard University, the principle of which had been decided in the summer of 1636 while Harvard himself was still in England; but at his death in 1638 he bequeathed half of his estate and all of his books to the college. The nature of his private library is described and discussed.

Books Across the Atlantic

It must go without saying that the story of John Harvard (1607–1638) is the first and most obvious of all the Anglo-American links across the broad expanses of the North Atlantic Ocean. It must also unite us in a further consideration of the contrasting conditions of England under the Early Stuarts with its combination of political and religious intolerance, and of the North American Colonies, especially in New England, in the first and the primitive stage of their social and economic development.

Until fairly recent times, John Harvard was "scarcely more than a name," and far less was known about his life in England, before 1637, than about his life in New England during the very short period before his death in 1638, when he was the first private benefactor to make substantial provision for the establishment of the incipient Harvard College: the first institution of higher learning and education in the new world. Thus, in 1842, an American named James Savage offered a reward of US$500 for anyone who could provide five lines of authentic information about John Harvard in any capacity, public or private. There were no takers. Today, we certainly know more about John Harvard: his life on both sides of the Atlantic. Back in 1702 "the reverend and learned" Cotton Mather, in his *Magnalia Christi Americana* could record little more than a brief note on Harvard dealing entirely with his American benefaction of all his books, and the sum of rather less than eight hundred pounds for the purposes of "Harvard College." "It soon found encouragement from several other benefactors."[1]

Since then, however, researchers have ferreted out a reasonable amount about Harvard's family and a good deal of this throws useful light on English social history for this distant period. John Harvard was born in Southwark, London, son of a fairly well-to-do butcher, Robert Harvard, who died of the plague in 1625. He went on, in his education, from Southwark Grammar School, to Emmanuel College, Cambridge, which he entered

74 Book Collections and Classical Training, 1638–1799

for the autumn term of 1627, when he was almost 20 years of age. He graduated BA there in 1632, and MA in 1635. Emmanuel College—founded by Sir Walter Midway in 1584 on the site of a former priory of the Dominican Order—was from the start a Puritan foundation; and, in the 1630s, a large proportion of its graduates sooner or later emigrated to New England. John Harvard was among these, although neither he nor his family was ever fanatic about Puritanism.

At any rate, he delayed his departure for the New World until after his marriage, on 19 April 1636, to Anne Sadler, sister of one of his College mates, John Sadler (1615–74). Massachusetts, of course, had already been started by the famous Pilgrim Fathers in 1620; and after 1630—when the High Church persecution of Puritans in England began—the emigration into New England steadily increased. Yet it was not until the summer of 1637—with the intensification of Archbishop Laud's efforts in England to suppress Puritanism—that John Harvard set off for the New World. There, under conditions of great hardship and privation, he very quickly gained for himself an established position, acquiring land, building a house, and preaching in the local church. Perhaps because of these unaccustomed tasks and responsibilities he died suddenly and unexpectedly on 14 September 1638, before he had reached his 31st birthday.

His was a short and comparatively uneventful life, therefore, which might scarcely have been remembered at all in the ampler annals of history, had it not been for the fact that he left so much of his estate for the benefit of what was soon afterwards known as Harvard College, the genesis of the senior and most prestigious of all the American universities. There has always been some doubt about the precise monetary value of John Harvard's bequest. But it seems reasonably certain that amounted to just under 800 pounds, a very substantial sum for those times. This John Harvard had gathered entirely from family inheritance, so that he can have had no economic motive or necessity for his trans-Atlantic emigration. It was solely for conscience.

Moreover, we have to be careful when we may assign to him the renown as "The founder of Harvard University." The latter had already been envisaged by Massachusetts, before his death. His bequest, therefore, although most useful was unexpected and it did not exactly initiate the project. As early as 1636 the proposal for a "College" of higher learning was accepted by the Colony of Massachusetts, which then proposed to endow it with the sum of 400 pounds, half Harvard's bequest. At the time of Harvard's death in 1638 the college was already in operation and a start had been made on the construction of its first permanent building. It follows, therefore, that John Harvard rendered secure and predictable the establishment of Harvard College; but he did not initiate the idea, a very remarkable one for so poor and struggling a North American colony.

Even today, perhaps, John Harvard remains a somewhat shadowy and elusive figure. Not a single letter of his has survived and there is no available portrait: those representations that do exist, as in the Chapel of Emmanuel College, Cambridge, being merely imaginative impressions. Nevertheless, the character that does obviously emerge, even from the meager historical data that is now at hand, combines financial acumen with an outstanding dedication to books and literary culture, which Harvard had no intention of relinquishing because of his long trans-Atlantic journey. Indeed, it is evident that despite his inability to conform to the religious orthodoxies of his times, he clung even harder to his beliefs in the traditional culture of his times. Thus between 1635 and 1637—when he left England for North America—he assembled for trans-Atlantic transportation a very remarkable collection of books, most of which in the end went to begin the Library of Harvard College. It is these books, therefore, that symbolize and epitomize the extraordinary addictions to literature and learning that united as much as they also divided both sides of the North Atlantic Ocean in this period.

Perhaps, even now, we may fail to observe the surprising fact of the Puritan determination to establish in the New World the best standards of book learning, despite their formidable problems of economy and society; the hazards alike of the climate and of the hostile aborigines. Lesser folk would have succumbed to the immense difficulties, and at first settled for primitive standards of living and the urgent simplicities of life: food, housing and material things. Not so the Puritan leaders of New England, however. Before Massachusetts had been in existence as a colony for ten years, the leaders were already actively engaged in the pursuit of culture, undeterred by extremely small money resources and the apparent dependence on an unyielding, truculent soil.

Culture, indeed, became an urgent priority for the earliest of the Colonial Fathers. They were not to be outdone by anything that the Old World could produce in humanism and book learning. By the year 1800 Harvard College had "a library of 5,000 volumes."[2] Evidently, therefore, the Puritans of New England were resolute in their policy of retaining, even expanding, the culture of the Old World, however much they might have been obliged to set aside its religion.

In that important process, too, John Harvard was both typical and crucial. It must always be an extraordinary fact that he contrived to convey across the Atlantic so many diverse and ponderous volumes of theology, literature, and history. After all, these could not then have been either the material necessities or the elementary equipment for a farmer's life in the New World, as then it was. Nevertheless, so carry them he did on a long and perilous sea voyage in the summer of 1637. Fortunately, we have a fairly adequate record of John Harvard's books, kept for us by Samuel Eliot Morison.[3] He eventually gave to Harvard College a total of 329 titles, amounting to some 400 volumes. Nearly three-quarters of these were theological works, mostly in Latin; but they were by no means all of a Calvinistic or even a Protestant sort. Thus, they included works by Chrysostom, Augustine, and St. Thomas Aquinas, as well as works by Luther, Calvin, Melanchthon, and Beza. "John Harvard evidently cared little for the polemical divinity that bulked so large in the Cambridge of his age."[4]

There is evidently a profound and varied curiosity about books and learning among John Harvard's surviving books. He was well read in the Classics, as well as in theology. Moreover, what is perhaps even more striking and extraordinary, he carried that assorted learning—and its requisite books—with him, even across the Atlantic Ocean. He was not to be separated from the seminal sources of his interests and his insights, mostly acquired at Emmanuel College, Cambridge, in the years between 1627 and 1635. The range of the human mind and imagination, then as now, could not be restricted even by such immense and daunting geographical barriers. From him, too, the legacy of books as the necessary vehicles of all civilization and humanism, went directly into the resources of the young Harvard College, for whose eventual educational purposes they became directive and formative.

Books so carried across the Atlantic, to be assimilated permanently in the New World, thus became at least as important for the ultimate destiny of American culture and education—the future for its emerging youth—as John Harvard's money ever was; although that also was certainly a noteworthy legacy, which only insight such as his could have conveyed transatlantically. John Harvard's library was not confined to the aridity of dogmatic or polemical theology; it contained editions of Pliny, Perseus, and Juvenal. It had North's Plutarch, Holland's Pliny, and Chapman's Homer. The existence therein of the major works of Francis Bacon (1561-1626) further indicated that John Harvard had not renounced the scientific thinking of England in the seventeenth century. He also had works by Descartes and Aristotle. He had Aesop's Fables and the comedies of Plautus and Terence. Altogether, therefore, this was a collection of books which, in its taste and range, reflected very validly the culture of an English gentlemen of those times; yet Harvard must have expended a large amount of time, effort and money, not only in gathering it, chiefly in London, but also in transporting it across those unpredictable waters until it could be housed again in his new home in New England. The motivation for all of that is perhaps both curious and significant: certainly, it could have operated only in the conditions of the seventeenth century. In present-day America, of course, there are books in plenty, perhaps even in some super-abundance. The literary resources of the New World, in Anglo-Saxon civilization, have long since supplemented and amplified those of Europe in general and England in particular. A reverse traffic in the transmission of ideas and intellectual appraisals has long since been established and made effective.

But it could never be so in the pioneering times of John Harvard. He went to the New World in its real and harshest beginnings; when books were unknown except in Europe, and so they had to be carried there across the Atlantic. Most immigrants in his times concentrated their attentions on such things as agricultural implements, seed, cattle, carpentry tools. These even John Harvard did not despise. But he also brought with him—what was much more unusual and remarkable—books, in a well-chosen and crucial collection. These we may even today pause to observe as the first sources of the literary culture of the New World, based as it so richly and evidently was, on the best of the traditional learning of Europe.

John Harvard, therefore, was very remarkable for his bookish attainments and expectations for the New World, as well as for the monetary gifts to the first American university. He made it clear that, as far as he was concerned, New England was never to renounce the Old Culture, even if it might wish to renounce the Old Religion; and so, it has been ever since. He may almost have begun that transatlantic traffic in books and the things of the mind which thereafter grew into a process of immense and protracted significance, binding together as well as sometimes dividing the two English-speaking civilizations of the UK and the U.S.A.

All of that process, of course—hugely important for the future of the world's power as well as its inherent civilization—John Harvard could never have foreseen or envisaged. But he largely began it in his own small way with his books and well-wishes for what became, as from 13 March 1639, Harvard College. Thus, his books, so valiantly conveyed across the Atlantic, retain for us even now a large measure of interest and meaning. They were almost the initial germ of all the ensuing literary culture of the New World. All in all, they were also remarkably up to date: over a quarter of them were printed after 1630. "That such a collection could be brought out to a Colony that was less than ten years old is striking evidence of the Puritan purpose to maintain intellectual standards in the New World."[5]

Notes

1. Cotton Mather, *Magnalia Christi Americana: Or, The Ecclesiastical History of New England*, 7 vols. (London: Thomas Parkhurst, 1702), 4: 126.

2. Allan Nevins and Henry Steele Commager, *America: The Story of a Free People* (Boston, Massachusetts: Little, Brown, 1942), 45.
   3. Samuel Eliot Morison, *The Founding of Harvard College* (Cambridge, Massachusetts: Harvard University Press, 1935), 264–66.
   4. Morison, 265.
   5. Morison, 266.

Further Reading

Mather, C. (1702), *Magnalia Christ Americana, or The Ecclesiastical History of New England*.
Miller, P. (1954), *The New England Mind: From Colony to Province*, Oxford.
Morison, S.E. (1935), *The Founding of Harvard College*, Harvard College Press, Cambridge, MA.
Nettels, C.P. (1938), *The Roots of American Civilization*, New York, N.Y.
Nevins, A. and Commager, H.S. (1942), *America: The Story of a Free People*, Oxford.
Stubbings, F. (1983), *Forty-Nine Lives: An Anthology of Portraits of Emmanuel Men* (Chap. 11: John Harvard).

Libraries in America to 1850

College Libraries

Elmer D. Johnson *and*
Michael H. Harris

The history of the college library in America stretches back into the seventeenth century nearly as far as that of the first private collections. Indeed, America's first college could be said to have begun with a collection of books. Harvard had been founded in 1636, so that young men could be trained for the Puritan ministry without returning to England, and it acquired its name in 1638 when the Reverend John Harvard gave the college some 280 books and a small endowment. Other gifts of books followed, including one of forty volumes from Governor John Winthrop in 1642, but the college library grew only slowly. Its holdings were largely theological and, even in 1723 when the first catalog was printed, it contained only 3,500 volumes. In addition to about two thousand religious works, there were titles in history, geography, classics, science, and languages, in that order.

In 1764, when Harvard College was more than a century and a quarter old, the library contained fewer than five thousand volumes and, in that year, it was burned with almost all of its book collection. After this tragedy, friends of the college came to its aid and the Massachusetts Legislature voted funds to replace the burned building. In addition, a popular subscription raised more money for the purchase of books, and with many gifts the library was back to its former size by 1775. Something of the nature of a Colonial college library can be gathered from the library rules at Harvard in 1765. The librarian was required to keep the library room open and heated only on Wednesdays, and only junior and senior students could take books from the library. If these rules sound strict, they were an improvement over the earlier ones which allowed only the seniors to have library privileges. After 1765 Harvard boasted an "undergraduate library," which was a collection of duplicates and more popular works set aside for the use of students. Perhaps the real intent of this move was to restrict student use to a small and more replaceable collection, preserving the majority of the library for faculty use.

A college and a college library were planned for the new colony of Virginia as early as 1620. A collection of books was gathered in the colony and others were sent from England to provide a library for "Henrico Indian College," to be established near the present site of Richmond. The Indian uprising of 1622 put an end to these charitable plans and Virginia did not acquire a college until William and Mary was founded in 1693. This founding was largely the result of the determination of James Blair to provide for the training of Anglican ministers in the college, and he appropriately became its first President. A few hundred books were gathered for the use of the college before 1700, but most of these were destroyed in a fire in 1705. The library was reestablished with a few gifts, but the private library of the Reverend Blair provided most of the reading for the first few decades. In 1742 the will of Governor Alexander Spotswood gave the college about two hundred volumes, and the next year, upon the death of Blair, his library, or most of it, officially became the college library. Even so, it is doubtful that the college owned more than two thousand volumes before the Revolution. Younger faculty members usually "kept" the library a few hours per week, and for some years only clerks were in attendance. No books circulated, and apparently only the faculty used the college library to any extent, while students generally relied on their texts and lecture notes.

New England's second college also began with a collection of books. The eleven ministers who organized a society for the formation of Yale College in New Haven in 1700 each donated a few books, and in the next decade other donations increased the collection to nearly a thousand volumes. In 1714 the Reverend Elihu Yale, for whom the college was named, gave three hundred books to its library, and in 1733 the Reverend George Berkeley of London sent a gift of some one thousand volumes, including many valuable folios. By 1742 the Yale library contained some 2,500 volumes, and the college president, Dr. Thomas Clap, in that year began to reorganize and catalog the collection with the aid of a tutor. He divided the library into two sections, roughly according to size, and numbered each book in each section, giving to each a fixed location. Next, he drew up three catalogs, or booklists: one alphabetically by author, one arranged as the books on the shelf, and a third by broad subject matter, using about twenty-five headings. By 1765 Yale's more than four thousand volumes were still heavily theological, although there were many volumes on history, classics, philosophy, and mathematics. Literature and science were neglected, and there were few books published in America, and in fact few titles published after 1725.

Among other Colonial colleges, the College of New Jersey [Princeton] was begun in 1750, but its library had only some twelve hundred volumes as late as 1764. Governor Jonathan Belcher of New Jersey gave his library in 1757, some 475 volumes, and other gifts came from friends in America and in England. When Dr. John Witherspoon became president of the college in 1768, he added three hundred volumes to the library, but it still contained fewer than two thousand when it was virtually destroyed by British soldiers during the Revolution. The University of Pennsylvania (then the Academy) had its library beginnings in 1750 also, but despite the enthusiastic support of Benjamin Franklin, and library fees charged to students, its book collection was not very large before the Revolution. King's College (later Columbia University in New York) was begun in 1757, and its major library patron was Reverend Bristowe of London, who donated some fifteen hundred volumes. Joseph Murray of New York, one of the college's founders, also left it his library and an endowment, so that by 1764 the collection was large enough for the appointment of its first librarian, who was also the professor of mathematics. Columbia's library, too, suffered at British hands during the Revolution, but some of the pilfered volumes were later restored. Rhode Island College (later Brown University in Providence) began about 1765, with some books collected by the Reverend Morgan Edwards, but still had only some 250 volumes in 1772. Other gifts were received, however, and the collection grew slowly. Fortunately, the Rhode Island students also had access to the volumes in the Providence Library Company, founded in 1753. In 1766,

80   Book Collections and Classical Training, 1638-1799

Queens College (later Rutgers) was founded in New Brunswick, New Jersey, but apparently its library, prior to the Revolution, consisted largely of the books belonging to the faculty. The last Colonial college was Dartmouth, where classes started about 1770 and where a library was begun several years earlier. Eleazar Wheelock, who founded the college as a school for Indians, had begun to round up books as early as 1764. Fortunately, Dartmouth in New Hampshire was little disturbed by the Revolution, and with other gifts being received, a librarian was appointed in 1779 to arrange and administer some twelve hundred volumes. In general, Colonial college libraries were small, made up almost entirely of gifts, managed on a part-time basis by an instructor, open only a few hours weekly, and little used, especially by students.

The few college libraries formed during the Colonial period suffered during the Revolution; in fact, higher education in general was set back seriously by the conflict leading to independence. Still another decade of uncertainty was to follow the Peace of Paris in 1783, but by the 1790s there was a definite improvement in colleges and college libraries and a few new colleges were begun, Growth was slow, however, for most college libraries until after 1850, and the Colonial tradition of opening the library only a few hours a week, with close restrictions on the use of books, was hard to outgrow, Not until after the Civil War, and indeed not until the late nineteenth century, did modern libraries begin to develop in the nation's colleges and universities.

Though forced to move from Cambridge to Concord during the early part of the Revolution, Harvard College saved its library and even added to it with books confiscated from fleeing Loyalists. It revived during the 1780s, and a foreign visitor, Francisco de Miranda of Venezuela, described it as "well arranged and clean ... contains some 12 thousand volumes, English generally, although not badly selected."[1] By 1790, it had reached the place it was to keep as the nation's preeminent academic library.

Note

1. Johnson and Harris did not specify the origin of this quotation, although we expect it is drawn from the reading list they supplied for the chapter, "Libraries in America to 1850," *History of Libraries in the Western World*, 3rd edition, completely revised (Metuchen, New Jersey: Scarecrow Press, 1976), 220-23.

Liberal Arts Colleges and Professional Education, 1800–1875

In the early years of the American experiment, collegiate education struggled to maintain its place and to expand its influence while nation builders focused on seemingly more pressing concerns. And yet the impulse to establish a college, with or without a college library, could not be contained even as many such efforts were doomed to fail. President John Tyler's phrase, "there is nothing like the elbow room of a new country,"[1] captured the spirit of the age, offering an insightful metaphor for the American ethos of expanding, reaching out, and starting all over in the great quest for fortune or fame or a more meaningful future.

John R. Thelin describes a spirit of innovation and consumerism, inhering in the national character, that resulted in a panoply of nearly two hundred colleges by the eve of the Civil War. Daniel J. Boorstin referred to these as "booster colleges," noting that the hallmarks of a town with big-city aspirations required, at a minimum, the establishment of a hotel, a newspaper, and a college. "While in Europe a college or university would be found in an ancient center, in the United States it was more likely than not to appear in a town whose population and prosperity lay all in the future."[2] Numerous small towns took advantage of the missionary spirit of the religious denominations which had launched colleges as part of a larger program to Christianize western settlements. These outposts, in turn, sought to grow, to point to futures bright with prosperity, and they solicited colleges typically out of an innate desire to become another "Athens of the West"; thus, by 1860, the states of Kentucky, Ohio, and Pennsylvania together had chartered sixty colleges.[3]

Yet the colleges did not follow, in rote fashion, the liberal arts model inherited from the Colonial Era. Urban centers like Boston, Philadelphia, and New York hosted medical schools with great variation in courses of study and often with minimal connections to academe. Similarly, law schools exhibited great variety, not requiring an academic pre-requisite but rather uneven combinations of education, apprenticeship, and licensure. In the 1820s, European visitors to the United States noted a striking abundance, even overabundance, of lawyers and law practices.[4]

Citizens in the new nation created colleges for a wide array of purposes. Colleges for women, for example, emerged especially in the Midwestern states of Michigan, Ohio, and Wisconsin, and were often known as academies, seminaries for women, or female institutes. Oberlin College in Ohio had been the first in the nation both to admit people of color and to adopt co-education. Mt. Holyoke, established in western Massachusetts to educate women (at about the same time Oberlin had admitted them), soon became a leader at integrating pedagogical functions into living arrangements. The United States Military Academy at West Point, New York, the Citadel in South Carolina, and the Virginia Military Institute were also established in this period, and they emphasized engineering and other applied sciences. The trustees of one of the oldest state universities, the University of North Carolina, proposed a broad curriculum, one that included agriculture and the applied sciences as well as traditional liberal arts subjects. And the religious denominations, led initially by Catholics, Congregationalists, Episcopalians, Lutherans, Presbyterians, and Unitarians were later joined by Baptist, Methodist, and Disciples groups establishing colleges. These latter three denominations had previously been content with unlettered clergy but their eventual responses to the expansive spirit of the age resulted in colleges of their own.

The authority on libraries of this period was Haynes McMullen. In tabular form, he identified libraries of all types in existence at chronological intervals from the Revolutionary years up to 1875. Many of the libraries were quite small even by the customs and expectations of the day; McMullen specified dates of founding and dates when a library was in existence. He discerned that a number of libraries, like colleges, operated a few years then disbanded, yet he also confirmed the expansive impulses of the nineteenth century. For the year 1790, for example, he identified 157 libraries of all types in existence in the United States, a number that had risen to 2,011 by 1860.[5] The backdrop for these seemingly large numbers was growth in the general population from approximately 3.9 million to 31.4 million for the same period, but also growth in urbanization, commerce, and intellectual life generally including the American book trade. McMullen found, further, that 804 college and professional school libraries were established from the Colonial Era through 1875.[6] While nearly two hundred of these libraries were in classical colleges, the vast majority of them were devoted to traditional professional pursuits such as law, medicine, and theology, but also such practical specialties as agriculture, business, engineering, and teaching.

Howard Clayton (1929–2009) has offered perhaps the single most comprehensive, insightful essay on the smaller group, the libraries in classical colleges during the early nineteenth century. He addressed the range of forces impacting the libraries—intellectual, pedagogical, social, and economic. Within these frameworks, the reader can grasp the significance of the library's dependence on gifts for collection growth, the limitations of service by underqualified part-time staff, and the hazards of uncomfortable and inhospitable facilities. At the same time, all these negatives were sometimes balanced by the relentless drive to build and to grow in the face of seemingly overwhelming odds. Michael H. Harris reprinted Clayton's essay in *Reader in American Library History* ([Washington, D.C.: NCR Microcard Editions, 1971]: 89–98).

Notes

1. Quoted in Edward P. Crapol, *John Tyler: The Accidental President*, Paperback edition (Chapel Hill, North Carolina: University of North Carolina Press, 2012), 237; and Daniel J. Boorstin, *The Americans: The National Experience* (New York: Vintage, 1967), title page. Republished from the 1965 edition.
2. Boorstin, 153.
3. Boorstin, 153; Thelin, 44. David F. Larabee described American colleges as "unusually independent of the state and unusually dependent on the consumers," claiming that robust growth in American higher

education depended on a strong market, a weak state, and a divided church. See *A Perfect Mess: The Unlikely Ascendancy of American Higher Education* (Chicago, Illinois: University of Chicago Press, 2017), 8, 26.

    4. Thelin, 54.

    5. Haynes McMullen, *American Libraries before 1876* (Westport, Connecticut: Greenwood Press, 2000), 48.

    6. Figure derived from Haynes McMullen, "The Founding of Libraries in American Colleges and Professional Schools before 1876," in *For the Good of the Order: Essays in Honor of Edward G. Holley*, ed. Delmus E. Williams, et al (Greenwich, Connecticut: JAI Press, 1994), 40.

The American College Library, 1800–1860

Howard Clayton

When compared to present-day standards, the academic library of 1800 is often thought of as an ineffectual appendage to institutions that were themselves objects of charity. To begin with, no college in 1800 had a collection of more than 13,000 volumes and the smallest of them, Rutgers, probably had a collection of no more than one hundred books (28). Moreover, such libraries had to wage a continuous battle against fires, wars, and pillaging, while relying for support on donations of people who lived far from the campus. Then, too, the college library of 1800 was hampered by severe physical limitations, for the crude furnishings found in most of these libraries must have seemed austere and uninviting even to the people who had grown accustomed to privations.

The academic library of 1800 was weak because higher education was weak. Indeed, the twenty-five colleges existing in the United States when John Adams left the presidency had no more than a foothold in the cultural and economic setting of early nineteenth century America. Moreover, this was as true for the state-supported institutions as it was for the private colleges; in fact, the relative stability of the latter, at least as typified by the nine Colonial colleges, contrasted sharply with the marginal existence of the three public universities in Georgia, Vermont, and North Carolina. One reason for this general impoverishment was that the nation had not yet developed a population large enough to supply colleges with students, faculties, and money. For example, only on the coastline between Virginia and Massachusetts did the population of 1800 range as high as from 18 to 45 inhabitants per square mile, and only four of the nation's largest cities could boast of a population which exceeded 10,000 persons. (34:51)

Yet, it should not be presumed that these institutions were impotent and without meaning. There is evidence, in fact, that considerable leadership came from among graduates of these colleges. Three of the five men who drafted the Declaration of Independence were graduates of the Colonial college; furthermore, four of the five members making up Washington's first cabinet were also products of these schools (33). Such circumstances indicate that even in pre–Revolutionary times, when theology was the cornerstone of its curriculum, the American college was entirely capable of equipping men of action and imagination for service in the demanding field of public affairs.

During the early part of the nineteenth century, then, the American college was playing a useful role though it was forced to operate on a subsistence basis. This Spartan approach to education meant that while all colleges wanted a library, no institution had the resources to provide for more than a small collection of books. But even if these schools had been able to tap great sources of wealth, they still would have had difficulty in building quality collections, for book publishing was but a tiny enterprise during the 1800s. Evans (11), for example, lists only 39,162 publications for the entire period, 1639–1800, and by their very nature many of these materials could not possibly have been available to all college libraries. The same situation obtained for periodicals, for even had libraries subscribed to every American magazine published in 1800, they would have found that the number scarcely exceeded a dozen[1] (3), (4), (6), (24).

Such a situation meant that many materials had to be imported from Europe and England. This in itself resulted in a scarcity of books for colleges prior to 1800; but, as serious as this difficulty was, it still did not have as deleterious effect as did the spirit of illiberality that hampered acquisitions work everywhere during this early time. In 1793, for example, an audit committee of the Trustees found that the purchase of Boydell's *Collection of Prints* by the College of New Jersey—later to become Princeton—was such "a very expensive and totally unnecessary article," that the bill would have to be charged to the president personally (26:304). Because such attitudes were commonplace, it is understandable that the collections at Princeton, Bowdoin, the University of Virginia, and Yale numbered only about 8,000 volumes each in 1829 (3).

Even the meager materials available in the academic libraries of the early nineteenth century were not very well used. Good teaching in that era was necessarily rare; in fact, the faculty had little opportunity to excel. Teachers were usually younger men who aspired to enter the ministry, and as such they were not only poorly paid and motivated but were often called upon to teach the full range of subjects as well. Furthermore, they had to popularize education, among both students and parents, for if the pupil left school it meant the end of a tuition-paying customer. The president's lot was hardly any better, since he was left with the task of being the sole administrator, of conducting religious services, of raising money, of recruiting students, and of teaching courses to the senior class.

The importance of libraries to education, then, was necessarily limited because men who comprised the faculty could rarely lead a scholarly life. Those who did not enter the ministry, and who could content themselves with a life of self-denial, often stayed with their institution forty or fifty years. In this process piety supplanted intellectual promise as the prime requisite for an outstanding faculty, and the result was almost always an absence of intellectualism, or spirit of scholarly inquisitiveness. Such a condition not only proved inimical to the academic library, but it also went a long way toward explaining the attitude expressed by Mark Hopkins when he said, "You read books. I don't read books, in fact, I never did read any books" (25:504). While modern-day historians would probably credit such an outlook to a naïve nineteenth-century faith in experience, rather than to a basic anti-intellectualism, it is nevertheless difficult to believe this concept did not work against the library's development. Therefore, from the standpoint of a librarian, Eliphalet Nott of Union College expressed an equally objectionable attitude when he said, "I care less for Greek than you do, and less for books, generally, as a means of educational discipline" (27:1:155).

If descriptions of early nineteenth-century methods of teaching are valid, it is not surprising that books were unimportant as a means of educational discipline. Classes began early and lasted through the day, being interrupted only by prayers. The customary fare was recitation and textbooks, with little more than singing and the writing of verse to break this cycle. The products of such an education supposedly received a mixture of classical scholarship and theological concepts, the former having come from Renaissance thinking and the latter from Reformation doctrine. Occasionally some far-sighted individual or group could be found who wished to break away from the pattern (2), (17), (19); but such efforts were rare, for the predominant mood concerning genuine liberalization of the curriculum was usually one of intolerance.

Another reason for the relative impotence of the academic library was that many pre–Civil War colleges were sponsored by groups who were neither intellectually minded nor economically affluent. As early as 1776, almost every popular religious sect had either planned or arranged financial backing for a college of its own. But while the training of clergymen supplied the motivation for such exuberance in college founding, not all of these sponsoring denominations actually favored a highly educated ministry. Such a paradox was especially prevalent among Methodists, Baptists, Disciples, and United Brethren groups where evangelical fervor took precedence over scholarship and bookish sources of learning. This is understandable when one remembers that the appeal of such sects was to the underprivileged, the rank-and-file, the frontier lay preacher, and the circuit rider. However, the result at many of the colleges founded by such groups was that a situation developed in which it was impossible to determine whether the suffering of the library's quantitative or qualitative standards was more acute.

The religious atmosphere generated at these small denominational schools could also be found at the tax-supported colleges. While many of the new states made constitutional provision for a public university, the schools that ultimately emerged from such foresight took on an atmosphere which in many ways was not very different from that of the denominational college. Twenty-one state universities were founded before 1860 (30:133); yet, because church sponsorship of higher education remained dominant throughout the Middle Period, it was not until after the Civil War that public universities became significant. Tax-supported colleges, then, were caught in the same educational and economic outlook as that which permeated the denominational campus, and because of this it is not surprising that they demonstrated no more zeal for a quality library than did the private schools. Nor is it any wonder that Charles C. Jewett saw fit to characterize American colleges of this time as "mostly eleemosynary institutions ... [whose] libraries are frequently the chance aggregations of the gifts of charity; too many of them discarded, as well-nigh worthless, from the shelves of the donors." (29:39) From this, it is easy to understand why the library in both types of colleges was typically a collection of gifts, old books, reference works, and standard editions, open only a few hours per week, managed by persons without professional training, and little used by students.

The example of the University of North Carolina is probably typical of the way library programs were developed in public institutions. From the Minutes of the Trustees (38), it would appear that the Board originally had an appreciation for the place of a library in its new university. Indeed, this attitude went beyond mere declarations because from later Minutes, viz., January 3, 1795, it can be seen that the Trustees took direct action in the library's behalf by specifically commissioning a bookcase and a bookplate for its use. Later in the same year, December 7, 1795, the Board went even further, for it then appropriated at least fifty dollars for the purchase of forty-six books whose titles they itemized in the minutes (39). As was the case in other colleges during the period, approval was given for the assessment of student fees so that books could be purchased.

Unfortunately, any good intentions further manifested by the Trustees during the early part of the nineteenth century proved to be short lived, for the period beginning with 1824 and lasting through Reconstruction was a distressing one for the North Carolina university library. As late as 1869, North Carolina's library was reported to have holdings of no more than seven thousand volumes, because at least 1,897 of these volumes were acquired in 1859, subsequent to the death of Prof. Elisha Mitchell in the preceding year. The library's plight during the second quarter of the nineteenth century is seen to be even more dismal when it is noted that from 1824 until 1869 the only other acquisitions were: a gift to the University of sixty volumes; twenty-five volumes from the Smithsonian Institution; 218 state documents; and 1,500 pieces from the federal government (7:5).

Thomas Jefferson was one of the first to be influential in establishing a college that would break this pattern. Jefferson brooded for many years about higher education's lack of concern for modern history, modern languages, and the applied sciences (16)[2]; moreover, he wanted colleges to espouse frankly the concepts of natural law, reason, and observation. At first, he hoped significant change along these lines could be effected at William and Mary; but, when such efforts came to nothing, he turned his thoughts toward the establishment of an entirely new university that would be structured around some of his most cherished notions.[3] This too, however, proved to be difficult and it was only after many years of frustration and disappointment that Jefferson finally saw his dream become reality in the establishment of the University of Virginia at Charlottesville.

Among the extraordinary educational achievements of Jefferson was the incorporation of a library into his plan of study. This was no token effort on the part of the nation's third president, for Mr. Jefferson personally planned the library building, chose the initial collection, arranged for its purchase, classified the materials, and played a large part in selecting the first two librarians (9). Great emphasis was placed on the acquisition of a good collection, and because of this Francis Walker Gilmer was sent to Europe to choose materials and arrange for their purchase. In addition, the book company of Cummings, Hilliard and Co., of Boston, was retained to procure other materials over an extended period of time. As a consequence, the University of Virginia library in 1826 probably contained all the material common to college libraries of the early nineteenth century, plus good holdings in English, French, German, ancient, and modern literature.

Jefferson was also concerned about how the university library would be serviced. With this in mind, he personally formulated rules for its governance and supervised the cataloging of books. The library began with an appropriation of $10,000, and soon thereafter Jefferson ordered another $15,000 worth of materials from Hilliard. In addition, the library subscribed to all the principal American and English reviews and owned the standard sets in law and medicine. Other innovations brought about by Jefferson included a library committee, a central location on campus for the building, and the concept of a collection with authoritative coverage in all fields.

Unfortunately, much of the enthusiasm for such an approach ended with the death of Jefferson. After 1826, the library at the University of Virginia went into decline because of lack of income, attention, and interest. With such elements missing, the program was soon curtailed; and, because the initial outlay for library materials and facilities was substantial, a low priority was given to further acquisitions. Even the personal library of Jefferson did not find its way to the college, for the majority of it went to creditors.

Ultimately, the university did receive 6,800 volumes of this collection, but this was the last contribution of any size until 1836 when James Madison left part of his library and $1,500 in money to the library as endowment (1:186–87). Inattention accorded the academic library during this era was the result of circumstances far more complicated than mere official unconcern. Money had already been mentioned as a problem, but it should be emphasized that the American colleges before 1860 were never far from bankruptcy. This was particularly true of the western colleges, for every one of them was reduced to begging from Easterners just so they could keep their doors open. And while it is true that John Lowell, John Jacob Astor, and Peter Cooper all made contributions to libraries and education before 1860, the huge gifts of the country's noted benefactors did not begin until after the Civil War. Then too, the decision in the Dartmouth case brought an end to public funds for private education, while those principles that came to be the hallmark of Jacksonian Democracy resulted in a further decline of popular support for higher education.

The latter point is especially important to anyone examining the sociology of higher education, for it illustrates an ambivalence toward advanced learning that has been a traditional part of American thought. Because hundreds of colleges were founded throughout this era, higher education must have been important to innumerable persons who had but little schooling of their own. Yet, a popular notion, simultaneously held, was that colleges were for America's privileged classes, and from 1800 to 1860 the climate of opinion increasingly became one in which domination by the common man was idolized and rugged individualism reigned supreme. The chief concerns of the country were not along intellectual lines, for the overwhelming majority of persons were more interested in physical work and in earning a living than in mastering theoretical refinements traditionally derived from bookish sources.

Clearing a wilderness, settling land, and fighting the adversaries of nature were typical American preoccupations throughout the Middle Period. This being the case, it is hardly any wonder that the concept of a gentleman-scholar, leading a life of leisure and contemplation, was not in favor. The American culture of this time had little need of a specialized labor force and it felt no regret for the absence of a tradition in art and music. Consequently, a hard-working population that was at least twenty percent illiterate (35:206) was in no mood to provide vast amounts of money for a college education that was believed to be largely superfluous.

The colleges for their part proved equally obstinate. Attempts to bring about only partial reform in the curriculum were stoutly resisted and all efforts to modernize a basically classical education proved fruitless. George Ticknor was one of the most notable advocates of change, but even he achieved only negligible results at Harvard. In 1823, this noted scholar gave it as his opinion that Harvard's twenty or more teachers, as well as its three hundred students, were busying themselves with the same things that obtained when the college had only a president and a few tutors (31:1:357). Ticknor was anxious to divide the college into departments, limit the choice of subjects and alter the proficiency examinations. He felt that until such changes were effected, instruction at Harvard would always be limited to making certain that prescribed lessons were learned by dealing out punishment when recitations were less than satisfactory.

While it is easy to scorn such teaching and curricula, it should be remembered that many colleges were founded in places where few if any secondary schools existed. This meant that colleges had to undertake a considerable amount of secondary instruction, and in many cases, even elementary training. With an educational program keyed to such a level, it is only natural that the usefulness of a quality library could be nothing more than limited, and in many cases even peripheral. Just how grim the actual situation was can be seen by reviewing a few of the reports which Horace Mann compiled for the Massachusetts Board of Education beginning in 1838 and continuing throughout the 1840s. This noted educator pointed out not only that the state's public schools operated on an average of no more than seventeen weeks per year, but that while 42,164 Massachusetts children did not attend school in the summer, there were at least 23,216 children who went to no school, at all, summer or winter (20:I:38). These reports further stated that because the legislature was operating the state's teacher-training institutions on impossibly low budgets, most public school teachers were less than qualified to face the classroom.

Conservatism and penuriousness, then, were significant factors in American education. Such characteristics might have been excusable had the country not been interested in improvement, or if it had been economically bankrupt. However, such was not the case; on the contrary, public and private funds were generously spent on such social and economic improvements as canals, railroads, and highways. Education, for its part, reciprocated by rejecting most suggestions that it contribute to the country's social needs, a circumstance which is reflected in the fact that during the building of the Erie Canal no college except West Point had an engineering program.

Yet, change was occurring. Rensselaer was developed as a special school to help farmers; normal schools appeared as early as 1839; Cooper Union and Brooklyn Polytechnic were opened in the 1850s for the applied sciences; and a municipal college was started as early as 1837 in Louisville. Obviously, learning was beginning to appeal to more than just the upper classes, a fact that was especially welcome on the frontier. While in the West such a trend seemed imperceptible, by 1815 there were at least twelve Kentucky towns, ten Ohio towns, and two Indiana towns with libraries. Equally important were the libraries in the Ohio Valley at such schools as Transylvania College, Kentucky Academy, Ohio University at Athens, Miami University, Cincinnati College, and Vincennes University, all of which were important enough to attract the attention of local chroniclers (40).

But as has always been the case, those schools which placed the greatest confidence in a classical curriculum showered contempt on those that addressed themselves to the needs of society. The most comprehensive assault on practical education and curriculum change was promulgated in the Yale Report of 1828 (42). This treatise not only denounced the work of reformers, but it stoutly championed the psychology of learning which emphasizes discipline of thought and furniture of the mind. It unabashedly proclaimed the value of the classics by claiming that only they could give a person what he ought to know. And, implicit in the report, was the remarkable reasoning that a single text with recitations is superior to use of the library.

The Yale Report was written by two men who were the personification of stability, conservatism, and caution—Jeremiah Day and James L. Kingsley. Day taught at Yale for sixty-nine years, Kingsley for fifty. Drawing on such lifetimes of service and confidence in the status quo, their Report specifically castigated education intended for mercantile, mechanical, and agricultural pursuits, labeling such teaching as outside the realm of college responsibilities. And of particular chagrin to present day librarians is the fact that it neither said anything for the value of a library in the educational process, nor for its importance to the curriculum. But whatever may be said against it now, in 1828 the Report served its purpose well, for it helped to suppress change until at least the 1850s and to make a permanent fixture of the curriculum until late in the nineteenth century.

But while its impact was shattering, the minority toward which the wrath of the Yale Report was aimed did not give up. A number of scholars had already traveled to Europe and while there they had discovered that libraries and library-centered methods could bring about decisive results. Among such travelers were John Motley, Edward Everett, George Ticknor, and Henry Longfellow. During their sojourns, they not only discovered how inferior American academic libraries actually were, but they also came to feel that high quality libraries in the United States would be necessary if there was ever to be receptiveness to intellectual endeavor among the public at large. A favorite place of study for these American students was Göttingen, and while there they must have been particularly aware of the contrast between European libraries and those at home, for the library at Göttingen contained over 200,000 volumes while the one at Harvard had only 30,000. The impact of a liberally administered academic library was also demonstrated to these men, and especially to Ticknor, for he mentions in his notes (31:I:72) how impressed he was by the fact that the Göttingen library loaned materials to students for as long a as necessary.

Ticknor's opinion was that American college libraries were 50 to 100 years behind those of Europe. He also came to feel that a library was the first necessity in education, a point on which he elaborated by stating that Harvard professors did not complain about inferior holdings because they were blind as to what a quality library really was (15:I:257). If Ticknor's indictment was valid, the statement left other colleges in an especially poor light because at this time Harvard easily had the best college library in the United States. Furthermore, the superiority enjoyed at Cambridge was not just a quantitative one, since there is evidence that Harvard had made conscious efforts to raise the quality of its collection. For example, the Ebeling collection of 3,200 volumes plus 10,000 maps and charts was acquired from Col. Israel Thorndike in 1818, and with this acquisition Harvard made its first gesture toward becoming a research library (12:I:xi). Even earlier, in 1815, an undergraduate library had been recommended, indicating that the college was enough interested in the collection to be willing to spend some time considering a different theory for its use (14). These combined factors point to the conclusion that Harvard did have a library program of some dimensions and may at least partially explain why literary societies did not flourish there as they did at most other colleges.

The effect of such forward-looking policies, however, should not be overestimated. For example, the undergraduate library did not become a reality until 1845 (13:1), and despite the fact that in 1821 the college boasted of a well-organized collection, the emphasis apparently remained on preservation rather than on use. This attitude can be seen from the sentiment expressed in a letter from Joseph Cogswell to George Ticknor of January 18, 1854, in which the former said, "At nine A.M. I take my stand inside the railing and I remain there as a fixture until half-past four. They all look wishfully at the books and ask, 'Can't we go into the alcoves and up to the second story,' and when I answer 'No.' they break out into a railing accusation. But it's no use, I tell them, 'You can't do it.' I know not what I should have done if I had not hit upon this plan of a close corporation. It would have crazed me to have seen a crowd ranging lawlessly among the books and throwing everything into confusion" (10:264).

It is true that this quotation is from a letter written by Cogswell when he was librarian at the Astor Library in New York, and not when he was at Harvard. Nevertheless, he had been one of Harvard's most noted librarians and there is no evidence that in the years before 1854 he was any more amenable to unsupervised use of the collection. Nor is there any reason to think that any of his earlier ideas concerning the composition of a high quality collection were different from the ones expressed in another letter to Ticknor at about the same date, "The readers average 100–200 daily, and they read excellent books, except the young fry who employ all the hours they are out of school in reading the trash, as Scott, Cooper, Dickens, *Punch*, and *the Illustrated News*. Even this is better than spinning street yarns, and as long as they continue perfectly orderly and quiet, as they now are, I shall not object to them amusing themselves with poor books" (10:264–65). Evidence that Cogswell's convictions, as expressed above, were representative of opinion generally can be found among the rules established by the trustees at the University of North Carolina. In Section VIII, Article 1, of the Laws of the University can be found the following, "…No person but a trustee or member of the faculty shall be admitted into the room of the library, without the presence of the librarian." But worse, Article 3 of the same Section states, "The encyclopedia shall not be taken out of the library by any student not belonging to the senior or junior classes; and no other shall ever consult them, except in the presence of some other member of the faculty" (37). It can only be hoped that such rules were necessary because books were difficult to procure, and not because those in authority wanted to limit free inquiry. Whatever the reasons, however, such an attitude was so widespread, and can be so easily documented, that one must conclude preservation of the collection was an over-riding concern of virtually all college libraries between 1800 and 1860.

Despite the conservatism which pervaded American higher education, and notwithstanding the fact that throughout the period 1800–1860 the idea of going to college was beyond the common man's needs or aspirations, the nation was nevertheless beginning to feel the need for more elementary education. One way in which this need was met was through the establishment of land-grant colleges. Although the land-grant movement did not come to fruition until after 1860, the idea was actually conceived much earlier. Such a concept was particularly beneficial to libraries because it stimulated the collecting and disseminating of information, publishing of journals, and writing of monographs on discoveries and experiments. Moreover, between 1800 and 1860 Congress became aware of its duty to education in other ways. West Point and Annapolis were both established in 1802, while interest in scientific research under government auspices could be seen in the creation of the Smithsonian Institution and the Geodetic Survey. Finally, as early as 1867 Congress established a Bureau of Education. These combined circumstances, when taken as a whole, meant that the nation was maturing intellectually, and that men such as Horace Mann, Henry Barnard, and William T. Harris had actually been successful in implanting the notion that popular education was of value to democracy.

One measure of education's impact on daily living can be seen by examining the nature of book publishing in the West. By reviewing the various checklists of imprints which represent publications issuing from printers in Pennsylvania and Kentucky during the period 1786 to 1815, and from printers throughout Ohio from 1796 until 1820, Peckham (23) found that no less than 481 books were published solely for purchase on the open market. Furthermore, in Indiana sixty-five such books appeared from 1804 to 1835, and between 1814 and 1840, printers in Illinois published thirty-two. In making this survey, it was reasoned that titles published with unsubsidized funds would reflect genuine interests in reading, since no printer would risk the capital unless he felt reasonably certain of a profitable return. If this conclusion is correct, it would indeed show that literary tastes did exist west of the Alleghenies and that attention to learning went beyond purely practical application.

It is, of course, easy to overestimate popular enthusiasm for such encouraging trends. Nevertheless, the extent to which reading was affecting America's intellectual awakening can be appreciated by noting that in 1825 the number of periodicals appearing in the United States had risen to 100, and by 1850 this figure was as high as 600 (22:34–42). Of this total, perhaps no more than three professional education magazines were appearing in 1826, although several periodicals of a general nature carried articles on the subject.[4] This number, however, increased significantly between 1825 and 1850, for more than sixty periodicals in the field of education appeared during this quarter century. While a positive correlation is not synonymous with cause and effect, it is nevertheless interesting to note that throughout the period 1825–1860 new public schools and colleges, as well as reading materials of all types, appeared with increasing frequency throughout the United States (36:352, 506–17).

With such a quickening interest in education, it may not be accidental that college libraries saw fit to extend their services to persons beyond the academic community (21). These libraries were probably the only substantial collections of books in large and sparsely settled areas, and their holdings undoubtedly included materials with appeal to the population at large. Such a circumstance is understandable when it is remembered that college libraries were in large part comprised of gifts, a fact which indicated that these books had first been of personal interest to lay donors. This would also account for the fact that religious materials were over-represented in academic libraries and those general stores which sold books in addition to everyday necessities (23). It is, therefore, not surprising that college libraries had holdings that were broad in subject matter but not entirely pertinent to the curriculum.

This lack of association with the classroom was largely because college libraries reflected education's emphasis on teaching rather than study, its preoccupation with students rather than scholars, and its disposition toward maintaining order and discipline rather than promoting learning. In such a restricted atmosphere as this, it is not surprising that during the antebellum period the academic library made little impact on methods of teaching, and even less on faculty involvement in book selection, seminar study, research projects, and interpretation of the collection. The college library reflected the aims and methods of the parent institution between 1800 and 1860 just as it does today and, because of this, it is understandable that in 1835 no academic library in the United States could have supported a study such as Gibbon's *Decline and Fall of the Roman Empire*, or Wheaton's *International Law*. For the same reason, the research for George Ticknor's *History of Spanish Literature*, as well as for the works of Bancroft and Prescott, was necessarily done in Europe.

Colleges during the Middle Period also contrasted sharply with those of today in that many of the era's leading scholars were not connected with higher education. For example, Prescott, Bancroft, Motley, and Parkman were neither teachers in the contemporary sense nor even men who spent much time on campuses in general. Moreover, Longfellow and Lowell, though affiliated with Harvard for a time, did no writing for scholarly journals. This may or may not have been one of the reasons why the study of literature was restricted to ancient and hallowed writers, but exclusion of contemporary writers was almost universal in higher education and this resulted in a significant lacuna in all library collections. Such conditions led to a general dearth of library holdings in English literature, and at Oberlin this attitude went so far as to result in the exclusion of works by Milton, Dryden, Cooper, Burns, and Southey.

In such a setting, one would expect at least some students and faculty to feel frustration. Just how many were concerned enough to voice an opinion is not known, but one faculty member at North Carolina University is reported to have said, "Not a volume has been purchased by the trustees during the last quarter of a century. No stranger is ever invited to examine our present collection" (41:12). And a Boston newspaper, the *Atlas*, complained in 1857 about the lack of enthusiasm for acquisitions at Harvard by commenting that the college was spending only $300—$400 per year for the purchase of books while it annually invested at least seven times that amount for the inspection of pickled fish (18:2). The editorial estimates that Harvard had only one book in fifty of those published during the preceding half century.

However, it is easy to be aggressively harsh in judging the college library of 1800–1860. The collections were probably as good as the endowments, the dormitories, the curricula. And if many libraries remained locked most of the time, while others struggled along with no room which could be locked, it should be remembered this was an era in which higher education looked to the past rather than the future. Reflective thinking and theoretical considerations were rare qualities in any college discipline before 1860. It follows rather naturally, then, that college libraries had only limited significance, especially since librarians of the time considered themselves practitioners and schoolmasters rather than scholars.

Few, if any, of the teaching approaches during this era had any relation to the library. It is difficult to over-emphasize the impact that methods of teaching make on use of a college library; consequently, in assessing the significance of the college library during the Middle Period it is important to remember that with isolated exceptions, even gifted history teachers had pupils memorize and recite words found in a text. After some of the noted educators of America returned from European study, the teaching of history slowly shifted from the memorization of such things as political episodes, military achievements, and intrigue to considerations of Darwinism, social evolution, and the inner life. Even so, it was probably not until the 1880s that history teaching in the leading colleges of America began to rival that of the European universities.

The studies that were offered also mitigated against any meaningful library program. Although science had gained a place in the curriculum by 1850, it was not until after the Civil War that the new technology found popularity through application to everyday problems. As late as 1880 much of the science taught in American colleges was still called "natural philosophy." And scientific equipment continued to be known as "philosophical apparatus." And, even though Newtonian science had gained importance as early as the eighteenth century, it is significant that Aristotelian terminology persisted until almost 1900.

The academic library was equally influenced by the number of disciplines that were not part of the curriculum. University training in anthropology, for example, did not begin until the very last part of the 1800s, and this same subject did not enter the undergraduate curriculum until at least 1920. Moreover, the profession of education, with its scientific orientation, and its emphasis on sociology, psychology, and methods was completely unknown during the first half of the nineteenth century. Nor were research centers part of university life before 1860, and those branches of knowledge which rely on sophisticated abstracting, indexing, and retrieving were far in the future. Finally, the study of literature was completely different, for mastery of various editions, evaluative tools, concordances, and analytical works played no part in the educational process of that era.

Even today the academic library is too often challenged only at the graduate level. Yet, it was not until 1852 that one of the earliest attempts at graduate education was undertaken at Michigan University, and this effort was far from a total success. However, with the advent of the seminar, students were able to come in contact with teaching that discussed sources, authorities, opinions, and established values. As a consequence, the library at last began to be as important as classes, dormitories, and compulsory attendance.

Conditions changed slowly, however, and because of this it is not surprising that reform in librarianship itself was slow. The Dewey Decimal scheme, for example, did not appear until 1876 and the Cutter system was not invented until 1891. Library science schools did not open until 1887, and Library of Congress catalog cards were not produced until 1901. Academic librarianship in the modern sense, therefore, is largely a creation of the twentieth century.

The contribution of early nineteenth-century college libraries was nevertheless worthy of respect. They were probably of greatest value when they attempted to provide the scholar with transactions of learned societies, for one of the oldest responsibilities in college librarianship is to maintain collections such as these. Moreover, it may be that these early libraries will be remembered not for their failure to develop large research collections and support elaborate teaching functions, but for their ability to work with what they had and to maintain themselves against an overwhelming array of adversities.

If their services and holdings were considered meager, their collections were at least as satisfactory as those that were owned by outstanding teachers, and they did reflect the educational thinking of the day. It may be that this caused the college library to duplicate rather than to supplement the teacher's personal collection which he kept at home, but at least it indicated to the student what kind of books should be owned by an educated man. No college before 1860 was content with itself if it did not have at least some semblance of a library. Perhaps this attitude was the greatest legacy these early institutions could leave, for without such an idea permeating today's colleges and universities, higher education would be quite a different enterprise.

Notes

1. Beer lists ten magazines that were started in 1800. Some of these lasted for less than one year and others failed to publish more than a single number. Combining such short-lived journals with those founded in previous years, Beer's *Checklist* indicates that a total of thirteen periodicals were available at one time or another during 1800. The *American Almanac* states that by 1810 this number had risen to twenty-six.

2. Letter, Thomas Jefferson to T.M. Randolph, July 6, 1787. (*Writings*: VI, pp. 165–69); Letter, Thomas Jefferson to John Adams, July 5, 1814. (*Writings*: XIV, pp. 144–51).

3. Letter, Thomas Jefferson to Peter Carr, September 7, 1814 (*Writings*: XIX, pp. 211–21); Letter, Thomas Jefferson to J. Correa De Serra, November 25, 1817. (*Writings*: XV, pp. 153–57).

4. A review of *Poole's Index to Periodical Literature, 1802–1881*, indicates that entire articles on the subject of education before 1826 were rare. *North American Review*, *Analectic Magazine*, and *Portfolio* (*Dennie's*) are representative of magazines that devoted some space to the topic.

References

Adams, Herbert Baxter. *Thomas Jefferson and the University of Virginia*. .. U.S. Bureau of Education, Circular of Information No. 1. Washington, D.C.: Government Printing Office, 1888.

96 Liberal Arts Colleges and Professional Education, 1800–1875

Amherst College. *The Substance of Two Reports of the Faculty to the Board of Trustees with the Doings of the Board Thereon.* Amherst, Mass.: Carter and Adams, Printers, 1827.
American Almanac and Repository of Useful Knowledge for the Year 1830. 2nd Edition. Vol. 1. Boston: Charles Bowen, 1833.
_____. *1841.* Boston: David H. Williams, 1841.
_____. *1860.* Boston: Crosby, Nichols, and Co., 1860.
Beer, William. *Checklist of American Periodicals, 1741–1800.* Reprinted from *Proceedings of the American Antiquarian Society* for October 1922, Worcester, Mass.: American Antiquarian Society, 1923.
Brewer, Fisk Parsons. *The Library of the University of North Carolina.* Chapel Hill: University of North Carolina, 1870.
Brodman, Estelle. "The Special Library, the Mirror of Its Society," *Journal of Library History*, 1, No. 2 (April 1966), 108–24.
Clemons, Harry. *The University of Virginia Library, 1825–1950: Story of a Jeffersonian Foundation.* Charlottesville: University of Virginia Library, 1954.
Cogswell, Joseph Green. *The Life of J.G. Cogswell, as Sketched in His Letters.* Cambridge, Mass.: Privately Printed at Riverside Press, 1874.
Evans, Charles. *American Bibliography: A Chronological Dictionary...* New York: Peter Smith, 1941.
Harvard University. *Catalogue of the Library of Harvard University...* 3 vols. Cambridge, Mass.: E.W. Metcalf and Co., 1830.
Harvard University. *Eleventh Annual Report of the Librarian of the Public Library of Harvard University, Made by the Examining Committee, July 11, 1842.* Harvard University Archives Library.
Harvard University. Memorandum from Andrew Norton, Librarian, to President Kirkland, 1815. Harvard University Archives Library, U A III 50.28.13.
Hofstadter, Richard, and Smith, Wilson. *American Higher Education: A Documentary History.* 2 vols. Chicago: University of Chicago Press, 1961.
Jefferson, Thomas. *Writings.* Library Edition. 20 vols. Washington, D.C.: Thomas Jefferson Memorial Association of the US, 1903.
Journal of the Proceedings of a Convention of Literary and Scientific Gentlemen, Held in the Common Council Chamber of the City of New York, October 1830. New York: Jonathan Leavitt and G. & H. Carvill, 1831.
"The Library of Harvard College," *The Boston Daily Atlas*, XXV, No. 2 (Feb. 26, 1857), p. 2.
Lindsley, Philip. *The Cause of Education in Tennessee: An Address Delivered to the Young Gentlemen Admitted to the Degree of Bachelor of Arts in Cumberland College at the Anniversary Commencement, October 4, 1826.* Nashville: Banner Press, 1826.
Massachusetts. Board of Education. *Report, together with the Report of the Secretary of the Board.* 1st—12th. Boston: Dutton and Wentworth, State Printers, 1838–1849. [Washington, D.C., 1947–1952].
McMullen, Haynes. "The Use of Books in the Ohio Valley before 1850," *Journal of Library History*, 1, No. 1 (January 1966), 43, 55.
Mott, Frank Luther. *History of American Magazines, 1741–1850.* Cambridge, Mass: Harvard University Press, 1939.
Peckham, Howard H. "Books and Reading on the Ohio Valley Frontier," *Mississippi Valley Historical Review*, XLIV (March 1958), 649–63.
"Periodical Literature of the U.S.," *North American Review*, XXXIX (October, 1834), 277–301.
Perry, Arthur Latham. *Williamstown and Williams College.* Printed by the Author, 1899.
Princeton University. Minutes of the Board of Trustees of the College of New Jersey, April 9, 1793. Princeton University Archives, 300–11.
Raymond, Andrew Van Vranken. *Union University, Its History, Influence, Characteristics and Equipment...* 3 vols. New York: Lewis Publishing Co., 1907.
Shores, Louis. *Origins of the American College Library, 1638–1800.* New York: Barnes & Noble, 1935.
Smithsonian Institution. *Fourth Annual Report of the Board of Regents... 1849.* Washington, D.C.: Government Printing Office, 1850.
Tewksbury, Donald G. *The Founding of American Colleges and Universities Before the Civil War.* New York: Archon Books, 1965.
Ticknor, George. *Life, Letters and Journals.* 6th ed. 2 vols. Boston: James R. Osgood and Co., 1877.
Union List of Serials in Libraries of the U.S. and Canada. 3rd ed. New York: H.W. Wilson Co., 1965.
U.S.Congress. *Biographical Directory of the American Congress, 1774–1961.* Washington, D.C.: Government Printing Office, 1961.
U.S. Bureau of the Census. *Abstract of the Fourteenth Census of the US, 1920.* Washington, D.C.: Government Printing Office, 1923.
_____. *Historical Statistics of the U.S., Colonial Times to 1957.* Washington, D.C.: Government Printing Office, 1960.
U.S.Department of the Interior. *Report.* (1869). Vol. II, *Report of the Commissioner of Education.* Washington, D.C.: Government Printing Office, 1870.
University of North Carolina. "Laws of the University of North Carolina Established by the Board of

Trustees at their Session, December 1799," *Faculty Journal*, 1814–1823. University of North Carolina Archives.

_____. Minutes of the Board of Trustees..., Dec. 3–13, 1792.

_____. Minutes of the Board of Trustees..., November 15, 1790—December 6, 1797.

Venable, William Henry. *Beginnings of Literary Culture in the Ohio Valley*. Cincinnati: R. Clarke & Co., 1891.

Wilson, Louis R. *Library of the First State University: A Review of Its Past and a Look at Its Future*. Chapel Hill, N.C.: North Carolina University Press, 1960.

Yale University. *Reports on the Course of Instruction in Yale College*; by a Committee of the Corporation, and the Academical Faculty. New Haven: Hezekiah Howe, 1828.

Formation of the University, 1876–1919

Historians who study the topic of higher education scarcely contain their enthusiasm for the confluence of forces that gave rise to the research university in the late nineteenth century. The structural outlines of the university emerged in the last quarter of the century and became solidified during the first two decades of the twentieth. Scholars had earned doctorates in Europe, Germany most prominently, and returned to American soil with the gospel of scholarship. Central to their mission was creation of the graduate program featuring original investigation and culminating in a finished product of scholarly or scientific writing. A thirst for knowledge, a deep desire to learn and to analyze something new, and to engage in a life of the mind drove the modern university to unprecedented heights. Early in the century, scholarship had been the purview of the independent amateur with wealth and leisure to amass a large personal library and to travel to the great centers of book production and research in Europe. By the end of the century, a comprehensive movement was underway, influenced by European and indigenous elements, that would redefine higher education and institutionalize original, specialized inquiry, thus transforming the academy into a permanent home for scientific research and professional scholarship.

Symbolic of this great movement was the establishment in 1876 of Johns Hopkins University, designed expressly for graduate study and research that would culminate, for the successful student, in a publishable product and the awarding of a Ph.D. Universities would forever incorporate the pursuit of new knowledge as an institutional value which, in many places, would come to overwhelm a school's mission to train undergraduates. Doctoral programs in the United States did not begin with Johns Hopkins but were already underway in places like Harvard and Yale and Michigan. As the universities expanded their horizons, advocates used terms such as "revolution" or "transformation" which did not constitute rhetorical overkill but, rather, interpreted accurately the magnitude of sweeping changes eventually envisioned, implemented, and internalized. As a harbinger of things to come, Ralph Waldo Emerson had observed (shortly after the Civil War) the arrival of a new era in higher education, one that represented a "cleavage … occurring in the hitherto firm granite of the past."[1]

A signal feature of graduate instruction was the seminar developed in German universities and adapted for American uses. Seminars were constituted of a professor and a small group of graduate students who prepared written and oral presentations, now a staple of graduate and upper division undergraduate classes but quite innovative in the late nineteenth century. Student work was then critiqued by the professor and the class as a whole. The in-class conversations amounted to a dialectic, a back-and-forth analysis of student topics. In the intellectually richest settings—the major universities in the forefront of doctoral research—graduate seminars took place in seminar libraries with contextual and, sometimes, original source material close at hand. The professional library literature contemporary with this period is, in fact, replete with references to seminar libraries.

Scientific, technical, and engineering research took a great leap forward in the 1840s with the birth of schools of science at Harvard and Yale although, as early as the 1790s, engineering had been taught in the United States Military Academy at West Point and, in the 1830s, at Rensselaer Polytechnic Institute. But the vast expansion of scientific and technical education came after the Civil War, complementing the Gilded Age movements of industrialization, urbanization, and immigration that exploded into the United States in the late nineteenth century. The research university emerged with a significant role in American society as industry often looked to the university to incubate technical discovery and innovation. Thus, seeds were planted for corporate-collegiate partnerships that have expanded into present-day programs.

Other disciplines adopted scientific terminology to describe their own work, and a term such as "scientific history" emerged, connoting a close examination of primary documents, complemented by a new level of exactitude with respect to observation, detail, and logic. The discipline of history and other humanities-oriented ways of knowing grew and matured along with the sciences, and scholars of history and literature began to refer to the university research library as a "laboratory" for the humanities, something comparable to the laboratory in basic and applied sciences. The library thus became part and parcel of the vast research engine of the major university and, as Lee Shiflett had noted, for the period from 1875 to 1925 some university libraries were able to expand their holdings five or ten or even twenty times.[2]

The social sciences were likewise energized. They had gathered impetus, in early iterations, from religious denominations committed to ameliorating the worst of the social problems engendered by the Industrial Revolution, concerns such as alcoholism, prostitution, theft, violence, child labor, illiteracy, and poverty. Social services gave practical opportunity to those seeking to improve quality of life for urban America, but the Social Gospel movement, although remaining in the churches, would soon give way to the professionalization of occupations such as social work, nursing, teaching, and librarianship. Thus, emerged education and training for the helping professions simultaneously with broad curricular reform already underway in the colleges. Moral philosophy, as the capstone of the classical undergraduate college program, declined in the face of robust specialization that spawned the separate subjects of business and economics, education, political science, psychology, and sociology. Newly minted doctoral graduates were becoming much more professionally conscious, organizing curricula and courses into academic departments, creating career ladders for promotion and tenure, and establishing national scholarly associations to advance their respective disciplines.

The rise of subject specialization became both stimulant and beneficiary of the course elective system pioneered by major universities, most notably Harvard under the direction of Charles W. Eliot who served as its president from 1869 to 1909. Growing numbers of disciplinary offerings coincided with greater flexibility for student choices at both undergraduate and graduate levels. Indeed, the entire project of higher education was undergoing a sea change with the adoption of course electives as a strong influence for democratization.

A further democratizing influence came into play, the land-grant college movement. In 1862 the Land-Grant Act (known commonly as the Morrill Act after representative and, later, senator Justin Smith Morrill of Vermont) set aside federal lands to establish new colleges or to induce existing colleges to create programs in agricultural, industrial, and technical fields. These schools expanded rapidly in the years after the Civil War, offering instruction, laboratory research, and extension services in subjects such as agricultural economics, agronomy, animal husbandry, botany, chemistry, horticulture, plant pathology, and veterinary medicine. Although not specifically designed to omit the humanities and social sciences, the land-grant colleges came to emphasize those disciplines that, by their nature, responded most directly to the economic and social needs of their age. The land-grant schools thus developed technical and engineering expertise for the great engine of the Industrial Revolution, fueling fresh opportunity for aspiring middle classes to pursue a life in industry as well as agriculture. The land-grant schools took higher education beyond classical roots for undergraduates and into far different curricula than even those of the older doctoral granting schools, emerging as a powerful symbol of democratic impulses for an expansive age.

Not surprisingly, the land-grant colleges established libraries with strengths in scientific and technical topics but with collections substantially smaller than the older universities that had begun years earlier with retrospective holdings in the humanities and social sciences. Writing in the mid-twentieth century, Arthur E. Bestor, Jr. (1908–1994) identified the main intellectual, pedagogical, and professional currents that, fifty to seventy-five years earlier, had swept the university into modern American life. In our next entry for this section, Wayne A. Wiegand considered the role of the professoriate in establishing the canon of authoritative sources within individual disciplines as academic cultures were coming to maturity at the close of the nineteenth century. The place of the research library had become not merely that of building retrospective collections and supporting original research, but also the thankless task of gathering those fugitive items rejected as marginal by previous generations. Thus, as matters of taste evolve, and changing values influence the rise and fall of genres and movements, the research library prepares for readers of the future by preserving things seemingly insignificant, overtly repressed, or simply underestimated.

Notes

1. Emerson, Ralph Waldo. Quoted in Walter P. Rogers, *Andrew Dickson White and the Modern University* (Ithaca, New York: Cornell University Press, 1942), 4.

2. O. Lee Shiflett, "Academic Libraries" in *Encyclopedia of Library History*, eds. Wayne A. Wiegand and Donald G. Davis, Jr. (New York: Garland, 1994), 10.

The Transformation of American Scholarship, 1875–1917

Arthur E. Bestor, Jr.

Judged by the direction which their writings take, scholars as a group are the greatest extroverts in modern society. The manager of a great corporation studies the organizational charts and the flow sheets of his own particular firm and may even hire a historian to tell him about its past. The citizen of a Middletown cannot escape some introspective probing of the inner structure of his own community, once the scholars have laid it bare for all the world to stare at. But who dissects the structure of scholarship itself or of the professional world within which the scholar works? Not the average scholar. He can generalize rather more subtly and objectively about how Papuans are initiated into manhood than about how the young scholar among us finds his way into a professional career. He can describe more accurately the functioning of the prytany in Athenian government than the role of the academic senate in the running of his own university. We historians are committed to the view that historical understanding of a particular institution has less value for the solution of its current problems, but, as one distinguished member of the profession recently put it, "What university or college history department is able to give a new instructor a useful history of the department, [or of] the undergraduate or graduate school in which it is located, to help him orient himself to his work?"[1]

No insuperable difficulties bar the way to an understanding of these matters. The organized structure of intellectual life is just as susceptible of analysis and historical treatment as is the organization of economic or political life, and a knowledge of the institutional pattern of scholarship and scientific research is fully as important for solving problems connected with the advancement of knowledge as is an understanding of the economic system for solving problems connected with the effective production and distribution of goods. The reciprocal relationship between scholars, librarians, and booksellers is a relationship that arises within the framework of organized scholarly activity in America today. This paper is designed to show what that framework is and how it came to be.

Intellectual life, considered as an organized social activity, embraces, of course, much more than the advancement of knowledge. It includes the transmission of already acquired knowledge, a major function, obviously, of schools and undergraduate colleges. It includes the diffusion of information and opinion to a wide public through newspapers, periodicals, and the radio, and the other agencies which we are coming to speak of as "mass communications." It includes the creation and diffusion of the imagination: of poetry and fiction, of music and the fine arts. In all these things, the library and the book trade play a significant part, and the scholar and the scientist have not only an interest but also measure of responsibility. But these are things which can be discussed only incidentally, if at all, in the present paper. Time requires us to focus our attention upon a limited segment only of organized intellectual life as connected with the advancement of knowledge, I am thinking primarily of five distinct matters: (1) How is the scholar or scientist trained for the work of advancing knowledge in his chosen field? (2) How is he supported while engaged in this task? That is to say, "what agency provides him with a living while he undertakes work that in itself is seldom directly remunerated?" (3) What institution furnishes the materials needed in his research or the means of access to them? (4) How does the scholar communicate with his fellow-workers in the same field? That is to say, "how does he function as a member of a profession, and what is the role of this professional activity in the advancement of his own personal career?" (5) Where and in what form does he present the results of his research, and how are these disseminated or applied by himself or others?

I present these questions in a more, or less, systematic fashion in order to indicate the matters that must be discussed in any attempt to analyze the organized structure of scholarly and scientific activity. I do not intend to answer them one by one, still less to deal with them statistically and quantitatively. My intention, rather, is to picture as clearly as I can the various institutional arrangements which, in each distinct period of time, provided the things that scholarly and scientific research required.

In each distinct period of time—the phrase is important, for the main theme of what follows is the fundamental transformation that has taken place in the organization of intellectual life in America in the last three-quarters of a century. No one, certainly, thinks of these years as static ones. Everyone is aware of the great changes that have occurred within the field in which he is particularly interested. But it is a curious quirk of the human mind that, even when it is most intensely aware of the fact of change in certain directions, it is apt unconsciously to assume that the situation in other respects was pretty much the same in the past as now. Most of the anachronisms which the historian uncovers as he attempts to correct men's picture of the past arise out of this understandable but nevertheless disconcerting psychological quirk. That the system as a whole may be undergoing fundamental change, as well as the individual parts of the system, is an idea that requires more than ordinary effort to grasp. The scholar, for example, knows that his predecessor of a century ago used materials very different from his own and used them very differently, but he is apt to envisage the materials themselves as reposing in a library much like today's only smaller. The librarian, on the other hand, is well aware that the library of a century ago was an institution vastly different from that of the present, but I suspect he pictures the scholar of the past going about his task in about the same way as the modern occupant of a cubicle in the stacks. The fact is, of course, that scholar and library have both undergone transformations, swept along in an intellectual revolution greater than either.

To understand the transformation of scholarship in the last three-quarters of a century, it is desirable at the outset to consider briefly who the scholar was and how he worked during the period before the forces of change began to gather momentum. The first point we need to recognize is that before about 1875 productive scholarship in the United States was not associated in any close or direct way with a career in college teaching. In the field of history, for example, the American writers of the early nineteenth century who first come to mind are Prescott, Bancroft, Motley, and Parkman. Except for Bancroft's brief service as a tutor in Greek at Harvard as a young man of twenty-two and Parkman's year as professor of horticulture in the same institution, long after his historical reputation was established, none of these historians held university positions. To look at the matter from the opposite direction, serious writing did come from the occupants of professorial chairs, but it had far less connection with the author's supposed academic specialty than it would have today. The professorships of modern language and literature which Longfellow and Lowell held undoubtedly influenced the direction of their literary work and suggested many of their themes, but these men felt no professional compulsion to write monographs or scholarly papers of the sort that their successors contribute to *PMLA* or the *Journal of English and Germanic Philology*. The career of George Ticknor offers perhaps the closest parallel to that of a twentieth century scholar in its close correlation of academic teaching with writing in the same field. Ticknor's monumental *History of Spanish Literature* (1849) appeared fourteen years after he had resigned his professorship (at the age of forty-three), and during the actual writing of the book he was dependent neither upon an academic salary nor upon the resources of the college library.

The lack of dependence upon the college library is what interests us particularly. The reason for it in Ticknor's case is obvious. His private library of some thirteen thousand volumes, which he had begun sedulously to build during his student days in Germany, provided him with the greatest collection of Spanish literature in the United States. "This work could be written, in this country," commented the librarian of the Smithsonian Institution, "only by one who was able to procure for himself the necessary literary apparatus."[2] Few scholars could hope to possess a library like Ticknor's, of course, but one responsibility which every serious scholar seems to have accepted without question was that of building up for himself the collection of books upon which his future would rest.

To supplement this, certain resources were indeed available. The historical societies preserved American manuscripts, newspapers, and pamphlets, which by reason of their uniqueness or rarity or bulk could hardly come within the scope of a scholar's collection. The academies of natural history or science maintained collections of books and specimens which, within their field, were probably closer in conception and purpose to those of a modern institution of higher learning than were the libraries and collections associated with the colleges. The latter, the college libraries, were probably the greatest value to the scholar in providing the transactions of learned societies, for one of the librarian's oldest professional responsibilities was maintaining collections like these. The general collection of the college library was more likely to duplicate than to supplement the scholar's own, for it was essentially a projection upon a larger scale of the kind of library which an educated man was expected to possess for himself. The good ones, at least, were such. The poor ones, to quote a blunt report of the Smithsonian in 1850, "were frequently the chance aggregations of the gifts of charity; too many of them discarded, as well-nigh worthless, from the shelves of the donors."[3] For serious works of recent date in all the secular fields of knowledge the scholar's best outside resources were in most cases subscription libraries, such as the Boston Athenaeum, or even the libraries of the undergraduate societies in the colleges.

The library resources available in the city of Philadelphia in 1875 provide a fair example of the general situation. Of its one hundred and two libraries, fifteen contained more than 10,000 volumes apiece. Tied for sixth place in the list was the University of Pennsylvania Library, with 20,000 volumes, or 25,573 if one includes the undergraduate society libraries and those in law and medicine. The two largest libraries in the city were several times this size: the Mercantile with 125, 668 volumes, and the Library Company of Philadelphia (which included the Loganian Library), with 104,000 volumes. Both of these were subscription libraries, and there were three others of this kind among the fifteen largest. In the natural sciences, there were four important collections, topped by those of the Philadelphia Academy of Natural Sciences (30,000 volumes) and the American Philosophical Society (20,000 volumes). Two historical societies, those of the Historical Society of Pennsylvania and the Pennsylvania German Society, stood at 16,000 volumes apiece. There were two substantial medical libraries, the largest of which, maintained by the College of Physicians, contained 18,753 volumes, more than six times as many as were in the medical department at the University of Pennsylvania. Neither in law nor theology did any single library attain the figure of 10,000. But the Law Association Library, with its 8,500 volumes, dwarfed into insignificance the mere 250 volumes in the law library of the university. The theological libraries were strictly denominational, hence, individually, they were relatively small; but there were at least nine (including denominational historical libraries) which contained between 3,000 and 9,315 volumes apiece. There was one entirely free public library of 21,000 volumes, the Apprentices' Library Company, but there was no college or academy library, aside from that of the university, which contained 10,000 volumes.[4]

These special types of libraries, widely dispersed except in major cities as Philadelphia, could only be supplements, and not very dependable supplements, to the scholar's own collection of books. It was on the latter that he had to depend for the long, steady pull. There are, as I see it, two fundamental reasons why a scholar is constrained, in any period, to build up a library of his own. The first is the more obvious of the two. Unless the materials he needs are available in some collection to which he has access, he must gather them himself. But there is a second reason, known best to those who have done research of their own. A scholar works *among* books; he can hardly labor effectively if he has to consult them one at a time and in isolation from one another. Every journey which a scholar must make in order to get at his material is time subtracted from the real accomplishment of his task, time subtracted not only by travel itself but by the elaborate note-taking, which is necessary with respect to a volume or a document that cannot be consulted again at will. If anyone is in doubt as to what I mean, let him try accurately to collate two variant texts or to compare two discordant narratives of a historical event while keeping one at home and the other in his office.

The American scholar of the early nineteenth century felt the full force of both problems. Many of the books he needed were in no collection available to him, and the standard books that he had to know well could be part of his working environment only if they were his own. The correspondence of earlier scholars records the continuous quest for books—for obscure volumes known only through citations, for good editions of standard works, for the latest books published in distant cities. The libraries of distinguished scholars and scientists which, by gift or purchase, came to swell the collections of the growing scholarly libraries at the end of the nineteenth century, testify to the money and effort that had gone into acquiring the literature of a field: early editions, long runs of less-known scholarly proceedings, collections of theses and monographs, and other specialized papers. The bookseller played a vital role in this enterprise; his relationship to the individual scholar was apt to be a continuous one, and his specialized knowledge was often the substitute for formal bibliographical tools.

Now the quest for books is to me a pleasant one, and the placing of them on shelves for companionship a continuous delight. If the older scholar's lot was hard, it had compensations which we today can rarely experience—the excitement of looking for the first time at a book which none of one's fellow countrymen has ever seen, the sense of victory as each elusive title is arranged in its proper place in a unique and growing collection. But efficiency, alas, is the foe of charms like these, and the pattern I have described was manifestly inefficient in bringing to the scholar the range of resources he needed. It has given place to a far more efficient pattern, and our business (for which we must be efficient, too) is to see how the newer one was woven.

Chronological limits in these matters are necessarily arbitrary, but it is perhaps safe to say that the new structure of scholarly and scientific activity was clearly worked out during the quarter-century from 1875 to 1900, that it established itself securely as the controlling pattern of American intellectual life in the period between 1900 and the first World War, and that it has expanded since then as a mature system, achieving new triumphs but also raising new problems by virtue of its very size and complexity. Unsatisfactory though such a precise delimitation of periods must be, it does at least provide convenient divisions for the discussion that follows. I would like to consider the first two of three periods, devoting most attention to the first because it was the seminal one.

The central fact in the reorganization of American intellectual life was the rise of what is sometimes described as the "new" university. The opening of Johns Hopkins University in the centennial year of 1876 is as representative an event as any, but a cluster of other developments signaled the effective beginning of the new era in the early 1870s: the opening of Cornell in 1868 under Andrew D. White, the inauguration of Charles W. Eliot as president of Harvard in 1869 and of James B. Angell as president of Michigan in 1871, and the reorganization of postgraduate work at Yale in the same year, to mention but a few.

The scholarly achievements of the great universities of Germany—Halle, Göttingen, Berlin, and the rest—were in the minds of those who commenced the reconstruction of American higher education. German example led to the introduction of the seminar as a vehicle for graduate instruction. (The stubborn refusal of the latter word to be anglicized into "seminary" is in itself indicative). Nevertheless, it is a decided error to think of the American university of this period as a new type of institution suddenly established upon foreign models or to underrate the elements in it which were not only of native origin but were also unparalleled in the universities of other lands.

The assimilation of educational ideas from abroad was merely part of a far larger process of assimilation. And this comprehensive process of assimilation was what, in the last analysis, brought the new American university into being. The unintegrated character of American intellectual life in an earlier period has already been indicated—the relatively slight connection between higher education and scholarship, the dispersion of library facilities among specialized agencies. Many more examples might be given of the separatist organization of the various branches of intellectual life. Scientific research had even less connection with the profession of teaching than did advanced humanistic scholarship, despite exceptions like Benjamin Silliman at Yale and Louis Agassiz at Harvard. The rigidity of the classical college curriculum led to establishment of wholly independent technological schools like the Rensselaer Polytechnic Institute founded in 1824 or to affiliated but separate agencies like the Lawrence and Sheffield scientific schools at Harvard and Yale. The relations between the professional school of law or medicine and the university were so tenuous as to be purely nominal. Graduate training in the nonprofessional fields of science and letters had to be sought outside American institutions entirely, through university study on the Continent. Finally, the dissemination of knowledge to a wider audience was not a recognized responsibility of the college. Such autonomy militated against the interpenetration of ideas, it stood in the way of the efficient accumulation of the resources upon which the advancement of knowledge depended, and it insulated one branch of professional activity from the influence of higher standards of training or performance in another branch.

The new American university brought these *disjecta membra* of the intellectual world together in a single great institution. This, to my mind, was the essence of the movement. The major ingredients that went into the amalgam had existed in America before. The undergraduate college was not sacrificed by any pushing down of its content into the high school or the Gymnasium, as had happened in Germany. The existing scientific and technical schools gradually assumed a co-ordinate place in the undergraduate curriculum. In the state universities, the training in "agriculture and mechanic arts" which the Morrill Land-Grant Act had prescribed "in order to promote the liberal and practical education of the industrial classes in the several pursuits and professions in life"[5] was likewise assimilated to and placed on a parity with the classical and scientific programs of undergraduate study. Thus, was Jonathan B. Turner's dream of a "people's university," separate and fundamentally different from the conventional college, rendered obsolete. The free-elective system, inaugurated by President Eliot at Harvard, made this assimilation easier, and opened the way for the introduction of new academic disciplines—particularly among the social sciences—much sooner after their birth than could have been expected under the older system.

Such a comprehensive synthesis of academic programs might have collapsed from the sheer insufficiency of trained academic minds, had the new university not closed at last the greatest gap in American higher education, namely its lack of adequately organized advanced training in pure research. The graduate school, dedicated to the task of educating men and women for the advancement of knowledge, was the capstone of the new university structure. Since there had been a real hiatus here, the new institution naturally drew more of its ideas from abroad than it was forced to do in the organization of other areas. Even so, the ideas were not newly imported. Ever since 1815, Americans in large numbers had studied at the various universities of the Continent and had brought back conceptions of how advanced work should be done. The opportunity to put them into effect was slow in coming, but, when it did come, the ideas were not alien to the minds of American scholars but familiar through at least two generations of meditation and aspiration. The ideal of a university as a company of scholars engaged both in the advancement of knowledge and in the instruction of students could not have been realized so rapidly had it not been for this long maturing process and for the partial realization of the aim in certain institutions, such as Yale (which awarded the Ph.D. degree as early as 1861), and Harvard, and others.

Professional education in law and medicine began to reflect the emphasis upon sound advanced training for which the new university stood. It is significant that the raising of standards came first in institutions that were part of the new university, like the Medical School of Johns Hopkins. In the long run, the greatest failure of the new university was probably its inability to impress its new standards of scholarship and competence upon the nation's system of training teachers for secondary and elementary schools. This failure belongs to the story of a later period, however, for in the final quarter of the nineteenth century the influence of the new university upon teacher training and high-school curriculums promised to be akin to its influence in other professional areas.

As if to compensate in advance for this failure, the new university went beyond the older boundaries of formal education and quickly assumed an unprecedented responsibility for the direct dissemination of knowledge, both to the learned world and the general public. The great series of university studies in various fields began to take their place alongside the transactions of the older learned societies, scholarly journals began to issue from editorial offices within university walls, and the university press came into existence. In the direction of popularization, the new institution seized upon the idea of university extension almost as soon as it was launched in England, it adopted the summer session which the Chautauqua movement had pioneered, and it undertook instruction by correspondence. All these activities were incorporated in the structure of the new University of Chicago, opened in 1892, the program of which summed up, as it were, the developments that had been taking place in American universities since the 1870s.

Around the new university, American scholarly and scientific activity in all its branches quickly reorganized itself. The new institutional pattern which it established is the one within which the scholars and scientists of today carry forward the task of advancing knowledge. This dominance was not achieved at a stroke, of course, but the pattern itself was fully developed by the end of the nineteenth century. Clarity of exposition can best be achieved by considering the main features of this pattern, deferring for a moment the history of its gradual working out in practice in the various fields.

The new pattern of intellectual life affected the work of the undergraduate colleges, of course, but it first began crucially to influence the professional life of the young scholar after he received his baccalaureate degree. Graduate training attempted consciously to inculcate the ideal of the university: that the advancement of knowledge was as sacred a responsibility of any institution of higher learning and of any scholar connected with it as teaching itself. The Doctor of Philosophy was intended as a public recognition that the scholar or scientist possessed such a command of the materials, the problems, and the methods of investigation in his field that he could continue the process of advancing knowledge already begun in his dissertation, the latter being proof in itself that he was capable of doing so.

The choice and support of the university faculty represented a second manifestation of the same basic ideal. Given its purpose of advancing knowledge, the university sought the men who were trained to do so, and the Ph.D. became the standard measure of this. The teaching load of a university professor was made compatible with the active prosecution of research, and published evidence of the latter became one criterion for advancement. Like all quantitative and mechanical measures of what essentially is a qualitative matter, these criteria had grave shortcomings, but—and I should like to emphasize this—not because they measured the wrong thing but because they measured the right thing badly. A university salary had been made, with deliberate intent, partially a subsidy for research, and the recipient was certainly under a moral obligation to demonstrate that he was accepting it for that purpose.

The importance of this kind of subsidy can hardly be exaggerated in any historical account of American intellectual life. As a result of it, the university soon replaced every other agency—the church had perhaps been the most important one from the Middle Ages to the mid-nineteenth-century—as the great patron of learning. Even individual patrons began to act through the university rather than directly, by making their gifts to university funds. And in the twentieth century government and private industry found that the most productive means of spending money for pure research was through contract with a university or its graduate schools.

The actual contributions to knowledge made by the faculties of universities provided one important measure of the value of this new way of subsidizing fundamental research. Another was the extent to which a university career became both the goal of men whose interest was in the advancement of knowledge and the context in which scholarly and scientific research was normally pursued. Every issue of a learned journal in one of the basic disciplines today testifies to the completeness with which the university has assumed the support of those who are making serious contributions to science and learning. Only a scattered few of the articles and book reviews are by scholars without a university connection, and these few are usually by men with advanced university training. The great majority of the books deemed worthy of review are by university-connected men, and a growing number bear the imprint of university presses. It is significant that in *Who's Who in America, 1950–1951* the largest single vocational classification is that of college professors, who constitute 11.2 percent of the persons included.[6] This is perhaps a fair measure of the attraction which a university career holds, by reason of its combination of research and teaching, to men of high intellectual capacity.

The concentration of scholars and scientists in so many fields upon the campuses of universities revolutionized the matter of providing the facilities and resources for research. The development of well-equipped scientific laboratories (for research and not mere demonstration), of great collections of specimens and artifacts, and of libraries, was a necessary corollary of the responsibility which the university had assumed. We are, at the moment, concerned with the last of these. The inadequacy of the older system of dispersed specialized collections of books—in historical societies, in academies of natural science, and the like—became apparent once the main corps of active research workers began to cluster about a single, integrated type of institution. Scholars continued, and will always continue, to use the unique materials preserved in many of these long-established collections, but teaching duties tied them too closely to their own campuses for them to use distant, independent collections as working libraries. The new ideals of critical, comparative scholarship, moreover, revealed in a sharp light the limitations of many of these older agencies, especially their antiquarianism and provinciality. One evidence of the latter was the experience of Herbert Baxter Adams, the Johns Hopkins historian, who found as late as 1881 that the basic set of Virginia statutes was not available in any of the libraries of the adjoining state of Maryland, or at least of its largest city, Baltimore.[7]

From every direction came the pressure to build the university library up into a genuine research institution. Historical seminars like Herbert B. Adams's were conducted in book-lined alcoves, and graduate students were sent into the library for the materials required for research papers. Scientists, proportionately more numerous than ever before on a college campus, demanded a shift in the classical orientation of the library and called for the scientific journals and monographs that their work required. Young Doctors of Philosophy went forth imbued with a mission to build up the library facilities for research in the colleges and universities to which they received appointments. The correspondence of a college professor reflected the quest for books, as the older scholars had, but now it was often for the purpose of developing the university library rather than his own. The bookseller continued to play the role he had played before, though the ultimate purchaser was often an institution rather than an individual. The acquisition of entire libraries that had been gathered by scholars working under the older conditions formed an important part of the process. The dragnet extended to Europe. Isadore G. Mudge has listed twenty-six important scholarly collections that were brought to America between 1870 and 1900, twenty of them by university or college libraries.[8]

The output of the new university scholars themselves contributed in a far from negligible way to the contents of the growing university library. The monograph was the characteristic product of the new research methods. In essence, it represented the critical study of one carefully delimited phase or aspect of a larger matter, a matter which the older scholar would have undertaken to wrestle with as a whole. The virtues and the grave defects of the monograph—and it has plenty of both—we have not time to consider. Certain implications of the new form, however, are important for the questions we are discussing. The subdivisions of subjects once treated comprehensively made easy a parceling out of topics to many hands and facilitated the rapid completion and publication of the results of research. The increase in the number of individual scholarly titles which a university library had to handle was thus much greater than the increase, itself prodigious, of men devoting themselves to the field. This was not all. A newly published comprehensive study tends to supersede and make obsolete the older ones on the same subject, but a new monograph does not have quite the same effect. It fills the interstices between other studies, or it corrects certain parts of older works, leaving other parts to stand unchallenged. This piecemeal way of advancing knowledge makes it necessary for the scholar to have at hand the whole range of monographic literature, not just the selected best of it, if his own work is to be in accord with the latest scholarship. In research libraries, consequently, the ideal of a well-selected collection of books had to give way to the ideal of virtual completeness. Moreover, the subdividing of topics made mandatory a more detailed and closer classification scheme for the library at the same time that it was making classification more difficult by encouraging studies, individual and cooperative, which concentrated upon the relationships between matters once thought of as belonging to quite different fields.

The new professionalized attitude toward scholarship manifested itself in one other new type of organization, the publications of which also swelled the collections of scholarly libraries. This was the new learned society, devoted to a well-defined special field, and composed largely of college professors working within that field. The American Chemical Society, founded in 1876, the Modern Language Association of America (1883), the American Historical Association (1884), and the American Economic Association (1885) are typical of the societies established contemporaneously with the rise of the new university. Well over a hundred such were founded in the single decade of the 1880s.[9] The new organizations were markedly different from their predecessors. The historical and scientific societies of an earlier period, like the Massachusetts Historical Society, founded in 1791, and the Philadelphia Academy of Natural Sciences, founded in

1812, concentrated their efforts upon building up research collections each in its special field, eagerly sought the support of citizens interested but not professionally engaged in the field, and represented in their meetings and publications community-wide (or, at least regional) participation. The new association, on the other hand, rarely established library or research facilities of its own. Its headquarters were merely the college office of the professor who happened to be its editor or executive secretary. Its membership, though rarely limited by any express provision, was composed overwhelmingly of university teachers and professional workers in the field.[10] And its infrequent meetings, customarily scheduled at Christmas time each year to fit the college holidays, were truly national gatherings.

For the university professor, tied to his campus during the full academic year and frequently in summer sessions also, this annual meeting was the time when his professional field became a personified reality to him. It was in these organizations that scholarship assumed what we might call—borrowing a phrase from the vocabulary of business combination—a horizontal structure, for it brought together men engaged in the same activity, whereas the structure of the university was vertical, in that it represented the co-operation of men engaged in a whole variety of scholarly activities. The professional society, moreover, became the one great vehicle of interuniversity communication, so far as individual faculty members were concerned. Committees sponsored by it undertook to canvass the resources in the field. They brought pressure to bear on governments and semipublic agencies to preserve, arrange and facilitate the use of their archives and to modernize and extend their research activities. They sponsored bibliographical projects and surveys of research materials, compiled lists of research in progress, or supported efforts by others to do so. Most important of all, they sponsored learned journals which undertook to publish contributions to knowledge that were of a briefer sort than the monograph, to bring the specialized literature of the field under regular review, and to provide, by means of news notes, a modicum of strictly professional communication. The number of these periodicals is almost beyond belief. Some thirty-five thousand different scientific and scholarly journals were being published in all parts of the world at some time during the first third of the twentieth century alone.[11] No one could say with assurance that a single one of them was without potential value to some scholar or scientist on a university faculty. To maintain an ever-increasing list of subscriptions to learned journals was a fixed responsibility of every university library and in itself accounted for part of the tremendous growth in its size.

Statistics are hard to follow in these matters, and I shall be sparing with them. The point is not so much the numerical growth as the fact that by 1900 the age of the great library had arrived in America, requiring the separate book stack (built first at Harvard in 1877),[12] scientific classification and cataloging systems, a large full-time professional staff, etc. The physical growth was characteristic of all types of libraries, of course. The Library of Congress reached a million volumes by 1900. Among university libraries Harvard was first with its 560,000 volumes and 350,000 pamphlets. But Harvard's leadership in this respect was the continuance of an old and great tradition. The truly spectacular developments were the building-up of great libraries from scratch by newly created universities and the rapid expansion of college libraries that in the recent past had accepted for themselves an extremely modest role. Two examples will suffice. The University of Chicago, only eight years old, counted 329,778 volumes and 150,000 pamphlets in its collections in 1900 and took rank next to Harvard. The University of Pennsylvania, whose unimpressive sixth place among the libraries of Philadelphia in 1875 has already been noted, rose to first place in that city in 1900, if its 160,000 volumes, 100,000 pamphlets, and 22,525 law books are combined to arrive at the total.[13]

With the arrival of the great research library, the profession of librarianship came into its own. The American Library Association was founded in the same year as Johns Hopkins University. I shall not rehearse the careers of the great librarians so well known to all of you, but I will continue, instead, to look briefly at the problems of librarianship that belonged to the last quarter of the nineteenth century. The problem of sheer physical size was, of course, pressing, and one after another the universities erected new library buildings only to have them fill up in a generation or less, to the point where new structures had to replace almost every one of them before the twentieth century was half over. The growth of librarianship, however, was a response to technical needs within the library rather than to the external problems of engineering and architecture. The kind of access which scholars required if the now enormous collections were to be useful to them raised, first of all, the problem of classification. In the smaller libraries of the past, the books had been arranged in alcoves, each devoted to a general subject.[14] To look over an entire alcove was no great chore for anyone interested in the subject; it was, after all, what he would do in his own library. From one to two thousand books would constitute the whole of almost any subject grouping in a library of twenty thousand volumes divided into ten or fifteen classes. A tenfold expansion in size, such as often took place in this period, would result in blocks of ten or twenty thousand volumes on an undivided subject—far too many for anyone to scan in quest of specific material. Closer classification was inevitable. But close classification raises problems of its own. The narrower the subdivision of a subject is made, the more books one finds which deal with two or more topics and which a reader might properly look for in any one of several equally appropriate places. A catalog becomes a necessary finding tool, not a mere record of holdings. Classification and cataloging were the first great problems of the new library profession.

Melvil Dewey's *Decimal Classification*, first published in 1876, was, in the long run, the most influential of the schemes proposed, but it, and C.A. Cutter's differing schedules, which began to appear in book form in 1891, were by no means the only ones. The librarian of Yale studied carefully at least six different systems, American and foreign, before devising his own scheme for that library in 1890.[15] Harvard also evolved its own schedules in the 1880s, after learning by experience that a fixed-location number, indicating the particular shelf upon which a book belonged, could not work with an expanding collection.[16] A fascinating chapter of intellectual history could be written about the philosophical presuppositions and the attitudes toward knowledge, its uses, and its inner relationships that are revealed in the development of schemes like these for the classification of books, but this is not the place to write it. Nor is this the place to tell the story of how card systems gradually won out over the great folio volumes, manuscript or printed, that had dominated past thinking on the problem. Suffice it to say that by 1901, when the Library of Congress began to sell its printed cards to other libraries for use in their catalogs, the general principles of classification and cataloging had crystallized in substantially their modern form just as definitely as the broader pattern of scholarly and scientific activity that we have been considering.

The ground plan of the new structure of scholarly and scientific life had been clearly laid down by the beginning of the twentieth century. The account I have given would be misleading, however, if it suggested that the building was finished and fully tenanted by that date. In truth, scaffoldings were still up all over the place, and the products it was designed to turn out—for it was, we must admit, a kind of factory—were as yet comparatively few. The years from the beginning of the century until our entrance into the first World War in 1917 were the ones in which the new system began to fully operate. Statistics show the increase in graduate students during the period, the growing proportion of academic posts filled by holders of the Ph.D., the swelling volume of scholarly publications, and the enlargement of libraries. But these I shall not burden you with. A few examples will illustrate the matter more clearly than figures can do.

Historical scholarship exemplified the developments that were taking place in every field. Between 1884 and 1889 the eight-volume *Narrative and Critical History of America* appeared, under the editorship of Justin Winsor. In its critical discussion of bibliography and sources and in its division of labor, it exemplified the new approach to scholarship. But, of its thirty-four authors, only ten were university professors, only two of these were in departments of history, and only one of the entire group had received formal graduate training in history. By contrast, the next great cooperative work on the subject, Albert Bushnell Hart's *American Nation*, published between 1904 and 1907, enlisted the services of twenty-four authors, all but three of whom were university professors and all but two of whom had done graduate work in history.[17]

The great *Quellenkunde der deutsche Geschicte*, which Fredrich G. Dahlman first published in 1830, which Georg Waitz enlarged and improved in 1869, and which continued, in successive editions, to keep the literature of German history under full bibliographical control, was a model that American historians knew well. Not until the end of the century, however, were they well enough organized to sustain a comparable effort. Channing and Hart's *Guide to the Study of American History*, published in 1869, and J.N. Larned's co-operative *Literature of American History* in 1902 laid the foundations, the latter in fruitful collaboration with the American Library Association. In 1902 appeared the first volume of *Writings in American History*, and from 1906 it went forward on an annual basis. Only a comprehensive bibliography of bibliographies could tell the full story of the great networks of bibliographical control that have since been woven in all the great fields of knowledge.

To the historian, of course, the manuscript records of the past were of major significance. By the middle of the 1890s the profession was sufficiently well organized to tackle co-operatively and systematically the problem of making these more fully known, available, and usable. In 1895 the American Historical Association appointed its Historical Manuscripts Commission (modeled after the British Historical Manuscripts Commission, which dated from 1869). Already, important work was underway in the Bureau of Rolls and Library of the Department of State, which began in 1893 to publish its great calendars of the papers of the founding fathers. Gradually this work passed to the Division of Manuscripts of the Library of Congress, created in 1897, to which these basic collections were transferred from the State Department, beginning in 1903. The Carnegie Institution of Washington, founded in 1902, financed the work of historians in preparing the first adequate guide (published in 1904) to the dispersed federal archives, then a series of guides to the leading archives abroad. To make the most important of these latter documents available without European travel was another desideratum, and in 1905 the Library of Congress inaugurated its program of transcribing and reproducing foreign manuscript collections, thus carrying forward and systematizing the work that individual scholars had done before. Agencies connected with universities were active in such efforts also, notably the University of Illinois, whose Illinois Historical Survey assembled photostats from a wide range of foreign repositories and co-operated in financing the calendaring of important collections in Washington not yet touched by historians. Thus, were taken, in the first decade or so of the century, the steps that eventually led to the creation of the National Archives in 1934 and to the vast programs of today for microfilming the archives of European countries.

The creation of the Carnegie Institution of Washington, already mentioned, was an example of a new direction which the endowment of science and scholarship was to take in the twentieth century. Most of the great single steps forward in university development between 1875 and 1900 had been the consequence of gifts made to create universities of the new kind: Cornell, Johns Hopkins, Clark, Stanford, and Chicago, for example. Other great gifts had made possible the creation of new research libraries like the Newberry, or the expansion of older ones. Research, in other words, had been endowed by endowing the agencies of research. In the twentieth century, however, foundations were conceived which would endow research more directly and specifically, independent of existing agencies with their multifarious commitments to other activities besides research. A new element was thus added to the pattern. But it was an outgrowth of, not a departure from, the basic intellectual structure which I have described. For its personnel, it depended on the graduate training of the universities and the participation of members of their faculties. For guidance in planning, it looked to the new scholarly and professional associations. And for its library resources it turned to collections which existing agencies were maintaining.

The period between the beginning of the century and the first World War saw likewise the first real examples of how the new institutions of science and scholarship might serve the general needs of society and the nation. One day in 1892 Herbert Baxter Adams at Johns Hopkins received the following letter on the stationery of the United States House of Representatives:

My Dear Sir: —

Please give me below every historical illustration you can recall of the cheaper money, iron, copper, silver, paper, shells, etc., driving the dearer out. Begin with the Grecian iron money, or earlier, and, if possible, omit no historical proof of this kind in any country or in any age, winding up with the Argentine Republic, Mexico, and all others in that condition today....

Yours truly,

Michael D. Harter

[P.S.] Kindly give name of history opposite each request in which I will find a full account.[18]

This request, certainly as breathtaking in its scope as any which a reference librarian has been called upon to answer, received a reply within three weeks. It foreshadowed the calls that were to be made for public purposes upon the scholar and the new scholarship in years to come. Among the characteristics which distinguished the Progressive Era of the decade before the outbreak of World War I from earlier periods of political and social reform, none was more significant than the role which professionally trained scholars—political scientists, economists, historians, and sociologists—played in analyzing its problems and proposing its solutions. The election of Woodrow Wilson brought to the White House for the first time a man trained in these disciplines in precisely the pattern of the new scholarship that we have seen evolving. The period I am

116 Formation of the University, 1876–1919

dealing with ended with the assembling by Colonel House of what was known of the "Inquiry," a body of trained scholars, mostly college professors, who were asked to study the basis for making the peace settlement at the end of World War I.

I shall not attempt to describe the development of science and scholarship since 1917. Along with its triumphs come many problems, as they do with any institutional system that grows into such size and complexity. Serious weaknesses there are in certain aspects of our structure of learning, notably in the lack of preparation by the lower schools for the complex intellectual problems which men today must meet by intellectual means. Alarming, too, are the apparently increasing gulf between the scholar and scientist and the general public, and the monopoly of the means of mass communication by those with no claim to enlightenment. Nevertheless, were I to continue the account until the present, I would not be inclined to end on a querulous note. The problems I have hinted at are merely problems, and there is no reason at all to consider them insoluble. The weaknesses are weaknesses only, not fatal flaws portending ultimate collapse. What disasters may fall upon scholarship and science from the warring world without, no man can well predict. But I see no symptom whatever suggesting unsoundness in the basic intellectual structure that the last seventy-five years have evolved. It is idle to say that scholarship and science alone can save us from disaster in the world crisis in which we live. But scholarship and science, and the institutions which embody them, are powerful and uncorrupted instruments that we as a nation and as a larger community of nations can use in saving ourselves. We must see that they remain powerful and uncorrupted; that universities and libraries and the varied enterprises of research are not sacrificed in the stringency of a war economy; and that the freedom to think, which means the freedom to think critically and to think differently, does not fall a victim to hysteria.

Notes

1. Elmer Ellis, "The Profession of Historian," *Mississippi Valley Historical Review*, XXXVIII (June 1951), 6.

2. C.C. Jewett, "Statistics of American Libraries," in *Fourth Annual Report ... of the Smithsonian Institution ... during the Year 1849* (Washington, D.C., 1850), p. 41.

3. *Ibid.*, p. 39.

4. *Report of the Commissioner of Education for the Year 1875* (Washington, D.C., 1876), Table XVI, "Statistics of Public Libraries," pp. 869–71.

5. *U.S. Statutes at Large*, XII, 503.

6. *Who's Who in America, 1950–1951*, XXVI (Chicago: A.N. Marquis Co., 1950), 11.

7. W. Stull Holt (ed.), *Historical Scholarship in the United States, 1876–1901: As Revealed in the Correspondence of Herbert Baxter Adams* ("Johns Hopkins University Studies in Historical and Political Science," Vol. LVI, No. 4 [Baltimore: Johns Hopkins University Press, 1938]), p. 436. This collection of letters makes clearer than does any other source I know, the characteristics of the new scholarly environment which the university was creating in the period.

8. W. Dawson Johnston and Isadore G. Mudge, *Special Collections in Libraries in the United States* ("United States Bureau of Education Bulletins," No. 23 [Washington, D.C., 1912]), "Chronological List of Imported Collections," p. 124.

9. Arthur M. Schlesinger, *The Rise of the City, 1878–1898* ("A History of American Life" series, Vol. X [New York: Macmillan Co., 1933]), p. 221 and note.

10. See Phyllis G. Wherley, "Statistical Data," in Frank Burdette (ed.), *Directory of the American Political Science Association* 2nd ed. (Columbus, Ohio: American Political Science Association, 1949), pp. 339–45. The American Political Science Association reports that today 52.6 per cent of its members are college teachers and another 12.4 per cent are university students (practically all at the graduate level). Men in government service constitute 17.6 per cent, many of them drawn, of course, from academic positions. Despite wide general interest in political and governmental problems, with which the association is concerned, only 16.0 per cent of the membership come from outside these areas of professional employment. Doctoral

degrees are held by 48.8 per cent of the members, and at least one graduate degree, by 79.1 per cent. At least 39.6 per cent of the members have published books or monographs. Most of the other learned societies have an even more exclusively academic cast than this.

11. *A World List of Scientific Periodicals Published in the Years 1900–1933* 2nd ed. (London: Oxford University Press, 1934), p. vii.

12. William C. Lane, "The Harvard College Library, 1877–1928," in Samuel Eliot Morison (ed.), *The Development of Harvard University since the Inauguration of President Eliot, 1869–1929* (Cambridge: Harvard University Press, 1930), pp. 609–10.

13. *Report of the Commissioner of Education for the Year 1899–1900*, I (Washington, D.C., 1901), chap. xvii, "Public, Society, and School Libraries," 946–1165. The rank of the libraries of Philadelphia by size depends upon how pamphlets are treated in the totals. The three other largest libraries were the Free Library of Philadelphia, with 207,585 volumes but no separately specified pamphlets; the Library Company, with 201,184 volumes and 31,000 pamphlets; and the Mercantile Library, with 185,000 volumes and 10,000 pamphlets.

14. Anna M. Monrad, "Historical Notes on the Catalogues and Classifications of the Yale University Library," in *Papers in Honor of Andrew Keogh* (New Haven: Yale University Press, 1938), pp. 260–61. The 20,515 volumes in the Yale Library in 1849 were so arranged, apparently with no numbering of the individual books.

15. *Ibid.*, pp. 275 and 283, n. 90.

16. Lane, *op. cit.*, p. 615.

17. Holt, *op. cit.*, p. 401.

18. *Ibid.*, pp. 573–74. The letter was addressed to President Gilman, who handed it over to Adams for reply.

Research Libraries, the Ideology of Reading, and Scholarly Communication, 1876–1900

Wayne A. Wiegand

Post–Civil War America experienced significant changes, not the least of which was the transformation of higher education from a rigid system emphasizing the classic languages and literature to an elective undergraduate system and the beginnings of graduate education and professional schools. Most scholars agree that the modern American university dates from this period. Its goal—to search for, identify, and communicate new knowledge—naturally influenced the development of research libraries, many of which are now numbered among the nation's best.

This paper will argue that the role the research library assumed in the scholarly communication system fostered by the American university in the last quarter of the nineteenth in large part determined the way the research library profession defined its responsibilities to the research community. Perhaps a discussion of this period can shed some light on contemporary problems with which the profession struggles today. Much of what is discussed here is derived from recent reading in the history of higher education generally and reading on what David Ricci calls "the academic culture" in particular.[1]

An understanding of the role the research library assumed in scholarly communication around the turn of the century must begin with a discussion of the ideology of reading that drove the library profession at that time.[2] Identifying the belief system about reading that governed the professional practice librarians structured for themselves during the last quarter of the nineteenth century is not difficult. Evidence for it can be found in reflections on books and reading by selected intellectuals, in self-help manuals designed to improve character, and in statements by librarians quoting the intellectuals and echoing the manuals.[3] Essentially the ideology consisted of two elements: how to read and what to read. How to read had several constituent parts. "Read with a purpose" was the first. "The best rule of reading will be a method from Nature, and not a mechanical one of hours and pages," Ralph Waldo Emerson wrote in his well-known essay on books. "Let him read what is proper to him," he continued, "and not waste his memory on a crowd of mediocrities." In *Advice to Young Men in their Conduct in Life* (1860), T.S. Arthur warned: "Mere reading ... does not give a man much power.... It is *study* that does this." Frederick Harrison wrote in his *Choice of Books and Other Literary Pieces* (1886) that "reading for mere reading's sake ... is one of the worst and commonest and most unwholesome habits we have." Ainsworth Rand Spofford, Librarian of Congress during this period, echoed these sentiments. "Have a purpose [in reading], and adhere to it with good-humored pertinacity," he admonished a class in Melvil Dewey's first library school at Columbia in 1887.[4]

"Read systematically and widely" represented the second constituent part of how to read. "Reading maketh a full man," said Sir Francis Bacon in a passage librarians loved to quote often. Emerson surmised that the opinions of Plato, Shakespeare, Milton, and Göethe, among others, carried weight with subsequent generations precisely "because they had means of knowing the opposite opinion." "Identify a course of reading," said Raymond C. Davis, director of the University of Michigan library, to Dewey's students in 1887. "It [will give you] a bird's eye view of lit[erature], and a faulty view is better than none." Spofford summarized all this neatly when he wrote in 1900: "to pursue one subject through many authorities is the true way to arrive at comprehensive knowledge."[5]

"Digest what you read" formed a third part of instructions on how to read. Authors on the subject of reading often used eating as a metaphor to describe the way the mind worked. "Some books are to be tested, others to be swallowed, and some few to be chewed and digested," said Bacon. Excessive reading, like overeating, ought to be avoided. Librarians, with many others, believed that readers ought not to introduce a new subject into their minds before digesting the one previously occupying its attention. And like the stomach, the mind had limits. "There is in many minds ... a point of saturation," warned William Mathews in an 1876 essay, "which, if one passes by putting in more than his mind can hold, he only drives out something already in."[6]

Knowing how to read took practice. Knowing what to read was simpler. Advice abounded. Much of it was reflected in the classical curriculum, which tradition had identified as contacting the appropriate cultural, intellectual and literary norms against which new works ought to be judged. It was a curriculum many late nineteenth-century library leaders had weathered themselves, so they took to it naturally. Books and speeches were filled with lists of recommended reading. Authors cited regularly included Plutarch, Shakespeare, Homer, Dante, Milton, Burns, Tennyson, Scott, Thackeray, Dickens, and Hawthorne. In *A Book for All Readers* (1900), Spofford echoed the thoughts of others by citing history, travel, and biography as much more important than fiction. He named essay writers Bacon, Newman, Emerson, and Holmes, and argued that poetry which "deals with the highest thoughts in the most expressive language," ought to be read over and over. His list of standard selections, he pointed out, was "designed to include only the most improved and well-executed works."[7]

Improving was a word often used by individuals writing on the subject of reading. Many believed with William Foster, of the Providence Athenaeum, that the undisciplined mind was vulnerable to a "great mass of indifferent, unimportant reading," which wastes the "limited time we have in which to read," and also has a tendency toward "positively vicious and injurious books." Disciplined minds, on the other hand, discriminated between good and bad books, and with repeated practice and sound advice made the most of their reading time. To improve one's reading, Emerson posed three rules: "1. Never read any book that is not a year old. 2. Never read any but famed books. 3. Never read any but what you like." Cast in terms of today's scholarship on the creation and perpetuation of cultural, intellectual, and literary canons, Emerson was warning readers to avoid new works that had not stood the test of time, that had not met the norms forged by centuries of tradition.[8]

How to read; what to read. The structure of an ideology of reading was clear, and the vast majority of librarians came to accept it almost without question. But like all ideologies, its shortcomings were invisible to its believers. This ideology failed to acknowledge that the mental baggage readers brought to a text significantly influenced the message they got from it.[9] But that part of the ideology was missing in the public library movement of the late nineteenth century, when librarians had to deal with masses of people they believed knew neither how to read nor what to read, and when they were convinced that bad reading (as they defined it) led to bad social behavior. Attempts to implement programs motivated by the ideology are easy to trace in public librarianship. In the research library movement, however, which grew out of the changes occurring in higher education in the last quarter of the nineteenth century, the impact of the ideology is much less evident. Nevertheless, it was equally powerful in influencing the way research libraries defined their responsibilities to research communities. To understand how, one must first look closely at changes taking place in higher education at this time.

Before 1876, almost all colleges offered a classical curriculum of preselected courses that students had to take. Faculty normally required students to recite and memorize important passages from a class text, or to translate important passages from texts written in their original languages. Thus, faculty determined what students read, and how they read it. The ideology of reading was certainly in operation on the antebellum American campus, but the reading activities reflecting the ideology were put into practice by the faculty, not by academic librarians.

College librarians seldom contested this authority. Instead, they directed their attention toward developing a library practice to mime instructional methodology. For example, because institutions and their instructors did not regard independent reading very highly, college librarians felt little pressure to build large collections. Instead, they merely guarded collections donated from estates of deceased faculty members or alumni. College libraries were open for only a few hours a few days per week, and borrowing privileges for students were heavily restricted, which only further demonstrates the power of the curriculum and its agents on the antebellum college library.[10]

Two important events occurred, however, that dramatically changed higher education. The first was the publication of Charles Darwin's *Origin of Species* in 1859. Darwin's work challenged scores of established theological certainties—many of which, of course, had been echoed in the classical curriculum—and posited the tenets of a scientific method of inquiry, calling for efforts to collect facts and study them without prejudice. The second event was passage of the Morrill Act in 1862, which determined that public lands be set aside in each state to subsidize, "at least one college where the leading object shall be, without excluding other scientific and classical studies, ... to teach such branches of learning as are related to agriculture and the mechanic arts, ... in order to promote the liberal and practical education of the industrial classes in the several pursuits and professions in life." Colleges like the University of Illinois and California began as a result of this act. Along with several others, like the University of Wisconsin, which "inherited" land grant status, they were strengthened by a second Morrill Act of 1890.

The land grant colleges anointed by these federal mandates grew quickly, and in time became inextricably linked with the scientific method of inquiry scholars found so convincing. Together the institution and the adoption of the scientific method created a new environment, an "academic culture." That culture consisted of experts whose job it was to find new truths to replace the old authority patterns Darwin had so successfully contested. Above all, the experts had to meet the new challenges to the social order posed by a rush of new technologies, by industrialization, by immigration, and by urbanization. The universities and faculties that evolved from this mix of forces had a different goal than their antebellum predecessors. They were charged to search for, identify, and communicate new knowledge. And that new knowledge had to be based on facts, not assumptions. Naturally, the best place to gather and contemplate these facts was within the walls of a university, where experts trained in the use of the scientific method could observe, digest, and measure their value.[11]

In history, for example, the quest for fact-gathering became a passion driven by the assumption that it was a "condition for a general advance of the discipline." Demands for more data led to the acquisition of major research collections. Spofford himself noted how the demand for Americana "has noticeably enhanced the prices of all desirable and rare books." In 1867, he had scored a significant victory in this area by acquiring the Peter Force collection for the Library of Congress. In the late nineteenth century, people like Lyman Draper and Reuben Gold Thwaites spent countless hours chasing down and acquiring collections of "facts" that members of the newly emerging professional academic discipline of history found necessary to the practicing of their craft.[12] Research libraries, mostly outside academe at that time, were in the vanguard of this quest.

Academics themselves also came to believe that amassing knowledge based upon analysis of facts somehow had intrinsic social value. For example, members of new social science disciplines like psychology, sociology, and political science advertised their work as a scientific form of social analysis. They suggested in the process that further study would surely uncover those elusive "truths" society needed to reestablish the certainties overturned by Darwin and to meet the problems of the Gilded Age. The truths, it was assumed, would eventually turn into a kind of knowledge that would improve both societies and individuals. One Johns Hopkins University professor recalled that the president, Daniel Coit Gilman, believed the university should offer its scholars, "the unique experience of having contributed some tiny brick, however small, to the Temple of Science, the construction of which is the sublimest achievement of man."[13]

To make the task of constructing the Temple of Science manageable, the faculty began to redirect its efforts into areas of specialization. Members of the academic culture formed a series of networks, or scientific communities, reaching from coast to coast. These networks found powerful voices in the many professional associations established during these years, whose primary purpose was to define common standards of professional conduct. Among them the American Historical Association (1884); the American Economic Association (1885); the American Statistical Association (1888); the American Mathematical Association (1888); the Geological Society of America (1888); the American Anthropological Society (1902); and the American Sociological Society (1905).

If the new university was a Temple of Science, and its academic employees the high priests of a new knowledge, the process still required a pulpit from which to disseminate these newfound truths to other members of the order. To address the needs of the academic culture, universities established and subsidized new systems of information exchange. In the new field of political science, for example, the Johns Hopkins University founded *The Johns Hopkins Studies in Historical and Political Science* in 1883. Three years later Columbia set up the *Political Science Quarterly*. In 1890, the University of Pennsylvania began the *Annals of the American Academy of Political and Social Science*, and a year later Columbia followed with *Studies in History, Economics and Public Law*.

Most professional associations and learned societies also began publishing journals. Together with university-sponsored journals, they offered forums for members to communicate the results of their fact-gathering activities. Each journal served to institutionalize a branch of learning; each helped to establish common vocational languages and to enforce occupational standards. The *American Journal of Mathematics* (1878); the *American Chemical Journal* (1879); the *American Journal of Philology* (1879); the *American Journal of Psychology* (1887); the *American Geologist* (1888); the *American Historical Review* (1891); the *Journal of Political Economy* (1892); and the *American Journal of Sociology* (1894) all began publication within a fifteen-year period.

To supplement this new army of journals, many universities also offered subsidized presses to faculty members in order to provide a conduit for lengthier scholarly studies, which commercial publishers found unprofitable. Between 1890 and 1910, Johns Hopkins, Chicago, Columbia, Harvard, Yale, Princeton and the University of California all established presses.[14]

The communication system supported by the modern university also provided members of the academic culture with a means by which to measure the worth of their peers. Academic journal and press editors, usually highly respected members of the academic culture, weighed the value of manuscripts submitted for publication by "objective" scientific standards. Some journals and presses, it was assumed, had higher standards than others. Any member of the academic culture who published in a press or journal that discipline consensus had determined was superior would raise his national reputation above those who published in presses considered less worthy. Academics soon began to build their campus reputations in large part on the basis of publications, to advance their careers on the basis of publications, and to establish national and international visibility on the basis of their publications. Because the specialized knowledge generated by the disciplinary communities accumulated so rapidly, a consensus quickly emerged that only one's disciplinary peers were capable of judging the quality of work in that discipline.

While most members of the academic culture subscribed to journals within their own discipline, and while most were able to purchase books issued from university presses, campus libraries were nonetheless expected to collect books and journals for faculty and student use as a matter of normal library practice. Thus, as a result of a greatly expended system of scholarly communication, and because research libraries had a responsibility to collect the products of the system, faculty members could generally assume that they and their students had access to "good reading" that had weathered a prepublication filtering process run by academic peers in whom they had confidence.

Consequently, as in the classical college, the authority to determine what to read was still being exercised by the faculty. However, that authority had been transferred from an individual who assigned texts on campus to a peer evaluation system, which largely took place off campus, and from which research libraries were excluded except as consumers. Members of the academic culture continued to determine quality; members of the research library community were charged to obtain quantity, and to impose some order on that quantity.

Academics openly recognized the nature of the situation. Only after about 1875, wrote professor Oliver Farrar Emerson in 1909, was "the buying of books [in academic libraries] ... put on a methodical basis by men who have known what was best in the particular fields." This attitude was echoed in the preceptorial system Princeton president Woodrow Wilson pushed for in the 1890s, in which "young doctors of philosophy would 'live in the dormitories and direct the reading and studies of the student' thus restoring 'something of the primitive democracy of college life.'"[15] In the marketplace of ideas, then, the research scholar looked upon the research library either as a place that had gathered the sources he chose to study and from which he determined prevailing truths, or as a reliable consumer that provided a reasonably stable market for the products of the scholarly communication system upon which he based his career. In either case, the scholar retained the most control. He chose what to study, and he and his peers determined what should be read by defining the canons of the disciplines. In response, research libraries continued to hunt for primary source collections, and universities that subsidized journals and presses recognized an obligation to adjust university library budgets to meet the increased needs generated by the accelerated scholarly communication system.

A parallel system for establishing literary canons also influenced research library development. Initially, this system functioned outside the university. Literary periodicals like the *National Review*, the *Saturday Review*, the *Athenaeum*, the *Critic*, and the *Atlantic* assumed responsibility for determining quality literature merely by process of selection. William Dean Howells, editor of the *Atlantic*, firmly believed that because of his editorial standards the best authors published in the *Atlantic* and lesser authors published elsewhere.

Naturally, the trade publishing world recognized the market value of the existence of a hierarchy that cemented literary canons into place. Richard Brodhead calls this "the establishment of a high literary zone." At Houghton Mifflin, James Fields began issuing the very successful Riverside Literature Series, which automatically selected the "best" American authors the nation had to offer. Brodhead argues persuasively that classic American literature, "as the nineteenth century knows it," was largely determined by Howells and Fields. They canonized some writers who met their standards of literariness, ignored or dismissed others, and thus had significant influence in identifying "the best reading." Thousands of numbers of the Houghton Mifflin Literature Series were purchased by libraries across the country, and references to the value of literary guidance provided by periodicals like the *Atlantic* are numerous in late nineteenth-century library literature.[16]

For a time, academics took their cues from this literary establishment operating outside academe, but gradually they assumed a greater role in formalizing, certifying, and legitimating literary canons within their own institutions. In 1896, Bliss Perry was still in the minority when he published an essay advocating the study of modern fiction in colleges and universities. Institutions of higher education had an obligation, he argued, "to send into this public, to serve as leaven, men who know good work from bad, and who know why they know it." A generation later, his views had achieved consensus. The literature professor was regarded as an authority on literature, and the university a place where good literature was identified and transmitted. That the authors whom literary scholars endorsed were generally Anglo-Saxon males, drawn from the native-born New England literary establishment, gave members of the academy little pause. Academics studied their texts to discover important truths, and the scholarly communication system naturally expanded to accommodate their findings.[17] Libraries dutifully collected the results of their careful research and actively sought "important" collections to support it.

The accelerated system of scholarly communication created an expanding body of knowledge that students could expect to find in their research libraries. Curriculum served as another important element in determining research library development. Recent scholarship argues persuasively that universities showed an impressive ability to accommodate new areas of investigation in the late nineteenth century simply by adding "fields" to their curricula. As long as money could be found to fund new positions, the field coverage principle proved an easy, comfortably self-regulating way to deal with expansion. It proved relatively painless for university administrators; new and old faculty members working within the same departments did not have to debate disciplinary issues with each other, because they did not work the same fields. Consequently, the power of each faculty member to decide what to study in his specific area of expertise, and to determine which were the authoritative works his students ought to study, went virtually uncontested. Debates on prevailing truths were reserved for externally operating scientific communities. This environment led to significant influence over collecting practices at research libraries.

The establishment of graduate programs gave faculty even more power over the direction of research library collections. Graduate students were expected to debate old assumptions by becoming acquainted with the latest research in the field under study; they were also expected to engage in wide reading. The seminar gave graduate students an opportunity to do some original research; it also created a need for easily accessible collections of primary source material. Naturally, graduate faculty pressed university libraries on their campuses to accelerate efforts to acquire larger collections of primary and secondary source materials for their students. And research libraries responded as best they could, some better than others.

Young PhDs who had successfully negotiated graduate programs took jobs in colleges and universities throughout the country, where they sought to duplicate the intellectual excitement of their alma mater. For example, by 1886—only ten years after opening its doors—Johns Hopkins had granted doctorates to sixty-nine people, fifty-six of whom went on to teach at a total of more than thirty colleges and universities.[18] In their new posts, they undoubtedly pressed for teaching and research facilities similar to those they found in Baltimore.

The influence of an ideology of reading, combined with the late nineteenth-century rise of an academic culture, significantly affected the development of research libraries. What students were assigned to read in higher education classes introduced them to a part of "the good reading" in a particular field. But to back up required reading assignments, academics could also count on whole libraries of good reading that had been approved for publication by peers in whom they had confidence. Research libraries were not a part of this process, except for the pressure they could apply as consumers.

An ideology of reading was still operating here, but to members of the academic culture, whether students or faculty, the research library was not perceived as an active participant. How to read was being evaluated by a system of grading that faculty members exercised on their graduate and undergraduate students. What to read was being determined by class assignments on campus, in judgments rendered on manuscripts submitted for publication in scholarly journals and presses, and in a reviewing process generated by off-campus authorities. Good research libraries had what students and faculty needed; poor ones did not. Faculty continued to determine the best reading, and from their perspective the research library had two major responsibilities. One was to remain part of the system of scholarly communication by supplying current periodicals and publications. The other was to garner as many collections of primary source materials as possible, so that research scholars did not have to travel great distances to conduct their research. Beyond these needs, faculty had little reason to concern themselves with the development of research librarianship.

To suggest that research libraries merely responded to the "supply on demand" nature of the scholarly communication system, however, distorts the total picture. At the center was an ideology of reading that governed the library's collection activities and allowed authority to remain largely in the hands of members of the academic culture. But by the late nineteenth century, the research library itself had evolved into a bureaucracy. It had developed systems of its own, tied to faith in a science of administration and in the development of a particular form of professional expertise. The library science that grew up in the last quarter of the nineteenth century called for a marriage of efficient institutional management with a unique expertise that imposed order on the cultural, intellectual, and literary objects libraries chose to collect and preserve.

Research libraries drew from this library science to fit their particular needs. They adopted or developed classification systems and subject bibliographies for patron use and hired staff to maintain the systems. They also acquired and developed impressive special collections of primary sources, along with the staff necessary to maintain these collections. And it is during this period that formal reference librarianship had its origins. Research libraries performed admirably here too. They established and developed reference collections, and again hired staff to maintain them.[19] But no matter how hard they tried, no matter the quality of their library science, research libraries had difficulty countering the "supply on demand" attitude of resident faculty as the latter's most important criterion for evaluating service. As long as the supply was satisfactory for those faculty who used the library, they had little reason to include the research library in their thoughts about research, learning, literacy, and higher education.

These conclusions may seem harsh, but they should not be taken to imply that the research library lacks a significant role in the system of scholarly communication. Far from it. This essay attempts to reconstruct the developing role of research libraries in the system of scholarly communication as viewed by members of the academic culture. But that view is myopic, because it fails to account for the major contributions of research libraries to the dynamics of scholarship.

New scholarship is challenging the "Temple of Science" mentality, arguing that the scientific objectivity supposedly exercised by members of the academic culture is and has been molded by that culture's own limitations. Recent works show how the exclusion of entire groups of people from cultural, intellectual, and literary canons has had a major impact on how a pluralistic society looks at itself and at the histories of its various parts. Gerald Graff, for example, notes that even though scholars were motivated by "a genuine democratic egalitarianism," the academic literary studies that developed during the Progressive era nonetheless "combined class, ethnic and gender prejudices." David Ricci concludes from his research on the late nineteenth-century political science profession that "any idea advanced in political science literature must be judged rather than accepted automatically because practitioners certify it as a valuable addition to our knowledge of public affairs." Richard Brodhead is more specific. "Traditions begin when the past is purged of irrelevance," he says. "They come into existence when the full past, the sum of what has been, is allowed to fall from mind; then, when a past worth remembering is selected and given memorable shape." Elaine Showalter is even more forthright: "Feminist critics do not accept the view that the canon reflects the objective value judgments of history and posterity," she says, "but use it instead as a culture-based political construct. In practice, 'posterity' has meant groups of men with the access to publishing and reviewing that enabled them to enforce their view of 'literature' and to define a group of 'classics.'"[20]

Over the years, these critics argue, members of the academic culture have tended to study white male wielders of power. As a result, the cultural, intellectual, and literary canons they created and perpetuated, which in turn are reflected strongly in the collections of research libraries across the country, systematically (but seldom intentionally) excluded whole groups of people.

It is here that the research library assumes a vital role in the scholarly communication system. The library has the potential to check the built-in limitations of scholarly truth-seekers. Brodhead argues that "canons do not become available for a new group's remaking until they have already lost their compelling reality for a strategic position of their original supporters."[21] As a new generation dismantles the set of old canons that served its predecessors, and as that new generation constructs a new set of canons more carefully tailored to its own needs, it requires data saved from the past in order to redefine the past for itself. Often that data is found in research libraries.

Some authors, such as Emily Dickinson, and entire genres of literature, such as female-authored mid-nineteenth-century romances, have been rescued from relative obscurity because a few research libraries saw fit to collect them, even though the works have not been legitimated by members of the contemporary academic culture. Some works have now entered the existing canons. But "literary institutions work in part by making literary pasts," Brodhead argues. "They institute a particular formation of literature by *making* some segment of previous writing to be the significant past—a past that, reinternalized by the readers and writers who inhabit that institution, helps neutralize and validate its definition of what literature is."[22]

Other authors, like Mrs. E.D.E.N. Southworth, await a restructuring of the canon to take into account the historical context in which they worked before they can be studied. "For a work to become a source of tradition, a later worker must locate it as a significant model," Brodhead says. Showalter echoes these sentiments. "As the works of dozens of women writers have been rescued from what E.P. Thompson calls 'the enormous condescension of posterity,' and considered in relation to each other," she writes, "the lost continent of the female tradition has risen like Atlantis from the sea of English literature."[23] The same dynamics are evident in the cultural and intellectual canons governing the direction of all academic disciplines.

Some authors, some books, and whole groups of subcultures, however, will never be studied, not because they do not merit analysis, but because records of their existence have not been preserved. Research libraries must share some responsibility for their absence. This situation will undoubtedly be exacerbated in the future when research libraries have to make decisions about which materials deteriorating on their shelves deserve to be preserved, and which should be allowed to deteriorate. If they must fall back on the canons of their own contemporary culture to make these decisions, they will be sentencing future generations to an increasingly narrow view of the past, from which those generations will reconstruct their own version of the past.

Research libraries, bureaucracies within universities supporting academic cultures, deserve some credit for saving segments of a larger cultural, literary, and intellectual heritage than the contemporary academic culture considers worthy of study; but it is also necessary to recognize that research librarians are products of an academic culture. They need to become much more aware of their shortcomings, so that they do not systematically (and certainly not intentionally) erase the record of existence of entire groups functioning almost invisibly within contemporary society and operating outside the confines of subjects being studied by members of the academic culture.

Librarians also need to become aware of the limits placed upon their professional vision by adhering to the traditional ideology of reading. The ideology is inherently flawed by the notion of identifying the "best reading," and it reverberates throughout the system of scholarly communication. For example, Spofford's belief that "the works most frequently reprinted in successive ages are the ones which it is safe to stand by" ignores the power of canons to control a circumscribed vision of the past. This power justifiably merits the criticism of Graff, Brodhead, Ricci, Showalter, and Hamerow, to name only those cited in this paper. An ideology of reading that aims at collecting the best, then, may hinder more than help the scholars of the future, but like all ideologies it will be difficult to challenge.

To expect members of the academic culture to admit openly that they may not have considered all relevant "significant models," or that they failed to consider problems inherent in the "enormous consideration of posterity," would run counter to human nature. After all, professors are employed as experts; they are supposed to know the right answers. Research libraries may, in fact, serve as uncomfortable reminders that over time their supposedly scientific answers show many unscientific flaws. It represents a curious dichotomy. On the one hand, research libraries provide the evidence that the academic culture needs in order to prove its own expertise. On the other hand, research libraries also provide the evidence to hold that expertise suspect. The easy way out is to ignore this dichotomy. Little wonder members of the academic culture tend to overlook research libraries in their discussion of research, learning, literacy, and higher education.

Research libraries also play a vital role in the activities of the academic culture through the indirect pressure they exert as consumers. Too often, members of the academic culture appear blind to the educational benefits that accrue in libraries, and that the research library makes possible simply because it is the major consumer of scholarly materials. The ideas professors develop in their publications are often introduced in their classrooms, where they help stimulate learning experiences. Because research libraries constitute the primary market for the majority of their publications, they can justifiably take some credit for the creation of these learning experiences.

A final reason for believing research libraries play a vital role in the activities of the academic culture relates to the evaluation system the members of the academic culture have invented to judge each other's work. Academic cultures—like most cultures of the intellect—consist, for the most part, of people with good minds, but good minds which can be improved. Here the evaluation process for scholarly publications serves a useful purpose, because the evaluation usually leads to revisions that often significantly improve the work's ideas.[24]

The system of scholarly communication exists, like it or not. Research librarians and other members of the academic culture have to deal with it. But perhaps they tend to concentrate too much attention on its faults, and to ignore its strengths. Research librarians often lament the pressure that numbers exert on research library collections yet forget the side benefits brought by the creation of these collections. Without research libraries to provide the market for these products, would the process be significantly inhibited? Many members of the academic culture have commented that colleagues who have not published for years after obtaining tenure often continue to espouse ideas that are no longer fit the times and no longer fit the needs of the students they teach. The evaluation process that precedes publication does have beneficial effects on higher education; those effects might be threatened if research libraries had to cut so far back on budgets that most products no longer had a market.

Research libraries are generally left out of contemporary discussion of research, learning, literacy, and higher education in America because most experts in the academic culture who discuss such subjects perceive research libraries either as depositories for the primary sources they wish to study or as a final resting place in the scholarly communication process. The evaluation, the determination of what is best, has in large measure already taken place before the scholarly work has found its way into the research library. That the authorities to whom society looks for expert opinion do not have research libraries primarily in mind may explain why the library profession does not command much power compared to the other professions.

In part librarianship has itself to blame. The profession has tied itself to an ideology of reading that in effect restricts its role in the canon-making process. The library is a cultural, literary, and intellectual institution that echoes the expert opinions of others by defining the parameters of collection building according to those expert opinions.

But one should not disparage this situation. Certainly, it has worked to the benefit of millions over the past century. Certainly one can demonstrate that the academic culture and the system that supports it have had a major and positive impact on society. And certainly, the process within academic culture leading to publication has beneficial spillover effects that ought to be accelerated and amplified.

But the situation also brings with it limitations, and research libraries need to be made much more aware of these limitations. If research libraries and their employees can augment that awareness, if they can turn some of their attention away from the administration of bureaucracy and the expertise unique to it alone, perhaps the research library can play an even larger, more active role in the process of canon-making. This would require, however, significant shifts in the ideology of reading, including an acknowledgment that people interact with texts differently, often much differently and in many more ways than the reviewer in *Choice*, the *American Historical Review*, or the *New York Times Book Review* can envision by him or herself. "Best" is a relative term; recognizing that fact may be a first step toward assuming a larger role in the process of scholarly communication.

Notes

1. David Ricci, *The Tragedy of Political Science: Politics, Scholarship and Democracy* (New Haven: Yale University Press, 1984). A good portrait of the closeness of this culture viewed from the inside is Merton Dillon, *Ulrich Bonnell Phillips: Historian of the Old South* (Baton Rouge: Louisiana State University Press, 1985). See also Burton Bledstein, *The Culture of Professionalism: The Middle Class and the Development of Higher Education in America* (New York: W.W. Norton, 1976).

2. I take my definition of ideology from Martin Seliger: a "belief system" that serves a group of people "on a relatively permanent basis." See Martin Seliger, *Ideology and Politics* (New York: The Free Press, 1976) 120.

3. A good bibliography of nineteenth-century self-help manuals can be found in Karen Halttunen, *Confidence Men and Painted Women: A Study in Middle Class Culture in America, 1830–1870* (New Haven: Yale University Press, 1982) 248–55.

4. Ralph Waldo Emerson, "Books," in *Society and Solitude: Twelve Chapters* (Boston: Houghton Mifflin Co., 1912) 194; T.S. Arthur, *Advice to Young Men in Their Conduct in Life* (Philadelphia, 1860); Frederick Harrison, *The Choice of Books and Other Literary Pieces* (London, 1886) 78. Spofford's lecture can be found in an unpublished manuscript: Francis Miksa, "Melvil Dewey's School of Library Economy, Columbia College, 1887–1888: Shorthand Notes of Classes," (1987): lecture 116, p. 1.

5. Francis Bacon, "Of Studies," in *The Essays or Counsels, Civil and Moral, of Francis Bacon*, ed. Samuel Harvey Reynolds (Oxford, 1890) 342; Ralph Waldo Emerson, "Culture," in *The Conduct of Life* (Boston: Houghton Mifflin, 1904) 141; Miksa, "Melvil Dewey's School of Library Economy," lecture 103, pp. 1, 2; Ainsworth Rand Spofford, *A Book for All Readers: Designed as an Aid to the Collection, Use, and Preservation of Books and the Formation of Public and Private Libraries* (New York: G.P. Putnam's Sons, 1900) 284.

6. Francis Bacon, "Of Studies" 342; William Mathews, "Professorships of Books and Reading, Part II," in U.S. Bureau of Education, *Public Libraries in the United States of America: Their History, Condition, and Management, Special Report, Part I* (Washington, D.C.: Government Printing Office, 1876) 242. This report is one of the library profession's landmark publications. For a recent discussion of the eating metaphor, see Catherine Sheldrick Ross, "Metaphors of Reading," *Journal of Library History* 22 (1987): 147–63.

7. Spofford, *A Book for All Readers*, chap. 1. See also Samuel Smiles, "The Companionship of Books," in *Character* (London: John Murray, 1907) 297, 322–23; and Newell Dwight Hilles, *A Man's Value to Society: Studies in Self-Culture and Character* (Chicago, 1894) 240.

8. William E. Foster, *Libraries and Readers* (New York: 1883) 20; Emerson, "Books" 196.

9. For example, see Jane P. Tompkins, ed., *Reader-Response Criticism: From Formalism to Post-Structuralism* (Baltimore: Johns Hopkins University Press, 1980); Susan R. Sulieman and Inge Crossman, eds., *The Reader in the Text: Essays on Audience and Interpretation* (Princeton: Princeton University Press, 1980); Judith Fetterly, *The Resisting Reader: A Feminist Approach to American Fiction* (Bloomington: Indiana University Press, 1977); Elizabeth Freund, *The Return of the Reader: Reader-Response Criticism* (London: Methuen, 1987); and especially Wolfgang Iser, *The Act of Reading: A Theory of Aesthetic Response* (Baltimore: Johns Hopkins University Press, 1978) and Stanley Fish, *Is there a Text in this Class? The Authority of Interpretive Communities* (Cambridge, MA: Harvard University Press, 1980). See also Janice Radway, *Reading the Romance: Women, Patriarchy and Popular Literature* (Chapel Hill: University of North Carolina Press, 1984) for a recent attempt to evaluate a literature through the eyes of the regular readers of that literature.

10. Frederick Rudolph, *Curriculum: A History of the American Undergraduate Course of Study since 1636* (San Francisco: Jossey-Bass Publishers, 1977) 69. See also Gerald Graff, *Professing Literature: An Institutional History* (Chicago: University of Chicago Press, 1987) 34–35. The standard history of the classical college library is Louis Shores, *Origins of the American College Library, 1638–1800* (New York: Barnes & Noble, 1934). See also Arthur Hamlin, *The University Library in the United States* (Philadelphia: University of Pennsylvania Press, 1981), chaps. 1–3; and Orvin Lee Shiflett, *Origins of Academic Librarianship* (Norwood, N.J.: Ablex, 1981), chaps. 1–2.

11. Ricci, *Tragedy of Social Science*, 33. See also Thomas S. Haskell, *The Emergence of Professional Social Science: The American Social Science Association and the Nineteenth-Century Crisis of Authority* (Urbana: University of Illinois Press, 1977) 65ff. Standard works on Darwin's impact include Richard Hofstadter, *Social Darwinism in American Thought* (Philadelphia: University of Pennsylvania Press, 1944); Cynthia Eagle Russett, *Darwin in America: The Intellectual Response, 1865–1912* (San Francisco: W.H. Freeman and Co., 1976); and Walter P. Metzger, *Academic Freedom in the Age of the University* (New York: Columbia University Press, 1955). The best overview of these developments is still Robert Wiebe, *The Search for Order, 1877–1920* (New York: Hill and Wang, 1967).

12. Theodore S. Hamerow, *Reflections on History and Historians* (Madison: University of Wisconsin Press, 1987) 48, 166–67. See also Spofford, *A Book for All Readers* 454; and Ricci, *The Tragedy of Political Science* 55, 67.

13. Edward Shils, "The Order of Learning in the United States: The Ascendancy of the University," in *The Organization of Knowledge in Modern America, 1860–1920*, ed. Alexandra Oleson and John Voss (Baltimore: Johns Hopkins University Press, 1979) 28. Gilman is quoted in Ricci, *The Tragedy of Political Science* 23.

14. Hamerow, *Reflections on History and Historians* 40; Ricci, *Tragedy of Political Science* 50; Graff, *Professing Literature* 62.

15. Oliver Farrar Emerson, "The American Scholar and the Modern Language," *PMLA* 24 (1909): appendix xc; John Kennedy Winkler, *Woodrow Wilson: The Man Who Lives On* (New York: Vanguard Press, 1933) 85, as quoted in Graff, *Professing Literature* 92.

16. Richard Brodhead, *The School of Hawthorne* (New York: Oxford University Press, 1986) 62, 86, 87–88, 101. Most research libraries still own numerous Riverside editions. For an example of the influence that periodicals occupying a high literary zone had on the acquisition of fiction by libraries, see discussion

of a new periodical entitled *Novel-List* in *Library Journal* 12 (1887): 537. See also Spofford, *A Book for All Readers* 243–44.

17. Bliss Perry, "Fiction as a College Study," *PMLA* 11 (1896): 84. American modernism's ability to encompass a wider range of intellectual, cultural, and literary canons did not seriously threaten the authority of academic and literary experts to determine the canon. For a wide-ranging recent discussion of modernism's many influences, see *American Quarterly* 39 (1987), a special issue on "Modernist Culture in America." See also Brodhead, *The School of Hawthorne* 60–61; and Graff, *Professing Literature* 68.

18. W. Carson Ryan, *Studies in Early Graduate Education: The Johns Hopkins University, Clark University, The University of Chicago* (New York: Carnegie Foundation, 1932) 32; Ricci, *Tragedy of Political Science* 35–36.

19. For a more extended discussion of the changing library bureaucracy at this time, see Wayne A. Wiegand, "View from the Top: The Library Administrator's Changing Perspective on Standardization Schemes and Cataloging Practices in American Libraries, 1891–1901," in *Reference Services and Technical Services: Intersections in Library Practice*, ed. Gordon and Sally Stevenson (New York: Haworth Press, 1983) 11–37.

20. Graff, *Professing Literature* 13–14, 173; Ricci, *Tragedy of Political Science* 291; Brodhead, *School of Hawthorne* 206; Elaine Showalter, ed., *The New Feminist Criticism: Essays on Women, Literature and Theory* (New York: Pantheon, 1985) 32. This literature continues to grow. See Kermit Vanderbilt, *American Literature and the Academy: The Roots, Growth and Maturity of a Profession* (Philadelphia: University of Pennsylvania Press, 1987); Jane Tompkins, *Sensational Designs* (New York: Oxford University Press, 1985); and Gerda Lerner, *The Creation of Patriarchy* (New York: Oxford University Press, 1986).

21. Brodhead, *School of Hawthorne* 206.

22. Brodhead, *School of Hawthorne* 83.

23. Brodhead, *School of Hawthorne* 176; Showalter, *New Feminist Criticism* 27.

24. In a recent article discussing the excessive number of historical inaccuracies and shortsighted, self-serving interpretations of the Age of the Discovery in popular American history textbooks, James Axtell makes the point forcefully. "Pressure the better journals into the regular reviewing of textbooks," he argues, and most of the sloppy delivery of information with disappear. See James Axtell, "Europeans, Indians and the Age of Discovery in American History Textbooks," *American Historical Review* 92 (June 1987) 632.

Experimentation and Redefinition, 1920–1945

The historiography devoted to higher education pays comparatively limited attention to the period between the first and second world wars, due largely to such robust and expansive developments having occurred on either side—before the 1920s and after 1945. The period of the interregnum was troubling; the optimism so abundant in the formative years could not be sustained. The good news was that grant dollars had expanded the potential, for those devoted to a life of the mind, to undertake an entire career in academe, teaching and pursuing a self-defined research agenda. John D. Rockefeller's General Education Board, established in 1902, began making grants to separate black schools and soon expanded into higher education generally, seeking to make the better colleges even stronger with contributions for endowments, salary increases, and faculty pensions. Likewise, the Carnegie Foundation for the Advancement of Teaching contributed millions of dollars, first to private colleges and, soon thereafter, to state universities. Carnegie largesse targeted faculty pensions with programs that eventually morphed into the establishment of TIAA-CREF (Teachers Insurance and Annuity Association and College Retirement Equities Fund). Member institutions of TIAA-CREF came to constitute most major research universities plus hundreds of colleges and smaller schools which collectively, through institutional and employee contributions, became the largest pension fund in the United States. These dollars, matched differently from one college to the next, have provided for the professoriate an income stream permitting basic dignity and comfort in the years after one's employment.

Support of this nature made higher education ever more appealing as a lifelong career. When professors taught young people, they provided a valuable social service, regarded by many as essential to the commonweal of the entire society. Professors with sufficient ambition, intellect, and training could also enjoy a middle-class lifestyle while engaged in academic pursuits. One might logically conclude that a combination of social utility and long-range financial planning could provide much encouragement. And to a certain extent that happened but other factors were at play, rendering the interregnum a time of disenchantment and anxiety.

As the 1920s roared into American culture, students became more obsessed than ever before with life beyond the curriculum. The second decade of the twentieth century offered increasingly powerful diversions: fraternities, sororities, and social clubs had evolved to chart the parameters of the undergraduate experience while planting the seeds fruitful for networking after college. In addition, the popularity of intercollegiate athletics rose to new heights, and an era of large arena and stadium construction was underway. One scholar posited that, in the 1920s, undergraduate males devoted ninety percent of their time to non-curricular activities.[1] Libraries, books, and undergraduate studies in general were relegated to the margins of campus life. Laurence R. Veysey described a loss of nerve and a fear of scarcity on the part of educators who were confronting a social pattern hostile to the entire curriculum.[2]

Higher education struggled throughout the Great Depression but could not look to the United States federal government for comprehensive relief. Proponents of the New Deal tended to regard the collegiate scene as elitist, thus colleges benefited in only two ways, highly selective building construction (typically through the W.P.A. [Works Progress Administration]) and direct support for students in work-study programs. Beyond these limited efforts, the picture for academe was often grim as budget reductions and personnel layoffs became the norm, and the foundations, though providing endowment and pension dollars, could not be expected to alleviate annual shortfalls occurring with painful frequency. And yet, out of the age of discontent and diminishing resources, emerged some of the more creative ways to think about undergraduate teaching and learning. John Dewey (1859–1952) proposed instruction that emphasized civic responsibility and social and family development, Robert Maynard Hutchins (1899–1977) and Alexander Meiklejohn (1872–1964) experimented with new theoretical constructs for the liberal arts, and honors programs emerged as intriguing options for undergraduates. Veysey was able to conclude that by the end of the 1930s "there seemed far more likelihood of widespread curricular rethinking than at any time in the preceding thirty years."[3]

Academic librarians were not without our own efforts at theory creation for it was in the 1930s that the nation's first doctoral program in librarianship (at the University of Chicago) began to produce graduates who became authors of groundbreaking dissertations, books, and articles. The sociological and historical research conducted at Chicago would redefine and redirect librarianship for decades and Chicago would stand alone as the only doctoral program in librarianship until after World War II. To the increasingly sophisticated library literature were added the earliest statements of the library-college concepts of Louis Shores and, in 1940, B. Harvie Branscomb's *Teaching with Books*, a study of sixty liberal arts college libraries from the viewpoint of pedagogical effectiveness rather than administrative efficiency.[4] While the Chicago graduates lifted library science research to unprecedented heights, and began mapping the discipline with fresh analysis, Shores and Branscomb (1894–1998) envisioned a vital new role for the college librarian as essential, coequal partner with the professor in teaching the critical thinking skills imperative to instruction in the use of books and libraries.

Philanthropic support held the capacity to vastly improve, even to redefine an institution in ways appreciated by most university citizens including librarians. In "Private Dominance in Black Academic Libraries," James E. Hooper shows the grant-supported black college libraries as having grown in vitally important ways, according to documentary evidence featuring Arthur Klein's 1928 report issued by the federal government. Southern whites were content for black colleges to benefit financially as long as northern philanthropists did not leverage grant dollars to challenge the mores of rigid racial segregation; Hooper analyzes these dynamics within the context of the traditionally delicate balance between donors and recipients. Our next essay, penned by Kenneth Carpenter, traces the influence of historian Robert C. Binkley (1897–1940) in his role as chair of the Joint Committee on Materials for Research.[5] Representing the Social

Science Research Council and the American Council of Learned Societies, Binkley and his committee expanded their vision to examine the entire enterprise of scholarly communication. They experimented with the new technologies of microform reproduction to safeguard the intellectual contents of decaying publications and to disseminate materials for research library collection development and preservation. Binkley also became a national leader and spokesperson for considering the macro-level concerns of scholarly information. As his work matured, he came to see its potential not only for humanities and social science scholarship but also for local history, for the enrichment of cultural life in cities and towns, small communities, and neighborhoods. Like J. Franklin Jameson, Binkley came to see the historian as custodian of a sacred trust, preserving the culture for the common good, and serving the interests of present and future generations.

Notes

1. David O. Levine, *The American College and the Culture of Aspiration, 1915–1940* (Ithaca, New York: Cornell University Press, 1986), 119.

2. Laurence R. Vesey, "Stability and Experimentation in the American Undergraduate Curriculum," in *Content and Context: Essays on College Education*, ed. Karl Kaysen (New York: McGraw-Hill, 1973), 9–14. See also Paula S. Fass, *The Damned and the Beautiful: American Youth in the 1920s* (New York: Oxford University Press, 1977); Helen Lefkowitz Horowitz, *Campus Life: Undergraduate Cultures from the End of the Eighteenth Century to the Present* (New York: Knopf, 1987); and Lynn Peril, *College Girls: Bluestockings, Sex Kittens, and Coeds, Then and Now* (New York: W.W. Norton, 2006).

3. Veysey (1973), 10.

4. Louis Shores, "The Library Arts College, a Possibility in 1954?" *School and Society* 41 (January 26, 1934), 110–14; and B. Harvie Branscomb, *Teaching with Books: A Study of College Libraries* (Chicago, Illinois: Association of American Colleges and American Library Association, 1940).

5. A photograph of Robert C. Binkley is published with Carpenter's essay, "Toward a New Cultural Design" in *Institutions of Reading: The Social Life of Libraries in the United States*, eds. Thomas Augst and Kenneth Carpenter (Amherst: University of Massachusetts Press, 2007), 284.

Private Dominance in Black Academic Libraries, 1916–1938

JAMES E. HOOPER

Significant political and economic changes influenced the development of black academic libraries between the two World Wars. After World War I, the reputation of big business led President Calvin Coolidge to say with proud sincerity: "The nation's business is business." In the same vein, Herbert Hoover extolled the virtues of rugged individualism, while other economists predicted an unending era of prosperity based on the triumph of private enterprise. According to business apologists, tremendous wealth at the top of the economic pyramid would filter down to the lowest productive class thus creating buying power which would uphold the mighty economic edifice. Although this philosophy held some validity, the southern black, at the lowest level of the economic pyramid, profited little.[1]

Two northern philanthropists believed that only through liberal and advanced education could blacks hope to compete in the modern world. John D. Rockefeller, Jr., of Standard Oil, and Julius Rosenwald, of Sears, Roebuck, and Company, sought to ameliorate the lot of the southern black and were persuaded that Booker T. Washington's promise of a black artisan class was obsolete. The Phelps-Stokes Survey of 1916 reported that virtually all education for blacks was in some way deficient. Largely as a result of the efforts of private philanthropists, black colleges experienced remarkable growth and profound alteration of their goals during the 1920s and 1930s.

Perhaps a shift of Fisk University's institutional values was underway in 1924 when Fisk University Librarian Fred R. Steiner directed a memorandum to his president demanding the ouster of "roomers" from the library, since the aroma of bacon frying in the morning had disturbed students in the reading rooms. In less affluent times, black college librarians tended to accept greater inconveniences (Atkins, 1936, p. 40).

A more prosaic, although perhaps more accurate, measure of the revolution in black colleges involved the termination of many pre-collegiate training programs that prepared young adults for higher education. Howard University set the pace, dropping its preparatory department in 1919 (Duncan, 1955). Shortly thereafter, many prestigious schools followed suit: Fisk, Lincoln University of Pennsylvania, Wilberforce, Virginia Union, Morehouse and Talladega. By 1930, even colleges such as Savannah, which offered no collegiate instruction in 1916, had discontinued their high schools (Regulus, 1955, p. 7). It was difficult to find even a demonstration school in black higher education by 1940, in large measure because of the successful efforts of the John F. Slater Fund, the Peabody

Education Fund, the Anna T. Jeanes Fund, the General Education Board (GEB), and Julius Rosenwald, in promoting elementary and secondary education of blacks (Franklin & Moss, 1994). In summary, Franklin and Moss write with approval that:

> The age of philanthropists contributed substantially toward bringing about a new day for education in the South. By conditional grants and aid to those institutions that had proved their worth, philanthropists did much to stimulate self-help on the part of the individual, the institution, and the states of the South. There was general approval of Northern philanthropy, when the white citizens of the South discovered that their benefactors showed little or no interest in establishing racial equality or upsetting white supremacy [pp. 381–82].

A further indication of the improvement of black colleges would be the decline between 1916 and 1938 in the number of distinct institutions calling themselves "college" or "university." In the preceding twenty years, the number of such institutions had increased by ten (Johnson, 1938). But the most impressive proof of the transitions underway in black higher education in the 1920s is Arthur J. Klein's 1928 survey, which, unlike Thomas Jesse Jones's survey of 1916 for the Phelps-Stokes Fund, was funded by the federal government and conducted by personnel in the Bureau of Education's Division of Higher Education (1928, p. 974). Although Klein handled individual libraries in rudimentary fashion, he far surpassed Jones's survey in perception and depth.

Rather than simply appraising property, Klein (1928) offered recommendations concerning the basic financial and administrative difficulties confronting the black college:

> The government and financing of Negro higher educational institutions are acute problems. They are interrelated. The question of support rests in a large measure on methods of control. Institutions with types of government inspiring confidence [tend to] make the most effective appeal for support [p. 5].

Having made this statement, Klein demonstrated its validity for the seventy-nine colleges surveyed. The nine privately supported institutions, owned, governed, and controlled by independent, self-perpetuating boards of trustees were found to have the highest average income, $261,082; the twenty-two state owned and state-operated schools governed by appointed boards were second, with an average of $109,752; the seventeen privately supported colleges, owned and governed by black churches, averaged $66,977; the thirty-one owned and controlled by northern white denominational church boards had the lowest average income, $61, 075 (Davis, 1933; Klein, 1928).[2] The total income that these figures represent, $2,283,000, was a four-fold increase over 1916, but the change Klein considered most important was the increase in black colleges' productive environments which portended "a growing conviction that Negro higher education [would] be placed on a permanent base, through the provision of stable annual income" (p. 32).

The federal government's aid to black education, largely over-shadowed in the 1920s by private philanthropy, continued to support Howard and retained enough interest to fund the Klein survey of 1928 and his 1930 survey of land-grant institutions, which included those for blacks. By the end of the 1930s, however, support for black education had grown to proportions not seen since the end of the Freedman's [aka Freedmen's] Bureau. This action may not have resulted from conscious policy, since President Franklin Delano Roosevelt (FDR) felt strongly the need to maintain support from the southern wing of the Democratic Party.[3] However, Eleanor Roosevelt, whose lack of constraint about opposing segregation was legendary, became the spiritual leader of large numbers of "New Dealers" who administered massive recovery programs. The New Dealers sympathized with the plight of the black and later, when it was politically feasible, emerged as equal rights advocates. During the 1930s, however, they found it necessary to court the southern power structure. In practical terms, this meant that the aid filtered from Washington to black college libraries was limited to amounts justifiable in general anti-depression programs and subject to numerous state controls.

Perhaps the single most significant variety of New Deal aid which reached the black college came from the National Youth Administration's Negro Division. Southern states were generally unresponsive to the needs of black college librarianship; the Public Works Administration (PWA), had constructed at least two libraries in black colleges in North Carolina (South Carolina Colored Normal and Mechanical College, 1936).[4] Although the state legislature refused to appropriate money for permanent improvements, President J. Ward Seabrook saved enough from the regular budget of Fayetteville State to secure a grant from the PWA. Eventually, Governor J.C.B. Eringhouse acquiesced to this procedure, and a $36,000 building was completed in 1936 (Jones, 1969).

The library of the Alabama Agricultural & Mechanical Institute benefited from regional development planning conducted by the Tennessee Valley Authority (TVA). In 1936, the TVA, [attempting] to organize educational facilities for its employees in the Huntsville area, contracted with the State A & M Institute at Normal for job training, recreation, library service, and general adult education (Lowell, 1942). By many such small increments, federal support for black college libraries increased. An indication of the future direction of support [during] the ensuing sixteen years is the failure of the Office of Education in 1940 to treat black libraries separately in general reports of college and university library statistics (U.S. Office of Education, Federal Security Agency, 1940). Equally significant is the fact that the first organizational unit within the Office of Education specifically responsible for library development was established during the Roosevelt administration under Ralph McNeal Dunbar.

Governing Bodies, Accrediting Agencies, and Library Associations

Klein's (1928) survey of black higher education reflects the tremendous improvement of black college libraries between 1916 and 1927. Of the seventy-nine libraries surveyed, thirty-five held more than 5,000 volumes. In ten institutions, the library occupied separate buildings. On paper, Hampton Normal and Agricultural Institute had outstripped Howard University in total volumes and in average expenditures for periodicals and salaries, although in total library expenditures for books, binding, and supplies, Howard still led the field (Havlik, 1968). Eight institutions, in addition to Hampton, surpassed Fisk's 12,400 volume collection; however, Fisk ranked third in two categories by a comfortable margin: an average total library expenditure of $4,789 and an average salary expenditure of $3,169 (Klein, 1928).[5] Twenty-two institutions averaged as little as $100 in annual expenditures for periodicals, while twenty-three spent less than $500 annually on libraries, and an additional seven lacked libraries altogether. Klein (1928) described conditions in black college libraries as dreary:

> it is found that in many cases the number of volumes reached the minimum standards for colleges or junior colleges but in these collections were found in many instances a large

number of useless works, the donations for the most part of retired clergymen and others ... the libraries contained very few public documents ... [p. 47].

Service provided by the library was not clearly understood in a number of schools, which had undue restrictions in the hours the library was open to students, and teachers tended to nullify their utility. Only occasionally did colleges fully appreciate that the college library should serve as a workshop for the teachers and students and that books and professional magazines were not intended merely for students.

Klein (1928) expressed optimism about the future of black libraries because the five years from 1922 to 1927 showed interest in improving service. He reported: "During this time sixteen colleges had increased their expenditures from 55 to 99 percent, eight from 100 to 199 percent, ten from 200 to 299 percent, and five over 300 percent" (p. 47). Of the remaining forty institutions, twenty-one recorded less than forty-nine percent growth while nineteen did not grow at all (pp. 948–50).

Library fiscal support and collection size varied substantially by forms of institutional governance. The collections of the nine institutions controlled by private, self-perpetuating boards all exceeded the 5,000-volume minimum recommended for senior college libraries in 1928. Funded largely by the federal government, Howard University, under the control of such a board, and having budgeted for library service for forty-two years, led black higher education in 1927 with expenditures of $11,985 (Klein, 1928).[6] The libraries of three other leading black colleges (Fisk, Atlanta, and Hampton), which had been founded by the American Missionary Association, prospered after the association relinquished control to private boards. Fisk, for example, accumulated an endowment of $9,000. Although also under a private board, Booker T. Washington's Tuskegee was slow to direct much of its support to the library. Even so, the library employed three full-time staff, two with library training, and spent $1,000 for books and periodicals. The total expenditure for library service at Tuskegee, $3435.41, represented seven percent of its institutional budget. Morgan College, one of the smallest schools controlled by an independent board, claimed only 6,500 volumes, "a fairly good selection of books for collegiate work in excellent condition" and expended 3.3 percent of its total institutional income for library purposes (Klein, 1928).[7]

A second group of colleges included the thirty-one governed by northern churches. Of the twenty-eight purporting to be senior colleges, fifteen held fewer than 5,000 volumes. The best-supported schools apparently were supported by the American Baptist Home Mission Board, due possibly to large Rockefeller grants to several Baptist colleges (Klein, 1928, p. 46).[8] The superiority of northern Baptist support for libraries merits reconsideration, however, in view of Klein's (1928) comment on Virginia Union:

The library contains an extraordinarily large list of old theological books of no value to college students and of doubtful value to theology students.... Excessive expenditures are being made for recent theological books as compared with books of direct college usefulness [p. 940].

A more likely candidate for top honors among white denominational organizations supporting black colleges, the Board of Education of the Methodist Episcopal Church, maintained a committee to supervise the libraries of colleges under its jurisdiction. This committee conducted two-week conferences for its librarians and periodically made "extensive purchases of books of college quality and distributed them to schools under its control" (Klein, 1928, p. 845). The committee approach benefited libraries: when

Methodist Episcopal and American Missionary Association colleges merged in Louisiana to form Dillard College in the 1930s and in Florida to form Huston-Tillotson in the early 1950s, the Methodist libraries held superior collections (O.D. Brown, personal communication, March 24, 1975; C.R. Taylor, personal communication, February 21, 1975).[9] The annual reports of the American Missionary Association (AMA) division of the Congregational Church did not mention library support, and not until the 1930s did the AMA allow $250 per annum budgets for book purchases in its institutions (Jeanetta Roach, personal communication, February 21, 1975).

Klein (1928) indicated that college libraries under black church control (thirteen of seventeen had fallen below the 5,000-volume standard) but also public institutions under black administrations did not have the same standard:

> Notwithstanding the deficiencies in the libraries of some smaller schools under northern church control, the outstanding weakness in view of size of enrollments of the institutions is found in the libraries of institutions under Negro administration [p. 46].

The plight of such institutions was typified by the African Methodist Episcopal (AME) Church's experience at Wilberforce when, in 1934, the administration applied for North Central Association accreditation. In his evaluation, Herbert S. Hirshberg, librarian of Western Reserve University, described the "book collection, ... its organization and administration, in relation to recognized standards applied to college libraries."[10] In April 1934, Hirshberg reported that the library was ninety-seven percent deficient and recommended:

> remodeling the building, redecorating the walls, floor covering, open shelves for all books and periodicals, an adequate budget, building up the collection on the basis of standard lists, discarding of useless gifts, and a change of personnel [Dunlap, 1941, pp. 6–7].

Bishop R.R. Wright and successive Wilberforce presidents responded to these recommendations with the generous support of alumni and the AME Church.

Of the twenty-two publicly funded black colleges, seventeen were land-grant institutions. Four of the remaining five were teacher training schools fully dependent on state appropriations (Carnegie Commission of New York & GEB, 1941).[11] Black land-grant schools also depended on state governments because federal law limited the funding to two-thirds of an institution's total income. Of library income, Klein (1930) reported that:

> one of the principal handicaps with which the libraries are confronted is the failure of the colleges to segregate their finances from the other institutional funds. Apparently no budget is maintained. By far the best method of financing the libraries is through direct state appropriations. When funds are furnished in this way they are available only for expenditure of the library and cannot be used for other purposes [pp. 889–90].

The case of South Carolina Colored Normal and Mechanical College proved the wisdom of Klein's recommendation for, despite library drives and student fees, the library showed no progress until 1933 when specific allocations were made by the state legislature. Until the specter of non-accreditation loomed, neither states nor most other governing bodies were seeking to correct the chronic circumstances of the black college library.

Although Howard University had been accredited by the Middle States Association in 1921, the vast majority of black colleges were under the purview of the Southern Association of Colleges and Secondary Schools. Jim Crow attitudes combined with the damning blow of the Jones survey to prohibit any southern black college from consideration for accreditation before 1929 except for state bodies or the black association formed for self-accreditation.

Arthur Klein's survey noted enough improvement in the quality of black higher education that in 1929 the Southern Association formed a committee to study accreditation for black colleges. Thereafter, other accrediting activities became meaningless. Constituted of Horace Macauley Ivy, John Henry Highsmith, and Theodore Henley Jack, the Southern Association Committee was initially funded with $35,000 from the General Education Board (GEB). For twenty years it held sway over the reputations of black colleges (Agnew, 1970, p. 28). Rather than granting equal status by accrediting the colleges, the Highsmith Committee merely "approved" them. Further, it divided those approved into the "A" rated institutions, which fully met Southern Association standards, and the "B" rated schools, which lacked only one requirement for accreditation. A.B. Beittle's impassioned speech before the conference at Houston in 1949 shows the burden felt by black college administrations since the "progressive action of twenty years ago" had become the "reactionary position" of the day (Southern Association of Colleges and Secondary Schools, 1949, pp. 214–16).

The first school to receive an A rating was Fisk in 1930, followed by Hampton, Atlanta, Morehouse, and Spelman in 1932. Fred McCuistion, executive agent of the Highsmith Committee, reported that the thirty-two A and B colleges in 1933 expended a total of $163,643 for libraries. He observed a "wide variety in the amount and quality of library service, some colleges having small but effectively operated libraries, while others have ample volumes but poor service" (Agnew, 1970, p. 8).

The great impact of accreditation on black colleges was recognized by Donald E. Riggs (1971) in his study of West Virginia's Bluefield State College:

> Perhaps the biggest boost for the library came in 1947 when the college received accreditation by the American Association of Teachers Colleges. Arbitrary standards brought forth by accrediting committees enabled the library to glean a larger share of the college's annual operating budget [p. 11].

Although the threat of suspension could produce results, the Southern Association was less effective than it ought to have been in improving libraries.[12] According to Wallace Van Jackson, the association applied separate standards for black libraries and tended to overlook serious deficiencies (Southern Association, 1935, pp. 38–39; W. Van Jackson, personal communication, June 1974).

White library associations were less effective than any other external agency in improving black college libraries. Jim Crow laws had excluded blacks from membership in local and state library associations in the South (J. R. O'Rourke, personal communication, March 19, 1975).[13] Until such laws were ruled unconstitutional, the ALA leaders could do virtually nothing, except as individuals, for the black college library. Perhaps the most important ALA contribution involved the Board of Education for Librarianship's recommendation of Florence Rising Curtis as director of the first library school for blacks.[14] Blacks formed library associations in North Carolina, South Carolina, and Texas, while in Virginia, black librarians met in conjunction with the Virginia Negro Education Association (M. Beal and L.R. Wilson, personal communication, 1925). Black academic librarians often assumed leadership in such associations but did not develop them widely across the South.[15]

Library Education, Organized Philanthropy, and Academic Librarianship

Perhaps the single most important detriment in the development of black college libraries between 1916 and 1938 was the lack of relatively large numbers of trained personnel. Florence Rising Curtis (1925), prior to her work as director of the Hampton Library School, surveyed the libraries of sixteen black colleges and concluded that:

> The chief reason for a poor and inadequate library in nearly every Negro college is the fact that the library is not a separate department with a budget which would provide for salaries, books, periodicals, and binding. The alumni of some institutions are making an effort to raise money for books; in others there is a disposition to make available from general funds a fair sum for immediate needs; while in others a book shower is mainly expected to provide something of value to teachers and collegiate students.... A well-educated librarian could build up and care for the collection, give proper reference help to teachers and students, and guide the students' reading by suggesting books of interest and amusement. In those sixteen colleges, there are but two colored librarians who [had] graduated from a library school [p. 2].[16]

One of the librarians to whom Curtis referred, sometimes known as the dean of black college librarians, was Edward Christopher Williams. A Phi Beta Kappa student from Adelbert College of Western Reserve University, Williams became librarian of Adelbert's Hatch Library soon after his graduation. In fifteen years as head librarian at Western Reserve, he expanded the collection from 25,000 to 65,000 volumes, developed a German collection, organized a staff association, corresponded with Charles Evans, became a charter member of the Ohio Library Association and, in one year's sabbatical, completed the two-year library course at Albany. After seven years as a high school principal in Washington, D.C., Williams assumed the position of librarian at Howard and retained it until his death in 1929. At Howard, Williams was unable to equal his accomplishments in Ohio although he managed to add 12,000 volumes, expand the Moorland Collection, direct the department of romance languages, and in 1928 begin work toward a Ph.D. (Josey, 1969). During his Howard years, the percentage of library expenses to total institutional expenditures slipped from the ALA-approved three percent to 1.5 percent (Duncan, 1955, p. 83). At the Hampton Library Conference in 1927, Williams expressed fear that the library at Howard would never develop into anything of importance (Carnegie Commission of New York and General Education Board, 1941, p. 69).

Before 1925, the corps of professionals serving black academic libraries included several whites. As late as 1939, however, when black institutions employed ninety-one black librarians, five black college libraries were still headed by whites who were more concerned with improving the libraries under their own direction than with black college libraries in general (Van Jackson, 1940, pp. 95–104). For example, Frances L. Yocom, employed at Straight College in the 1920s, concentrated on cataloging and weeding the 7,000-volume collection. Without adequate supplies or clerical help, she had little opportunity to provide other services (F. L. Yocom, personal communication, September 6, 1974, Chapel Hill, NC; Taylor, personal communication). Mabel Grace Robb at Knoxville College and Sister Bernadette at Xavier met with similar circumstances (L. N. Clark, personal communication, February 26, 1975; Curtis papers, 1939).[17]

Louis Shores's service at Fisk University may be offered as a model of academic library practice for the era. In 1929, the Fisk Library had operated under a budget for two years and employed three professional staff members. Shores directed the library,

142   Experimentation and Redefinition, 1920–1945

Gertrude Aiken oversaw cataloging, and Anne Rucker supervised circulation and reference. Two other staff members, Margaret Reynolds and Onilda Taylor had received Rosenwald grants for library study. Student assistants did most of the work. Shores's tenure included the formation of an undergraduate library school, the housing of the Negro Collection, the union of the Fisk and Meharry collections, and the construction of the Erastus Milo Cravath Library (Fisk University, 1929–33; Shiflett, 1996, pp. 17–41).

Too few white librarians would serve in low-paying black colleges, and too few presidents and deans of those colleges "realized that librarians should be professional workers on a par with teachers and not be expected to act in a clerical capacity or look after the mail" (Curtis, 1926, pp. 472–74). Trained black personnel were rarely available to black colleges. The only library education available to blacks in the South before the opening of the Hampton Institute School in 1925 was the training course of the Colored Branch of the Free Public Library of Louisville, Kentucky.

James Hulbert (1943) labeled the work of the Hampton School "the greatest impetus to library development" in black higher education (pp. 623–29). Of the products of the school and of Curtis, Edgar W. Knight (1937) had only praise:

> The record of high achievement of this school is acknowledged throughout the country. Here as at other library schools for whites and Negroes the cost of training librarians has been high, but the work at Hampton has been of the finest order and the graduates of this school have given a splendid account of themselves in so far as college and public library administrators have allowed them to operate. The Director of this school is recognized as one of the most able of all the directors of library schools in the southern states ... [and] she has stood for more rigid limitation of students than any other director [p. 53].[18]

Fortunately, Hampton earned a good reputation for, by 1939, when it ceased operation, the school had graduated 138 black librarians, most of whom were employed by colleges, usually as the only trained librarian in the institution (Carnegie Commission of New York and General Education Board, 1941, p. 67; *Directory of Negro Graduates of Accredited Library Schools*, 1900–1936).

Virtually every state-funded black college employed a Hampton graduate as its first professionally trained librarian. The 1930 Klein survey, implying tightened control on federal monies, provided a strong incentive for college administrations to improve library services. The devotion and quality of their first librarians varied. James R. O'Rourke notes that the library at Kentucky State at Frankfort "became an organized collection of books" under the direction of three Hampton graduates: Olie Atkins Carpenter (1929–30), Emma Lewis (1930–34), and Anne Rucker Anderson (1934–43). From 1,000 volumes (of which 630 were discarded) in 1929, the collection began to grow to a well-cataloged 12,000 volumes by 1939. Periodicals were bound; odd furniture was replaced with Library Bureau equipment; the library was expanded and redecorated; and a course in librarianship for high school teachers was offered. O'Rourke credits library growth to President Rufus B. Atwood, clear evidence of the powerful influence of the black college presidents (J. R. O'Rourke, personal communication, March 19, 1975).

At least four Hampton graduates spent their entire professional careers in the libraries of land-grant colleges: Camille Stivers Shade at Southern, Ollie Lee Brown at Alabama State College, Martha Brown at Tennessee Agricultural and Industrial Institute, and Athelma Nix at South Carolina State. Faustina Jones writes of Ollie Lee Brown: [She] served the faculty, students and community unselfishly and commendably ... she collected and preserved an appreciable amount of Black America's heritage, ... the bulk of the Library's Collection of Afro-Americana ... (personal communication, March 4, 1975).

From 1930 onward, Ruby Stutts Lyells may have been the most influential Hampton graduate to serve in a publicly funded college library (G. J. Beck, personnel communication, March 3, 1975).[19] She organized and built the collection at Alcorn A & M, introduced library clubs, established faculty library committees, and practiced other techniques learned under Florence Curtis. More importantly, Lyells furthered the development of black college libraries through graduate work under Louis Round Wilson in the 1940s. Her thesis on the library in black land-grant colleges provoked the association of presidents of those colleges to focus their 1944 conference on library improvement.[20]

In private institutions, too, Hampton graduates served with distinction, although seldom for such long periods (F. L. Yocom, personal communication, September 6, 1974; M.S. Grigsby, personal communication, February 18, 1975; Battle, 1960).[21, 22] Several Hampton graduates and future faculty of the Atlanta University School of Library Service had first served black college libraries.[23] As the practice of employing black librarians became widespread and scholarship funds became available from the GEB and the Rosenwald Fund, blacks began to attend library schools in the North and to return to black colleges to make further contributions (Grotzinger, Carmichael, and Maack, 1994, pp. 27–104).[24]

Opinions of the quality of work of Hampton's library school graduates are divided. Virginia Lacy Jones, dean of the Atlanta University School of Library Service, stated that Curtis exerted enormous personal influence upon her, and the Hampton graduates were able to provide the essential service for black colleges of the period, building and organizing collections for the training of teachers (V. L. Jones, personal communication, May 23, 1974). Wallace Van Jackson, despite personal fondness for Curtis, felt that Hampton turned out too many "desk watchers" who did not "know books." Hampton failed to produce scholars equal to the college's professors or to teach proper methods of service for students and faculty (W. Van Jackson, personal communication, June 1974).

The work of organized philanthropy, felt first in black college libraries during the 1920s, accelerated during the 1940s and 1950s. The great virtue of foundations like the GEB was their support only for specific purposes within realistic general policies (Jeannetta Roach, personal communication, February 21, 1975).[25] Until trained librarians became available it was not feasible for foundations to make direct gifts for books. Therefore, in 1926, they cooperated to provide trained staff to acquire and make effective use of such gifts. The Hampton Institute Library School was established with a grant from the Carnegie Corporation; scholarships for its students were funded by the GEB; and the ALA Board of Education for Librarianship fully accredited it as a senior undergraduate library school in 1930 (Curtis, 1927, p. 378; S.C.N. Bogle, personal communication, May 10, 1930).

In 1927, when the Julius Rosenwald Foundation fund began to provide matching funds for the purchase of books for black colleges, Curtis, as a paid agent of the fund, approved lists of books sent by the colleges and forwarded them to Samuel Leonard Smith for purchase (F. R. Curtis, personal communication, November 10, 1933).[26] The benefits of the Rosenwald program were three-fold. Between 1927 and 1932, at a cost to the fund of about $60,000, nearly $350,000 flowed into forty-one black college libraries. The Fund would pay one dollar for every two dollars spent by the schools for book purchases, but it required that a trained librarian be employed to organize the books and that adequate library housing be provided (Smith, 1950).

Representatives of the GEB and the Carnegie Corporation attended the first conference of black librarians held at Hampton in March 1927. Foundations subsequently sponsored one such conference at Fisk in 1930 and three at Atlanta in the 1940s. In addition, they funded training programs for school librarians beginning in the summer of 1930 at Atlanta University and from 1936 to 1939 at Fisk, Hampton, Atlanta, and Prairie View (V. L. Jones, personal communication, May 23, 1974).

The most visible programs of organized philanthropy in black college libraries featured three attempts by the GEB to create research libraries in black universities. The GEB supported the union of the Meharry and Fisk collections in 1930 and provided funding for the $400,000 Cravath Library. In 1932, the GEB committed $600,000 to Atlanta University to endow a joint library for black colleges in the city of Atlanta (Kuhlman, 1966, p. 65).[27] The third effort for black college library cooperation followed the formation of Dillard, and it attempted to pool the libraries of Dillard, Xavier, and Southern University in New Orleans (V. L. Jones, personal communication, May 23, 1974). Louis Round Wilson, compiling "Statistics of Southern Negro University Libraries, 1938–1939" included only Fisk, Atlanta, Dillard, and Howard; the four had essentially been created by the GEB.

Although Jim Crow begot many monstrosities, it is pleasing to note that the libraries of our traditionally black colleges and universities became monuments to human hope. The dedicated work and sacrifice of individual blacks and whites overcame inadequate resources, prejudice, hatred, and the fear of one's enemies, as well as ignorance, authoritarianism, and the condescension of one's friends. Black academic libraries, although transformed in the latter part of the twentieth century, have been constructed on the foundations of scholarship, service, flexibility, and promise, attributes developed in an earlier, more difficult era.

Notes

1. The crash of 1929 and the Great Depression demonstrated, among other things, that too little income had reached the consumer.

2. This figure may be misleading since the 1930 *Survey of Land-Grant Colleges and Universities* indicated these state schools used only 1.9 percent of their income for library purposes.

3. FDR's desire for the support of the southern bosses allegedly prompted the quip to Hopkins, "they may be SOBs but they are our SOBs."

4. Athelma Nix promoted a request to the South Carolina legislature that a PWA library be considered for SC State but was refused.

5. Lincoln, PA, 40,000; Talladega, 25,000; Tuskegee, 21,167; Atlanta University, 16,243; Virginia Union, 15,000; Johnson C. Smith, 13,500; West Virginia State, 13,078; and Wilberforce, 12,912.

6. 1.8 percent of its fiscal 1927 budget.

7. 69–900 passim.

8. One of six American Baptist Home Mission Board schools was below standard, as were four of six run by the American Missionary Association of the Congregational Church, six of eleven by the Methodist Episcopal, one of three by the United Presbyterians, two by the United Christians, and one by the Catholic Church.

9. Dillard was formed from New Orleans University and Straight College in 1935 and Huston-Tillotson in 1952.

10. Klein's judgment is here brought to question since in 1927 he found that collection to be well-selected for reference and for collateral reading in support of the curriculum, even lacking the Shaw list, which was perhaps too generous.

11. One president reported: "Sometime after I went to the University I had a very good friend in the state senate who followed me through a number of experiences with the governor and with [the] legislature. Then I called on him for a grant of $10,000 for books for the library. And he called on me and said, 'See here Professor, you know I have supported you for eight or ten years in your program at the university, but I just

can't go with you on this program, because you know, and I know, and everybody knows that college students are supposed to buy their own books.'"

12. Livingstone College was placed on probation in 1935.

13. The librarians at Kentucky State in 1939 were apparently excepted from this general rule (Louis Round Wilson interview). Until Jim Crow laws were lifted in southern hotels, permitting blacks and whites to use the same facilities, southern cities were excluded from consideration as ALA convention sites.

14. A telegram from Carl H. Milam to Louis Round Wilson dated 27 April 1925 reads like a secret memorandum: "Can you undertake at our expense to visit Tuskegee and Hampton to obtain for the Board of Education for Librarianship information about library administration, standing with faculty, staff income, and presidents' probable attitude towards a school for librarianship if a few thousand dollars were given for such a school? It is important to have a report before May 1st, if possible. You are authorized to use this telegram as credentials. Avoid publicity. Wire direct."

15. The first officers of the North Carolina Negro Library Association were college librarians: President, Mollie Huston, Shaw; Vice President, Mollie Dunlap, Winston-Salem; Secretary, Josephine Sherrill, Livingstone; and Treasurer, Pearl Snodgrass, St. Augustine's.

16. The report entitled "The Library of the Negro College" was based on visits in the fall of 1925 to Howard, Atlanta, Morris Brown, Spelman, Johnson C. Smith, Morehouse, Greensboro A & T, Bennett, Shaw, Winston-Salem, Allen, Benedict, Claflin, SCC N & M, and Petersburg N & I. Curtis elsewhere indicates that only one Negro held a professional degree in 1925.

17. Perhaps the most effective white librarian who served in this period was Wilhelmina E. Carothers, a graduate of the University of North Dakota and the University of Illinois who presided over the merger of New Orleans University and Straight College libraries from 1935 to 1940.

18. Arthur Klein recommended in 1930 that the Hampton Institute Library School be reduced to a junior undergraduate library school. Curtis's spirited defense, outlining the errors of such a course of action, prevailed (Undated letter to Arthur J. Klein).

19. Lyell's activities did not stop with libraries for she gave bond for one of the first sit-ins, was an active supporter of the Freedom Riders, and in other less controversial ways served her community.

20. Association of the Presidents of Negro Land-Grant Colleges *Proceedings of the Twenty-Second Annual Conference, October 24–26, 1944* (Chicago, IL: n. p., 1944). Featured speakers included Robert Bingham Downs, Ruby Stutts Lyells, Eliza Atkins Gleason, and Charles Harvey Brown.

21. Yocom was not impressed for, when she replaced a Hampton graduate at Fisk in the mid-thirties, she found a large box of unprocessed books shoved into a corner. The librarian at Meharry quipped that those were probably the hard ones. Yocom reported, "They weren't."

22. Theodus Gunn is exceptional, for he shares with Camille Shade, of Southern University, Baton Rouge, Louisiana, the record for longest continuous service to a Negro college library, forty-one years. See "A History of the Carnegie Library at Johnson C. Smith University" (Master's thesis, University of North Carolina, 1960).

23. Eliza Atkins Gleason, Winston-Salem; Virginia Lacy Jones, Atlanta; and Wallace Van Jackson, Virginia Union.

24. Wallace Van Jackson, Ruby Stutts Lyells, Eliza Atkins Gleason, and Arna Bontemps attended Chicago; Zenobia Coleman, O.J. Baker, and Parepa Watson Jackson attended Columbia; and Mollie E. Dunlap graduated from Michigan.

25. Even generous benefactors could be extravagant on occasion. While in the 1940s the Woolworth Library still suffered for lack of funds at Tougaloo, Eva Hills Eastman had special library furniture flown in from California (Franklin & Moss, 1994, p. 379). Rockefeller by contrast gave the GEB $53 million to expend as it saw fit.

26. Curtis, in a letter to Wilson dated 10 November 1933, stated that although Rosenwald monies had dried up, lists of books were still sent to her for approval. Interview with Jones and Thomas Rankin Barcus, *The Carnegie Corporation and College Libraries, 1938–1943* (New York: Carnegie Corporation of New York, 1943). Grants for library purposes, begun in the 1920s by the GEB, were supplemented by the Carnegie Corporation in the 1940s and by the Ford Foundation in the 1950s.

27. Served jointly were Atlanta University, Clark, Morehouse, Morris Brown, Spelman, and Gammon Theological Center.

References

Agnew, D.C. (1970). *Seventy-five years of educational leadership*. Atlanta, GA: Southern Association of Colleges and Schools.

Association of the Presidents of Negro Land Grant-Colleges. (1944). *Proceedings of the twenty-second annual conference (October 24–26, 1944)*. Chicago, IL: The Association.

Atkins, E. (1936). *A history of the Fisk University Library and its standing in relation to the libraries of other comparable institutions*. Unpublished Master's thesis, University of California.

Barcus, T.R. (1943). *The Carnegie Corporation and college libraries, 1938-1943*. New York: Carnegie Corporation of New York.
Battle, M.E. (1960). *A history of the Carnegie Library at Johnson C. Smith University*. Unpublished Master's thesis, University of North Carolina.
Carnegie Commission and General Education Board. (1941). *Library Conference held under the auspices of the Carnegie Commission of New York and General Education Board, March 14-15, 1941*. Atlanta, GA: Atlanta University.
Curtis, F.R. (1926). The library of the Negro college. *The Southern Workman*, 55, 472-74.
Curtis, F.R. (1927). The contribution of the library school to Negro education. *The Southern Workman*, 56 (August), 373-78.
Curtis, F.R. (1925-1930). The library of the Negro college. *Papers*. Hampton, VA: Hampton Institute.
Davis, J.W. (1933). The Negro land-grant college. *Journal of Negro Education*, 2 (July), 312-28.
Directory of Negro graduates of accredited library schools, 1900-1936. (1937). Washington, D.C.: Columbia Civic Library Association.
Duncan, A.M. (1955). *History of the Howard University Library: 1867-1929*. Rochester, NY: University of Rochester Press, ACRL.
Dunlap, M.E. (1941). Carnegie Library, Wilberforce University. *Wilberforce University Quarterly Alumni Journal*, 4 (February), 6-8.
Fisk University. (1928-1945). *Annual reports, 1929-1933*. Unpublished manuscript.
Franklin, J.H. and Moss, A.A. (1994). *From slavery to freedom: A history of African Americans* (7th ed.). New York: McGraw-Hill.
Grotzinger, L.A., Carmichael, J.V., Jr., and Maack, M.N. (1994). "Women's work: Vision and change in librarianship: Papers in honor of the centennial of the University of Illinois Graduate School of Library and Information Science" (*Occasional Papers* No. 196/197 of the Graduate School of Library and Information Science, University of Illinois). Urbana-Champaign, IL: Graduate School of Library and Information Science, University of Illinois.
Havlik, R.T. (1968). The library services branch of the U.S. Office of Education: Its creation, growth, and transformation. In M.J. Zachert (ed.). *Library History Seminar No, 3 (Proceedings, 1968)*. Tallahassee, FL: School of Library Science, Florida State University.
Hulbert, J.A. (1943). The Negro college library. *Journal of Negro Education*, 12 (4), 623-29.
Johnson, C.S. (1938). *The Negro college graduate*. Chapel Hill, NC: University of North Carolina Press.
Jones, M.P. (1969). *History of Fayetteville State College*. Fayetteville, NC: Fayetteville State College Press.
Josey, E.J. (1960). Edward Christopher Williams: A librarian's librarian. *Journal of Library History*, 6 (2), 106-12.
Klein, A.J. (1928). *Survey of Negro colleges and universities* [Bulletin, 1928, No. 7, U.S. Department of the Interior. Bureau of Education]. Washington, D.C.: USGPO.
Klein, A.J. (1930).*Survey of Land-Grant colleges and universities* [Bulletin, 1930, No. 9, U.S. Department of the Interior. Bureau of Education]. Washington, D.C.: USGPO.
Knight, E.W. (1937). *A study of Hampton Institute, Part 1*. Chapel Hill, NC: University of North Carolina Press.
Kuhlman, A.F. (1966). *Preliminary report on some problems and opportunities of the Atlanta University Center*. Nashville, TN: Vanderbilt University Press.
Lowell, M.H. (1942). *College and university library consolidations*. Eugene, OR: Oregon State System of Higher Education.
Regulus, H. (1955). *An evaluation of the Savannah State College Library, Savannah, Georgia*. Unpublished Master's thesis, Atlanta University, Atlanta, GA.
Riggs, D.E. (1971). Bluefield State College Library history and development. *West Virginia Libraries*, 24 (January), 10-12.
Shiflett, O.R. (1996). *Louis Shores: Defining educational librarianship*. Lanham, MD: Scarecrow Press.
Smith, S.L. (1950). *Builders of goodwill: The story of the state agents of Negro education in the South, 1910 to 1950*. Nashville, TN: Tennessee Book Company.
South Carolina Colored Normal and Mechanical College. (1936). *Annual reports of the President*. Orangeburg, SC: South Carolina Colored Normal and Mechanical College.
Southern Association of Colleges and Secondary Schools. (1935). *Annual report*. Atlanta, GA: SACS.
Southern Association of Colleges and Secondary Schools. (1949). *Annual report*. Atlanta, GA: SACS.
United States Office of Education, Federal Security Agency. (1940). *Biennial survey of education in the United States, 1938-1940*. Washington, D.C.: USGPO.
Van Jackson, W. (1940). Negro library workers. *Library Quarterly* 10 (1), 95-108.
Wilson, L.R. (1925). *Papers, 1933-1981*. (Southern Historical Collection). Chapel Hill, NC: University of North Carolina, School of Library Science Library.

Toward a New Cultural Design
The American Council of Learned Societies, the Social Science Research Council, and Libraries in the 1930s

Kenneth Carpenter

In the late 1920s, the scholarly world was experiencing signs of a publishing crisis. Would the philanthropic foundations continue to provide sufficient subsidies to cover rising costs? At the same time, scholars were experiencing needs for source materials that libraries were unable to provide, and libraries, in addition, were finding that many of their existing holdings were crumbling. American learned societies in the humanities and social sciences responded. Through their umbrella organizations, they formed a joint committee, which to this day continues to be the only instance in which scholars of many sorts took a long and hard look at what might be called the infrastructure of academia. The committee was active through the 1930s, almost all of that time chaired by the visionary historian Robert C. Binkley.

The Joint Committee on Materials for Research initially focused on these problems of scholars and libraries, with emphasis on the possibility that the new technologies of reproduction, in both paper and film, could solve them by creating a new pattern of communication. They could, Binkley envisioned, diffuse among libraries the source materials for research, and then inexpensively disseminate the results of the scholar's work, even assist in the note taking and document gathering inherent in that process.

As the decade progressed, Binkley came to see wider possibilities for the developing technologies. He came to believe that they could create a new cultural design. With use of the new technologies, every town, many families even, would find that individuals were able to research, write, and then disseminate histories within the small, interested circle. Or towns could have their published poet; art would then be public as were music and visual art, through local bands, choral societies, and art shows. Binkley also anticipated collaborations in scholarship. With some individuals pursuing research not to write it up themselves, but to aid professional historians. High school teachers, especially, he envisioned, would become researchers. The web would also be furthered by local historical societies using the technologies to record their holdings and even to disseminate copies.

Binkley wished to further what he called "history for a democracy."[1] "History," he wrote, "nourishes the spirit of any institution." "It creates a conception of relationship with ... [the] past," and furthers "a feeling that our present activity has some meaning in the scheme of time" (198). Binkley's development of the implications of historical knowledge was, as the title of his essay indicates, stimulated by fear of the spread of totalitarian regimes. He was, however, explicitly opposed to a purely celebratory history of democratic institutions, to the inculcation of any particular view of the past. Such a history would resemble that of the fascist regimes. He urged, on the contrary, that "investigators [must be] free to follow wherever the evidence leads them ... even if it should be discovered that the heroes of democracy were villains, and that the institutions of democracy did not function as the well-wishers of democracy would have preferred" (201). It was not a nationalistic history that he wished, but rather a history that would "nourish and sustain ... the value of the individual personality and the protection for him of a maximum zone of freedom" (202), within the framework of "groups of all kinds, organized in all ways" (202). Indeed, he saw the "federative organization of society" (202) as protecting the freedom of the individual against a centralized state. It was not the group that had to be protected against an excess of individualism, but rather the group that was necessary to maintaining the freedom of individuals—to the end, Binkley explicitly stated, that the "people" rule themselves. They "must act with a keen respect for facts, for knowledge, for enlightenment. They must be willing to get together on the common platform of discovered truth, wherever that platform may be" (202). In other words, it was the process that was crucial.

Binkley saw three kinds of history as preserving these values. One was a "history of individuals," that is, family history. The history that would preserve our federative structure was local history, and the "history that will preserve the basis of government by ourselves is history written by ourselves" (203), which, he noted, "implies participation in scholarship," since that induces "respect for truth and understanding of the methods by which it is investigated" (203). The amateur was thus a vital part of the web of scholarship. As he wrote in his conclusion to "History for a Democracy," "Let us therefore have history of the people, by the people, and for the people." Or, as he concluded his essay "The Cultural Program of the W.P.A.," in which he called for the schools to use documentary materials in teaching, "ultimately, the American people will be more conscious of the possibilities of the democratization and enrichment of our culture."

Although Binkley did not, he might have applied an expression employed by Horace Mann in his third (1839) report as Massachusetts Commissioner of Education to describe the important function of libraries: formation of "a powerful and exemplary people."[2] Binkley stood in a line that in fact went back beyond Mann to the early days of the Republic, and through him and the Joint Committee on Materials of Research, the American Council of Learned Societies (ALCS) and the Social Science Research Council (SSRC) attempted in the third decade of the century to change both American scholarship and American society.

The ACLS and the SSRC did not have in mind such a broad agenda when they created the Joint Committee in 1929, and the Joint Committee began with attention to scholarly problems. These were, however, not so much signs of weakness as of the transformation of scholarship in the 1920s. The Great War marked a divide. In its aftermath, the United States moved from being an outpost of scholarship into a leading role—in the minds of some, even the nation primarily responsible for maintaining the traditions of Western culture. Thus, as early as May 1919, the American Association of University Professors drafted a plan for an International Catalogue of Humanistic Literature, and the Carnegie Endowment for International Peace was asked for $50,000 for an "International Congress for the purpose of laying plans to produce an Apparatus of Scholarship that would be of value to the scholars of the world in the field of the Humanities to supplement the International Catalogue of Scientific Literature now being revised by the Royal Society of London."[3] The bibliography was never undertaken, but humanistic scholarship and international peace were clearly linked in this call for a humanistic project that was analogous to one in the sciences. Implicitly, the letter states, balance must be maintained in the world of learning, and that has been lost. The Carnegie Endowment, on January 28, 1919, had appropriated $5 million to the National Academy of Sciences, which placed the National Research Council, established in 1916 during the war, on a permanent basis. It became the second foundation-funded institution devoted to scientific research, the first being the Rockefeller Institute for Medical Research, established in 1901. The message was not lost on the Carnegie foundations. Both the Carnegie Corporation and the Carnegie Foundation for International Peace supported the American Council of Learned Societies.[4] A few years later, in 1923 (incorporated 1924), the social scientists, following the earlier examples, formed the Social Science Research Council, with major support again coming from foundations, especially those of the Rockefellers.

The foundations, besides assisting learned societies, had two major possible ways to further the advance of knowledge. One was to create, outside universities, research institutions devoted to humanistic or social science studies, as they had done in the sciences. The Brookings Institution is an example of such an institution, but the foundations also decided to support research in universities. They recognized that universities were no longer only teaching institutions serving undergraduates. They had changed, in part thanks to funding for pensions and salaries as well as to gifts for endowment from the various Carnegie and Rockefeller foundations, donations that also stimulated support from individuals. With both stronger finances and a new sense of their mission, the major universities could be partners of the foundations in creating new knowledge.[5]

The emphasis on research created a need for subventions for publishing the results of research. The need was brought to the attention of the foundations, as in the December 1926 "Report of the Advisory Group" of the Rockefeller-funded General Education Board, which called for "general subventions to periodicals, and series of monographs, [plus] special aid for the publication of individual books."[6] They did support publication, but the learned societies were uneasy about whether subventions would continue. Today's crisis in scholarly publishing is not a new phenomenon. The anomaly was the post–World War II era when scholarly publishing flourished, thanks to the expansion of well-funded libraries and to the growing number of academicians.

Just as increased funding for research led to manuscripts worthy of publication, it also created a need for source materials as well as access to an ever-wider range of scholarly monographs and journals. The problem was acute. Except for some traditional fields in which the need was for a limited body of currently produced publications, such as classical and medieval studies, few libraries had adequate research collections. Even for the publications issued in the United States, no library equaled the comparable holdings of, say, France's Bibliothèque Nationale, which had long been the beneficiary of copyright deposit in a highly centralized nation. No union catalogue, not even on cards, then existed, so a scholar could not determine if and where a book was held, without turning to colleagues and librarians. The possessing library might lend, but otherwise the option was either travel or a photostatic copy, if the library had one of those quite new machines. The great microfilm collections, which brought together holdings from many libraries, did not then exist, let alone today's online versions. The scholar in 1929 would only just have been able to determine where a file of a journal might exist, thanks to the *Union List*. Library directors, both professional librarians and library faculty directors, had long been aware of the inadequacy of collections. With exceptions, particularly at the Library of Congress, the New York Public Library, Harvard and Yale, and some specialized libraries, the accepted wisdom was that the necessary research materials could be brought to this country only by dividing up collecting areas. For example, Library X would emphasize Spanish literature, while Library Y built Italian. Library directors could not implement such coordination. Even if a few directors had sufficient power and money to participate, their numbers were small. In almost all institutions, funds were controlled by a faculty library committee whose main function was to divvy them up among the academic departments. To set some aside for a national plan would have required a consensus impossible to reach, and, of course, librarians themselves were eager to have their allocation for reference books or for special purchases be as large as possible.[7]

The problem of collections was, in fact, intellectual as well. What appropriately constituted library materials, and what did scholars really need? Scholarly monographs and journals, both current and back files, were indisputably desirable, as were editions of the works of canonical authors and most kinds of earlier printed source materials for historians, especially if obtained by gift. But manuscripts? Ephemera? Material in fields not taught? Material published outside the book trade, such as state and municipal publications? Some such material for the social scientist was outside the ken of the humanistically trained librarian, who was accustomed to serving the social scientist who pursued traditional historical and a priori approaches. Some social scientists who sought to develop general laws that would result in improved conditions of life wanted to obtain "knowledge and understanding of the natural forces that are manifested in the behavior of people and of things," and they were not sure they needed libraries very much at all. Beardsley Ruml, the powerful director of the Laura Spelman Rockefeller Memorial, was one such, and an influential 1924 report that he commissioned advocated field work and statistics.[8] Others did emphasize materials,[9] and a major statement was made at the August–September 1929 meeting in Hanover, New Hampshire, of the Council of the SSRC. It drew up a list of "ultimate objectives" and detailed the "specific policies and procedures" for obtaining them.[10] Seven methods were listed, followed by specifics. The seven, which "came to be reverently referred to … as The Seven Roman Numerals,"[11] were

    I. By improvement of research organization
    II. By development of personnel
    III. By enlargement, improvement and preservation of materials
    IV. By improvement of research methods
    V. By facilitation of the dissemination of materials, methods, and results of investigations
    VI. By facilitation of research projects
    VII. By enhancement of the general appreciation of the significance of the social sciences.

Two of the seven, numbers 3 and 5, have to do with materials, and the "specific policies and procedures" spelled out under those headings demonstrate a keen understanding of relevant issues relating to materials:[12]

> III. Enlargement, Improvement and Preservation of Materials
>
> Since scientific progress in all fields is conditioned by the existence of a constantly enlarging body of research materials and by its availability to investigators, one of the primary duties of the Council is to promote such objects and to concern itself with the improvement and preservation of research data. In carrying out these purposes the following courses of action are appropriate:
>
> A. Initiating and participating in plans for making more comparable and more widely serviceable the classifications of social and economic data, for making more precise the significance of the data, and for otherwise improving such records
> B. Helping to lay out a plan for the nation-wide development and coördination of existing archival collections and for the building up of new research collections along special lines at strategic scholarly and geographical centers
> C. Initiating and participating in plans for constructing union finding lists and calendars of the resources of existing research libraries, with particular reference to their social data, so as to make them more available to scholars
> D. Initiating and participating in plans to discover, select, edit, publish, or otherwise reproduce basic data in the social sciences, which are difficult of access to students or likely to perish
> E. Calling to the attention of individuals and of governmental, business and other institutions and agencies the importance of preserving their records for future analysis and study
> F. Encouraging the adoption and widespread use of those varieties of paper and other materials used in the making of records which promise a maximum durability
> G. Initiating, encouraging and participating in plans to develop the research uses of historical, industrial and social museums; and encouraging the building up of new collections with these purposes in mind.
>
> V. Facilitation of the Dissemination of Materials, Methods and Results of Investigations
>
> Social research is directly aided by the publication and distribution of the results of investigations to research workers and by opportunities for fruitful contact among investigators. The following types of activity are appropriate to these ends:
>
> A. Publication:
>   1. Encouragement in all types of publication of (a) the prompt issuance of advance summary notices of research results for the information of other workers in the same field, following the practice of the natural sciences; and (b) the making available in some form for the full data on which published reports are based
>   2. Study through conferences and other means of their service rendered currently by social science journals, including the problem of adequate technical reviewing
>   3. Possible development under the Council of a reprint and bulletin service similar to that of the National Research Council

4. Encouragement of the assembly of research abstracts in specific fields of research
5. Study of the need for monograph series in various fields of inquiry
6. Representation to the universities of their responsibility in making doctoral dissertations generally available
7. Coöperation with State and Federal agencies in the more prompt dissemination of the results of investigations made under tax-supported auspices
8. Study of the problem of the publication of social science material including textbooks, by university presses and commercial publishers in so far as such publication affects the range and adequacy of the material made available

B. Interchange of information through conference and other informal means:
1. Development of ready informational interchange of points of view, research experience and data among (a) the departments, including the pertinent natural sciences, in a given university; and (b) research agencies of all kinds, including commercial agencies in a given geographical location
2. Development of formal conferences, including (a) active coöperation with the various associations in the Christmas meetings; and (b) the sponsoring of carefully planned meetings of workers on a given problem at centers at which active work on this problem is going forward.

The SSRC Council also voted to ask the ACLS to join in forming a committee.[13] The ACLS agreed, and the first meeting of the Joint Committee was held on February 17–18, 1930, at SSRC offices in New York. It was chaired by Dr. Solon J. Buck, superintendent of the Minnesota Historical Society. The other initial members were N.S.B. Gras, professor of business history at the Harvard Business School (also involved with the Mediaeval Academy); Clark Wissler of the American Museum of Natural History; Waldo G. Leland, permanent secretary of the ACLS; Harry Miller Lydenberg[14] of the New York Public Library; Arthur H. Quinn, professor of English at the University of Pennsylvania; and Robert C. Binkley, professor of History at Western Reserve University.

Binkley could not make the meeting, but he contributed in advance of it a four-page single-spaced memorandum, "Possibilities for Enlargement, Improvement and Preservation of Research Material." It began by noting three research problems in chemistry and technology—paper manufacture, paper preservation, and "miniature photography and projection"—that, "if solved … will affect much of the practical development of policy." Binkley's evident capacity for hard and thoughtful work continued to be demonstrated, and in September he was appointed secretary of the committee; then in 1932, after Buck asked to be relieved of the chairmanship, Binkley was selected chairman. He continued in that role until his death from cancer of the esophagus in the spring of 1940.

Binkley was, along with Lydenberg, his closest colleague on the committee, a pioneer in concern about preservation. Although the American Library Association had established a committee to look into paper quality in 1912, concern about paper had not gone beyond the doors of libraries. Lydenberg changed that. He wanted scientific research, and when the National Research Council argued that research into paper quality was a library problem, Lydenberg retorted that librarians were not scientists, that the chemistry of paper was a problem for scientists.[15] He was instrumental in getting the Carnegie Corporation to make a grant of $10,000 on October 15, 1929, to carry out the scientific work. Lydenberg may also have been behind the ACLS Council considering, on January 26, 1929, "the imminent danger of the loss of much manuscript and printed material through disintegration of the paper on which it was printed."[16]

Lydenberg and Binkley had in fact met over the issue of preservation.[17] In 1927, Binkley, then an instructor at New York University, sent his undergraduates to the New York Public Library to comb through the library's holdings of Public Record Office publications on the Spanish armada; and the student use was so heavy that it was brought to the attention of Lydenberg, perhaps by Keyes Metcalf, who was Lydenberg's deputy. Lydenberg got in touch with Binkley and asked him to come by to talk over the problem his assignment was creating. Years later, Lydenberg recorded Binkley's "first words when we met showed intensity, zeal, appreciation of the other man's point of view, willingness to adjust himself to conditions, and at the same time confidence in his cause and insistence on its rightness. The first impression grew more attractive the longer I came to see and talk with the man."[18]

For Binkley, this encounter made vivid the "problem of reconciling maximum use of research materials in the present, with their preservation for future generations"[19] and he, ever the historian, was stimulated to look into the question historically. The result was "The Problem of Perishable Paper," delivered at the First World Congress of Libraries and Bibliography, held in Rome in June 1929.[20] He wrote that upon the first introduction of writing, durable material had been used. This meant that libraries were able to serve the twin goals of disseminating texts and preserving them. No conflict existed between those two goals—not until the second half of the nineteenth century. Binkley was well aware of the irony of the timing of the introduction of wood-pulp paper. "The nineteenth century made us more conscious of our duty to history." We came to "understand that an accurate knowledge of all aspects of our past was essential to clear thinking upon the present. And having thus taught us the value and sanctity of all records, it began to print its records upon highly perishable paper!" Now the two duties diverge, because the writing materials are no longer durable. The librarian of today, is, as a result, "unable to do what ... [earlier generations] have done, for the records of our time are written in dust" (170–71).

After putting forth the need for research on paper quality and for working out a means whereby publishers would produce some copies of printed material on durable paper, Binkley turned to salvaging what was already in libraries. He concluded that the cost-effective way was by reducing a photographic reproduction to "microscopic proportions and reading it by projection or by some other optical device" (177). That paper was delivered before a learned audience concerned primarily with books and libraries, but as early as January 1929, right in the period when Lydenberg was striving to obtain scientific assistance on the problem of poor paper, Binkley had also written for a scientific and more popular readership. In that essay in *Scientific American*, he proposed as a solution, "photographic copying ... on a reduced scale, to be read back again with a magnifying glass or by projection on a screen."[21] That paper was condensed in *Reader's Digest* in February 1929, the month after its appearance in *Scientific American*, thus showing both the novelty of the topic and the belief that it would be of interest to an audience beyond the learned.

Binkley was not the first to advocate photographic copying, but he was perhaps the first to urge "reduced-scale photographic copies" and to call for "coordination of the salvaging efforts of the libraries of the world" (178). Although microphotography was then known,[22] by 1930 it had barely been mentioned with respect to libraries. Photography had, however, entered into the world of libraries in the second decade of the twentieth century,[23] and by 1921 at least a few librarians had the idea of using photography for collection building—even doing so cooperatively, albeit on a small scale. The Newberry Library, as early as June 1921, distributed a list of titles that it was considering obtaining as photographic reproductions. It asked in part for bibliographical information on the books, as well as for locations of copies (there was not yet a *National Union Catalog*), but the goal behind publishing the list was larger. The Newberry sought to determine whether other libraries might wish "to co-operate in the enterprise to obtain prints for their own collections."[24] It noted that the Modern Language Association had appointed a committee to look into the question of photographic reproductions. An attempt was even made, by Frederic Ives Carpenter, a professor of English, to summarize American thinking and activities at this time. This 1921 essay included a "suggestive letter," dated July 5, 1921, of George Parker Winship whose responsibilities in the Harvard Library included the Widener Memorial Rooms and the Treasure Room. In his letter Winship went beyond the idea of buying copies of various books in a number of areas. His vision was that libraries would, after acquiring a collection of originals, systematically use photography to complete the holdings of those materials.[25] A programmatic step was taken by scholars, in that the photographs obtained via the committee of the Modern Language Association, mentioned in the Newberry pamphlet, were being centrally deposited at the Library of Congress. There the librarians involved undertook to make these photographs, as well as others, available through a union list of them. Their 1929 catalogue recorded about one thousand titles reported by libraries across the country, including the ninety-six deposited in the Library of Congress through the MLA.[26]

Besides exploring photography as a means to acquire materials, scholars and librarians were also beginning to see a role for photography in disseminating the products of scholarship. Thus, the American Council of Learned Societies *Bulletin* no. 8 (October 1928) contained "An Inexpensive Method of Reproducing Material Out of Print."[27] No author's name is attached to the essay, which describes a "method known variously as the zincographic, planographic, or off-set process." It records that the United States Government Printing Office established early in 1927 a zincographic department for producing out-of-print material,[28] and it concludes by stating that the Executive Offices of the ACLS can supply "names of concerns ... samples, and the most recent quotations." If the GPO could use the process for out-of-print material, it could also do so for new publications.

Although only a few pioneers envisioned that printing from raised type would lose its monopoly as a means of disseminating substantial numbers of copies of a text, handwriting had long since lost its monopoly in making individual copies. The typewriter was by then common in libraries,[29] and it could be used to create masters for duplicating or making multiple copies. Among the many processes, some, such as the hectograph and mimeograph had been developed in the 1870s and 1880s.[30]

It was inevitable that someone would see the possibility of microcopying text and then projecting it for the scholar to read. The first such proposal seems to have been Robert Goldschmidt and Paul Otlet's *Sur une forme nouvelle du livre: Le livre microphotographique*, Institut international de Bibliographie, publication no. 81 (Brussels, 1906).[31] Although this publication was available in the United States and the Institut international de Bibliographie was itself well known—and controversial—in the 1920s, it may be that the example of the cinema was more important in drawing attention to the possibilities of microphotography. In fact, the term "projecting" was used to describe what machines for reading microfilm would do, and the film itself that was employed for "micro-copies" or "film-slides," was initially the same film used in movies.

Because Binkley linked preservation and the reproduction of texts, including microfilm reproduction, he was an ideal member of the Joint Committee. More than that, though, Binkley—the scholar and former librarian—saw the possibility of newly developing technologies for disseminating source material. He knew firsthand that printed materials, even those of recent times, can be exceedingly rare and worthy of preservation and dissemination. Binkley had, immediately after the war, assisted in France in collecting material on the war on behalf of Herbert Hoover. Then, while pursuing a doctorate in history, he worked as reference librarian from 1923 to 1927 in the Hoover Library on War, Revolution, and Peace, which preeminently among libraries was collecting modern source materials.

The year after receiving his Ph.D., 1928, Binkley published an article in *Historical Outlook*, "Revision of World History," in which he argued that historical writing changes in response to the interests of successive periods and that archival policy should take into account successive shifts—ideas that were not then truisms a decade before the Society of American Archivists was formed. In 1929, the thirty-one year old [scholar] was also a rising star in the historical profession. Not only was he highly productive as a scholar; his "Ten Years of Peace Conference History," published in the December 1929 issue of the *Journal of Modern History*, had, according to its editor, "aroused more comment and evoked more praise than any other contribution to the *Journal*." Binkley began his career at New York University. When Sidney B. Fay moved to Harvard from Smith in 1929, he suggested Binkley as his successor, calling him "the most promising man in the field of modern European history." Binkley spent a year there before moving to Western Reserve in the fall of 1930, where he repeatedly returned after teaching stints at Harvard (1932–33) and at Columbia (1937–38).[32]

Binkley the observer of the academic world also saw that the developing technologies of reproduction would make it possible to publish for the ever-smaller scholarly communities that Binkley the historian saw as an inevitable consequence of the development of academic disciplines. The advent of printing, argued Binkley, enabled the "moderately wealthy man" to afford "a fairly complete collection of the materials he desired" (181).[33] And since what the individual scholar desired was identical to what others also wished, the means of reproduction of texts meshed with the needs of the scholarly world. As, however, learning markedly advanced in the eighteenth century, specialization also developed. Then, in the nineteenth century significant change took place in the economics of book production and distribution. Cheap and abundant paper was introduced about midcentury, and that, combined with mass literacy, altered the economics of book production, making large editions necessary in order to absorb the costs. In this world, the scholar could easily obtain what everyone else also wanted, but "the body of documentation that was once the common ground of all learning and culture [had] … lost its cohesion," and scholarly publication had become "a relatively unimportant element in the total bulk of publication" (182). The scholar's problem came to be to get what no one else (or only a few) "would think of looking at" (182). Subsidies to publishers served only to alleviate the problem, not solve it.

To Binkley, the general framework of two types of materials applied as well to libraries. Some holdings, ideally, were identical in all libraries, as is implicit in a work such as C.B. Shaw's *A List of Books for College Libraries* (New York: Carnegie Corporation, 1931), to which he referred. Others, even though printed, more nearly resembled archives in their rarity. He termed these "special collections" and stated that they required a new approach: "The great generation of librarians now passing away saw the problem of internal library administration solved. We will have to think of library systems rather than separate libraries. That generation dealt chiefly with two classes of material passing through our hands. They knew only one way of acquiring a book—to purchase it, and only one way to service it—to lend it.... Our problems will be far more intricate than theirs, and also, I believe, far more interesting."[34] Binkley envisioned a number of methodologies within a world of library systems, but foremost was, as with scholarly production, the employment of new technologies to reproduce material.

Since Binkley viewed technologies as essential to solving the problems of scholars and libraries, to gather information about them and to make it available were priorities. His first effort was *Methods of Reproducing Research Materials: A Survey made for the Joint Committee on Materials for Research of the Social Science Research Council and the American Council of Learned Societies* (Ann Arbor: Edwards Brothers, Inc., 1931). The 139-page book, with various inserted reproductions, had on its title page a statement that immediately let the reader know what was at hand: "This edition published by Edwards Brothers, Ann Arbor, by the photo-lithographic process from author's own manuscript, pica double space typescript, reduced one-half." Only one hundred copies were printed. Most of these, the author wrote, were for those who had assisted him in preparing the book. Although he did not say so, he probably wanted to demonstrate the feasibility of printing in small numbers at low cost. The 1931 edition was, in effect, an internal document meant to inform those involved with the two Councils and to obtain their support for his ideas. Binkley, characteristically, assumed he would have it and he promised a subsequent edition for wide distribution. It did appear in 1936, in an edition of 1,500 copies,[35] also published by Edwards Brothers. The 1936 publication had a slight but important title change. Two words were added, so that the title read *Manual on Methods of Reproducing Research Materials*. That suggestion of a detailed handbook was accurate. In this edition, he worked out the cost structure of each method of reproduction in relation to number of copies, and through rich detail, including 55 tables, 73 illustrations, and even product samples, he made utterly convincing the case that new and viable means of reproduction existed.

Covered was standard printing from raised type; the Multigraph process photo-offset; the standard typewriter as well as the Varityper and Electromatic typewriter; carbon paper copying; the hectographic process, both gelatin and liquid; mimeograph techniques; blueprinting, photostating, and allied techniques, including the Dexigraph; the issue of non–Roman characters, tabular matter, diagrams, and illustrations, including photoengraving, half-tones; Photogelatin or Collotype; Intaglio processes, Aquatone and Pantone, Dermaprint, photosensitive paper processes; paper permanence; binding, vertical filing, and film storage; reduced scale photographic and photolithographing including Peters' Miniature Abstracts and Theses, the Fiske method, Film-stat reproduction, Bendikson procedure, the Van Iterson device, the Folmer Graflex Recording Camera, and the True-Vue apparatus; microcopying and projection reading; photographic and projecting apparatus, including the Cinescopie and Photoscopie, E.K.A. camera and Lemare Ampligraph, Leica and Contax equipment, the Argus, Ansco Universal Still-Film Copying Camera, Ludwig camera, Matson camera,

Filmograph and Kennedy cameras, Draeger camera, Folmer Graflex camera, Recordak bound-book copying cameras, Recordak camera, Newspaper Recordak, and, of course, projector reading machines, as well as projector-and-enlargement equipment.[36]

All of these methods were tested, and all were considered from the standpoint of aesthetics and legibility, as well as costs. Even large-scale microfilming received its test: the 315,000 pages of the records of the Agricultural Adjustment Administration and the National Recovery Administration, filmed under the supervision of T.R. Schellenberg, the Joint Committee's executive secretary. Unforeseen problems arose, and these were duly reported.

The section on microfilm also reported on the Bibliofilm service, which provided on-demand copying in the library of the US Department of Agriculture, and Binkley noted that the Library of Congress, the New York Public Library, Yale, and the Huntington had all installed cameras, as had the Preussische Staatsbibliothek. He dealt with the issue of copyright, which was crucial to the use of microfilm, and he reprinted correspondence with W.W. Norton, president of the National Association of Book Publishers. These letters constituted a "gentleman's agreement" that outlined the conditions under which microfilming of copyrighted material was permitted. Binkley also discussed the use of microfilming in making union catalogs[37] and in what he called an "assembled catalogue," that is, microfilm copies, in one location, of the cards of individual libraries. He envisioned that individual scholars could also assemble microfilm copies that would constitute complete coverage of a given topic, and he considered this a "new unit of intellectual activity" (159–60).[38] He believed that it would be beneficial to scholarship if the effort of some scholars were diverted to this activity, but he recognized that "one of the greatest obstacles to this diversion of effort lies in the academic convention which honors any publication, but accords no recognition to the gathering of material if publication does not issue from it."[39]

In this merging of collecting and publishing, he expected the small libraries to become participants. Each unit in the "library system" would perform a task "proportionate to its resources." This idealist scholar believed that libraries would become not merely collectors of existing records, but that the "library of the future [would] ... reduce to writing information that would otherwise go unrecorded." His faith in ordinary people throughout the country, his desire to see a vast apparatus of contributors to historical learning, led him to conclude the section on microfilm with a paean to the possibilities open to those in small towns: "There is no community so small that it does not offer to a sensitive mind aspects of human life that are worthy of record, and facts that should be entered in the dossiers of scholarship" (160). Indeed, he concluded his book (202) with the same vision: "The same technical innovations that promise to give aid to the research worker in his cubicle may also lead the whole population toward participation in a new cultural design."

Not that Binkley and the Joint Committee failed to devote attention to the scholarly world. To be sure, the technology could serve all, but technology alone, he came to recognize, would not change scholarly publishing. A failed attempt to change the structure of scholarly publication was instructive. At the January 29, 1932, meeting of the ACLS secretaries of constituent societies, the secretaries requested the Council "to investigate the subject of printing costs, with a view to effecting further economies in printing from type and to developing other methods, especially for small editions."[40] Subsequently, the Joint Committee devoted much of its energies to drawing up a project providing "for the establishment of a central agency, which would [18] receive the manuscripts of proposed publications, selected and sponsored by the various constituent societies of the two Councils, would determine the method of publication—by planograph or type-setting—would estimate its cost, and would canvass the prospective purchasers, both libraries and individuals, in order to ascertain whether the demand for the work in question is sufficient to meet the expenses of publication. The agency would also be charged with procuring the publication and distribution of works that might finally be selected."[41] This idea of advance orders determining the method of reproduction fit perfectly with Binkley's analysis of the specialization of academic work, and it was a favorite of his.

No such project was ever established, but Binkley did not give up. His 1936 *Manual on Methods of Reproducing Research Materials* was a further stage in the battle, and it was having influence, to judge from a letter of Waldo G. Leland, permanent secretary of the ACLS, to Frederick P. Keppel, president of the Carnegie Corporation, dated June 9, 1937. Written with the aim of persuading Keppel to use his influence with the American Philosophical Society to organize a conference on the publishing problem, it stated: "Meanwhile, the idea of non-conventional publication is gaining ground rather rapidly and as the various methods of such publication are perfected, and especially as reading machines are made available at moderate prices [a reference to microfilm], I believe that in another year we shall be much nearer such solution of our problem as it may be possible to reach." That ungrammatical, albeit tactful phraseology, did indicate that opposition remained, as another letter of July 11, 1937, indicated: "I confess that the Executive Offices of the Council have a somewhat different view of the matter than that held by many members of the Council itself."[42] Besides that conservatism, familiar to advocates of electronic publishing in lieu of print, was the fact that it was difficult to obtain advance orders, and the effort, of course, entailed costs. Binkley also realized that demand for a book would continue, so he continued to hope for a method of publication on demand.[43]

More successful was the Joint Committee's role in the Historical Records Survey of the Works Progress Administration. It seems that Francis S. Philbrick of the University of Pennsylvania's Law School, who chaired the American Historical Association's Committee on Legal History, wrote to Binkley in January 1934 and proposed a national survey of state and local archives, to be conducted by unemployed white-collar labor. Binkley then got to work to try to solve the problem inherent in carrying out a project with thousands of individuals when the product that was wanted needed to be comparable across the country. At an early point he called a conference, and, then he and Schellenberg, executive secretary of the Joint Committee, drew up a plan.[44] In 1935, President Franklin Roosevelt established the Historical Records Survey under the WPA, with Luther H. Evans as National Director (he was later Librarian of Congress), and throughout the life of the WPA Evans and Binkley worked closely together to frame the rationale behind the Historical Records Survey and to obtain ongoing funding.[45]

As part of his WPA work, Binkley was able to obtain funds to experiment with abstracting and indexing. In this, he followed his standard practice, which was to develop a methodology and determine costs, and he did so using Cleveland newspapers as a demonstration. Although he hoped that newspaper indexing would become a widespread part of a Depression-era relief program, followed by microfilming the newspapers, he anticipated that interested individuals would also do such work on their own. The model consisted of a forty-four-volume abstract/index of Cleveland newspapers from 1818 to 1935. (The project also compiled a list of the currently published foreign-language press, as well as the Jewish and African American press in Cleveland).[46]

Binkley never urged that the foundations make grants to libraries for the acquisition of materials; and although from 1930 to 1932 he had considerable correspondence on library cooperation, particularly in the collection of government publications, he dropped that line of activity. Another early activity that he dropped was the effort to enumerate the categories of research materials as needed by scholars in various fields, which was the work of a subcommittee chaired by N.S.B. Gras of the Harvard Business School. Although the constituent societies were asked to consider "how new material for research in the humanities and the social sciences can be discovered and collected, and how all materials, both new and old, can be made available for research," the committee had to admit that "few research workers have given thought to the possible expansion of the resources of their fields in research materials."[47] The meager responses, supplemented with statements by a few other individuals, did enable the committee to issue a 91-page mimeographed volume.[48] Its concrete result was to turn the subcommittee in the direction of education.[49]

That effort was based on the Joint Committee's awareness that research materials were to a considerable extent produced by various institutions, such as business and law firms as well as government bodies, as a more or less incidental part of their activities. The goal, then, was to educate the creators of the records to preserve them. A pamphlet about business records was widely distributed; it went through three editions. One reason to urge the creators of the records to preserve them was that few university libraries had archival programs, and, in any case, Binkley calculated that libraries were already struggling to house a quantity of printed research materials that was doubling every twenty years (his figure).

Educational efforts were also directed at the public. Binkley wrote for various journals, but so did other committee members. The English professor Arthur H. Quinn published "New Frontiers of Research" in *Scribner's Magazine*.[50] Beneath the title was: "In an old trunk in your attic may be records, documents, or diaries which should be preserved. Libraries and research organizations are taking an added interest in anything which illumines the study of American institutions and American life." This article concludes in a Binkley-like manner: "To this enterprise the co-operation of every citizen of the United States is invited, and there are few indeed without the power to make their contribution." Lydenberg also produced a popular essay, "The Collector's Progress," published in the *Journal of Adult Education* (1940).[51]

Although it is possible to see much of the work of the Joint Committee through the framework of education (the *Manual*, of course, aimed to inform), Binkley had no single approach, certainly no plan of action. He would seize on whatever would come along that offered possibilities. His support of union catalogues is another example. The paths gone down, the dead ends encountered, are more numerous and varied than can be described here. One explanation is that he saw himself in the role of advocate and intermediary, what is sometimes called today "the big-picture guy." He did not want to become tied down to operations. Perhaps he saw himself this way because it fit with his personality. Harry Miller Lydenberg recounted in a sketch published after Binkley's death a statement of a fellow worker, made when those in a room down the hall heard a door open, followed by footsteps: "Here comes Binkley, all five of him."[52]

Closest to his heart, though, was microfilming, especially on a large scale. It was how to get that accomplished on which he was flexible. Early on, in 1935, he seems to have had some hopes that the library community would, with some foundation support, be able to undertake large-scale microfilming of early material. Keyes Metcalf, then director of the Reference Division of the New York Public Library, drew up such a plan on August 13, 1935, "Proposal for Reproduction of Research Material on Film."[53] It called for 100,000 exposures of various types of materials: newspapers of both the United States and Europe, early American printing, English printing before 1640, incunabula, medieval manuscripts, manuscripts relating to American history from the Library of Congress, material listed in Henry Harrisse's bibliography of Americana. Metcalf's proposal, which called for initial financing by a foundation and ongoing support by subscribing libraries, did not get off the ground. Binkley's hopes for tying newspaper filming in with newspaper indexing, all with WPA funds, also did not work out. Later on, by 1938, Binkley had apparently given up on librarians as a group and on foundations and was supporting Eugene B. Power, who resigned from Edwards Brothers on July 1, 1938, in order to devote full time to his own company, University Microfilms.

Appointment of Archibald MacLeish as Librarian of Congress in 1939 enabled Binkley to dream even more boldly. He hoped that the Library of Congress would pursue massive copying of materials, printed and archival, in European institutions. He proposed beginning with copies of the printed catalogues of the great libraries of Britain and France, plus the German *Gesamtkatalog*, then getting copies of the Swiss, Dutch, and Danish union catalogues, combining them into one, and then using that catalogue to obtain microfilm copies of materials, selected by scholars, that were not in any American library.[54] MacLeish was cautious, one reason being that the plan called for American libraries to check their holdings against lists provided by the Library of Congress, then make purchases of the copies the Library had filmed. The caution was justified.

Microfilming on the scale envisaged by Binkley did not happen, but this memorandum, plus another one of November 27, 1939, "A National Acquisition Policy," fed into the discussions that ultimately led to the Farmington Plan, the postwar cooperative acquisition program that aimed at increasing American coverage of the publications of Europe. Also feeding into the Farmington Plan was the work of librarians, which Binkley kept MacLeish apprised of, when on December 11, 1939, he sent him a proposal from Metcalf, chairman of the ALA committee on photographic reproduction of library materials. It included a proposal "to request $100,000 from Rockefeller to microfilm on a large scale irreplaceable European materials, including any American archives not already covered by Project A of the Library of Congress, all English books printed before 1640, early printing from other European countries, classical and mediaeval manuscripts at least up to the year 1500, the 15,000 volume index of the Public Records [sic] Office, all material that has been moved from the British Museum and other London libraries into the country for safety, and the same for material from Paris and other cities." To this MacLeish replied on December 14, 1939, "Metcalf's proposal seems to me a sound one—at least it is a nibble at the cake."

The parties could not come to consensus on a plan of action, but the war in Europe had provided a new impetus to think boldly. "America must be in a position to keep western culture alive." So wrote Binkley in his memorandum of October 30, 1939. With that statement, the circle closed, and the United States had returned to seeing libraries and scholarship in the same way as in 1919, after the First World War.

Four months later, on April 11, 1940, Robert Binkley died; so, he did not see the vast postwar growth of academia and libraries that was stimulated by the belief that they served a great national purpose—not merely keeping Western culture alive but keeping civilization itself alive in the era of the Soviet threat.

Just before Binkley's death, in his early forties, he connected with a development that was to be even more portentous. Stuart Rice, the statistician, told him that Vannevar Bush, the MIT electrical engineer, was working on a machine to index microfilm. Binkley wrote to Bush on January 23, 1940, to ask for more information about the "micro-selector"; and Bush replied on February 14, 1940,[55] with an account of the "rapid selector" machine that five years later he described in print in his pioneering essay, "As We May Think,"[56] which inspired many who subsequently developed hypertext.

It is clear that the world of microfilm, which, of course, continued on its own,[57] had stimulated development of the new technology that is now replacing microfilm for many uses. Bush may even have been influenced by Binkley to think about the new technology in broad terms. The essay "As We May Think" has no footnotes, but it is organized in a way that suggests Bush had been reading "New Tools for Men of Letters," which Binkley had published in the *Yale Review* in the spring of 1935. Bush began his essay as Binkley had, by emphasizing the specialization that had occurred. The second of his eight sections is about photography, and it emphasizes the possibilities of microphotography and then reading the text by projection. Bush notes especially that microphotography, through duplicating vast resources, creates a need for access, not just to extract but to select. To Bush, the ideal method of doing so involved not indexes with their rules, but rather a system that worked by association. That will be done by a machine that he calls the memex. Thus, the scholar's workstation will consist of a screen that permits reading of microfilm, to which access is made available by the memex. Provision is also made for photographing notes, memoranda, photographs, and the like. The "associative indexing" is done by creating a code entered into a code book, with the code also appearing at the bottom of the microfilm image. Tapping on it will bring up other instances in which that code has been used. Then Bush writes, as Binkley would have, that in providing access to the past, his system would elevate the human spirit.

Binkley, the prophet, died before entering the promised land. He only saw from afar the possibilities of a new technology that made microfilm largely into an intermediate technology, save for its durability when reproduced under high standards. He was right about microfilm and preservation—technically—but nowhere in the files does he or anyone else indicate awareness that not all "copies" of a book are the same or that a given copy may not be complete. Similarly, nowhere in the files has there been found an indication of microfilm's limits, that not all texts will be readable, let alone convey what they do on paper—and that microfilm created for libraries the issue of preserving at least one copy on paper.[58]

Perhaps Binkley the scholar, the historian, would have come to see that microfilming actually entailed the possibility of loss, not preservation, when carried out in a culture dominated by the need—very real—for cost effectiveness, but where the guidelines developed to ensure that goal were created by managers distanced from the materials.[59] If Binkley did not see the dark side of microfilm—and it is the fate of advocates trying to change the world to be single-minded—we have him to thank for his help in bringing about the positive. Whoever consults a digital version of a book or newspaper that was earlier on microfilm is indebted to this pioneer.

Binkley's legacy is, however, broader than that. His example as a scholar thoroughly engaged in a disinterested way in libraries and the infrastructure of scholarship raises the question for us of how to further such involvement today. Binkley's ideas, put forth with clarity in a simpler age, bear ongoing examination. His recognition that libraries should be seen as a system can always be profitably considered. His insight into the specialization of scholarly interests as the fundamental cause of the publishing crisis leads to consideration of the factors inherently behind the problems of university presses today.

Binkley is relevant as well for reasons other than his example or his insights. His goal of a new cultural design brought about by technology continues to intrigue and challenge. Yes, we have a new cultural design brought about by technology. We even have the technology used to research and make available local histories, autobiographies, volumes of poetry, and the like. The fact that the technology is used this way does not mean that we have the new cultural design envisaged by Binkley. The question remains as to how our libraries, educational institutions, and scholarly societies can further a cultural design that is consonant with the most positive values of our history.

Notes

1. Robert Binkley, "History for a Democracy," *Minnesota History* 18 (1937): 1–27. This was presented on January 18, 1937, before the Minnesota Historical Society. Page numbers in parentheses refer to *Selected Papers of Robert C. Binkley*, ed. Max H. Fisch (Cambridge: Harvard University Press, 1948).

2. *Common School Journal* 2 (15 April 1840): 120. Binkley did not need to read Horace Mann to come by his views; they were experientially derived. His father, a high school teacher, one-time secretary to Joaquin Miller, was also a published poet who learned Chinese and built up a working library for Chinese studies. Also, crucial may have been the experience of driving from California to New York in 1927. In that era before the interstates, the Binkleys experienced firsthand town after town. Fisch, in two paragraphs obviously based on an interview with Mrs. Binkley, recounted the trip and the conversation; see Fisch, "Robert Cedric Binkley: Historian in the Long Armistice," *Selected Papers*, 11–12.

3. Letter from Yale's Secretary to the "Carnegie Peace Foundation," 26 May 1919; Yale Librarian Papers, Box 5, folder 43 (RU, 19ND-A-233).

4. It was officially formed on February 14, 1920, at a meeting in the office of the Institute of International Studies, an organization funded by the Carnegie Endowment. That meeting was chaired by the institute's director, Stephen P. Duggan, who was also involved in the bibliography.

5. Roger L. Geiger, *To Advance Knowledge: The Growth of American Research Universities, 1900–1940* (New York: Oxford University Press, 1986; New Brunswick, NJ: Transaction Publishers, 2004) is crucial to understanding this period, especially chaps. 1, 3–5. No indication has been found that foundations turned to universities because they possessed in libraries the tools of scholarship. See also Frederick P. Keppel, *The Foundation: Its Place in American Life* (New York: Macmillan, 1930), where the discussion on pp. 87–88 indicates consideration of the two options for foundation efforts to advance knowledge.

6. In Yale Librarian Papers, box 37, folder 413, General Education Board.

7. The problem, with concrete examples, was spelled out by Princeton's librarian, James Thayer Gerould, in a letter of 25 January 1932 to Robert C. Binkley. It reads in part: "The primary task of every library is to meet the current demands of its constituency, demands, which, in most of them are seldom fully met. No library can or should accept a program which makes it impossible for it to meet reasonable requests for books from the men actually on the ground. So long as the universities which the libraries serve do not delimit their fields, so long as they do not recognize the necessity for the development of American scholarship on a national basis, so long as we maintain institutional particularism, no very significant results can be expected. Every effort thus far made to secure cooperation, except as the plans have been related to institutions within particular cities, has failed. A committee of the Modern Language Association which, for several years, has been attempting to secure agreements as to the distribution of Spanish periodicals, was compelled, at its last meeting, to confess its powerlessness and to ask for discharge. A similar attempt of the psychologists, a number of years ago, and efforts which I personally have made to distribute the responsibility for the purchase of files of the French and German local historical, archaeological and literary societies, have had no result. Everywhere there is a recognition of the importance of the task, but there is equal unanimity in the claim that there are no funds which can be used for the purchase of books that are not in immediate demand."

8. For a discussion of Ruml's role and of Lawrence K. Frank's report, "The Status of Social Science in the United States," see Geiger, *To Advance Knowledge*, 149–56.

9. Librarians and scholars, as well as foundations, were concerned. For example, the Laura Spelman Rockefeller Memorial requested a report on "what is being done for the collection and preservation of material of all sorts that may serve to illustrate and record the various phases of contemporary life"; and the Association of American Universities sponsored a study of libraries (George A. Works, *College and University Library Problems, a Study of a Selected Group of Institutions Prepared for the Association of American Universities*, 1927). In 1926, two of the five committees of the SSRC were the Committee on Publication of an Index and Digest of State Session Laws and the Committee on Abstracts of Social Science Periodical Literature, which was also working with a League of Nations subcommittee seeking to develop a "plan for a general analysis of social science literature."

10. Council of the SSRC, *Fifth Annual Report, 1928-1929* (November 1929), Appendix B, 42–46.

11. Elbridge Sibley, *Social Science Research Council: The First Fifty Years*, 162, which is available online, following Kenton W. Worcester's *Social Science Research Council, 1923-1998* (New York, 2001), on the SSRC website.

12. I have been unable to determine who was responsible for the detailed plan laid out in roman numeral III.

13. The precise steps in setting up the new committee are unclear. The *Fifth Annual Report* covering 1 July 1928, to 1 September 1929, records the existence of a Joint Committee on Enlargement, Improvement and Preservation of Data, a name that Robert S. Lynd, permanent secretary of the SSRC, used in a letter to Harry Miller Lydenberg, on 7 January 1930, when the new committee should have been formed (NYPL Archives, RG6, ser. 2, box 3, Lydenberg: December 1929—February 1930). The only difference between the membership of the two committees is that Quinn and Binkley had been added. It is possible that changing the name was crucial, since the use of "data" has a definite social science ring.

14. Lydenberg's title was Reference Librarian, a term that meant he was head of the Reference Library at 42nd Street.

15. New York Public Library, Director's Office, Edwin Hatfield Anderson papers, Series 1: General correspondence, 1915–1928, Box 12, National Research Council folder.

16. ACLS *Bulletin* no. 11 (June 1929): 38.

17. Although it may be that Lydenberg suggested Binkley be appointed to the committee, Binkley's appointment may have been the result of his earlier acquaintance with Robert T. Crane, who succeeded Lynd as permanent secretary. Binkley had studied under Crane at Stanford, and the relationship is indicated by the fact that Crane was one of the few people to address Binkley as "Bob." Binkley never used Crane's first name in correspondence. Crane's support was, in any case, crucial in the work of the Joint Committee.

18. Fisch, "Robert Cedric Binkley," in *Selected Papers*, 12, quoting from Lydenberg's memorial statement in American Council of Learned Societies, *Bulletin* no. 33 (October 1941): 56–59.

19. Fisch, "Robert Cedric Binkley," 12–13.

20. This paper is published in Primo Congresso Mondiale delle Biblioteche e di Bibliografia, *Atti* (Rome: Libreria dello Stato, 1931), and reprinted in Binkley, *Selected Papers*, 169–78. Binkley attended the conference as representative of the Hoover Library.

21. In this essay, Binkley also likened the process of deterioration to "slow fires": "That is to say, the composition of wood-pulp paper is chemically identical with the burning of a log in the fireplace, except that the process goes on at a lower temperature and takes a longer time." C. Binkley [sic], "Do the Records of Science Face Ruin?" *Scientific American* 140 (January 1929): 29.

22. Allan B. Veaner, ed., *Studies in Micropublishing, 1853–1976: Documentary Sources* (Westport, CT: Microform Review Inc., 1976), 81–99.

23. Mentions in Harvard annual reports document this point. In the 1914–15 *Reports of the President and Treasurer of Harvard College* (p. 149), the acting dean of the Harvard Law School, Austin Wakeman Scott, wrote about "probably" photographing occasional laws by the "new photostatic process, at a moderate expense," wording that suggested a future direction. In the 1920–21 *Report* (p. 229), the librarian of Harvard College, William Coolidge Lane, wrote that the Harvard College Library was supplying photostats made by the photostat operator of the Massachusetts Historical Society. In the 1920s, Harvard libraries began to record gifts of photostat copies; see the searchable file of annual reports at http://hul.harvard.edu/huarc/refshelf/.

24. See *Proposed Reproductions of Rare Books and Manuscripts* (Chicago: Newberry Library [1921]), i–iii.

25. Frederic Ives Carpenter, "The Photographic Reproduction of Rare Books," *Papers of the Bibliographical Society of America* 15 (1921): 35–46. It was also reprinted and distributed separately. The Winship letter is on pp. 41–42.

26. *A Union Catalog of Photo Facsimiles in North American Libraries: Material So Far Received by the Library of Congress*, comp. by Ernest Kletsch, Curator of Union Catalogs of the Library of Congress (Yardley, PA: F.S. Cook & Son, 1929). Interest in photographic reproductions of manuscripts was not confined

to this have-not nation across the Atlantic. Indeed, the British took another step toward a systematic effort by surveying library policies and facilities for copying in countries around the world. The answers to the August 1921 questionnaire that the British Foreign Office had distributed were compiled and printed as *Photographs of Manuscripts: Reports from His Majesty's Representative Abroad Respecting Facilities for Obtaining Photographs of Manuscripts in Public Libraries in Certain Foreign Countries* (London: Stationery Office, 1922).

27. "An Inexpensive Method of Reproducing Material out of Print," ACLS *Bulletin* no. 8 (October 1928): 11–15.

28. The essay, in mentioning that the GPO had reproduced a sixty-page brochure on Joseph Pennell for the Library of Congress, emphasized that zincography could be used by libraries and scholars for current publications.

29. It seems that typewriters came to be adopted in library work in the 1890s and 1900s. Thus, the University of Rochester Library acquired its first typewriter in 1898; see http://www.library.rochester.edu/. Penn State bought its first typewriter for producing catalogue cards in 1902; see http://www.libraries.psu.edu/tas/cataloging/dept/history.htm.

30. Many machines are described and pictured at http://www.officemuseum.com/copy_machines.htm. The website is based on a variety of printed works, among them Barbara Rhodes and William W. Streeter, *Before Photocopying: The Art & History of Mechanical Copying, 1780–1938* (New Castle, DE: Oak Knoll Press, 1999), and T.A. Russo, *Office Collectibles: 100 Years of Business Technology* (Atglen, PA: Schiffer, 2000).

31. A translation appears in Veaner, ed., *Studies in Micropublishing*, 100–08.

32. Fisch, "Robert Cedric Binkley," is the source of the biographical information about Binkley.

33. Robert C. Binkley, "New Tools for Men of Letters," *Yale Review*, n.s. 24 (1935): 519–27; rpt. in *Selected Papers*, 179–97.

34. Robert C. Binkley, "The Reproduction of Materials for Research," in *Library Trends: Papers Presented before the Library Institute at the University of Chicago, August 3–15, 1936*, ed. Louis Round Wilson (Chicago: University of Chicago Press, 1937), 225–36; rpt. in *Selected Papers*, 224–35. The quotation is part of the concluding paragraph.

35. The number comes from Alan Marshall Meckler, *Micropublishing: A History of Scholarly Micropublishing in America, 1938–1980* (Westport, CT: Greenwood Press, 1982), 23 and his n. 22 citing box 67 of the ACLS Records at Library of Congress. The number, writes Meckler, was increased from 1,000 because of demand.

36. Binkley was also aware that print's monopoly of the means for mass communication was past. Although he envisioned that the other media could have a role in scholarly communication ("Television may render long-distance reading a possibility" [177]) and in special areas of research (folk music in particular), he was also interested in radio and cinema as historical source materials of wide cultural significance. Chapter 13 of his 1936 *Manual* is "The Recording of Sound."

37. He was influential in furthering the Philadelphia-area union catalog since he showed that technology could help in the process of copying cards.

38. These and the page numbers hereafter refer to the *Manual*.

39. Binkley considered this in an undated statement "An analysis of the resources available for the improvement of research materials with suggestion for their use," in Joint Committee Archive, box 1, folder Correspondence on Library Cooperation.

40. *Bulletin* no. 18 (October 1932), 138.

41. *Bulletin* no. 20 (December 1933).

42. These letters are in Carnegie Corporation Archive, III. A., Grant Files, American Council of Learned Societies folder, at Columbia University. Leland had brought the *Manual* to Keppel's attention on November 9, 1936.

43. The most important effort at publishing on demand was Robert J. Kerner's *Northeastern Asia: A Selected Bibliography* (Berkeley: University of California Press, 1939). For this two-volume work of some 1350 pages, the Committee was able to cover by advance subscriptions almost all of the $1,700 cost of a master photo-offset copy, which permitted a considerable saving from the subsidy of $10,000 that would have been required for a printing from type. Of course, Binkley tried to further on-demand copying on microfilm. He supported the National Agricultural Library in its on-demand copying, and he advocated that other libraries, especially the Library of Congress, do likewise. The American Documentation Institute, Binkley hoped, would further on-demand filming and also push the issue of copyright, and for a time he was on its board, until he came to see the Institute as acting contrary to the interests of scholarship in general.

44. In a letter to Binkley of 31 August 1934, Philbreck referred to "our proposed state surveys," so he continued to be involved; see Joint Committee files, box 34.

45. For a brief account, see David L. Smiley, "The W.P.A. Historical Records Survey," in *In Support of Clio: Essays in Memory of Herbert A. Kellar*, ed. William B. Hesseltine and Donald R. McNeil (Madison: State Historical Society of Wisconsin, 1958), 3–28. Smiley used Record Group 69 of the National Archives,

which is the correspondence relating to the Historical Records Survey. Boxes 16–22 of the Joint Committee Records specifically concern the WPA—in general and also in Ohio.

46. A small portion of the multivolume index to the general Cleveland newspapers has been digitized. http://web.ulib.csuohio.edu/SpecColl/annals/. The portion that has been digitized suggests that such abstracts and indexes would significantly increase the body of source materials on which students of the history of American culture draw.

47. *Bulletin* no. 15 (May 1931), 110 and 74.

48. *Committee Memorandum on Categories of Materials for Research in the Social Sciences and the Humanities. Prepared by the Sub-Committee on Categories of Materials* [n.p., 1933]. Later, Binkley confessed that he had never been able to find a methodology that would satisfactorily encompass the world of research materials.

49. ACLS *Bulletin* no. 22 (October 1934).

50. Arthur H. Quinn, "New Frontiers of Research," *Scribner's Magazine* (1935): 95–97.

51. Harry Miller Lydenberg, "The Collector's Progress," *Journal of Adult Education* 12 (April 1940): 133–37.

52. Fisch, "Robert Cedric Binkley," 30n.

53. Keyes Metcalf, "Proposal for Reproduction of Research Material on Film," 13 August 1935, in Joint Committee papers, box 34.

54. Robert C. Binkley, "Memorandum," 30 October 1939, "Mr. MacLeish, Librarian of Congress," in Joint Committee papers, box 34.

55. Binkley's letter to Vannevar Bush, 23 January 1940, reads: Stuart Rice has told me some fantastic things about a micro-selector or something of that kind that you have been contriving.

I am interested in its possible application to fields in the orbit of interest to the Joint Committee on Materials for Research. Could you give me a little bit more of a clue as to what it is?

Bush's response of 14 February 1940, is:

Your letter of January twenty-third has been forwarded to me from the Massachusetts Institute of Technology. The rapid selector which is being built at MIT may indeed have applications in the field in which you are especially interested. I talked with Stuart Rice about the matter, for at the present time several of us are puzzling over the problem of introducing this equipment in some favorable way for the handling of scholarly material. It has commercial usage, this aspect of the matter will be taken care of normally, but on the scholarly applications it may be possible to accomplish something quite unusual.

Without going into detail, the device is a mechanism for rapidly running over a large number of items on microfilm and selecting out by code any desired items, which it then photographs on a separate small strip of film. The principal point is that it can survey these items at the rate of 1000 per second and it does not need to stop to make the photographic duplicate, so that it is very fast. The coding can be very detailed, and in fact on the present machine there is provision, I think, for ten alphabets.

I will be very happy indeed to tell you more about the matter if you wish. It may be that you will have some questions and, if so, I will be glad to reply to them as far as I can. If you should happen to be in the vicinity of Cambridge the most effective way of looking into the subject would be to visit the laboratory where the development is being carried on. This I think you will find it well worthwhile to do so simply from the standpoint of the interest which the development has even although [sic] no specific applications were in mind.

I am grateful to the manuscript division of the Library of Congress for sending photocopies of the letters.

56. *Atlantic Monthly*, July 1945, available on the website of the *Atlantic Monthly*.

57. Microfilm and the learned societies were also linked by the Joint Committee on Microcopying Materials for Research, joint with the ACLS, the American Council of Education, and the National Research Council, this last meaning involvement of the scientific community. The consolidated lists of SSRC committees, available on its website, indicates that it, too, was a sponsor of the committee. The NRC's representative on the committee was W.H. Kenerson. Although Kenerson is not recorded as being among Bush's correspondents, Archibald MacLeish and Bush were in touch over many years, as indicated by the Library of Congress finding aid. MacLeish and Binkley had had numerous contacts, and MacLeish was also a member of the Joint Committee on Microcopying Materials for Research. It had been appointed in 1940 to carry out the recommendations of the Conference on Microcopying Materials for Research in Foreign Depositories. Its report for 1941 in ACLS *Bulletin* no. 35 (October 1942) recorded that it endorsed a plan "submitted for advice by another agency, for a National Division of Library Cooperation" within the Library of Congress. That division was established but it seems to have issued only one publication, Herbert A. Kellar, *Memoranda on Library Cooperation* (September 1941); the division is there called "Experimental Division of Library Cooperation."

58. Nicholson Baker, *Double Fold: Libraries and the Assault on Paper* (New York: Random House, 2001). Baker only mentions Binkley, no doubt because the widespread filming and discarding of newspapers occurred after Binkley's death.

59. The danger exists that large-scale digitization will be carried out under guidelines based on similar assumptions about the original and that holders of the originals, whether of the copy filmed or of other "copies," will discard the printed items, perhaps out of ignorance or space pressures. A digital copy is, however, by its nature more accessible than a microfilm copy, and that, combined with recognition of the dark side of microfilming, may limit destruction.

Expansion, Science, and Technology, 1946–1988, Part I

In World War II the United States and our allies reigned victorious, and the U.S.A. emerged thereafter as an undisputed world power. Such was confirmed in contemporary accounts and subsequent analysis of the period. And yet the postwar era, while grist for historical interpretation, is also recent enough that it resides in the popular imagination of baby boomers (born from the mid–1940s through 1964) and even some of their parents, informing the rhetoric, ideology, policy, and potential for higher education and libraries. Demobilizing the military had yielded a flood of veterans, young people, accomplished and confident, returning to American shores, seeking opportunity: peace time employment, affordable housing, and the promise of higher education. Federal legislation supported collegiate study for returning veterans who swelled the ranks of American institutions of higher learning. The total resident college enrollment nationwide had been 1,494,203 in prewar 1940 and 2,659,021 in postwar 1950. Post-war growth continued unabated and by 1970 total enrollment had reached 8,498,000.[1] Between 1940 and 1964, enrollment increased from fourteen percent to forty percent of the nation's college-age population.[2]

What all this meant for academe was unusually hurried growth, clearly unprecedented, often precipitous. Expansion necessitated enlargement of existing programs, the addition of new academic departments and specialized institutes, and the establishment of entirely new colleges and universities, public and private. On-campus housing became impossibly scarce, and thousands of quonset huts were repurposed from military barracks to serve as residence halls for students or, alternatively, as laboratory, instructional, or administrative space. Thus, in the immediate postwar years and through the mid–1960s, academics came to regard growth as a constant and inexorable determinant.

Returning veterans constituted only one of several factors stimulating growth in higher education. In 1957 the U.S.S.R. launched a satellite, challenging Western nations and the U.S.A., in particular, to compete for supremacy in outer space. The American legislative response, in the context of international tensions engendered by the Cold War (featuring the looming threat of nuclear annihilation), produced a vast expansion in collegiate education, especially in those fields most closely connected to military prowess: science, technology, engineering, and mathematics (STEM). Federal support for science and technology grew at breakneck speed. Agencies such as the National Defense Research Committee, the Committee on Medical Research, and the Office of

Strategic Research and Development, all established just before or during World War II, enlisted universities in technological innovation in general and, more specifically, in development on behalf of military advantage. The National Science Foundation and the National Institutes of Health further broadened the purposes of federal largesse in the postwar period. By 2012 the federal government was providing sixty-one percent of R. & D. dollars for colleges and universities in the United States; higher education had become essential in making the U.S.A. a world power economically, intellectually, and militarily.[3]

The impact on academic libraries was equally transformative. From 1959 to 1970 the number of academic libraries grew from 1,951 to 2,535; the number of total volumes from 176 to 371 million; and expenditures from $176 to $737 million annually.[4] By 1990 these figures had risen to 3,274 libraries; 717 million volumes; and $3.3 billion respectively.[5] Brick and mortar expansion was the rule of the day from the postwar years until the economic contractions of the 1970s. Libraries in major research universities had become integrated into on-campus mechanisms for cultivating federal support, and many faculty had come to see their academic library, not as a competitor for departmental funds but, rather, as an essential partner in their own enterprise as scholars and researchers.

Technological innovation created new platforms for resource sharing. Both the *National Union Catalog* and the Library of Congress program of catalog card distribution had been launched in the early twentieth century. Standardized practice for bibliographic description followed eventually, with widely adopted protocols undergirding the creation in the 1960s of MARC (machine readable cataloging) records. MARC facilitated the establishment of bibliographic utilities, among them OCLC (Online Computer Library Center), RLIN (Research Libraries Information Network), WLN (Washington Library Network), and UTLAS (University of Toronto Library Automation Systems). The utilities—through the mechanism of regional networks and numerous consortia large and small—have enhanced profoundly the ability of local libraries to create and maintain online records of holdings, and to implement integrated modules for a variety of functions including acquisitions, serials control, and circulation. Online records, moreover, have stimulated dramatically the growth of interlibrary lending (ILL) and borrowing transactions, which every year total in the millions. The high numbers reported for ILL reflected the vast expansion in the infrastructure for networked information, also presenting an essential response to the financial straits of the 1980s. Subsequently, librarians adopted a new phrase, "just in time rather than just in case," to emphasize a new, more affordable, service model of access over ownership—a strategic response to budgetary contractions and financial instability.

Still, the impact of online records in networked environments, specifically their capacity to redefine and to reshape the functions and services of academic libraries (including technical services but also reference information services and user instruction programs) constituted a great achievement as librarians approached the final decade of the twentieth century. In their essay, Philip D. Leighton and David C. Weber, with firsthand knowledge of Stanford University, took a micro-level view, examining the impact of computer driven adjustments in constructing and remodeling academic library buildings during the 1960s, 70s, and 80s. With the pre–1990s as historical context, we can benchmark our authors' accuracy at projecting the future, testing it against our own experience, but also appreciating the service implications and cost benefit complexities of everyday minutia. The Leighton-Weber references to local area networks and CD-ROMs seem remotely quaint even to those of us who lived through these transitions. Writing in 1989, they illustrated the kinds of technology which libraries had adopted and adapted in the not too distant past, underscored the importance of flexibility in planning and design, and predicted what the 1990s might hold.

NOTES

1. 1. John S. Brubacher and Willis Rudy, *Higher Education in Transition: A History of American Colleges and Universities*, 4th Ed. (New Brunswick, New Jersey: Transaction Publishers, 1997), 378.

2. Daniel Bell, *The Reforming of General Education* (New York: Columbia University Press, 1966), 104.

3. James Axtell, *Wisdom's Workshop: The Rise of the Modern University* (Princeton, New Jersey: Princeton University Press, 2016), 328, 333.

4. U.S. Office of Education, *Digest of Education Statistics 1966* (Washington, D.C.: USGPO, 1966), 110, Table 139; and National Center for Education Statistics, *Digest of Education Statistics 1977-78* (Washington, D.C.: USGPO, 1978), 191, Table 188.

5. Jeffrey Williams, National Center for Education Statistics, *Academic Libraries: 1990* (Washington, U.S. Department of Education, Office of Educational Research and Improvement, 1992), iii.

The Influence of Computer Technology on Academic Library Buildings
A Slice of Recent History

PHILIP D. LEIGHTON
and DAVID C. WEBER

> We never confine ourselves to the present time. We anticipate the future as too slow in coming, as it were, to hasten its course; or we recall the past, in order to stop it as too ready to go: so imprudent, that we wander into times that are not ours, and do not think on that alone which belongs to us; and so vain, that we meditate upon those periods that have vanished, and allow the sole moment that subsists to escape without reflecting upon it.
> —Pascal, *Thoughts*

Computer-related technology is revolutionizing library operations. It is also having a strong influence on library buildings. Information technology systems and the telecommunications and power they require force building accommodations. Wiring, lighting, acoustics, environmental controls, and furniture must change to meet these systems' needs. More fundamentally, there are altered functional relationships, new library services, new social circumstances, and greatly expanded information expectations and capacities. Change seems constant and rapid.

What has been the experience and what are the current expectations for changes in academic library buildings? We begin by looking at the 1960s and 1970s to see how computer technology first influenced library building accommodations. We then review contemporary institutional adaptations and experiences forced by rapidly expanding computer applications. And finally, we take a somewhat hazardous look, five to ten years into the future, when this technology may constitute an even stronger influence on the design of new or remodeled academic library facilities.

Twenty years ago, it was commonly thought that the computer would result in dramatic changes in library facilities. But as time passes, each change by and large hardly appears dramatic; and in most cases, with a little consideration of the factors involved, the changes seem as though they could have easily been imagined in advance. As in other historical reviews, however, the change from day to day is subtle and may hardly be perceptible, whereas cumulative adjustments over a period of even a couple of decades may actually be dramatic.

While a historian of the cultural context of science and technology might draw comparisons with the gradual changes in society brought about by the development of the radio, the electric light bulb, the phonograph, or even the elevator, each technological advance has its own unique characteristics and unanticipated consequences. Each grows within a context of economic, political, geographic, social, and organizational factors.[1] Furthermore, when a technology is in a rather early stage of development, and we do not know where to place it on a maturation curve, we later find some of the extrapolations of predicted change to be quite wild, while others turn out to be quite close to the mark.

The fifty-year history of academic libraries using computer technology, or at least a mechanical version of it, began with data processing applications, where staff used equipment usually located in quarters outside the library. For example, in February 1936 the University of Texas Library Loan Department began processing Hollerith punched cards using IBM electric sorting machines located in the registrar's office. It is the online system and the nationwide and worldwide digital networks, however, that truly influenced building design, space allocations, and furnishings. These online systems for libraries originated during the 1960s. The last twenty years have seen rapid advancements, notably the phenomenal growth of the Online Computer Library Center (OCLC) as a descendant of the joint catalog card production effort of the medical school libraries of Yale, Columbia, and Harvard, and the unique computer-reliant services of the Research Libraries Group (RLG) as the outgrowth of initiative by Yale, Columbia, Harvard, and the Research Libraries of the New York Public Library.

When the development of a technology is on a rapidly increasing maturation curve, we cannot then know when the rate of change slows. The pattern of historical development can be viewed accurately only when the conditions stabilize. Even with the attainment of a degree of stabilization, we may not realize the full effect of a new technology for a considerable period of time (as was the case after Gutenberg's use of movable type). Will these first fifty years of the influence of computer technology on library building design span the major significant changes? Or are we only half-way toward what, in another fifty years, might be seen with hindsight as a rapid early development toward relative stability? All we can say with certainty is that the rate of progress continues to be rapid. The future influences of computer technology on library buildings will certainly continue to be very significant for another ten years, and more likely for twenty years. What have we experienced so far in this history?

The 1960s and 1970s

In looking back twenty years, it is evident that the first influences of computers on facilities were minimal. Buildings as a whole were not adjusted to computer technology, but rather, the technology was accommodated by retrofitting individual spaces and systems for the computer. We have selected a few college and university libraries to illustrate that phase of this history.

In the early 1960s, libraries as disparate and as distant as Harvard University and Reed College used early IBM equipment. Susan K. Martin has written that in the early 1960s, during the Widener Library shelf list conversion project, Harvard University identified and renovated space to accommodate the new systems office and nine IBM keypunch machines. Later, arrangements were made to house one of the computing center's IBM 1401 computers in the library near the systems office, and further renovation was necessary. While neither the keypunch machines nor the 1401 initially required communications lines, they needed air conditioning and acoustic treatment. This treatment required that space separate from other library functions be assigned to the operations using this equipment. That was the first space in the library to become air-conditioned. With the circulation department following closely behind to safeguard its punched card and batch processing equipment.[2]

The Reed College Library in 1965 started its first automation project: bookkeeping records and purchase orders printed from punched cards on the college's IBM 1130. All the work was done at the computer center and required no library space alteration. As reported by Luella Pollack, Reed's next venture was joining OCLC in 1977. OCLC use required rearrangement in the catalog department for three terminals, which entailed a compressing of functions in a large open area and the installation of an additional phone line. From the point of view of the building at Reed, there were three problems: (1) the available area forced the terminals to face a bank of windows to the east, which necessitated heavy screening; (2) there were serious problems with static, despite the static-free carpet installed after several other solutions had been tried—the problem was aggravated by prevailing winter east winds; and (3) because the OCLC line went through the college's switchboard, a campus power outage would disable the line.[3]

At Stanford University, the principal change in the late 1960s, stemming from the adoption of an acquisitions and cataloging system (the prototype for today's Research Libraries Information Network system), was the installation of a terminal cluster used by support staff. This "data control" group was located a floor above the rest of the technical processing staff because of the need for adequate staff space, group training, supervision, sound isolation, and inputting efficiency. Ironically, Stanford's first air-conditioned library spaces were not for computers but, rather, for production photocopying operations where there was a chronic problem with heat and curling paper. Air-conditioned computer rooms were always outside the library.

In most libraries, the addition of computer terminals at staff desks and the space consumed by these terminals represent perhaps the most visible changes. Except for the addition of new power circuits, carpet, and an early form of "landscape" office partitions (thought of as bank partitions, after the glass-topped panels frequently seen in banks of that era), library buildings were not significantly modified. In planning for the new technologies, staff reacted by stages to the different equipment needs by introducing appropriate tables, desks, and counters to replace earlier makeshift arrangements.

As terminals were introduced to public service desks, two arrangements became common. The first placed the terminal on a lazy Susan so that after a search the staff member could turn the screen toward the reader. The other was to place the terminal at the end of a counter so that the staff member and the library patron could stand side by side to view the screen.

Noise was often a serious factor. Terminals and printers made one kind of noise; training staff and others to use the new systems generated another. In most cases, dealing with noise led to its isolation or simply acceptance. At service points, where transactions traditionally create noise, this sound was not too much of a problem. Technical processing areas, however, became nearly intolerable with the clicking and buzzing of printers. Libraries first grouped terminals (resulting in what we call the fishbowl effect), then dispersed them (resulting in the difficulty of finding an open terminal), and finally clustering them, but with a modest amount of visual and some acoustic treatment. More recently, the introduction of softer surfaces (carpeted floors, acoustic panels, and, occasionally, acoustic ceilings) and quieter printers has reduced noise problems in technical processing areas.

The association of noise with computers is in part related to human nature, for where there is no mechanical-auditory feedback (particularly with a system that is used for the input of large amounts of information), there may be a sense of feeling lost. The clicking of the keys gives useful feedback to the user of the tactile/audio system. For example, many readers have had the experience of owning an inexpensive calculator that has no tactile feedback. Without a click, the only way of knowing something is entered (and not entered twice) is to look, which may be fine at an automated teller or possibly at a public catalog terminal. But where there is a resulting need to watch the computer screen while inputting a lengthy quote from a manuscript, the computer operator would be frustrated without tactile/audio feedback.

Fans in microcomputers also create noise, a disturbance to some even when the equipment is located in a private office. Both ink jet and laser printers can be disturbing, even though they are much quieter than the typewriters and impact printers they replace. Thus, we conclude that the nature of the technology, both in terms of its relation to humans and in terms of the physical requirements of the technology itself, will always be surrounded by some sound.

Electrical circuits represented another typical building problem because the quantity, and occasionally the quality, was frequently inadequate. Extra electrical power had to be added to all library buildings, even those designed shortly after the Second World War. To permit vertical runs from basements or ceiling spaces below, librarians arranged for coaxial cable to be pulled (sometimes using pneumatic tube runs), for abandoned central vacuum system tubes or dumbwaiter shafts to be used, or for holes to be drilled though concrete slabs. The location of columns and walls (which served as surfaces for exposed runs of conduit and surface-mounted outlet boxes) often dictated placement of equipment. "Wire management" became a necessary art.

One of the most common electrical power problems was inadequate or improper grounding. In some older buildings, the third wire required for the ground connection was not present in the AC electrical outlets or building wire plant. In others, grounding of the wires (normally through the cold-water pipes or to a ground rod driven into the earth or connected to a grounding system) was not adequate. Terminals, computers, and related equipment are susceptible to many problems associated with grounding, ranging from "ground-loop" voltage, which induces errors in data transmission, to power isolation failures, which may destroy electronic components.

When the University of California at Berkeley began to use online systems, the impact of future technologies had already been anticipated, and both the acquisitions and cataloging departments were completely renovated with office landscaping, horizontal, and vertical chases for wiring, and "closets" for modem pools.

Russell Shank stated that at the University of California, Los Angeles (UCLA), "We have done what a lot of libraries do—strung coaxial cables to walls at the corners of rooms and along baseboards, plugged too many microcomputers, printers, etc. into two receptacle outlets, added circuits in walls where possible for electricity, and allowed the phone company to do whatever it does to expand circuits. We have a few coaxial cables running through steam tunnels between buildings and have drilled a few holes through thick concrete floors when it appeared necessary."[4]

As Cornell University changed to automated systems, there were problems with inadequate electrical outlets, telephone wiring, and shortages of workspace and furniture as more and more microcomputers and terminals were installed. These problems continued to tax the ingenuity and patience of staff and administrators. Catherine Murray-Rust notes: "We have lived through our fair share of traumatic experiences: installing wires in foot-thick stone walls; cut cables; endless waits for the telephone company; wires shorted out when floors were washed or waxed; once attractive offices filled with cables resembling huge piles of spaghetti; and we have survived."[5]

During the 1960s and 1970s, new library buildings were occasionally fitted with Q-decking (a flooring system with a steel pan forming the underside of a concrete slab where the steel is itself formed with lateral wire chases), cellular floors, raised floors where a mainframe might eventually be located, and knockout plugs in anticipation of additional major cabling requirements. Cable trays above the ceiling were specified. And organized vertical chases with service closets on each floor became part of building planning, but these tended to be centralized rather than distributed, and the capacity of main ducts quickly became filled.

Lighting problems were another category of adjustment in the early accommodation to computer technology, CRTs must not have light reflected on the screen from bright sources behind, or dramatic contrast or glare from light sources in front of the reader, nor should they be under intense direct overhead light. "Landscape office" furniture dividers were brought into many locations as a way of modifying existing space to moderate those lighting problems, and local task lighting became much more prevalent. However, architects, administrators, and designers really did not adequately address lighting problems and ergonomics until the 1980s.

In the 1970s staff complained about the duration of an individual's terminal time, uncomfortable chairs, the height of tables, the emission of rays from CRTs, and noise and heat produced by CRTs. Late in the decade the lessons of ergonomics were applied to the workplace. Strongly advanced by airplane cockpit design during the 1950s, ergonomics is the engineering of space and equipment design in response to the physical and psychological requirements of humans. The computer and related devices have brought an array of relations with new tools, and many of the human factors in these relations were usually overlooked. Thus, designers studied and adjusted lighting, posture, head inclination, arm reach, and tactile and audio feedback; they also accommodated social interactive needs of those learning and applying these new systems.

In many library applications of computers, staff in technical processing units commonly had assigned times to use a shared terminal. Training quickly became more routinized and equipment more familiar, leading to a more widely spread distribution of terminals in technical services. As David McDonald (University of Michigan) has stated, some libraries seem to prefer installing one or two individual terminals in a great many locations, while others install larger banks of four, six, or even eight terminals in one place.[6] (Berkeley just completed the installation of a terminal at each cataloger's desk, which certainly suggests that soon the size of groupings will be a moot issue). And these terminals take up ever-increasing space in all areas of the library. The cumulative effect is that older buildings are more crowded with equipment. Furthermore, work areas generally need modification in order to accommodate terminals under suitable ergonomic conditions.

Building design during the 1970s anticipated trends deriving from some of these factors. A case in point is the card catalog area in the Green Library at Stanford University, which was designed to accommodate at least eight online public access catalog (OPAC) terminals, and to provide special desk-height segments in each stand-up consultation counter for these terminals. In 1983 this configuration facilitated easy installation when the Socrates online catalog was made available to the public. (Elsewhere at Stanford, nearly all OPAC terminals are on counters). Lighting problems, even in buildings designed in the late 1970s, remain to a large extent to be improved in the future.

The 1980s

The past years may be characterized as accommodating older buildings and equipment to the new requirements of automation. Retrofitting was sometimes easy and was at other times difficult. What then are the current conditions?

The most significant is a recognition that building utility services must be adequate to support new requirements. Telecommunications is an issue noted by Susan K. Martin at Johns Hopkins University. "Even though the building is only twenty-four years old, the conduits are becoming full of the various wiring that has been installed in support of OCLC, RLIN, and the local system."[7] A number of publications deal with telecommunications, notably [those of] Heathcote and Stubley.[8] Those involved with planning libraries have provided new buildings with far greater power capacity. Data communication lines are now recognized as a utility, so that they are being brought to all college and university library buildings. In a number of instances, lines are being carried to faculty studies and graduate student cubicles within these library buildings.

Even at the present time, with over twenty years of library experience with online computer systems, some of the earlier difficulties of retrofitting buildings for computer systems are still being experienced. Of problems associated with materials used in buildings, asbestos is one of the most difficult as it has prevented or made prohibitively costly the addition of cabling for computer networking in a number of older buildings. And in Stanford's Green Library, installation of lines was frustrated by the presence of metal reinforcement or metal studs in the walls, making the attachment of external cable channeling difficult.

A more extensive example is Columbia University, where Paula Kaufman has stated that office automation activities in the Butler Library began in the mid-1970s and accelerated with the introduction of microcomputers. These devices "required considerable space juggling and the installation of additional power lines" because work sites are widely dispersed on the perimeter of a very large building. While it was not difficult to make these installations, often "one found (and still finds) insufficient power on one floor and must go up or down several floors to reach the right conduits. The simultaneous introduction of RLIN terminals required more extensive efforts, and terminals were placed not always for the convenience of staff but to preserve wood paneling and floor coverings and to utilize existing power lines."

In the 1980s, Kaufman continues, "the most troublesome installation in Butler was outside the main reading room in a circulation lobby, where we finally installed twelve CLIO (OPAC) terminals. Initial plans called for the cables to be pulled to the sixth floor, dropped through the reading room's false ceiling, and run through the existing closet. This proved to be impossible: there was no way to pull the cable without damaging ornate ceiling and wood panels, and the cost of erecting scaffolding was prohibitive. The ultimate solution was to pull the cabling up through the stacks and install it under the floor, bringing it to the wall opposite the circulation desk; this meant that we had to place the machines at a site different from the original one. Campus architect's approval to do the work, which required trenching into the marble floor base beneath the original floor covering, was required and delayed the project by several months. The original floor pieces were saved and replaced."[9]

With difficulties, even in the last couple of years, Columbia was nevertheless able to overcome many aesthetic as well as technical obstacles. At Harvard, Y.T. Feng reports the same type of problems being faced in the Widener Library.[10] As in most academic libraries, lack of space, inflexibility of original design, and lack of an installed utility capacity make some of the problems formidable.

Regarding wiring, we are learning that the average staff work position needs at least four electrical power outlets, which will quickly be exhausted by the terminal, modem, monitor, printer, desk lamp, electric pencil sharpener, fan, calculator, clock, electric eraser, and so on. For each workstation, what is desirable is a double grounded outlet for computer or other "electronic equipment" on a dedicated circuit for such use and one or even two separate double outlets for "electrical" appliances such as lights and fans.

In older buildings, flat wire and carpet tiles sometimes are an attractive way to provide access to power and signal throughout an open space. Flat wiring (e.g., ribbon cables) may have different electrical characteristics than the frequently required coaxial or twisted pair wiring which generally may not be substituted for computer signaling or networking applications. A form of phone cable and coaxial cable is available in a "flat wire" format. However, the impedance, noise immunity, and noise canceling properties of twisted and/or shielded wire are critical in many network applications and dictate the wire types. Matching the wiring to the application becomes generally more important as the distances become larger (i.e., more than a few feet). Certainly, any new facility requires many more circuits and a much broader network of distribution to provide for this need.

It is essential not to run signals together with power. Further, power circuits must be separate from those used for lighting, particularly if the lighting circuits are to be turned off each night, since certain computer systems require power to maintain their memory and thus must be left on. Indeed, a microcomputer file can be lost if lights are blinked to warn readers before the building closes.

In addition to power, computers need links to networks accommodated via twisted copper wire pairs, fiber optic cable and/or coaxial cable. At this time the library can expect both twisted pairs and coaxial to be distributed to each computer station. Fiber optics will certainly enter the library building, but currently they terminate in a "node" located in a closet or phone room. The need for a wiring closet of substantial size is increasing, and phone rooms in older buildings will become increasingly difficult to deal with in the future because of a typical lack of space for both wire/cable connections and for equipment. These distribution closets must not only be larger but must have environmental controls and power for active electronic components. Further, the vertical chases and service closets are becoming more widely distributed in large buildings to ease the future connections to computer-linked systems.

Networking in buildings has become as necessary a service utility as the telephone. To provide effectively for this new utility, the institution needs to adopt a building signal wiring standard that provides a harness, that is, telephone, computer, terminal, and video services preferably at a single wall outlet. In the past, networks have been installed in buildings on a piecemeal basis and tailored to the needs of the client, often after the building has been constructed. Because of his piecemeal approach, managers have on occasion made mistakes and caused inefficiencies in installing communications facilities in buildings. Links to other buildings on campus and off campus are now required.

Designers can reduce or eliminate problems by integrating the planning and installation of these communication services. Experience at Stanford indicates that savings of as much as forty percent of the wiring costs are possible when compared with separate telephone and local area network (LAN) installation. There are additional benefits, too. The delivery of multiple services to a single wall plate is not practical unless the design and installation are done as one project. Documentation and maintenance of signal distribution systems is simplified. And integrity of the installation is higher because the probability of damage to one system in the course of installing another is reduced. Therefore, at Stanford University, the telephone and network wiring for new buildings, like the other utility facilities that are part of the building, is now combined under a single standard and included as part of the capital cost for each building project.

There have been some difficulties in combining computer and other electronic technologies with certain book detection systems. In some cases, the computer terminal itself will set off the detection system or the detection system will interfere with the operation of the computer. Reducing the sensitivity of the detection system, moving the terminal away from the detection screen, or adding special shielding to the computer terminals has solved this problem in most cases.

A second concern with security systems deals with the floppy disk. Some libraries (Washington State University is an example) have made arrangements to pass the disks around security detection screens even though the vendors of the security system claim this is not necessary. It is very clear however that any magnetic storage device must be kept well away from the security system device that alters the magnetism of a strip of material in the book. This procedure should not present an overwhelming problem until there is a substantial number of books with floppy disks in them. In this case, there must be special handling of materials associated with magnetic memory devices in the checkout process.

Heat became less of a concern as vacuum tubes gradually gave way to transistors and solid-state circuitry, yet equipment grouped together can still create a serious problem. File servers on local networks and/or minicomputers produce a considerable amount of heat as well. Reed College Library indicated that one reason for choosing a particular automated system was the fact that it did not need a climate-controlled environment. Yet, with Reed's microcomputers in a large catalog department space, the combination of lights, people, and computer equipment generates enough heat to create unpleasant working conditions in the summer.

Online catalogs with printers are found in growing numbers of libraries (including Stanford's), and laser jet and ink jet printers make it possible to provide that service without noise difficulties in most public parts of the library. In the current building design for Mills College, the library is planning all online catalog consultation stations to be at stand-up counter height in order to discourage users from spending unnecessarily long periods of time at the terminal. Typically, libraries have at least two-thirds of the OPAC terminals on stand-up counters, with a very few at sit-down height; the latter can be sought out by an individual with a long and complex task or by a patron in a wheelchair. OPAC terminals are also placed on stack floors and in periodical reading rooms. Sunken circulation counter areas for automated equipment are reasonably common. Reference desks can now obviate the need for a lazy Susan by merely plugging in a patron monitor screen. Thus, the staff can search at the control terminal while conversing with a patron who watches the slave monitor faced in the opposite direction across the desk or counter.

At Pennsylvania State University Library, as described by Bruce D. Bonta, "One of the most critical issues ... is the physical placement and arrangement of new CD-ROM equipment. Since we believe that these indexes and services should be placed in close conjunction with the print volumes that they complement, we are having a lot of problems accommodating them physically. The reference room provides a spacious, effective area for the use of about 40,000 reference works, hundreds of indexes and abstracts, many on large index tables, and special areas such as the reference microfiche area. Opened in 1972, the room does not allow for the power needs, data transmission, or other communication possibilities that the CD-ROM technology requires. Most of the room has a coffered concrete ceiling, the floor is a 16" thick concrete slab that defies drilling, and the only power is available at the concrete support columns 22' apart. The present placement of the (library automation system) terminals, microfiche readers, CD-ROM stations, plus other electronic equipment used by patrons had taken nearly all of the available column locations. Placing a CD-ROM product that includes a data transmission feature from a remote computer, such as the WilsonDisc services, will be difficult for us without a lot of construction costs."[11]

For interlibrary lending services, the computer offers an alternative means of transmitting information. Libraries commonly transmit photocopies by mail. A few libraries have experimented with telefacsimile machines to transmit pages, but the staff time, telephone expense and length of transmission time have ordinarily made it difficult to justify this technology. The computer, with the ability to transmit large amounts of information digitally, offers a communication technology that will be advantageous to interlibrary loan.

While use of computer software requires training, the nature of the training will vary depending on the nature of the program as well as the people involved. There is a need within the academic institution for spaces where organized instruction can be provided. Such space can be thought of as being part of the library function in ways similar to bibliographic instruction. Both computer instruction and bibliographic instruction are necessary for access to and manipulation of information. For faculty, a separate room is sometimes provided for self-education, arranged in such a way that one can seek help and yet not feel embarrassment. However, Drexel University, which originally had a separate faculty room, found that separation was soon not needed. Students accept training as part of a course, but if it is not required, they also usually prefer a self-help environment.

In many libraries, typing rooms or small classrooms have been converted to microcomputer labs or to online classrooms for bibliographic and computer instruction, and for computer-assisted general course work. Cornell transformed two small public reading rooms into such facilities, and, while the renovations were modest, the educational effect of these facilities was substantial because of their heavy and successful use. At Cornell, Michigan, Stanford, and elsewhere, libraries have student microcomputer labs and public access terminals with more than 100 pieces of equipment and with some additional number available for faculty. Yet, at Williams College, Phyllis Cutler indicates that the library refused to give up reader space for personal computers (PCs), believing that noise would be a problem and that reading spaces should not be reduced in number; it did put thirty PCs in enclosed conference spaces.[12] Librarians must help determine whether provision of PCs should take up more space in academic libraries, or whether separate facilities apart from the library should be the norm. Increasingly, terminals are located in residence halls, with a student guru to provide local help, to decentralize general access to computer technology.

The social and privacy aspects of using computer technology are unresolved. Observation suggests that some students and many faculty are actually quite shy when they first face computer technology. They prefer to have semiprivate quarters in which to learn and perhaps to stumble while using the system. Steven Pandolfo of Mills College believes that those performing searches appreciate real privacy as well as quiet.[13] At UCLA, however, there are no places where there are private facilities and, as Russell Shank reports, "if the faculty are troubled in any way, they don't let us know."[14] At some institutions such as Reed College, the privacy aspect has been met by facilitating access to the catalog via modem from any faculty office on campus and from home.

People are social creatures, and there is a clear social aspect of many computer processes. Both library staff and library users need help and wish to discuss their experiences. Some people need little privacy and tolerate sound and commotion, and others feel quite the opposite, and libraries must accommodate this diversity. People interact more when using computers than when using most earlier technologies dealing with information. This socializing is due to a number of factors, including the reaction when the wrong key is hit, the waiting for something to happen (a fine time to say hello to your neighbor), the general confusion and lack of certainty (and thus the desire to ask "what now") as new computer users learn the systems, and so on. When computer-related activities are being introduced, conversation and teaching should be facilitated at some workstations since the need for help may occur at unpredictable times.[15]

If the first ten or fifteen years of online computer systems in academic libraries was a period of modest adjustment, recently there has been greater change (notably stemming from the OPAC and microcomputer clusters) and much better understanding of how people and automated systems interact. Spaces have been much more satisfactorily adjusted to accommodate the human needs. New buildings and the renovation of older buildings have led to less awkwardness in using new technology. Further, as Harold W. Billings reports of the University of Texas, "the ubiquitousness of the microcomputer/terminal throughout the library is, of course, obvious, but the hegira of the library terminal to non-library locations (and the lack of a need to provide large areas for a central library computer, as we believed we would require ten years ago) is quite striking."[16] And what of the future?

The 1990s

We project that the next five to ten years will see the equipment supporting computer technology becoming so common in staff offices and public areas that people will view computer access and transmission devices as an unsurprising advance over the combined services of the typewriter, the telephone, the photocopy machine and others in the extended family of information systems. Among changes coming about from multitasking and distributed processing and standards for linking technologies is the capacity through a single workstation to connect with a variety of databases and information systems. A person will be able to move easily back and forth, without having to deal with a different piece of hardware and a different query structure for each system.[17]

Carrying that a step further, we can expect that the workstations and information systems they connect with will be developed in a variety of models, some of which have great power and system elegance. Designers will create furniture to house the microcomputers that will be much more appropriate and flexible.[18] The personal workstations will have a keyboard integrated into a comfortable chair, with a printer attached and facsimile transmission capabilities included. Architects will design improved space and environmental conditions for workstations.[19]

There will continue to be rationale for traditional access to library materials (walking to the shelf and fetching a book, for example) and using computers for bibliographic control. Only to a very limited degree will computers be used for full text until late in the next decade. However, electronic publishing of heavily used materials, such as journals and major reference works, will come more rapidly than for the general collections, which tend to be much less heavily used than computer technology would economically support at this time.

Concerning seating for readers, the traditional functions of the library will continue and will be supplemented by the computer to a larger extent. Significant changes will result in the configuration and operation of reading areas, the reference areas, service points in general, and interlibrary loan, as well as spaces outside of the library by way of which one will be able to access information managed by or through the library.

And where and how will students use the PCs in class written work? With the ability to transmit digitized information comes the ability to manage that information and use it directly in the process of creating a paper for a classroom assignment. Initially the writing process may be heaviest within the library, simply because that is where access to the necessary networks and databases will be provided and facilitated, both in terms of the physical equipment and connections and staff assistance. As these devices will continue to be used along with traditional materials, the library as a site for this function makes a lot of sense for some students, though not for many others.

One postulate is that because of access to computers in the dormitory, the student culture will change to the degree necessary to support study in dormitories (a practice that at most times—exam time being an exception—has been virtually impossible because of student activities), and that the need for study space in libraries will diminish in the future, to be replaced with a need to provide facilities to supplement the student's PC capacity. These facilities may consist of publishing centers, training centers, a reserve desk for assigned software packages, and computer clusters. These clusters may have configurations supportive of networking, language practice, use of extensive computational equipment, or other activities seldom available on individual computers. Many of these functions are already visible in libraries.

We believe, on the other hand, that students will continue to find ways to disrupt serious study in the dormitory and that other sites—particularly the library—will continue to be in heavy demand for serious reading in quiet spaces and for the use of computers in support of study, course work, and research.

The large reference collection of thousands of volumes may in the future be reduced as more services are available and used online. Already in the 1980s, indexing and abstracting services are much less used in print form, and optical disk stations will take some of that space. We believe that the use of the reference room will increase demand upon space, rather than diminish it, as the need for database searching, teaching, and other computer-based work will not be easily offset by any possible reduction in the collections. And we are quite sure that the traditional book as we know it will remain, even in the reference room.

In relation to further design adjustments in library space planning, there are many questions. Will some staff work at home? Can the location of the catalog department be on a different floor from the main public catalog, or even in a different building? Will the technical processing functions be decentralized to a greater degree than at present? Can the interlibrary loan service be remote from the reference collection and the public catalog? Will library quarters include online classrooms? Will seating in libraries as a percentage of enrollment decrease slightly as students use a local area network to access information systems from distributed microcomputer laboratories and dormitory rooms? Will libraries need to accommodate portable computer devices brought in by library users for note-taking purposes? Will public workstations in libraries need to be arranged to accommodate considerable diversity in the physical and environmental preferences of readers? Will security of institutional equipment continue to be a significant concern?

The answer to each of these questions is yes, to some degree. Technological advancement, ease and simplicity of use, and financial considerations will strongly influence the rate of progress and the exact shape of the development.[20]

Let us expand this point by commenting on one aspect: portability. Currently, computers are not easily portable, and it is unlikely that staff will soon wish to read a computer screen while taking the bus to work, despite lap models with thin liquid crystal (LCD) screens. Computers occasionally carried by library users will be small, battery-powered and quiet; they will, despite some sound, be used even in an open reading room to record notes, quotations, or citations. Although workstations can be on wheels for greater portability, dependable links to communications lines are necessary and the faster systems of communications will be on networks that are considerably more sophisticated than the present common phone line. Each phone jack may also have a computer jack, and the computer can be taken from station to station when those jacks remain constantly "hot" (a practice currently discouraged by the pricing of telephone service through the Gandalf data switch but commonly free on campus network connections).

Thus, it seems reasonable to predict that, over the next decade, the computer will not be an instrument that is carried around more than was the portable typewriter in the 1950s. The real workhorse for readers as well as staff will remain a unit that is not portable. In using ubiquitous stationary equipment, people will carry information in the form of floppy disks, optical disks, at least for the near term. Or they will call up their data from a centralized file server to the workstation at which they are currently seated, and it will be sent over a high-speed communication network.

The general lack of portability also suggests that the book and notebook will be with us for a long time. Even if cost is not an acceptable argument for the desirability of traditional over high-tech formats, there are very practical reasons supporting the traditional technology—the book. It is a universally familiar format, compact, portable, attractive, often indexed, and readily accessed to any chapter or page. It facilitates, much more easily than does a database, the scanning or creative serendipity of reading a volume. And all one needs is adequate light for reading anywhere in the world. Meanwhile with a growing level of computer literacy and use, the computer will extend the capacity to know of the existence of books and other units of information, to find these items, to copy and transmit them, and to expand greatly the manipulative handling of information. Libraries, therefore, will not shrink, but rather grow and add an entirely new information management technology, expanding the library function and requiring a host of building adjustments.

At present, the concept of "smart buildings" is emerging. Smart buildings, sometimes called "intelligent buildings," have sophisticated technology, including computer-controlled card entrance and egress, computer-controlled environmental management, sophisticated data reception both on dedicated lines and by microwave transmitters, and electric power and data line outlets in every room in a number of locations with enough capacity for double or triple the current maximum requirement of the typical high-tech library office.[21] In the coming decade this electronically advanced design may be a strong influence over library building planning, especially planning to accommodate computer technology.

In smart library buildings, multiple vertical shafts with horizontal distribution ducts will be common for adapting to future change. Designers will provide spaces, probably on each floor and in many cases, several on each floor, for the equipment required to change from fiber optic transmission to coaxial or wire transmissions. These wiring closets of the future will be air-conditioned, for they may house network servers (computers, storage devices, etc.), and electronics. The library must house line filters or surge suppressors, often centrally in the wire closets. Lighting, including light levels, should be designed for computers and controlled by computers. Computers will monitor and control energy use. And the budget and the competition for space will more likely limit the capacity to install computer-supported systems than will power and signal (which seldom were truly limiting factors in the past). Technological skill will continue to make the computer smaller, cooler, easier to read, easier to use, more ergonomic, and so on. All of which suggests that the technology itself is changing more dramatically than the facilities that use and house the technology.

Operational changes in the library will come about as the technology requires or permits. Librarians will use card catalogs only for specialized uses such as miniaturized illustrations of prints mounted on cards. Library systems staff offices will remain in the building and grow in size as staff increases. There will be common use of machine-readable user cards, card-key controlled access to restricted areas, and printers distributed as photocopiers have been; and it can be hoped that digitized full-text transmission directly from bound materials will be economically provided. Despite use of battery-powered computers, outlets will need to be widely available for terminals that library users carry. Desks, counters and tables, and chairs, will take on new configurations in accommodating to the human activities of an advanced technological era.

Thus, in conclusion, it is evident that libraries are only beginning to move into the sophisticated age of information technology. The next ten years will see many further subtle changes in the workplace, some few significant functional relocations in new library buildings, and a more human-sensitive environment for using microcomputers and terminals. These developments will not come without cost. Perhaps the biggest unknown is the influence on this rate of development that derives from the national economy, as suggested below.

There can be little question that computer systems as they benefit library management and services are still developing at a rapid rate. They have not reached maturity by any means. And the rate at which laboratory developments can be turned into practical operating systems will also be conditioned by the profit possibilities of systems that are of interest to libraries. Unless the particular system is broadly supported in the general commercial sense, it probably will be too expensive for libraries to support.

It is therefore anyone's guess whether the world of higher education and scholarship can have funds available to enable libraries on college and university campuses to use the technology as fast as it is developed. If, in fact, there is a demonstrable benefit to the educational process, either in terms of the quality or rapidity of learning, or if the economics of higher education can be significantly improved, then one can suppose that funds would be available to advance information systems rapidly. On the other hand, if those benefits do not materialize or if the general economy is weak, it may be a long time before the more sophisticated advances in the laboratory are available in academic libraries.

In the meantime, there is every reason for enthusiasm about the advances that have been and are being made. The progress of the past three decades constitutes an exciting slice of library history.

Many items must be considered when planning a new building. Lighting issues involve the elimination of glare and the provision of power for computers separate from lighting circuits. Acoustical issues include the social aspects of computer use as well as the mechanical noise produced by the equipment, and the need to control or minimize the influence of noise on the more traditional use of libraries. Planners must consider the interaction of computer terminals with other systems, such as book security systems and information transmission systems, because they may be affected by electronic noise and power lines. General issues include space, portability, ergonomics, signal distribution, control of static electricity, power access, and security. The concept of a "smart" building may influence future building planning.

What is the effect of automated systems on other operations such as card catalogs, technical processing, access to remote databases by scholars, the function of the reference desk, and the process of teaching scholars how to use the computer effectively in support of research? The ability to transmit information and to access information from computer terminals will affect the way scholars use a library. And finally, but perhaps most importantly, what ramifications will emerge from the fact that the traditional book, book stacks, and reading areas will continue to be required as far into the future as we can see?

Notes

1. Professor Thomas Parke Hughes, writing in *Networks of Power: Electrification in Western Society, 1880–1930* (Baltimore: Johns Hopkins University Press, 1983) describes five phases in the evolution of complex technological systems. First comes the invention and development. Second is the process of technology transfer from one application and society to others. Third is system growth through resolution of system irregularities, critical problems, and component lags. Fourth comes substantial momentum providing an inertia of direct motion, often with rate accelerating and influenced by government agencies, professional

societies, educational institutions, and strong business concerns. And the fifth phase finds financiers and technologists expert in very large systems coping with problems of maturing growth (see pp. 14–17).

2. Susan K. Martin, Director, Milton S. Eisenhower Library, The Johns Hopkins University, letter to author, September 1987.

3. Luella R. Pollack, Director, E.V. Hauser Memorial Library, letter to author, September 2, 1987.

4. Russell Shank, University Librarian, University of California at Los Angeles, letter to author, September 8, 1987.

5. Catherine Murray-Rust, Assistant to the University Librarian, Cornell University Libraries, letter to author, September 17, 1987.

6. David R. McDonald, Systems Librarian, University Library, University of Michigan, Ann Arbor, letter to author, August 11, 1987.

7. Susan K. Martin, letter to author, September 1987.

8. Denis Heathcote and Peter Stubley, "Building Services and Environmental Needs of Information Technology in Academic Libraries," *Program* 1, no. 1 (January 1986): 26–38. See also Peter Stubley, "Equipment and Furniture to Meet the Requirements of the New Technology," paper read at the Eighth International Federation of Library Associations and Institutions, Seminar on Library Buildings, Aberystwyth, Wales, August 1987.

9. Paula T. Kaufman, Acting Vice President for Information Services and University Librarian, Columbia University, letter to author, August 26, 1987.

10. Yen-Tsai Feng, Librarian of Harvard College, telephone conversation with author, September 1987.

11. Bruce D. Bonta, "CD-Rom in the Social Science Reference Room," paper presented at International Federation of Library Associations and Institutions, Brighton, England, August 1987.

12. Phyllis L. Cutler, Director, Williams College, telephone conversation with author, September 1987.

13. Steven P. Pandolfo, College Librarian, Mills College, letter to author, August 21, 1987.

14. Russell Shank, letter to author, September 8, 1987

15. The social influence has also been dealt with in a paper at the ACRL Seattle conference: David C. Weber, "The Impact of Computer Technology on Academic Library Buildings," in *Academic Libraries: Myths and Realities*, ed. Suzanne C. Dodson and Gary L. Menges (Chicago: Association of College and Research Libraries, 1984), 202.

16. Harold W. Billings, Director, University of Texas Libraries, Austin, letter to author, November 18, 1987.

17. Carrol D. Lunau, "The Use of Electronic Mail and Interlibrary Loan Automation in Canada," paper presented at International Federation of Library Associations and Institutions, Brighton, England, August 1987.

18. See especially Margaret Beckman, "Library Equipment in a Changing Library Environment," paper read at International Federation of Library Associations and Institutions, Brighton, England, August 1987.

19. Heathcote and Stubley, "Building Services"; Stubley, "Equipment and Furniture."

20. Some general guidance can be found in Elaine and Aaron Cohen, *Automation, Space Management and Productivity* (New York: Bowker, 1981) and in Roscoe Rouse, Jr., "Planning Tomorrow's Library Building Today," paper presented at the Oklahoma Network of Continuing Higher Education Leadership Seminar, Norman, October 3, 1986.

21. One treatment is by Dean Schwenke, *Smart Buildings and Technology—Enhanced Real Estate* (Washington, D.C.: The Urban Land Institute, 1985).

Diversity and Retrenchment, 1946–1988, Part II

Unrelenting speed and force of expansion in scientific, technological, and military prowess were matched by equally dramatic changes in the social, cultural, and political makeup of modern America. Foremost among these developments was the Civil Rights movement for freedom, fairness, and equality of opportunity for American people of African descent. The context for this movement involved an acceleration of sentiment on behalf of blacks who had served in World War II, fighting fascism, waging war on behalf of freely elected Western democracies. Why would a black soldier, some reasoned, forcibly liberate Europe yet willingly forego basic liberties on American soil? Access to public accommodations, equal opportunity in education and employment and housing, and the right to vote, all were strategically and tragically abridged in postwar America especially in the South, the states of the former confederacy. A landmark event occurred in 1954 when the United States Supreme court ruled, in *Brown v. Board of Education of Topeka,* that racially separate educational facilities were inherently unequal, and that public education should proceed on an integrated basis.

Sustained, intensified pressure from black activists drove the society to slowly, painfully open up to people of color. In the early 1960s, freedom riders risked their lives to test separate court rulings that had outlawed segregated buses, trains, and terminal waiting rooms; such rulings had been systemically ignored, especially in southern states and municipalities, but activists eventually forced the federal government to take legal and protective measures on their behalf. Restaurants, theaters, and other venues began to accommodate blacks equally without the use of secondary seating or separate restrooms. Likewise, service stations, department stores, and other retail outlets integrated restrooms, water fountains, and lunch counters. Having accepted equality in providing customer services, businesses eventually adopted policies of minority hiring.

In 1964 federal legislation outlawed segregation based on race, color, sex, national origin, or religion; the law was designed to eliminate discriminatory practices in education, public accommodations, and labor and housing. The voting rights act of 1965 was equally sweeping, as it struck down racial discrimination in voting, thus allowing black access to the ballot box according to provisions of the 15th amendment to the U.S. Constitution. The voting rights law directed the federal government to join with black citizens in overturning repressive and intimidating measures such as poll taxes, literacy tests, and other devices created by state and local officials to deny suffrage to people of color.

We realize that many individuals, reading in the twenty-first century, find these legal necessities difficult to comprehend. Surely, people reason, the privileges and responsibilities of citizenship in the "land of the free and the home of the brave" should have been transparently applied to every legal resident of the United States. But such ideals have often been fraught with oppositional realities, and repressive codes and other discriminatory practices had become widespread especially at local and state levels. Such practices were challenged, of necessity, with direct action marches that were intended to be peaceful and respectful but that often drew responses that were aggravated, intense, violent, life-threatening, even murderous. In effect, dominant white power structures would not yield positions of privilege without dissembling, deceiving, subverting democratic processes, or resorting to violence.

Institutions of higher education, with mounting hopes and ambitions for a significant role in American society, were not immune to these overwhelming forces. Sometimes, the colleges functioned as center stage for civil rights activists bent on transforming American life. The force of law, occasionally accompanied by state or federal troops quelling civil unrest, was required to make integration a reality at the University of Georgia (1961), the University of Mississippi (1962), and the University of Alabama (1963) to cite three examples. The entering students, their legal representatives, and governors of their respective states temporarily became household names as the national press covered major civil rights events. Colleges and universities across the nation eventually integrated, if not initially to honor constitutional protections then certainly to obtain grants and long-term loans by complying with new civil rights regulations. During the 1970s, educators programmatically befriended people of color, launching affirmative action plans and aggressively recruiting blacks and other racial minorities as students, professors, and administrators.

The new legislation eventually gave blacks unprecedented access to American higher education. (They had, decades earlier, turned to the HBCUs and to resources such as the United Negro College Fund but the more robust, better funded research universities beckoned to everyone including students of color). The major universities offered wide and deep curricular options, world-renowned graduate programs, and deeply connected professional experts. Fortunately for higher education and libraries and for the entire nation, segregation was losing legal, political, and economic viability, and options for minority enrollment all across the country were expanding at unprecedented speed especially in the late 1960s and throughout the 1970s.

Encouraged by the success of civil rights activists, multiple social movements began to influence the society, redefining structural and personal relationships. Higher education often stood front and center as a national institution undergoing radical change. In 1964 the "free speech movement" emerged at the University of California where students challenged university restrictions on political activity. Free speech as a strategically defined political act subsequently spread to campuses across the nation with students speaking out, opposing the American war in Vietnam and protesting other social problems. Students denounced racism (a number of white students had joined black counterparts, for example, in the widely reported Mississippi Freedom Summer project of 1964). Fresh support emerged on behalf of equal rights for women, many of whom complained that their own contributions to civil rights and antiwar initiatives had been systemically overlooked by male-dominated leadership. Student activism had launched far beyond campus, routinely challenging values that marked the nation as a whole. Thus, did young people experiment with communal living arrangements and hallucinatory drugs, and begin to question American capitalism, militarism, patriarchy, and other characteristic interests.

Students eventually rebelled against the universities themselves as impersonal, overly bureaucratic, and insensitive to their concerns; and they transitioned from teach-ins and peaceful demonstrations to direct action. They successfully challenged *in loco parentis*, and they attacked the rigidity of the undergraduate core curriculum which, at various intervals, has undergone major revision. In colleague with the professoriate, students pressed for an expanding curriculum to incorporate African American (sometimes called black) studies, also Latino and other ethnic and immigrant studies, and women's studies. From these perspectives, scholars began to challenge the white male dominated, top-down American national narrative, and to re-examine history, literature, and the social sciences using a wider, more colorful lens. Eventually, the students' moral fervor became one essential force in the national decision to begin withdrawing American troops from Vietnam. But in the process of becoming radicalized and experimenting with alternative lifestyles many students, along with professorial sympathizers, cost their universities the political and financial support of voting citizens who came to regard them as elite and self-focused, lacking appreciation for the opportunities at their disposal. These realities came full force during the economic contractions of the early 1970s, taxpayers' revolts of the late 1970s, and throughout the 1980s. Private universities would, thereafter, rely increasingly on shifting combinations of tuition increases, federal grants, and the largesse of their donor base. Public universities encountered the same parameters and pursued similar solutions but, with shrinking appropriations from the states, the publics were forced to expand development operations and to begin raising money as never before.

The impact of the larger society, especially in economics, management, politics, and institutional culture, was felt throughout academic librarianship. David Kaser discussed these currents, describing the irrepressible optimism of the early-mid 1960s as constituting unrealistic expectations. According to Kaser, the public and the press had come to expect expansion of library computer driven services; college presidents expected librarians to cut costs; faculty expected to obtain whatever resources they needed; students expected round the clock service; and staff expected regular increases in compensation. But the economic conditions that had given rise to such lofty visions proved not to be sustainable as the decade of the 1960s drew to a close. Library directors could sense the coming dislocations, perhaps earlier than could the constituents they served, and Kaser noted that, during 1966–68, ARL member directors fell, one after another due to "coronaries and other stress-induced diseases."[1]

In discussing the late 1960s, David Kaser reviewed the movement for shared governance, launched from a congeries of impulses floating across academe, with students opposing the war and the military draft, challenging elected and appointed authority in general, and demonstrating and sometimes occupying university buildings in ways that were violent and life-threatening. Kaser noted that the drive for power was often predicated on the misconception that some entity—university or library administrator—actually held power that it was reluctant to share. The reality, according to Kaser, was that managerial circumstances were quite complex, fraught as they were with many more constraints than were apparent to those on the outside looking in. He identified various models that he expected to guide academic librarians in the 1980s and beyond, predicting that faculty status, rather than a corporate management or collective bargaining model, would emerge as the dominant strategy for stabilizing and expanding librarian influence in academe.

The main political and social currents of the 1960s and 70s yielded a vibrant professional literature of which Fay M. Blake's (1920–2011) retrospective is but one superb example.[2] Blake connected the librarians' drive to serve the previously underserved with the strong impulse to achieve faculty rank in the academy. She argued that enhanced librarian status had become essential to efforts to raise the status of information seekers, essentially claiming the librarian's role as an advocate on behalf of the information interests of the student on campus and the citizen in the community. We included Edward G. Holley's essay on the history of ACRL in the interest of reprinting essays with only the broadest possible interpretation. (Thus, we have not reprinted articles devoted to individual librarians or to individual libraries). We did, however, reprint this one history of an institution, which Holley described as the fifth largest library association in the world. The breadth of ACRL's interest in teaching and researching and publishing offers keen insight into the issues of the era, and Holley's finely-honed analysis traces the association's struggle for a federated rather than a dependent connection to ALA, and examines ACRL's programs on collection development, user services, management, and other defining functions of academic library practice. The scope of ACRL activity offers a glimpse of the ambition and commitment marking academic librarianship during the four plus decades of the postwar period.

Notes

1. David Kaser, "The Effect of the Revolution of 1969–1970 on University Library Administration," in *Academic Libraries by the Year 2000: Essays Honoring Jerrold Orne*, ed. Herbert Poole (New York: Bowker, 1977), 65.
2. David M. Battles, *The History of Public Library Access for African Americans in the South Or, Leaving Behind the Plow* (Lanham, Maryland: Scarecrow Press, 2009); Bruce D. Bonta and James G. Neal, eds., *The Role of the American Academic Library in International Programs* (Greenwich, Connecticut: JAI Press, 1992); Patricia Senn Breivik, *Open Admissions and the Academic Library* (Chicago, Illinois: American Library Association, 1977); James V. Carmichael, Jr., ed., *Daring to Find Our Names: The Search for Lesbigay Library History* (Westport, Connecticut: Greenwood, 1998); Robert S. Freeman and David M. Hovde, eds., *Libraries to the People: Histories of Outreach* (Jefferson, North Carolina: McFarland, 2003); Kathleen Heim and Kathleen Weibel, eds., with assistance from Diane J. Ellsworth, *The Role of Women in Librarianship, 1876–1976: The Entry, Advancement and Struggle for Equalization in One Profession* (Phoenix, Arizona: Oryx, 1979); Suzanne Hildenbrand, ed., *Reclaiming the American Library Past: Writing the Women In* (Norwood, New Jersey: Ablex, 1996); E.J. Josey, ed., *The Black Librarian in America Revisited* (Metuchen, New Jersey: Scarecrow, 1994); E.J. Josey, ed., *New Dimensions for Academic Library Service* (Metuchen, New Jersey: Scarecrow, 1975); E.J. Josey and Kenneth Shearer, eds., *Politics and the Support of Libraries* (New York: Neal-Schuman, 1990); Cheryl Knott, *Not Free, Not for All: Public Libraries in the Age of Jim Crow* (Amherst, Massachusetts: University of Massachusetts Press, 2015); Claire K. Lipsman, *The Disadvantaged and Library Effectiveness* (Chicago, Illinois: American Library Association, 1972); Eric Moon, ed., *Book Selection and Censorship in the Sixties* (New York: Bowker, 1969); Eric Moon and Karl Nyren, eds., *Library Issues: The Sixties* (New York: Bowker, 1970); Toni Samek, *Intellectual Freedom and Social Responsibility in American Librarianship, 1967–1974* (Jefferson, North Carolina: McFarland, 2001); Patricia Glass Schuman, ed., *Social Responsibilities and Libraries: A Library Journal/School Library Journal Selection* (New York: Bowker, 1976); John Mark Tucker, ed., *Untold Stories: Civil Rights, Libraries, and Black Librarianship* (Champaign, Illinois: Graduate School of Library and Information Science, 1998); Kathleen Weibel, "The Evolution of Library Outreach 1960–75 and Its Effect on Reader Services: Some Considerations," University of Illinois, *Occasional Papers*, 156. (Urbana, Illinois: Graduate School of Library and Information Science, 1982); and Shirley A. Wiegand and Wayne A. Wiegand, *The Desegregation of Public Libraries in the Jim Crow South: Civil Rights and Local Activism* (Baton Rouge, Louisiana: LSU Press, 2018).

In the Eye of the Storm
Academic Libraries in the Sixties
Fay M. Blake

We remember the Sixties most vividly for the turmoil on university and college campuses, but somehow libraries on those campuses seemed to stand aside from what was happening. Like the eye of the storm, the academic library remained mostly serene in the midst of turbulence. Barbara Anderson, who was at San Francisco State in the period of a bitter and violent strike in 1968, writes in "Ordeal at San Francisco State College":

> The library became the choice vantage point for demonstration watching.... Depending on the particular day's activities, great crowds would congregate at the windows on all three floors to watch the happenings from the safety of the building, and many of the television photos were taken from library windows. On this side of the building, the noise of the loudspeakers and the shouting and yelling was often so disturbing that little work could go on; however, on the other side of the building which faced the street, work proceeded as usual except when a student assistant would burst in with stories of the events taking place outside.[1]

While momentous events were taking place outside, events with important political significance—the realization of the overlooking of nonwhite students' needs, the catapulting of a vocal, beret-bedecked university president into the Senate in Washington, and the occupation of a college campus by police—the library itself remained a place from which to review the events. To Anderson: "Despite the picketing, shouting, and bloodshed, we continued building our book collections" and "we still managed to continue doing things that come naturally to librarians; we kept a bibliography of articles about the strike, a giant scrapbook of the news clippings was prepared, and collections of leaflets and broadsides ... were sorted out and arranged...."[2]

Anderson's article is eloquent testimony to the "natural" function of the academic librarian: to continue building and arranging "our" collections without regard to the changes taking place in the world around us. There is a certain admirable strength in such stubborn distancing. As the strike on the San Francisco campus wore on, the library became the object of harassment by frustrated or mischievous strikers—bomb threats, stink bombs, "bookins" in which hundreds of volumes were deliberately taken from shelves and misplaced, damage to the card catalog. But those librarians and student assistants who remained at work carried on, and all of us are intellectually the richer for the bibliographies and scrapbooks they produced. This is not meant to belittle the ideas or the efforts of the academic librarians who did not participate in the strike.

Some of the Black Student Union's "non-negotiable" demands were outrageous and simply impossible to grant. The violence was unacceptable (violence precipitated by both sides: fires and bombs and injuries to both strikers and policemen); moreover, supporters of the students' demands were not necessarily in accord with the demands and actions of the American Federation of Teachers, which joined the strike. Undoubtedly those librarians who continued to work in the midst of the confusion had examined the issues, but the inevitable conclusion must be that the issues were really extraneous to the library. Its natural functions—acquiring, organizing, and distributing information—existed apart from the surrounding society.

If the librarians considered the library to be an Olympian haven, the FBI certainly did not, as the case of Bucknell University in 1971 revealed. The FBI used an undercover informant in the university library to spy on the activities of librarians there. Boyd Douglas, recruited out of the penitentiary at Lewisburg, was paid by the FBI to use his position as a work-study student in the library to report on social activities which Reverends Daniel and Philip Berrigan and Sister Elizabeth McAllister attended. Zoia Horn and Pat Rom, head and assistant head of the Reference Department at the Bucknell Library, were subpoenaed to testify before a grand jury on Douglas's sworn—and forsworn—testimony. And Horn eventually went to jail for three weeks when she refused to be a government witness during the Berrigan trial.[3]

Most of those academic librarians who participated actively in the tumultuous events of the Sixties began with an assumption that no individual and no institution can, or should, stand apart from the surrounding society—that standing apart really meant supporting the status quo. Whether that assumption is borne out is probably impervious to anything but empirical evidence, but the small minority of academic librarians who attempted to influence change left a mark on the academic libraries of this country. Some of them had been active around social issues all of their lives but found it simpler or even necessary to separate social action from professional action. Lonely as it may have been to participate in a silent picket line at the Federal Building in Los Angeles against the War in Vietnam in the early Sixties, that was still easier for a librarian to do than to stand in silent protest with only one faculty member on the UCLA campus while colleagues from the library passed by with heads averted. And sending resolutions against the war was far easier in the church or the fraternal organization to which one belonged than trying to bring a resolution on Vietnam to the floor of the American Library Association. "The war has nothing to do with libraries," we heard. "ALA doesn't get involved in broad political issues."

As the national political scene began to heat up, however, it became clearer that even in the academic library the need for change was becoming critical. Although the academic library was shielded from the intensifying problems of the public library, college and university librarians began to fear that their professional functions were shriveling. While questions about the usefulness and ultimately the continued existence of the public library were beginning to surface, academic libraries were still perceived as essential, even if only to satisfy academic accreditation procedures. But the librarians in the academic setting—never regarded as equals, or even as full professionals—were in danger of losing even the minimal control they could still exert over the acquisition, organization, and distribution of resource materials.

Librarians have historically been perceived as less than professional by university administrators and faculty. Their role in the university was outside the traditional functions of research and teaching, and therefore they were something of an anomaly in the collegial brotherhood. To library users, too, the librarian was a lady behind the desk who told you how to get to the reserve book room or confirmed that the book you wanted wasn't available. Paul Wasserman describes the user's view of the librarian:

> The librarian is seen as essentially a custodian of books. Indeed, the client does not see himself as a client. For in a client relationship, he is prepared to solicit the services of an expert consultant in whom he has faith. When there is faith in librarianship, it is almost exclusively related to locating a published work or citation, seldom to problem-solving.[4]

Many librarians themselves accepted this subordinate "handmaiden's" role and some had even entered the profession in order to *not* be burdened with professional challenges. It was a notorious fact that library schools were full of "retreads," who came to librarianship after they had failed in other, more demanding, professions; and, that library school curricula as well as selection procedures provided havens for genteel bookish types who didn't want to cope with demanding clients or theoretical concepts or organization infighting. (See also Bundy, "The Social Relevancy of Library Education." In Bundy and Stielow, eds., *Activism in American Librarianship, 1962–1973* [New York: Greenwood, 1987]).

Reinforcing the subprofessional status of the librarians was the built-in institutional hierarchy under which they operated. Library directors usually, but by no means universally, were accepted as part of the academic community. Yet their underlings were usually seen as precisely that—employees who work under the same rules as the university's secretaries, file clerks, or custodians. Since work schedules were prescribed by administrators, the professional function in which decisions about the way a client's need could be met became an impossibility. Even the lowliest lecturer on campus determined what went on in his or her own classroom, even if constrained by certain limits. Librarians had their jobs described for them by their next higher supervisor.

In addition to the heavy hand of historical precedent which delimited the professional function of the librarian, a new threat was rapidly developing. It was beginning to be clear in the Sixties that library and information technology was evolving so quickly that the incoming generation of librarians would soon be facing a radically different environment. Machines, especially computers, would be taking over many manual functions and would soon be making a more efficient job of it. Many of the librarians' most intricate procedures were easily being adapted to machine processes. Consequently, it looked as if even the very limited decision-making by librarians would be turned over to computer experts who could either learn what librarians knew about the client-professional relationship or who didn't need to know it to make data processing decisions. Fay Blake, reflecting on the circumscribed role of academic librarians, calls them "rather a useless lot":

> Now let's try to imagine what would happen if every academic librarian in the city or the country went out on strike—or was suddenly struck down with leprosy—who would know or care? The population as a whole? Not likely. They don't know we exist. The faculty? In a pig's eye. They regard us as nuisances anyway. The university administration? Don't you believe it. The only time they think of the library is just before an accreditation team swoops down, and you can always divert them to a new cyclotron. The students? Well, maybe a few who use the library, but only if the libraries closed down and our clerical staffs could probably run them quite well without us.

Blake means her rather acid assessment to shock and goes on to indicate ways in which the academic librarian could and should become a useful member of the academic community. She exhorts them to "learn how to become scholars—not pedants, but scholars in areas of real social concern … how to discriminate between useful scholarship and arid scholarship."[5]

As the upheavals of the Sixties proceeded, some academic librarians began to translate the need for social change into the necessity to change themselves into professionals recognized as a valuable part of the academic community. This may seem to be rampant self-aggrandizement and did appear so to many librarians at the time. Undoubtedly an element of self-seeking did propel some of the actions. The possibilities for improved working conditions, better pay, and sabbaticals were attractive lures, but at least some of the agitation for changes in the status of academic librarians was powerfully stimulated by the desire to provide better services to the academic community. Librarians, who sincerely wanted to meet professional challenges, recognized that they could do so only by changing the way they were forced to work.

The recognition that the ability to make independent professional decisions was necessary to improve library service led to the recognition that librarians, like teachers on campus, needed academic or faculty status. They needed tenure in order to protect them from being dismissed for unorthodox professional decisions or from arbitrary or prejudiced administration action. They needed sabbaticals, educational leaves, and access to research grants in order to deepen their understanding of both their own discipline, librarianship, and the disciplines of the students and scholars they helped. They needed more flexible work schedules away from desks and among the public they served. They also needed a more equitable salary scale congruent with their educational backgrounds and experience. Perhaps, more basic than all these was the need to participate democratically in decisions about the campuses where they worked.

Without formally recognized academic status, most librarians were excluded from academic senates and were unable to discuss issues with their colleagues, not even issues that vitally affected the library. The howls of anguished opposition to academic status for librarians began immediately—from faculty, from university administrators, from library administrators, and from librarians themselves. Most of the objections emphasized the differences between librarians and faculty; librarians didn't teach and weren't required to publish the results of research. Some librarians were vocal about their contentment with the status quo. They didn't teach or publish and didn't want to. Counterarguments began to appear in the library press, in educational journals, at library conferences, even in academic senates when librarians could inveigle invitations.

Librarians *did* teach informally in the library when they showed clients how to find materials, in classrooms where they were invited to teach classes how to make effective use of the library, and in their own classrooms where they taught courses on the intricacies of research in the library. At the University of California at Berkeley, for example, librarians staffed a course on bibliography and research in which more than a thousand students a year enrolled. Librarians there also taught faculty seminars in which research techniques in various disciplines were demonstrated, a course so popular with the faculty that it required preregistration. Librarians also published though they usually had to research, write, and publish on their own time after their regular stints in the library. But arguments for academic status also pointed out that on many campuses faculty were not required to publish, and that it would be possible to develop other criteria for the evaluation of librarians based on their knowledge, expertise, and performance.

As the librarians' drive for academic status began to develop, they realized that not only was their function on campus anomalous but that their status was, more often than not, undefined and undefinable. In 1962, for example, then President Clark Kerr of the University of California suddenly announced that university librarians would now be considered academic personnel. Robert B. Downs, in one of his annual reports on the status of university librarians, cited Kerr's laconic announcement as evidence of the improving situation for academic librarians.[6] When librarians at the university tried, however, to find out precisely what this meant, they discovered to their dismay that they had gained nothing and had, as a matter of fact, lost ground. Personnel actions for librarians were still handled by non-academic personnel officers, but the few perks to which non-academics were entitled—overtime pay, grievance and appeal procedures—would not be available to librarians. Requests for more substantial changes in status, even requests for clarification, were summarily refused.

Other academic librarians throughout the country began to have similar experiences. Attempts to regularize academic status were almost uniformly rebuffed with a few honorable exceptions, such as Ohio State University and the unique University of Illinois, where the professional staff had obtained academic status back in 1944. It gradually began to dawn on academic librarians that improvement in their status would not be given but would have to be fought for and that any possibility for a successful fight lay not in individual but in collective action.

It became clear that academic librarians were unorganized. True, the Association of College and Research Libraries represented academic librarians in the American Library Association, and it even had a Committee on Academic Status established in the late fifties. But no one could discover that the committee of the ACRL or the ALA had ever taken any action on the status of librarians; nor did they seem particularly eager to take any action when approached by librarian members. It also became clear that ACRL was led by and predominantly represented library directors and top administrators, a group uninterested in or hostile to formal academic status for librarians. Further, it was evident that most librarians were not members of ACRL or ALA or their state library association and were in great measure excluded from much of the activity of these organizations, precisely because they did not have the advantages of faculty status. As a subspecies on campus, most of them had little access to travel funds or paid leave for attending conferences or committee meetings. Becoming active in the librarians' associations meant digging into one's own poorly lined pocket.

In spite of such difficulties a number of librarians did try to work through the ACRL for recognition of their need for academic status. They wound their weary way through resolutions, lobbying, floor debate, committee reports, and the rest of the organizational procedures under General Roberts's straitjacket. The process took years. One measure of the difficulties in getting action out of ACRL was the fact that the first publication from ACRL about academic status did not appear until 1970, and almost every article in that publication was by a library director.[7] None of the dozens of librarians who had worked during the previous years marshaling the arguments, gathering the evidence, and enduring the parliamentary maneuvers was asked to contribute to Lewis Branscomb's collection.

At the same time as the librarians were trying to elicit some sort of response from ACRL and ALA, they were beginning to experiment with other forms of organization and collective action on campuses across the country. At the University of California at Berkeley, librarians formed a chapter of the University Federation of Teachers AFL-CIO in May 1965 soon after the Free Speech movement shock waves.[8] They were primarily concerned with formal grievance procedures, overtime pay, and career advancement. In 1968 the union chapter presented a full-scale Library Improvement Program to the new university librarian. This proposed not only tenure and promotional opportunities for librarians but also improved service hours and other suggestions for making the library more responsive to students and faculty. This sense of responsibility and obligation to the academic community permeated almost every contribution to the discussions around academic status.

No matter what form their organization took, academic librarians accepted their responsibility to improve service to their clientele. Many argued that improvement in the status of librarians was a necessary preliminary to making the library more useful. Robert Haro, writing about the growing trend toward collective action in academic libraries, noted the almost universal demand for a "guarantee of librarian participation in the formulation of policy both within the library and the institutions."[9] He stressed the growing militancy of the librarians not only around issues of economic injustice but for a share in the educational process and predicted that democratic participation will result in "higher levels of productivity."

Although there were a few other examples of union organization among university librarians, most academic librarians turned to other forms of collective organization. At the University of California, librarians began for the first time in the history of that institution to organize a librarians' association. The effort began almost casually at the Los Angeles campus in early 1967, but very soon it became apparent that the combined strength of librarians on all nine campuses of the university would be a more potent force for collective action. It was also clear that only a university-wide organization would have any chance of formal recognition by the university—a type of association parallel to the Academic Senate, since librarians were not about to be accorded membership in that august body. To everyone's surprise, the idea took hold, and by April 1968 the more than 550 librarians at the University of California had elected representatives to the first meeting of the Assembly of the Librarians Association of the University of California. The objectives of the fledgling association were:

    1. To create a forum where matters of concern to librarians at the University of California may be discussed and an appropriate course of action determined;

    2. To set and enforce professional standards and the rights, privileges, and obligations of librarians at the University of California;

    3. To promote full utilization of the professional skills and abilities of librarians, to improve the library service and collections, and to protect librarians at the University of California;

    4. To propose to the University administration, at the earliest possible date, that this organization be recognized by the University of California as the official statewide body within the University structure where librarians have the opportunity to participate in the deliberative and decision-making process of the University. This group would function for librarians in a fashion similar to the manner in which the statewide Academic Senate functions for officers of instruction.[10]

This last objective was to involve many years of effort by many librarians in the system and scores of meetings, discussions, reports, and debates before it became a reality.

LAUC [Librarians Association of the University of California] gave tremendous impetus to all the librarians in their efforts to define their status and functions. At UCLA, for example, a conference of librarians was organized in early 1969 at which a series of papers was presented for discussion. The UCLA Librarians Association, "formed in response to general pressures of unrest," was seen as offering "new opportunities [to librarians] for participation in University affairs."[11] The papers dealt with salaries, peer evaluation, tenure, grievance procedures, sabbaticals and other pressing issues.

Other academic librarians were organizing, too, and one of the new tactics became joint actions in which organized librarians supported each other. While university librarians in California were developing their association, librarians in the state college system had already become involved in a fight for recognition. In 1965, California state college librarians were presenting their proposals for faculty status and developing their State College Librarians Round Table.[12] Eventually they persuaded their colleagues in the California Library Association to act collectively against the utterly recalcitrant administration for the state college system. For the first and only time in its history the CLA invoked sanctions against the state college system for refusing to act even after the federal senate had voted overwhelmingly in support of academic status for librarians. University and state college librarians shared experiences, position papers, demands, and arguments. They supported each other's resolutions in the California Library Association and worked together in the ACRL. In fact, for academic librarians the conferences of state and national library associations became convenient places to meet and to plan joint actions, and librarians found themselves coming together more frequently and in more substantive ways.

As a direct result of the flurry of action among academic librarians, there began to appear new proposals and discussion about improving the functions of the academic libraries. Most of the discussions centered on two areas: the improvement of services to the traditional library clientele and the extension of services to hitherto unserved and disregarded clienteles. Improvement in the status of librarians would lead almost inevitably to better service for scholars on campus. Librarians enabled to improve their own scholarship and skills would better understand the problems of users. Librarians responsible for the acquisition of scholarly materials and able to confer collegially with the users of such materials would provide more and better resources. Current awareness services could apprise scholars of what new materials were available in their disciplines. Improved document delivery would provide scholars with material more rapidly. Centralized and, therefore, consistent cataloging would make libraries easier to use.[13]

Academic librarians were also making it clear that the undergraduate student population ought to be served in new and more effective ways. Discussion on the efficacy of undergraduate libraries surfaced. Librarians were studying undergraduates' use of the library and their need for instruction in the use of the library. There was a new and revived interest in establishing advisory student library committees or bringing students even more directly into library governance through appointments to library policy committees, in addition to putting students in charge of browsing collections, regularly soliciting their suggestions, and including their contributions in the evaluation of librarians. Librarians were being charged with the responsibility of helping linguistically, academically, or financially disadvantaged students through the maze of college life.[14]

Academic librarians were also responding to the issues that were surfacing explosively outside the campus in the Sixties. The superbly orchestrated civil rights campaign, the heightened actions against many forms of racism, the evolving feminist movement were all having an impact within the libraries; first, of course, in broadening the acquisitions of academic libraries in support of, and occasionally even in advance of, the expanding curriculum. Black studies, ethnic studies, and women's studies programs were being reflected in library resources. But, in addition, the question of an expanded clientele and expanded responsibility began to be discussed.

What, if anything, did the campus library owe to the community outside its carefully guarded gates? Bill Hinchcliff called on college libraries to provide "able, socially responsible staff members ... to focus the college's available knowledge and skill upon the removal of obstacles to the advancement of the people of the community."[15] He cited war, racism, and urban problems as some of the community issues the library should be attacking. Fay Blake advocated the development of library-based programs not part of the orthodox curriculum and the inclusion of Blacks, browns, the poor, and other outsiders on library policy committees.[16]

The most eloquent argument for extending use of the academic library to the outside community came from E.J. Josey, who moderated a symposium on community use of academic libraries in 1967. Coming as he did from a predominantly Black college in the South, he recognized how essential an information resource the college library could be to many not formally enrolled. In the face of objections raised by other academic librarians—security, legal limitations, staff shortages, or added strains on budgets—he pleaded for discarding outworn traditions and for a concentrated imaginative effort to overcome difficulties and to put the college library at the service of the whole community.[17]

The salient question arising from this spate of theoretical and practical activity must be: Did it do any good or was it just a blast of hot air leaving the academic library essentially where it had been? There is substantial evidence that many things changed. Academic status and its prerequisites are no longer the outrageous novelties they were when the concept was introduced and debated in the early sixties. By 1973 more than half the academic librarians in the country had some form of academic status, and many more were enjoying various constituent benefits. Peer evaluation has become the norm rather than the exception. Educational leaves (if not sabbaticals), access to research grants and travel funds, and tenure are not unusual. Even where they do not exist, the idea is not brand-new heresy. Librarians know these benefits do exist and that academic libraries in which they are the practice have not fallen apart. Unfortunately, in some institutions where the benefits have been obtained there are now significant administrative efforts to withdraw or diminish them. These developments in no way lessen the value of the librarians' efforts. They only serve to emphasize once more that no struggle is ever fully won.

The right and the necessity for librarians to engage in collective action is now so broadly accepted that it no longer involves the massive organizational efforts of the sixties. Many academic librarians now have membership in their campus academic senate or, as in the case of the University of California, have their own equivalent, a librarians' association officially recognized by the university administration. Librarians' unions, not very widespread among academic librarians, nevertheless continue to function. At the University of California, a majority of librarians recently voted for the union to represent them, and negotiations for a contract are proceeding at the time of this writing. There is little question any longer that librarians need grievance and appeal procedures and the protection of collective action.

The hope for full professional status for librarians has not been entirely realized. Inflexible work schedules, hierarchical organizations, and routinized work assignments persist. With the prevalence of machines some academic librarians find themselves sitting before a screen all day, far removed from the challenging decisions a professional should be making. Pay scales lagging behind other campus jobs also persist despite the valiant work of comparable worth campaigns.

Sparked by the pioneer theoretical work of the feminist movement, the concept has grown that predominantly feminine professions, such as librarianship, are consistently underpaid and should be compensated at a comparable scale to those professions in which men predominate. Some recent court decisions, for example, against the state of Washington and in the city of San Jose, California, are significant. So far public librarians rather than academic have benefited from the decisions, but the battle continues.

There is very little left of the hope that academic libraries would develop alliances with their outside communities and would become part of the struggle against racism. Community colleges in many areas are fighting for their continued existence, and many colleges and universities have limited instead of expanding their services to the community. Economic exigencies, white backlash, a right-wing renaissance actively supported by our national administration, all tend to erode the surge of democratic anti-racist actions of the sixties. But the stirring ideas and ideals of that period survive. No one today—not even the most benighted bigot—could hope to use a return to segregation as a rallying cry. The reality is bad enough. Under the Aesopian cover of "reverse discrimination" or "quotas" or "law and order," advances in affirmative action and against discrimination are being reversed, but they cannot be eradicated.

Undoubtedly there will come a time for new struggles, new tactics, new messages for a democratic society without war, without racism, and without hunger, and undoubtedly academic librarians will participate in those actions. The work their predecessors did in the sixties will help them succeed.

Notes

1. Barbara Anderson, "Ordeal at San Francisco State College," in Patricia Glass Schuman, ed., *Social Responsibilities and Libraries* (New York: R.R. Bowker, 1976), p. 293.
2. *Ibid.*, p. 295.
3. Paul Cowan, "Bearing Witness: Some Thoughts on Zoia Horn, in Schuman, ed., *Social Responsibilities and Libraries*, pp. 7–11.
4. Paul Wasserman, *The New Librarianship: A Challenge for Change* (New York: R.R. Bowker, 1972), p. 237.
5. Fay M. Blake, "The Useful Academic Librarian," in Schuman, ed., *Social Responsibilities and Libraries*, p. 303.
6. Robert B. Downs, "Status of University Librarians—1964," *College & Research Libraries* 25 (1964): 253–58.
7. Lewis C. Branscomb, ed., *The Case for Faculty Status for Academic Librarians*, ACRL Monograph 33 (Chicago, Illinois: American Library Association, 1970).
8. Eldred Smith, "Librarians and Unions: The Berkeley Experience," *Library Journal* 93 (1968): 717–20.
9. Robert P. Haro, "Collective Action and Professional Negotiation: Factors and Trends in Academic Libraries," *ALA Bulletin* 63 (1969): 994.
10. Eldred Smith, "The Librarians' Association at the University of California," *ALA Bulletin* 63 (1969): 363.
11. Marcia Endore, ed., *Goals for UCLA Librarians* (Los Angeles, California: UCLA Librarians' Association, 1969), p. 3.
12. R. Dean Galloway, "The Quiet Revolution," *ALA Bulletin* 63 (1969): 1257–61.
13. Richard Dougherty, "The Unserved—Academic Library Style," *American Libraries* 2 (November 1971): 1055–59.

14. See, for example, Stith M. Cain, "Student Library Committees," *College & Research Libraries* 26 (1965): 493–94, 536; Gorham Lane, "Assessing the Undergraduates' Use of the University Library," *College & Research Libraries* 27 (1966): 277–82; Joseph H. Reason, "The Academic Library in Urban and Rural Areas," in Laurence L. Sherrill, ed., *Library Service to the Unserved* (New York: R.R. Bowker, 1970), pp. 37–43; and Robert P. Haro, "College Libraries for Students," in Schuman, ed., *Social Responsibilities and Libraries*, pp. 298–301.

15. Bill Hinchcliff, "Ivory Tower Ghettoes," in Schuman, ed., *Social Responsibilities and Libraries*, pp. 285–89.

16. Blake, "The Useful Academic Librarian."

17. E.J. Josey, "Community Use of Academic Libraries: A Symposium," *College & Research Libraries* 28 (1967): 184–202.

ACRL's Fiftieth Anniversary

For Reflection, for Celebration, and for Anticipation

Edward G. Holley

> We want to link the past with the future, and the 100th anniversary of the College Library Section gives us an excellent opportunity for reflection, for celebration, and for anticipation of the next 100 Years.
> —Martha A. Bowman, cochair, ACRL Fifth National Conference, *Research Libraries in OCLC: A Quarterly*, Autumn 1987.

Reflection: The Birth of College & Research Libraries

When A. Frederick Kuhlman edited the first issue of *College & Research Libraries* (December 1939), he pronounced its aims in the authoritative manner that was his hallmark. *C&RL* was to serve as the communications medium for the new ACRL, but the journal was to do much more than that. The quarterly was also to produce articles from convention speeches, to serve as a clearing house for educational research, to bridge the gap between college administrators/faculties and librarians, to serve as a bridge with other agencies and learned societies, to review and abstract books of interest to ACRL members, to stimulate research on improving library service and publish the research results, and to "help develop the ACRL into a strong and mature professional organization."[1]

Those were ambitious goals, to say the least. But in retrospect it is amazing not only that Kuhlman's aims and goals have been achieved in the last fifty years, but also how similar those aims and goals are to the current ACRL Strategic Plan.[2] Indeed, A.F. Kuhlman would probably be amazed, surely gratified, at how far academic librarians have come since the days when he did battle with ALA Executive Secretary Carl Milam (1920–48) and the ALA establishment. For Kuhlman and his colleagues were anything but reticent about ALA's neglect of matters that concerned academic librarians.

At the heart of the disagreement was the ALA headquarters staff's lack of understanding of the nature of higher education and the academic library's relationship to scholarship and learning. Academic librarians believed the way to success in the academic library was to be more like the faculty, interested in scholarship, concerned about teaching, and devoted to research and publication. In that effort *C&RL* was to play a crucial role. As David Kaser, one of Kuhlman's successors as editor (1963–69) later commented, "C&RL was a periodical intended at once to be [ACRL's] news bulletin, scholarly journal, and its forum."[3] At various stages it served all three functions well. Today, after the spin-off of the news to *College & Research Libraries News* in 1966, *C&RL* is primarily a scholarly journal, indeed often the most cited and highly rated among all the scholarly periodicals in the field of librarianship.[4] But ACRL and *C&RL* have been a long time reaching that eminent position.

Academic Librarians and ALA: The ACRL Background

Despite the fact that college and university librarians had formed the first ALA section in 1889, there is little doubt that public librarians dominated the association's leadership well into the second half of the twentieth century. True, the first three ALA presidents could be regarded as academic types: Justin Winsor (1876–85), who had been Boston public librarian for nine years before transferring his allegiance across the river to Harvard in 1877; William Frederick Poole (1885–87), whose strong commitment to the public library did not preclude historical scholarship; and Charles Ammi Cutter (1887–89), librarian at the Boston Athenaeum, whose "delicate and accurate scholarship" in his famous catalog was well recognized in the scholarly community. But it was chiefly to the rapidly expanding public libraries that the association looked for leadership during its first 100 years; it was public library concerns that occupied most of the association's attention.

Of course, there were scholars who assumed the presidency of ALA during its first century, e.g., Reuben Gold Thwaites, William Warner Bishop, Louis Round Wilson, but their presence did not alter ALA priorities. As Wayne Wiegand and Dorothy Steffens have noted, there were forty-five public librarians among the first 100 ALA presidents (1876–1986), outnumbering academic librarians 2.6 to 1.[5]

After World War I academic librarians expressed increasing disillusion with ALA's neglect. Criticism began to be voiced after William Warner Bishop's presidency (1918–19) and the failed ALA effort in 1919–20 to secure funds for massive improvement in library service. This "Enlarged Library Program" has been described by historian Dennis Thomison as ALA's short-lived experiment as a welfare organization.[6]

For the next two decades academic librarians' dissatisfaction grew until it finally culminated in the birth of ACRL in 1938.

The College and Reference Library Section

From its beginning in 1889, the ALA College Library Section was mainly a small discussion group of academic library administrators. To accommodate reference librarians, the section changed its name to the College and Reference Library Section in 1897. However, though the section began electing officers early in the twentieth century, it remained small until 1923 when it adopted its first set of bylaws. Growth was rapid after that, from ninety members in 1923 to 800 in 1928, though membership declined after 1928. Still, throughout the twenties, the College and Reference Library Section had obviously begun to attract attention. Growth of the section doubtless reflected both the changes in American higher education and the growth of colleges and universities in the first quarter of the century. With larger enrollments came expanded libraries and more librarians.

The section's programs reflected perennial issues in academic librarianship: personnel and faculty status, teaching students the use of the library, standards, interlibrary loans, and on-and- off-campus services. Though formal and informal discussion of these issues continued until 1938 (and indeed throughout ACRL's fifty-year history), many academic librarians—both behind the scenes and occasionally in public—began to argue for a stronger professional organization that would emphasize bibliographic and scholarly activity to meet their needs in serving an expanding higher education community.

In 1921 Ernest J. Reese and his library school students began a series of articles, "College Library News," in the *Library Journal*. The articles offered current information on personnel changes, publications, buildings, gifts, and appointments for the period covered. This series continued through the mid-forties. *C&RL* began publishing the series in 1943 but dropped it in 1945.

Other events in the twenties promoted a sense of need for a stronger forum for academic librarians. George Works's *College and University Library Problems* (1927), the result of a survey financed by the Carnegie Corporation, drew attention to the status of academic libraries and had a tremendous impact on librarians and some university administrators.

The emergence of the Graduate Library School (GLS) at the University of Chicago, another major Carnegie venture, offered both hope and skepticism in the library community. GLS aimed to prepare leaders through a program of research at the Ph.D. level, and thus to do for librarianship what Harvard had done for law and Johns Hopkins for medicine, to use Carnegie President Keppel's phrase.

The first significant open disagreement with ALA came from Frederick Telford's study of library staff classification and pay plans in the mid-twenties. ALA had employed Telford to do for librarians what was already being done by the federal government for civil service workers: define jobs and establish pay scales.[7] What happened was a not-so-subtle revolt of the academic librarians in ALA. They believed that Telford didn't understand academia (he didn't) and that a plan that might work well for public librarians would not work at all for academic librarians. Consequently, a subcommittee was appointed, under the leadership of Charles Harvey Brown (1875–1960), to develop a supplementary plan for librarians in higher education. Charlie Brown, who would later defend a higher status for academic librarians in the "Library" section of the US Bureau of Education's massive study of land grant colleges and universities (1930), went to work with typical zeal and developed a separate report—*Budgets, Classification, and Compensation Plans for University and College Libraries* (1929)—adopted as a supplement to the Telford plan for public librarians.

By the late twenties the section began to consider its future seriously. High among its priorities were bibliographic tools and a publication that would address the specific needs of academic librarians. Thus, began the short-lived *College and Reference Library Yearbook* (1929–31). The *Yearbook* was dropped after only three years, ostensibly because it didn't pay its way (probably a result of the Great Depression) but also because a suitable editor couldn't be found.

The Carnegie Corporation, responsible for GLS's emergence, also expanded its interest in academic libraries.[8] The Corporation sponsored surveys, standards, book collections, and basic book lists by underwriting the Charles Shaw and Foster Morhardt predecessors to *Books for College Libraries*. The Corporation's efforts gave added emphasis to the ALA's neglect of such matters. These activities have been well covered in Neil Radford's book, *The Carnegie Corporation and the Development of American College Libraries, 1928–1941*, ACRL Publications in Librarianship, no. 44.

Partly in response to the unrest among academic librarians, especially their request for a college library specialist at ALA headquarters (turned down for financial reasons), ALA established a College Library Advisory Board (CLAB) in 1931. Despite the board's membership of librarians from such notable institutions as Michigan (Bishop); Vassar (Borden); Iowa State (Charles Brown); and Penn State (Lewis), the board was not very effective, chiefly for financial reasons, according to Radford but also because of lack of interest on the part of ALA headquarters staff, according to Blanche McCrum (1887–1969), Washington & Lee University librarian, who found her services as chair of CLAB frustrated by headquarters.[9]

CLAB did not stop the growing discontent in the thirties as the Carnegie Corporation, chiefly influenced by Bishop at Michigan and Louis Round Wilson at GLS, invested not only in research and bibliographic compilations but also in grants for college library book collections.

In 1932 university library directors disbanded their recently formed Administrators Round Table in favor of a separate Association of Research Libraries where they could discuss problems of large libraries.

By the mid-thirties a number of leading academic librarians were pushing for a reorganization of ALA to reflect the diverse interests of the association through stronger subunits. In 1936 the section approved a committee under Brown's leadership to study reorganization. The *ACRL Organization Manual* (1956) called the Brown committee's report of 1937 "the key document of ACRL history."[10] Acceptance of the report was to result not only in "a radical reorganization" of the section (Brown's phrase), renaming it the Association of College and Reference Libraries in 1938, but also in ACRL's becoming the first ALA division in 1940.

The restructured ALA emerged from implementation of the report of its Third Activities Committee, which Brown also headed immediately upon completion of his report on the College and Reference Library Section. Brown had served on the Second Activities Committee and subsequently was to be ALA president in 1940–41, so he could see that his four years' work on ALA restructuring was neither neglected nor hindered by headquarters.

The ALA activities committees were an outgrowth of criticism leveled by that perennial gadfly and founder of the separate Special Libraries Association, John Cotton Dana. In 1919 Dana, in a stinging criticism, had said that the chief ALA problem was "the lack of brains on the part of the members." He followed that criticism with another letter in 1927 that was highly critical of ALA's efforts in library education. The result had been the First Activities Committee, which reported in 1930, and another activities committee that reported in 1934. Neither the first nor the second committees' recommendations had resulted in significant organizational change, however. The Third Activities Committee was different, though the results would not be apparent for a decade. The difference came from the political skills of Charles Harvey Brown and, subsequently, ACRL's 1945–46 President, Blanche Prichard McCrum.

While the Third Activities Committee's achievement was, in form, the "radical reorganization" that Brown intended, it never resulted in a federation-type organization that brought in separate library organizations like SLA in an umbrella arrangement, as Brown desired. The reorganization did give major ALA units semiautonomous status, however, and after ACRL's threatened secession in 1946, an executive secretary of its own—the long-desired college library specialist at headquarters.[11] Subsequently, despite the partial success of the Cresap, McCormick, and Paget management/organizational study in the mid-fifties, and the failure of ACRL President Ralph Ellsworth's second attempt at secession in the early sixties, ALA did move toward much stronger divisions.[12] Much later, after the turmoil of the late sixties and early seventies, realistic self-determination came only after the change in the ALA dues structure in 1974.[13]

Leadership: Presidents and Executive Secretaries

The obvious leader of the new Association of College and Reference Libraries (the name was changed to Association of College and Research Libraries in 1957, when the reference librarians departed to form their own division) was Charles Harvey Brown. When Brown declined to be selected as ACRL's first president, it was not because he was reluctant to assume that responsibility. His reasons were clear: he wanted to see the recommendations of the Third Activities Committee implemented, and he did not intend to leave that to chance. What he did do was to convince Frank K. Walter to become the first ACRL president and thus assure continuation of the thrust that had already been established. Correspondence in the ALA archives and in Brown's other letters indicates well his manipulation of the process. He had conducted an exhaustive survey of the ALA membership, spoken and written extensively on ALA restructuring, and was confident that decentralization of ALA was desired by the membership as well as desirable for academic librarians. Fortunately for him (though fortune probably had little to do with it), Brown was elected ALA vice president in 1939 and served as president in 1940–41. Thus, he was in the enviable position of assuring that his reorganization plan was carried out. In J. Victor Baldridge's terms, Charlie Brown was truly a "Machiavellian change agent" for ALA and ACRL.[14]

In the intervening fifty years, ACRL has had some remarkable leaders. After the secession movement of 1946, led by Blanche McCrum and Ralph Ellsworth, there were frequent tensions between ACRL and ALA. Many members did not believe that ACRL could trust the parent ALA to do the right thing by its major division. The strongest of that group was undoubtedly Ralph Ellsworth, the only person to have served two terms as ACRL president (1951–52; 1961–62). A leader in the 1946 battle, Ellsworth was a frequent ALA critic. In an oft-quoted article, "Critique of Library Associations in America," in *Library Quarterly* (1961) on the eve of his second ACRL presidency, Ellsworth reiterated his criticisms of the organization.[15] While recognizing the importance of ALA's battles for intellectual freedom, federal legislation, international relations, and the welfare of all librarians, he also thought the organization was too bureaucratic, too big, too indifferent to specialized interests of academic, public, and special librarians. He argued once more for ALA as a workable federation of library associations.

In response to this critique, ALA Executive Director David Clift noted that Ellsworth would soon have the opportunity to try to bend ALA to his will, because he would shortly be ACRL president again. Ellsworth himself did not think that would occur, and it didn't.[16] His dream of a separate ACRL and a federation of library associations was delayed another decade, until the ALA changed its dues structure, transcended the old arguments, and became, in fact if not in theory, a federation.

That old attitudes die slowly was clear to this author when he joined several persons to testify before the ALA Executive Board in support of ACRL's request to hold a second national conference. Talk of secession *if* the board declined to grant permission was again in the air on the night before the meeting—political naïveté. Few boards willingly confront a phalanx of distinguished representatives from their largest unit without giving them what they want. The ALA Executive Board usually backs down under strong protests from its smallest unit; there was no likelihood of turning down a request from its major division.

What kind of persons have led ACRL in the last fifty years? Among the leaders one should certainly include presidents and executive secretaries, but also those who have edited its journal, *C&RL*. An examination of the leaders' backgrounds and interests is revealing (see Addendum A for a list of ACRL presidents and executive secretaries/directors).

From the beginning university librarians have been the most numerous among ACRL presidents. Starting with Frank K. Walter at the University of Minnesota and continuing through Joseph W. Boisse at the University of California—Santa Barbara, in 1988–89, they constitute a remarkably strong group of leaders—this despite the competition from ARL, which, it has often been said, drained ACRL of the real academic library leadership. Of course, not all of these presidents came from ARL libraries, but many have—including a number of the most recent presidents.

Not surprisingly, in view of the fact that approximately fifty percent of the membership comes from university libraries, those institutions account for 35 of the 50 persons who have served as ACRL presidents.[17] Eight came from college libraries, one from a community college library, two each from public libraries and other types of libraries, and two from library schools. Of the college librarians, three were from women's colleges. Most of the ACRL presidents have been library directors.

Five ACRL presidents have subsequently been elected ALA presidents, as has one ACRL Executive Director.

Women and Minorities in Leadership Positions

In a gender-conscious age, one should note that only sixteen of the presidents have been women, though six of those served in succession 1982–1988.

Beverly Lynch, who became executive secretary in 1972, was the first woman to hold that office. Since that time all executive secretaries/directors (the title was changed to executive director in 1980–81) have been women.

For reasons not clear to this author, no woman has ever served as editor of *College & Research Libraries* nor has one ever served as editor of *ACRL Publications in Librarianship*. However, one should note that a number of gender studies indicate that women librarians have not been as active in publishing as men. Cline's study indicated that males accounted for an overwhelming 80 percent of the contributing authors and 73 percent of the cited authors in *C&RL* during its first forty years.[18]

Two well-known reference librarians, Mabel L. Conat, Detroit Public Library, and Winifred Ver Nooy, University of Chicago (and the 1944–45 president who initiated the protest of 1945–46), have served as president. Female presidents from college libraries are Blanche McCrum (Wellesley); Eileen Thornton (Oberlin); Helen Brown (Wellesley); and Anne Edmonds (Mount Holyoke).

Two black persons have served as president: Joseph H. Reason of Howard University and the late Louise Giles from Macomb County Community College, Michigan.

Executive Secretaries/Directors

One of the strong arguments for separate status had included the need of having a college library specialist at ALA headquarters. Many persons familiar with ALA's bureaucracy believe that ACRL has been especially fortunate, not only in the quality of persons serving as executive secretaries/directors but also in capable headquarters staff who did not stay too long, as did two ALA executive secretaries, Carl Milam and David Clift.

The first executive secretary, N. Orwin Rush, stayed only two years (1947–49). He was succeeded by "young Arthur Hamlin, fresh from the University of Pennsylvania," under whose tenure new publications emerged, including the first ACRL monograph in hard cover, Charlie Brown's *Scientific Serials* (1956). Hamlin served for seven years (1949–56). Both Richard D. Harwell, 1957–61, and J. Donald Thomas, 1968–72 (the period of the revolting librarians), served four-year terms. Mark Gormley, 1961–62, and Joseph Reason, 1962–63, were really interim executives. George Bailey, 1963–68, served five years as did Beverly Lynch, 1972–77.

The three women executives, Beverly Lynch; Julie Virgo, 1977–84; and JoAn Segal, 1984, have served during a time of transition for ALA divisions and a period of extraordinary growth for ACRL. During their tenure the publications programs, standards and guidelines, continuing education programs, and the national conferences have either been initiated or expanded. The executives have also been effective in seeking and maintaining divisional relationships with other professional and scholarly associations in higher education, a matter often talked about but frequently overlooked in the face of more pressing concerns.

While terms of seven years or less may be a cause for congratulation, short terms are scarcely the chief reason for their success. Each person has brought a strong background in academia and has understood the aims and goals of academic librarians. Each has also been supported by strong presidents. Housed as they were at ALA headquarters, each executive also had to balance the unique ACRL interests against the interests of ALA as a whole—often not an easy task. Nor was strengthening the ties between chapters and ACRL headquarters easy, since visits and speeches by staff and ACRL presidents are both necessary and time-consuming. By any objective standard leadership at headquarters has been excellent. One can only be amazed that so much good work is done by so few persons.

Publications and Their Editors: College & Research Libraries

Kuhlman aimed for *C&RL* to be both a communications medium and a vehicle for scholarship. Initially, the journal did both, first under Kuhlman himself (1939–41), then under Carl M. White (1941–48), followed by the long-term editorship of Maurice F. Tauber (1948–62).

Begun as a quarterly, *C&RL* became a bimonthly in 1956. Tauber's successors include a series of well-known librarians who worked steadily to improve the quality and scholarship of the articles: Richard B. Harwell, David Kaser, Richard M. Dougherty, Richard D. Johnson, C. James Schmidt, and Charles Martell. During the expansion of higher education in the sixties, ACRL approved a separate publication for the news section. *ACRL News*, later renamed *College & Research Libraries News* was first published in March 1966. In its 22 years of existence *C&RL News* has grown to an incredible 748 pages per year and now publishes opinion pieces and short research articles, as well as news, ads, and official ACRL information eleven times a year. Meanwhile, *C&RL*, continues as a bimonthly of approximately 650 pages a year.

Gloria S. Cline, in evaluating *C&RL*'s first forty years, noted that the journal has been a leading library science periodical since it first appeared.[19] She also reported that *C&RL*'s scholarliness improved over the period 1939–79 so that it compares very favorably with journals in other disciplines, especially in numbers of references per article and in up-to-date citations. Positive changes have occurred in the quality of manuscripts accepted and cited, and also in adhering to other high standards of scholarly publishing.

But Cline found a weak core of productive authors: only 17 out of 4,000 cited authors appeared often enough to be considered an "author core." Of those, three of the most cited were also leading contributors to *C&RL*. Six who contributed ten or more articles during the forty-year period include the familiar names of Robert Downs, Keyes Metcalf, Robert Muller, Ralph Ellsworth, Ralph Shaw, and Maurice Tauber. Also, though there was increasing collaborative authorship (a notable factor in science publishing) in the seventies, the vast majority of articles during the period had no coauthors.

Other ACRL Series

Two other series came into being in the fifties. The first was ACRL Monographs, designed, as Maurice Tauber had suggested, for papers either too long for *C&RL* or too limited in interest for the journal. The first monograph (1952), a photo offset item that sold at $.35, was Joe W. Kraus's "William Beer and the New Orleans Libraries, 1891–1927." Over the years the monograph editorial board, while highly selective in the titles chosen (only forty-five have appeared in thirty-six years), did include a number of collections of essays. Therefore, in the early seventies, the editorial board decided to change the title to ACRL Publications in Librarianship. While the series is eclectic, most of the titles have been well received by reviewers.

The second series, initiated under Lawrence S. Thompson's editorship, was the ACRL Microcard Series. Chiefly a collection of master's theses and papers from library schools, the microcard series lasted from 1953 to 1969, and served, according to Charles Hale, "as an outlet for aspiring young college librarians."

In 1980 the College Libraries Section began a new series called Clip Notes (College Library Information Packets), containing "data and sample documents from academic libraries to assist librarians in establishing or refining services and operations." Ten have now appeared. Like other ACRL series titles, CLIP Notes has been highly successful.

Another major contribution ACRL has made to academic library advancement is the publication of library statistics. Non-Association of Research Libraries university statistics have been published every other year since 1978. ACRL has also published HEGIS (Higher Education General Information Survey) data collected by the federal government in 1984 and 1986. The Association also collected and published statistics of some colleges and universities in an out-of-series mode in 1984 and 1986. The latter series will reportedly not be continued. In the decline of federal government publication of library statistics, ACRL's provision of accurate comparative statistical data has been welcome.

Choice *and* Books for College Libraries

Perhaps no publications have served a more useful function than *Choice* and *Books for College Libraries*. By the mid-sixties, when the Great Society programs were just beginning, ACRL had already been at work for five years on a review journal to help college librarians and faculty in their selection of the best books for college libraries. Access to high quality faculty who could assist in the reviewing led to *Choice*'s location in Middletown, Connecticut, near the Wesleyan University campus.

Thanks to a grant from the Council on Library Resources, the first issue of *Choice: Books for College Libraries*, appeared in March 1964. Under the editorship of Richard Gardner, *Choice* quickly earned a place of importance among the book reviewing media. Drawing upon the expertise of faculty for subject reviews and librarians for reference reviews, the magazine focused attention on authoritative evaluation of new titles for the expanding enrollments in colleges and universities. A recent article indicated that *Choice* reviewed more books per year (about 6,600) than any other publication. Especially popular was the spinoff *Choice Opening Day Collection*, a list of about 1,800 titles regarded by the editors of *Choice* as essential in any new college library.

Soon after *Choice* began publication, ALA published a major bibliographical tool, *Books for College Libraries* (*BCL*). The current reviews of academic books published in *Choice* was foreseen as a complementary, supplemental service to a basic booklist. There had long been a desire for a successor to the Shaw and Mohrhardt lists. The establishment of new campuses in the University of California system had led to compilation of a basic list of titles under the editorships of Melvin J. Voigt and Joseph H. Treyz. This list of 53,000 titles became the basis for the first edition of *BCL*, published in 1967. ACRL and ALA Publishing collaborated on the next two editions, 1975 and 1988. The latest edition, with understandable hyperbole, is advertised as "the most authoritative academic library collection development and evaluation tool available today." In a six-volume format, as well as online and on magnetic tape, *BCL3* will likely be as popular and useful as its predecessors. In this way ACRL has fulfilled one of its major purposes.

Standards and Guidelines

Important for academic librarians over the years has been the development of standards for college library collections and guidelines for library personnel. Not surprisingly, standards and guidelines remain a major priority for ACRL's membership.

ACRL standards and guidelines have had a strong impact on higher education despite the fact that regional accrediting agencies have not been willing to adopt the ACRL standards as their own. Nonetheless, accreditation visiting teams often take note of how a college has used such documents. Moreover, a number of higher education boards used the earlier "Standards for College Libraries," (1959) as a measuring device for improving their state-supported college libraries, just as they have used the 1975 standards, and no doubt will use the 1986 revision, for the same purpose. Board staffs routinely refer to the ACRL standards as the "ALA Standards," which may deny ACRL the credit but is technically correct since ALA delegates to its divisions responsibility for standards in their individual areas of expertise. The 1975 Standards for College Libraries broadened evaluation to include staff and space as well as collections and have had a salutary effect in encouraging states with weaker college libraries to upgrade their library resources and services.

Although measuring the impact may be difficult, this author believes that both the standards and the various guidelines have resulted in significant progress for small colleges and medium-sized universities, but probably have had less success in large universities.

The standards and guidelines most difficult to develop and maintain have been those involving personnel. The long battle of academic librarians for faculty/academic status has, at best, been only moderately successful. The debate over faculty status in the fifties between Robert B. Downs, a firm believer, and some other university librarians (at best, skeptical), resulted in a collection of essays published as ACRL monograph no. 22, *The Status of American College and University Librarians*, in 1958. ACRL adopted the Downs approach of full faculty status as the ideal. However, convincing academic administrators to adopt even the halfway house of academic status with rank and titles has not been achieved in most research universities. Moreover, there has clearly been some retrogression in the late seventies and early eighties.

In 1975 ACRL published *Faculty Status for Academic Librarians*, a collection of policy statements and articles in defense of faculty status. A new edition, *Academic Status: Statements and Resources*, has just appeared in 1988. In the current climate of higher education, one can predict that the battle for academic librarians to maintain their status and position on campus will continue. Unfortunately, their colleagues, especially administrative colleagues (sometimes even library directors), are often their worst enemies. As the above paragraphs indicate, the battle to secure a vital role for the library in the teaching and research process is never ending.

Conferences and Awards

Over the fifty-year period, the ACRL presentations at ALA conferences have attracted increasing numbers of registrants. In recent years the ACRL President's Program has suffered from the same problem of all similar organizations: how does one plan a program on a substantive topic that embraces everyone, from the neophyte from library school to the sophisticated and experienced professional? The answer is "with difficulty." The result has been to focus more on the program of ACRL's fourteen sections, but even there the large numbers can present a problem. Section programs generally result in good attendance because of their more specific topics. To communicate effectively with members, all except two sections have now begun newsletters and the other two are giving consideration to some form of publication.

Since the Rare Books and Manuscripts Section's preconference programs began in 1958, the unit has attracted such interest that it has had to limit attendance. RBMS conference papers and symposia have often been published, adding significantly to the literature in this important area. Recognizing the growing importance of its Rare Books and Manuscripts Section in 1987, ACRL began publishing a new semi-annual serial, *Rare Books and Manuscripts Librarianship*.

Preconference continuing education courses are now a regular part of ACRL's programs at ALA, as they are for a number of other ALA divisions. They have grown in popularity, as more and more members recognize their need for updating skills in bibliographic instruction, management, and technology areas.

ACRL was the first division to conduct a national conference apart from the ALA conferences. The Boston conference, in 1978, was designed for presentation and discussion of research and professional papers of high quality and *no* business sessions. With an attendance of over 2,600, the 1978 conference exceeded expectations. Subsequent conferences have been held in Minneapolis (1981), Seattle (1984), and Baltimore (1986). By all accounts the conferences have succeeded in presenting current issues and research results well, though research papers have been fewer than professional papers.

At the fortieth anniversary conference in 1978, ACRL, with support from the Baker & Taylor Company, presented its first ACRL Academic or Research Librarian of the Year Award to two giants in the profession: Robert B. Downs and Keyes D. Metcalf. Two other pioneers, Henriette D. Avram and Frederick G. Kilgour, shared this honor in 1979, but the following years have seen this award made to only one person.

In 1921 friends of Eunice Rockwood Oberly established a memorial award to honor the compiler of the best bibliography in the field of agriculture. ACRL now administers this biennial award, which technically might be called ACRL's oldest. However, the Academic or Research Librarian of the Year was ACRL's first major award.

Recent Developments: Planning

In 1982 ACRL established an Academic and Research Libraries Personnel Study Group to assess the division's current personnel programs and priorities. This group commissioned Allen B. Veaner to prepare a paper focusing on "working librarians, not chief administrators," in light of changes taking place in the academic libraries' environment. Veaner's paper, "1985 to 1995: The Next Decade in Academic Librarianship," was published in the May and July 1985 issues of *C&RL*, with comments by four librarians.[20] His observations on the types of knowledge, skills, and abilities, and attitudes which academic librarians will need during the decade have led to considerable discussion, especially among library educators, and have contributed to ACRL's planning process.

Strategic planning, the current buzzword in academia and the corporate world, has had its impact on ACRL. Planning for the decade began in 1981 when ACRL appointed an Ad Hoc Committee on an Activity Model for 1990.[21] Soon thereafter ACRL mission, goals, and objectives were adopted; afterwards an ACRL Strategic Planning Task Force was appointed to develop a strategic plan.

At the 1986 ALA Conference, the task force presented the results of its work to the ACRL Board of Directors, which adopted it. The plan's basis came from top priorities identified by the ACRL membership: publications, continuing education, standards and guidelines, alliance with other professional and scholarly associations, and chapters.[22]

The introductory mission statement reads well in the light of ACRL's history: "The mission of the Association of College and Research Libraries (ACRL) is to foster the profession of academic and research libraries to serve effectively the library and information needs of current and potential users."

Major goals for carrying out the plan are

1. To contribute to the total professional development of academic and research librarians,
2. To enhance the capability of academic and research libraries to serve the needs of users,
3. To promote and speak for the interests of academic and research librarianship, and
4. To promote study, research and publication relevant to academic and research librarianship [*C&RL News*, January 1987].

One reads this summary report with a keen sense of appreciation for how well the task force accomplished its work. Not only has the task force outlined subgoals and strategies in clearly understood prose, but [it has] also analyzed the Association's strengths and external environments in a commendable way. It is easy to concur with [the plan's] assessment, "We now have a clear sense of our mission, a strong set of goals for the next five years, specific objectives, and strategies for meeting them."[23] The ACRL Board has also initiated procedures to review the plan annually.

Another heartening aspect of ACRL's recent activities is its leadership in ALA divisional planning. ACRL, with help from the ALA Goals Award, managed the first divisional leadership enhancement program in 1984. The association has continued to work closely with other divisions in hammering out a new operating agreement with ALA. The Strategic Plan points out the significance of ACRL's position within ALA "not only in the symbolic recognition of the importance of one association for all types of libraries and library activities, but also in dollars...." The willingness to improve relationships and to recognize those common goals of all librarians as well as carry out goals specific to types of libraries and library activities augurs well for ACRL's future.

ACRL Today: Celebration

The facts are clear. ACRL on its fiftieth anniversary is far and away the largest, the most effective, and most prosperous of the ALA divisions. Representing almost one-fourth of the total ALA membership, ACRL had led the way in divisional national conferences, in continuing education, and in noteworthy publications. Among the *separate* library/information associations in the country, only the Special Libraries Association has a larger membership, by a thousand or so members. A 1983 *ALA Yearbook* article noted that ACRL membership placed it as the fifth largest library association in the world!

Organizationally, the ACRL of today reminds one of the ALA itself. ACRL is a complex organization with a strong programmatic thrust. There are now fourteen sections, all with vigorous and active programs; thirty-nine chapters; seventeen discussion groups; forty-nine ACRL level committees plus numerous section and discussion group committees; an active publishing program that would do justice to any major professional association; and a continuing education program both at ALA conferences, among chapters, and in grant-funded conferences for improving the quality of humanities programs in libraries.

ACRL has a sound budget plan and a firm financial base. In 1988–89 there will be a headquarters staff of about ten FTE, and a general budget of $1.1 million. At Middletown, Connecticut, *Choice* will have a staff of twenty and a budget of $1.4 million. Reserve funds for major projects like new editions of *BCL* are approximately half a million dollars. With a membership of 9,044 personal and 1,126 organizational members (as of August 31, 1988), ACRL is in a strong position to celebrate the accomplishments of its first fifty years.

ACRL: Anticipation

From the above recital, one can certainly conclude that ACRL members have a firm foundation for "Building on the First Century." The fifth national conference in Cincinnati is an appropriate place to launch ACRL's next 100 years, as cochair Martha Bowman has noted. Looking at the current and proposed ACRL programs one would be hard put to argue that the division is precluded from doing anything it wants to do. The battle for autonomy in its own programs, with its own staff, budgets, and conferences, is over. In the unlikely event of a major challenge, any future ALA Executive Board would clearly be the loser and so would the library profession.

One can argue persuasively, as Charlie Brown, Blanche McCrum, Ralph Ellsworth, and other academic librarians did, that librarianship needs an umbrella organization for common concerns such as access to information, national legislation/funding, intellectual freedom, public awareness, and personnel resources (the ALA Priorities). One can also argue, as they did, that library/information science needs separate units to serve specialized interests.

ACRL contributes substantially to all of the ALA priorities in its specialized context, the academic library/information center. One need only mention the ACRL Standards for College Libraries recognized unofficially, if not officially, by accrediting bodies and various higher education boards. ACRL publications are regarded as a contribution to the scholarly community, whether one is talking about the prestigious book selection journal, *Choice*, or the ACRL Publications in Librarianship Series, or the various publications of the Rare Books and Manuscripts Section. *College & Research Libraries* has long been among the top research journals in the library/information science field.

ACRL could now become a separate association if it so wished, but there is little incentive for it to do so. The future looks bright for the association's next hundred years. Charlie Brown, who used his political skills to secure a semiautonomous ACRL division under an umbrella ALA, and that small giant Blanche McCrum, whose "marching orders" sent her troops into the battle from which stems ACRL's current success, would both be proud.

Bibliographical Note

The sources used for this paper came from a variety of places which have not been cited unless there was some special reason to do so. There are numerous letters on the

214 Diversity and Retrenchment, 1946–1988, Part II

early ALA-ACRL controversies in the ALA Archives at the University of Illinois, especially in the folders for the College Library Advisory Board and for *College & Research Libraries*. The author has not examined these files for the period beyond 1948. The documentary record for the period after 1949 is extensive. That period also covers the time of the author's involvement with ALA-ACRL, and this essay necessarily reflects his own interpretation of the events from that perspective. Particularly helpful are issues of the two journals, *College & Research Libraries* and *C&RL News*, as well as issues of the *ALA Yearbook, 1976—*. One should also not overlook the collection of *C&RL* articles edited by Richard D. Johnson for the ALA Centennial, *Libraries for Teaching, Libraries for Research: Essays for a Century*. Chicago, Illinois: American Library Association, 1977. ACRL Publications in Librarianship, no. 39.

The definitive history of ACRL is yet to be written, but Charles Edward Hale's Indiana University dissertation, listed in the references, is a good starting place for basic data. Perhaps as ACRL looks ahead to its next hundred years, the board might consider encouraging research on a definitive history of the association.

Notes

1. A.F. Kuhlman, "Introducing 'College & Research Libraries,'" *College & Research Libraries* 1: 7–10 (Dec. 1939).
2. "ACRL's Strategic Plan: The Mission, Goals, and Objectives of the Association of College and Research Libraries," *College & Research Libraries News* 48: 21–25 (Jan. 1987).
3. David Kaser, "A Century of Academic Librarianship as Reflected in Its Literature," *College & Research Libraries* 37: 123 (Mar. 1986).
4. Gloria S. Cline, "*College & Research Libraries*: Its First Forty Years," *College & Research Libraries* 43: 208–32 (May 1982). An excellent study based on her doctoral dissertation.
5. Wayne A. Wiegand and Dorothy Steffens, "Members of the Club: A Look at One Hundred ALA Presidents," University of Illinois. *Occasional Papers*, 182. Urbana, IL: Graduate School of Library and Information Science (April 1988), 30p. The reason that there were only 100 presidents in the 110-year period is that four persons served more than one term.
6. Dennis Thomison, *A History of the American Library Association, 1876–1972* (Chicago, Illinois: American Library Assn., 1978), p. 72–83.
7. Richard Rubin, "A Critical Examination of the 1927 *Proposed Classifications and Compensation Plan for Library Positions* by the American Library Association," *Library Quarterly* 57: 400–25 (Oct. 1987).
8. Neil A. Radford, *The Carnegie Corporation and the Development of American College Libraries, 1928–1941*, ACRL Publications in Librarianship, no. 44 (Chicago, Illinois: American Library Assn., 1984). 257p.
9. For example, see Blanche McCrum to Charles Harvey Brown, 9/14/35 and 1/21/36; Brown to McCrum, 9/16/35 and 1/16/36, ALA Archives, University of Illinois, College Library Advisory Board, 22/2/5, Box 1.
10. Association of College and Research Libraries, *ACRL Organization Manual* (Chicago, Illinois: American Library Assn., 1956), p. 8.
11. These events are discussed at some length in Edward G. Holley, "Charles Harvey Brown," in Wayne A. Wiegand, ed., *Leaders in American Academic Librarianship: 1925–1975* (Pittsburgh, PA: Beta Phi Mu), p. 28–36, Beta Phi Mu Chapbook 16, distributed by American Library Association for Beta Phi Mu, 1983; and his "Mr. ACRL: Charles Harvey Brown (1875–1960)," *Journal of Academic Librarianship* 7: 271–78 (Nov. 1981). See also Betty Ruth Kondayan, "Blance Prichard McCrum: A Small Giant," *Journal of Academic Librarianship* 8:73 (May 1982), and her "Blanche Prichard McCrum," in Wiegand, p. 201–03; Edward R. Johnson, "Ralph E. Ellsworth," in Wiegand, p 112–15; and Charles Edward Hale, "The Origin and Development of the Association of College and Research Libraries, 1889–1960" (Ph.D. diss., Indiana Univ., 1976), p. 155–66. Hale's dissertation is a valuable compilation of data on the association, its programs, and its organization for the period covered.
12. Thomison, p. 195–203. See also Ralph Ellsworth, *Ellsworth on Ellsworth* . . . (Metuchen, N.J.: Scarecrow, 1980), p. 123–29.
13. Edward G. Holley, "Federation: An Idea Whose Time Has Come?," *Library Journal* 99: 335–38 (Feb. 1, 1974). Holley and Frank B. Sessa, "The New Personal Dues Proposal," *American Libraries* 5: 257–58 (May 1974). For a recent report, see ACRL Executive Committee, "ACRL and Its Divisions: Relationships Past, Present, and Future," *College & Research Libraries News* 48: 318–20 (June 1987).
14. J. Victor Baldridge, "Rules for a Machiavellian Change Agent: Transforming the Entrenched Professional

Organization," in J. Victor Baldridge and Terrence E. Deal, *Managing Change in Educational Organizations: Sociological Perspectives, Strategies, and Case Studies* (Berkeley, California: McCutchan, 1975), p. 378–88.

15. Ralph E. Ellsworth, "Critique of Library Associations in America," *Library Quarterly* 31: 382–95 (Oct. 1961); with a reply by David Clift, 395–400.

16. *Ellsworth on Ellsworth ...*, p. 128.

17. Ralph Ellsworth served twice as ACRL president, and hence the number of presidents is fifty instead of fifty-one.

18. Cline, p. 227.

19. *Ibid.*, p. 208–32.

20. Allen B. Veaner, "1985 to 1995: The Next Decade in Academic Librarianship, Part I," *College & Research Libraries* 46: 209–29 (May 1985); "1985–1995, Part II," (July 1985) with "Reactions...." 46: 309–19.

21. JoAn S. Segal, "The Association of College and Research Libraries: What It Can Do for Academic Libraries in the 80s," *Show-Me Libraries* 36: 11–12 (Oct./Nov. 1984). The ACRL articles in the *ALA Yearbook* also provide information on the planning process.

22. "ACRL's Strategic Plan...," p. 23.

23. *Ibid.*, p. 25.

Addendum A: ACRL Presidents (beginning 1938)*

1938–1939	Frank K. Walter	1948–1949	Benjamin E. Powell
1939–1940	Phineas L. Windsor	1949–1950	Wyllis E. Wright
1940–1941	Robert B. Downs	1950–1951	Charles M. Adams
1941–1942	Donald Coney	1951–1952	Ralph E. Ellsworth
1942–1943	Mabel L. Conat	1952–1953	Robert W. Severance
1943–1944	Charles B. Shaw	1953–1954	Harriet D. McPherson
1944–1945	Winifred Ver Nooy	1954–1955	Guy R. Lyle
1945–1946	Blanche Prichard McCrum	1955–1956	Robert Vosper
1946–1947	Errett Weir McDiarmid	1956–1957	Robert W. Orr
1947–1948	William H. Carson	1957–1958	Eileen Thornton
1958–1959	Lewis C. Branscomb	1974–1975	H. William Axford
1959–1960	Wyman W. Parker	1975–1976	Louise Giles
1960–1961	Edmon Low	1976–1977	Connie R. Dunlap
1961–1962	Ralph E. Ellsworth	1977–1978	Eldred R. Smith
1962–1963	Katherine M. Stokes	1978–1979	Evan I. Farber
1963–1964	Neal R. Harlow	1979–1980	LeMoyne W. Anderson
1964–1965	Archie L. McNeal	1980–1981	Millicent D. Abell
1965–1966	Helen Margaret Brown	1981–1982	David C. Weber
1966–1967	Ralph E. McCoy	1982–1983	Carla J. Stoffle
1967–1968	James Humphrey III	1983–1984	Joyce Ball
1968–1969	David Kaser	1984–1985	Sharon J. Rogers
1969–1970	Philip J. McNiff	1985–1986	Sharon Anne Hogan
1970–1971	Anne C. Edmonds	1986–1987	Hannelore Rader
1971–1972	Joseph Reason	1987–1988	Joanne Euster
1972–1973	Russell Shank	1988–1989	Joseph A. Boise
1973–1974	Norman E. Tanis		

*Formerly College Reference Section. Name changed by vote of section, June 1938. Approved by ALA Council, Dec. 1938.

Addendum B: ACRL Executive Officers

1947–1949	N. Orwin Rush	1963–1968	George M. Bailey
1949–1956	Arthur T. Hamlin	1968–1972	J. Donald Thomas
1957–1961	Richard B. Harwell	1972–1977	Beverly P. Lynch
1961–1962	Mark M. Gormley	1977–1984	Julie A.C. Virgo
1962–1963	Joseph H. Reason	1984—	JoAn S. Segal

Addendum C: ACRL's Fourteen Sections

Anthropology and Sociology Section (ANSS)
Law and Political Science Section (LPSS)
Art Section (ARTS)
Rare Books and Manuscripts Section (RBMS)
Asian and African Section (AAS)
Science and Technology Section (STS)
Bibliographic Instruction Section (BIS)
Slavic and East European Section (SEES)
College Libraries Section (CLS)
University Libraries Section (ULS)
Community and Junior College Libraries Section (CJCLS)
Western European Specialists Section (WESS)
Women's Studies Section (WSS)
Education and Behavioral Sciences Section (EBSS)

Digital Expansion, 1989–2015

The period of digital expansion is at once the easiest to present and the most challenging. Much can be brought forth from memory but, in ways eerily resembling contemporary journalism, the cautionary tale is that every word, every idea, and every assertion can be readily subject to immediate rebuttal in social media. Only a few predictions from the 1990s have prepared us for the disruptions of the twenty-first century. For example, at the end of the twentieth, many were concerned about a problem known as Y2K; some readers will immediately conduct an online search to find out what all the fuss was about. The problems inherent in the Y2K phenomenon required computer programming fixes in the billions of dollars, and yet the problems and their solutions, taken together in the U.S.A. and worldwide, seem trivial compared to the discord and unrest to which we are now, unfortunately, accustomed.

Rapid and sometimes chaotic change has accelerated into the years currently experienced by academic librarians, by academe at large and, indeed, the entire U.S.A. Many would mark the terrorist attacks of 11 September 2001 as a convenient line of demarcation after which Americans began to view the world in dramatically different ways. We certainly concur with readers as to the role of these events in forcing a reappraisal of life in the United States in its countless iterations. But we suggest that two earlier events, both from 1989, offered a sort of directional glimpse into what the 1990s and beyond eventually held and what has since come to pass. The first of these, occurring in the People's Republic of China, was a series of peaceful demonstrations and hunger strikes by university students, professors, and labor organizers, who were pursuing a more open society intellectually, politically, and economically. The Chinese government forcibly overthrew the demonstrators in what western journalists came to describe as the Tiananmen Square [located in Beijing] Massacre. The lesson for our purpose is not that a repressive regime stamped out democratic impulses but rather that students and labor activists had come together, organizing their movement, in part, by using electronic bulletin boards and email systems. Observers could soon discern the potentially powerful transitions of internet technology from military and scientific applications into something much wider—political, social, commercial, and educational operations, organizations, and movements.

Within a few months after the events at Tiananmen Square, the Berlin Wall was destroyed amidst the rise of democratic initiatives in Eastern Europe. East and West Germany were reunited, and the U.S.S.R. was soon dispersed into individual nations. These developments heralded the potential for economic and intellectual exchange in unprecedented ways, holding out hope that citizens could increasingly transcend the barriers of geopolitics, ethnicity, and language in order to engage in education and commerce across the globe. One of the immediate byproducts of the collapse of the Berlin Wall and of the U.S.S.R., was the emergence of the U.S.A. as the world's sole superpower, a designation the importance of which and even the actual existence of which remain sometimes controversial; that said, a fresh sense of freedom and possibility fueled a robust optimism spurred by unprecedented technological innovation.

The internet has redefined how the world works, and some of the nation's wealthiest and most influential companies came to flourish only with the arrival of the World Wide Web, and widespread adoption of internet technology throughout the 1990s. As early as the 1940s and 1950s, Frederick Terman (1900–1982) in his capacity as Stanford University dean of engineering and, later, provost had been encouraging students and former students to launch their own companies with the skills and tools of technological innovation they had begun learning at Stanford. Terman mentored William Hewlett and David Packard who formed their company in 1939, eventually converting it into a multinational corporation specializing in computing development, software design, networking hardware, and data storage. The trajectory of Hewlett-Packard illustrates the symbiotic relationship between Stanford University and companies devoted to high tech innovation. Stanford and the adjacent region of Silicon Valley had emerged as national leaders in imagining, creating, improving, and delivering technological products that shape modern life throughout the U.S.A. and the world. Silicon Valley–based companies include Agilent Technologies, Cisco Systems, eBay, E*Trade, Fairchild Semiconductor, Google, Intuit, LinkedIn, Netflix, Sun Microsystems, and Yahoo to name just a few. Silicon Valley accounts for one-third of the venture capital in the United States, and more than 5,000 public relations firms trace their origins to Stanford faculty and students or Stanford ideas.[1]

Higher education adopted the new technology for administrative operations, soon thereafter making adaptations for a variety of teaching, learning, and research functions. Students and faculty accessing multimedia library resources had historically relied on an array of technological tools from microform readers and reader printers to photocopiers, record players, and audio, video, and CD players; researchers located library resources through OPACs (online public access catalogs) which had replaced card catalogs during the late 1980s and early 1990s. Several of the multimedia formats would diminish in popularity with the development and widespread adoption of graphical interfaces, making the internet ubiquitous and transforming forever the way modern societies communicate and, more specifically, the way universities and university libraries conduct business.

A major development in digital scholarly communication was the establishment of JSTOR in 1995. It is a collection of scholarly journals, digitized in PDF (portable document format), completely retrospective and with full text searchability, with the intent of preserving intellectual content and expanding accessibility. JSTOR was conceived at Princeton University and funded, initially, with grant support from the Andrew W. Mellon Foundation. Drawing its name from the concept of journal storage, JSTOR is a non-profit organization since merged into its parent, Ithaka Harbors, likewise a non-profit entity, committed to preserving the scholarly record and nurturing sustainable resources in support of teaching and research.

The immense popularity of JSTOR is indicated by the fact that in 2013 it had more than 8,000 subscribers from one hundred-sixty countries. On the micro-level, JSTOR gives researchers the ability, when using high-quality rag content paper, to reproduce an article more durable than the original, and thus support the expansion of office files; these have historically been commonly used tools for the scholar in the humanities. On the macro-level, JSTOR greatly enhanced the potential of the academic library to develop a new business model for journal literature, improving the library's capacity to control the costs of access to scholarly and scientific information. The core of the JSTOR backlist serves most directly colleges and universities with curricular strength in basic liberal arts and sciences. While JSTOR has steadily added titles that support graduate and professional education, the more expensive specialized STEM journals have not been incorporated into JSTOR collections. Finally, JSTOR allowed the library to discard thousands of retrospective issues in paper form, yielding substantial amounts of square footage and, subsequently, contributing to conversations for reenvisioning library space in unprecedented ways. We cite JSTOR as a prominent example a full-text online database; today it is one of many such resources available through nonprofit and for-profit vendors.

By the turn of the century, it had become clear that widespread support for higher education as a common good was a thing of the past. Broad taxpayer support for public higher education had emerged immediately after World War II, flourished in the 1950s and 1960s, and begun to wane in the 1970s never again to return. But the internet-based technologies had given rise to new forms of preservation and access, making the mid-late 1990s a time of excitement and optimism. The optimism proved to be overinflated, especially in the for-profit sector, eventually morphing into a period of excessive speculation and resulting in a serious stock market correction in 2001. The national mood turned sharply following the attacks of 11 September 2001, and the venture capital invested in digital entrepreneurship began to shrink. While the dot-com bubble of 2001 was a smaller version of the housing-related crash of 2007–2008, an era of increasing anxiety had marked the new century and continues into the present.

In the face of growing economic volatility, university libraries began to cast a jaundiced eye at the rising costs of the journal literature, especially in STEM subjects gradually being taken over by for-profit publishers. The costs of scholarly communication had grown precipitously due to transformative growth in graduate programs after World War II and the expansion of federal financial support. Biomedical and related fields were the most egregious in terms of price increases; in the early 1990s, it became commonplace for the price of a journal subscription to quadruple within three years of its appearance, to exceed by several times either the national rate of inflation or the inexorable increase in tuition and fees. The professional literature since the 1990s is replete with reports of exorbitant increases exacted by multinational corporations purchasing the rights to journals and then raising prices. The library response, even at elite research universities, involved massive subscription cancellations.

Conventional economic principles have not been effective at reducing costs. That a decline in demand would result in a decline in cost is a principle that simply has not functioned with respect to current scientific and scholarly literature. When libraries dropped subscriptions, journal publishers increased prices on those subscribers who remained, continuing to expand profits. While a university library values the dissemination of information, a for-profit publisher values growth in profit margin. Libraries must pay for expensive journals due to the high expectations of the clienteles we serve. The pressure for high-prestige universities and high-profile professors to publish their work in top-tier journals is a powerful feature of academic culture. John M. Budd refers to this phenomenon as a "kind of academic arms race."[2] The professor seeks tenure and promotion and solicits a grant to support his or her research. The university, using a variety of funding sources, has hired graduate researchers and constructed laboratory space from which the professor operates. The professor pays a fee (especially in the sciences) to publish in a prestigious journal, and then gives the journal publisher rights to his or her intellectual property. The publisher, as copyright holder, charges a high subscription price which the university library cannot afford. On the downside, the university has produced the intellectual content and given it away, a business model crying out for disruptive revision. On the upside, all these elements have supported the faculty-driven concerns of teaching and research, promotion and tenure, and academic freedom, values not easily quantified or rendered in financial terms.

A growing response to the high cost of scholarly communication, especially in the journal literature, seems to have coalesced in the open-access movement. The fundamental principle of open access is that the results of scientific and scholarly research should be freely and widely available, rather than hidden behind walls of high subscription costs, computer protocols, or copyright protections. Conversations about open access content were occurring simultaneously with the emergence of open-source software development. With grant dollars from the Mellon Foundation, once again, and the Hewlett Foundation, MIT launched DSpace in 2002 as a digital repository with open-access source codes. Universities could download the software program at no cost and were, thus, invited to participate in its improvement and maintenance. DSpace and other open-source platforms offered a digital option for faculty seeking to preserve and access their intellectual products: lecture notes, lab reports, data sets, white papers, and research abstracts and articles.

But the institutional repository offered something more than a venue for contemporary learning and research materials. It has also emerged as a vast new expansion of digital storage and retrieval for documents, papers, and publications unique to each individual university, thus enriching the capacity for storytelling that goes to the heart of institutional identity and purpose. The library's department of archives or special collections, then, has become something of a growth industry over the past twenty years, strengthening both the library's campus-wide visibility and its potential for new liaisons with curricular revision and institutional advancement. The academy has known for a long time that it would become possible to share source code across institutional boundaries, but is now also discovering fresh power in the ability to share the results of intellectual labor itself, a much better bargain than giving away content and then buying it back at exorbitant prices.

One initiative from the open access movement exemplifies the sort of change that has become possible, the birth of SPARC (Scholarly Publishing and Academic Resources Coalition). SPARC is an international alliance of some 800 institutions incubated by the Association of Research Libraries and intended to support the creation of new models for reducing costs and improving dissemination of scholarly research in ways that benefit all stakeholders—authors, publishers, and libraries. Thus, the new era of digital formats and digital repositories has yielded fresh opportunity for the knowledge producing and consuming entities—universities and research libraries—to better balance the equation of return on investment in scholarly and scientific research.

Despite the hope and promise of the open-access movement, sweeping change is not likely to occur in the short term. The major cultural determinant in higher education remains with conventional faculty career ladders: grant support, research and publication, promotion and tenure. Professors in the baby boom generation made their mark in these settings, and now hold positions of senior leadership in committee structures that mentor younger professors. Baby boomers came up the "hard way," subjecting the products of their academic labor to the process of double-blind refereed assessments prior to publication in journals issued in paper form. Thus, adoption of institutional repositories has been slow to catch on, in spite of well publicized endorsements by university senates and other representative bodies that impact promotion and tenure. Questions arise such as "how does one guarantee academic quality in an institutional repository," particularly one that also includes lab reports and lecture notes? What are the implications for academic prestige, impact studies, and professorial reputation? How can a free (rather than expensive) full-text online journal mature to the point that it has a strong academic reputation? And how can the institutional repository hold greater appeal as a venue for one's research than a journal issued by a learned society or commercial publisher?

These questions go to the heart of institutional culture and to the intellectual work of the academy as a whole, and they must be addressed by supporters of institutional repositories and advocates of open access. We concur with John Budd that short-term solutions are unlikely, given the projected costs of operating institutional repositories, inadequate support from university administrations, stagnant state appropriations for public higher education, and the complex economics of knowledge production.[3] As perpetual optimists, we believe that the equation for producing scholarly communication will eventually tilt in favor of knowledge producers, the universities, and that as essential members of the academy, academic libraries—with our whole-campus points of view—will reap the benefits. We suspect, however, that we ourselves will not live long enough to see this new day on the horizon. For our section on the period, 1989–2015, we reprinted a piece by Rikk Mulligan, "Context and Background," that provides broad and deep perspective on scholarly communication, recounting the factors of economy and technology that, in recent decades, have stimulated change, all the while improving conditions for stakeholders seeking to confront challenges and to plan for the future. The character of academic information, the intellectual contents, containers, conditions, parameters, and potential for dissemination, after all, constitute our central and defining purposes.

Rationales for our optimism stem from interpretations like those of Beverly Lynch who had come to regard library professionals as early adopters, as proficient in the practice of self-examination in order to achieve economies of scale or to improve an existing service or launch a new one. The librarians' willingness, even desire, to change is exemplified in the movement, particularly after the turn of the century, to establish the information commons, also known as the learning commons, enlarging the range of services a library offers. Librarians partner with various other professionals to create new public space and to enlarge our definition of the library, accommodating, welcoming, even promoting multiple services to expand and enrich learning outside the classroom. Components of the learning commons might include but are not limited to traditional library print and digital services and resources, but also printing support, technology support, a writing center, a café service, film production capacity, collaborative workspaces, maker spaces, faculty development services, and any number of emerging options.

A leading thinker in this movement is Scott Bennett, formerly library director at both Johns Hopkins and Yale universities. Bennett has forged a new conversation about the purposes of the academic library, particularly about the uses of academic library building space. In his award-winning article, "Libraries and Learning: A History of Paradigm Change," he discerns the existence of three historical periods, reader-centered, book-centered, and learning-centered. For contemporary practice, he prefers the latter which, he claims, is rooted in the premise that we have knowledge abundance rather than knowledge scarcity. He urges librarians to focus on the art and science of learning, to think more like educators and less like service providers. He encourages us to enact learning rather than merely support it, and to view our physical setting less as a repository and more as a center where students create their own content, engaging in the enterprise of intentional learning.[4] Bennett also produced two landmark studies through the Council on Library and Information Resources, *Libraries Designed for Learning* (CLIR Publication no. 122, 2003) and *Library as Place: Rethinking Roles, Rethinking Space* (CLIR Publication no. 129, 2005) designed to recalibrate twenty-first century thought about library purpose and library building space. Bennett proposes that librarians collaborate with our partners in the academy, and he does not displace the centrality of scholarly communication but rather urges a more strategic use of it. How we store and retrieve scholarly information, and how we nurture and facilitate its effective use on behalf of students and faculty, remain at the core of who we are as a profession and of how we hope to influence academic life and the world beyond.

Notes

1. See Ken Auletta, "Get Rich U," *The New Yorker* (30 April 2012), 38–47. See also John Carreyou, *Bad Blood: Secrets and Lies in a Silicon Valley Startup* (New York: Knopf, 2018); Emily Chang, *Brotopia: Breaking Up the Boys Club of Silicon Valley* (New York: Portfolio/Penguin, 2018); and Arun Rao, *A History of Silicon Valley: The Greatest Creation of Wealth in the History of the Planet*, 2nd Ed. (Scotts Valley, California: CreateSpace, 2013).

2. John M. Budd, *Six Issues Facing Libraries Today: Critical Perspectives* (Lanham, Maryland: Scarecrow Press, 2017), 77.

3. Budd (2017), 81–82. The loss of public support for higher education has been confirmed by Charles Peterson of the Cornell University Department of History. Peterson noted that state investment per student dropped by twenty-six percent between 1990 and 2010. He also cited data assembled by the UC Berkeley Labor Center to the effect that in the fifty years since 1969, tenured and tenure-track positions in higher education in the U.S. have declined from seventy-eight percent to thirty-three percent of the total number of faculty. See "Serfs of Academe," *New York Review of Books* 57:4 (12 March 2020), 47.

4. Scott Bennett, "Libraries and Learning: A History of Paradigm Change," *portal: Libraries and the Academy* 9: 2 (April 2009), 181–97.

Context and Background [on the Transformation of Scholarly Communication]

Rikk Mulligan

Scholarly communication is the process of producing, evaluating, disseminating, and preserving the research findings of scholars and scientists shared with academic communities and other interested parties. This process helps shape academic disciplines, legitimize lines of inquiry and research methods, and influence public policy; it requires not only the availability of published materials, but also their review, use, and reuse as part of an active and evolving exchange of ideas. Scholarly publishing, the journals and monographs at the core of scholarly communications, has faced a series of challenges over the past few decades: discoverability, collection and preservation, and especially publication and production. Since the mid–20th century, new technologies have been and are being created to meet these challenges, yet many solutions have quickly become obsolete or spawned new problems, such as the attempt to reduce costs by using the Internet to distribute digital publications creating complications involving intellectual property rights, discoverability, and citation. Although the Internet initially appeared to offer a way to reduce the costs of scholarly publishing, particularly in the global north and other portions of the developed world, today, more than twenty years after its advent, its potential to deliver innovative modes of transmission and new communication formats remains largely untapped. Digital publishing has become a form of scholarly communication using PDF and ePub versions of articles and monographs, yet these remain tied to the long-struggling traditional publishing industry, particularly in the West, while more experimental and hybrid forms of scholarship remain on the fringe of student use and faculty acceptance.

Although scholars have always communicated with one another, the system of scholarly communication began with the formation of learned societies in Europe and quickly spread to colonies and centers of learning throughout the world. Groups of philosophers, observers, and experimenters formed societies to help them work together to increase their knowledge and define common goals by sharing discoveries and experiments. Formal scholarly communication in the English language began in the collection of the notes and letters of the members of the Royal Society of London and their publication in a scholarly journal, *Philosophical Transactions of the Royal Society*, in 1665. In addition to notes and letters, scientific articles quickly became the standard form used within such journals to disseminate observations and findings among society members, patrons, and sponsors. The system continued to evolve and expand as these societies proliferated, diversified, and grew. Journals became serial publications whose increasing number and volume required the development of indexing and cataloging practices in libraries and peer and editorial review processes by the societies to manage their production. However, because the audience for these works was relatively small and specialized, seldom were sales enough to cover production costs and labor. Scholarly publications therefore became the product of a gift or prestige economy rather than that of a strictly commercial market. Much of the labor surrounding scholarly publications, writing, editing, and peer review, was and is essentially exchanged for reputation and prestige, factors that became and remain important in the assessment, promotion, and tenure process of modern higher education.[1] The system of scholarly communication continued to grow and evolve beyond the journal as the landscape of higher education changed.

The passage of the Morrill Act in 1862 brought about the creation of the land-grant university system and shifted the focus of higher education in the U.S. toward research and improving the economy. More than just increasing the number of students and faculty, the range of scholarly disciplines expanded as did large-scale research projects that necessitated a new long-form of scholarly communication: the scholarly monograph, a specialist work on a single subject by a single author, a format that has since become inextricably linked with the system of assessment, promotion, and tenure for those in the humanities and social sciences. The 1887 Hatch Act placed greater emphasis (and access to funding) on experimentation and the 1914 Smith-Lever Act on sharing knowledge and information with the public, suggesting a greater emphasis on publication by professional scholars.[2] The monograph was intended to meet this need, rather than provide a source of revenue or even cost recovery, so it fell to universities to augment the efforts of the scholarly societies by also becoming publishers. The economics of the monograph meant that these new university presses also came to depend on the same prestige economy that already supported journal production.

Surprisingly, journals and monographs became profitable in the second half of the twentieth century after the GI Bill and the "space race" fueled a greater expansion of higher education and the rapid conversion of teachers' colleges into universities. Publishing had to expand to meet the burgeoning needs of a growing faculty and body of scholarship, along with increased interest in new science and technology, leading libraries to purchase more works, and then to physically grow as they required more storage space. This activity was largely funded by government grants and programs in the post-war decades, especially in the STEM disciplines (science, technology, engineering, and mathematics), yet society and university presses could not keep up with the demand, attracting commercial publishers to the now lucrative academic market, creating what some have called the golden age of academic publishing. However, because most of this production was supported by public funds rather than the scholarly market (student use, library holdings, or for use in promotion and tenure review),[3] when federal and state budgets were eventually cut in the 1970s, sales faltered, and scholarly publishing began to suffer.

The changing roles and mission of libraries and the spreading influence of digital technology began to radically alter scholarly communications in the 1980s. While libraries tried to maintain the strengths of their collections, and preservation efforts and bibliographic control, they also moved to automate processes as computer and information technology developed. Library experts such as Martin Cummings and David Lewis considered the costs of automation and the changing nature of the library, its holdings, and services, with Cummings addressing automation and cataloging, and Lewis forecasting not only the way research might change, but also how scholars and students might use the library differently (if at all).[4] Cummings added to the voices of others in pointing out that the cost of publications had risen faster than the consumer price index since the late 1970s and libraries had started to develop "resource-sharing schemes" even as publishers began to look to new online sales of information services for profits.[5] In 1986 Cummings saw the advantages of preparing and storing information electronically to increase access, availability, and preservation, although this was before consumer-based challenges appeared such as media evolution and the rapid obsolescence of formats (floppy disks, video tapes, CD-ROMs).[6] By 1988, although Lewis was looking at the library, his comments reflect changes needed in the system of scholarly communication as the "power of new media and the failings of the old system [of print publishing] are driving scholarly institutions toward change."[7] Things were beginning to change, slowly, and the advent of the Internet created greater disruption of both scholarly communications (including all forms of publishing) as well as research libraries.

Decades before the Internet was created, librarians and others began to envision networked texts, data, and scholarship that would propel research in the future—the activity that became the conceptual basis for the World Wide Web. Before J.C.R. Licklider of MIT published his report outlining such a vision, *Libraries of the Future,* he described how data, programs, and information might be accessed by people using computers from anywhere in the world; he called this concept a "Galactic Network" in 1962.[8] The first steps to creating this global network, what would become the Internet, began with DARPA and the ARPANET in 1969. By the mid–1980s it was common for students in the sciences and engineering to dial-in to their institutional mainframes and libraries. By the end of the 1980s, network providers including America Online, CompuServe, UUNet, and PSInet, among others, provided access to the growing free and commercial network of servers. The text-based Internet with its electronic billboards, chat relays, and early use-nets all suggested that the potential Lewis had described as the future digital library was within reach and most university students were now expected to own and use computers in their research and scholarship. 1992 is marked by many as the point at which the World Wide Web became open to the public thanks to the invention of Mosaic, the precursor to Netscape Navigator, a graphical user interface that could present the contents (initially limited to text and images) of these early websites—the first web browser.

1992 also marked the publication of an influential book on the need to transform how the library delivered its services at the dawn of the digital age and of a study commissioned by the Andrew W. Mellon Foundation on the changing and possibly troubled economics of the research library. Michael Buckland's *Redesigning Library Services: A Manifesto* articulated how library services—providing access to knowledge—needed to be considered in terms of the paper library, automated library (where Cummings and Lewis had placed their focus), and the fast-growing electronic library. Even though Buckland's vision did not immediately integrate with the emerging World Wide Web, it did suggest how networked data might help libraries take advantage of extended, interconnected catalogs, bibliographies, and digital texts. The report commissioned by the

Mellon Foundation, *University Libraries and Scholarly Communication*, emphasizes this moment of flux by suggesting that the entire system of scholarly communication was about to change in part because it was no longer sustainable in its present form. The roots of this study lay in the ARL Serials Prices Project (1989), the findings of which so concerned the Mellon Foundation that it launched its own multi-year study[9] to better understand major trends in research library spending, including the portion spent on journal subscriptions versus book purchases, the share for new acquisitions versus the cost to preserve and catalog holdings, and to consider how new technology had recently affected the work of librarians and archivists as well as to envision future changes in not just libraries, but also those needed to sustain scholarly communications more broadly. Scholarly publishing had long coped with a series of issues that one press director characterized as a "chronic illness" going back to at least the 1970s, but also continued into the 1990s as libraries bought fewer books and journal subscriptions.[10]

In the early 1990s libraries had already been under tremendous strain because of increasing journal subscription fees, the proliferation of cross-disciplinary journals, the growing demands for ever-more specialized monographs for tenure and review (even though fewer were selling to libraries), and the burgeoning amount of scholarship being produced by faculty under greater demands to publish more and faster. As Buckland's manifesto suggests, libraries were also under pressure to alter the way they provided services to readers who were quickly being redefined as "users." The Internet spawned the open-source movement for computer code, which provided a model for new initiatives pushing for the free and open access to information—including scholarship and the vast field of gray "unpublished" literature. The Internet also quickly offered novel options to disseminate research and create new forms of scholarship and revolutionary experiments in academic narrative and argument as hybrid or emerging scholarship. Between the economic instability of the traditional print forms and the need for libraries to use the latest technology to fulfill their core services, both short-form and long-form scholarship had to transform. This transformation started with digitized forms made available online, but quickly began to evolve new features and hybrid forms.

Notes

1. Stanley Chodorow, "Scholarship & Scholarly Communication in the Electronic Age," *EDUCAUSE Review* 35, no. 1 (January/February 2000): 88–89, http://www.educause.edu/ero/educause-review-magazine-volume-35-number-1-januaryfebruary-2000.

2. Board on Agriculture, National Research Council, *Colleges of Agriculture at the Land Grant Universities: A Profile* (Washington, D.C.: National Academy Press, 1995), 9–10.

3. Chodorow, "Scholarship & Scholarly Communication in the Electronic Age," 89.

4. David Lewis, "Inventing the Electronic University," *College & Research Libraries* 49, no. 4 (1988): 298, doi:10.5860/crl.76.3.296.

5. Martin M. Cummings, *The Economics of Research Libraries* (Washington, D.C.: Council on Library Resources, 1986), 26–29.

6. *Ibid.*, 58–65.

7. Lewis, "Inventing the Electronic University," 296.

8. Barry M. Leiner et al., "Brief History of the Internet," *The Internet Society*, accessed May 4, 2015, http://www.internetsociety.org/internet/what-internet/history-internet/brief-history-internet.

9. Mary M. Case, "Scholarly Communication: ARL as a Catalyst for Change," *Portal: Libraries and the Academy* 9, no. 3 (July 2009): 383. doi: 10.1353/pla.0.0050.

10. Sanford G. Thatcher, "Thinking Systematically about the Crisis in Scholarly Communication," in *The Specialized Scholarly Monograph in Crisis or How Can I Get Tenure If You Won't Publish My Book?* edited by Mary M. Case (Washington, D.C.: Association of Research Libraries, 1997).

ADDITIONAL REFERENCES

Brown, Laura, Rebecca Griffiths, and Matthew Rascoff. "University Publishing in a Digital Age." Ithaka Report. July 26, 2007. http://sr.ithaka.org/research-publications/university-publishing-digital-age.

Buckland, Michael. *Redesigning Library Services: A Manifesto*. Chicago, Illinois: American Library Association, 1992. https://archive.org/details/redesigninglibra00buck.

Bush, Vannevar. "As We May Think," *Atlantic Monthly* 176 (July 1945): 101–108. http://www.theatlantic.com/magazine/archive/1945/07/as-we-may-think/303881/.

Cummings, Anthony M., Marcia L. Witte, William G. Bowen, Laura O. Lazarus, and Richard H. Ekman. *University Libraries and Scholarly Communication: A Study Prepared for the Andrew W. Mellon Foundation*. Washington, D.C.: Association of Research Libraries, 1992.

De Roure, David. "The Future of Scholarly Communications." *Insights* 27, no. 3 (November 2014): 233–238. http://eprints.soton.ac.uk/370703/.

Fitzpatrick, Kathleen. *Planned Obsolescence: Publishing, Technology, and the Future of the Academy*. New York: New York University Press, 2011.

Licklider, J.C.R. *Libraries of the Future*. Cambridge, Massachusetts: MIT Press, 1965. https://archive.org/details/librariesoffutur00lickuoft.

Historiographical Futures
Imperfect But Possible

Historical writings devoted to academic librarianship have advanced mightily and matured in dramatic fashion since the U.S. Department of Education issued its massive report, *Public Libraries in the United States of America: Their History, Condition, and Management* (Washington, D.C.: Government Printing Office, 1876). At the time, college libraries—as a distinct category—were included in treatments of public libraries, and editors S.R. Clark and S.N. Warren analyzed college libraries in a sixty-six-page review incorporating historical references, donor information, and volume counts for library holdings. Additional topics that included academic librarianship appeared in wider discussions of administration, cataloging, and facilities, and an instructional component known as the professor of books, but early institutions and landmark events were those summarized by Clark and Warren. Though sometimes connected with the universities, libraries devoted to law, medicine, science, and theology were examined in separate essays. Taken together, these contributions, coupled with other landmark events of 1876, offer a convenient starting point for considering historiographical issues.

The modern era dates from the 1930s when the Carnegie Corporation provided financial support to establish the nation's first doctorate in library science at the University of Chicago. Faculty and graduates of the Chicago program redefined scholarly work in librarianship, taking it to unprecedented heights of historical and sociological inquiry. Doctoral study expanded further after World War II and library schools began to produce scholarship more fruitful for historical insight and professional expertise. As a metaphor for the maturation of library scholarship, consider Grosvenor Dawe's *Melvil Dewey: Seer: Inspirer: Doer, 1851-1931* (Lake Placid Club, New York: Melvil Dewey Biografy, 1932), comparing it to Wayne A. Wiegand's *Irrepressible Reformer: A Biography of Melvil Dewey* (Chicago, Illinois: ALA, 1996). We intend, in this comparison, to highlight the transition from hagiography to insightful, evaluative narration, an approach which has finally emerged, and which must remain routinized.

The public library holds much greater appeal than the academic library as a subject for historical research. We explore some reasons for this trend in our introductory essay—that the public library facilitates treatment of the large themes of democratic principles and human rights while the story of the academic library leads to, what some regard, as an inevitable outcome. But we have sought to balance this equation, identifying for future historians the heroic ideal of the academic research library—the striving for completeness through wide-ranging methods of acquiring, borrowing, lending, scanning, and distributing print and digital resources in the great national project of

230 Historiographical Futures

both creating new knowledge and of preserving neglected resources for generations yet unborn. These ideals require a continual search for clarity, rooted as they are, according to Wayne Bivens-Tatum,[1] in the enlightenment virtues of discovery and experiment, intellectual freedom and liberty. They also necessitate a public presentation, something we have sought to create in this book, toward an expansion of our audience, an enlargement of the core of academics and educated readers devoted to the enduring values of the academic research library.

The matter of who has written the history of the academic library goes to the heart of the reputation and status of the community of library historians. Our scholarly output has emerged primarily from those with a doctorate in LIS (more recently degrees from I Schools) and with work experience as LIS professors and/or academic librarians. These histories are written from the perspectives of insiders, and Weiner proposes that the story of the academic library be told by scholars most directly impacted by library collections and services: literature or history, for example. We have confirmed Weiner's analysis and we do not take issue with her proposal. In fact, we have assembled our own collection with a purpose quite similar, to enlarge the corps of those who read and write our history and who take a diligent stakeholder's interest in the health and longevity of the research library. As library historians, we seek and welcome input from multi-disciplinary perspectives but, with historical events as our guide, we must conclude that the lion's share of our story will continue to be written by those of us who have taught and practiced in the fields of librarianship.

The impulse of the community of library historians to reach beyond informal mid-twentieth century origins is suggested by name changes. The ALHRT became the LHRT, and the *Journal of Library History* became *Libraries & Culture*, since becoming *Information & Culture*; it has long been issued by the University of Texas Press. And a new journal has arisen, published by Penn State University Press, *Libraries: Culture, History, and Society*. Beginning with volume one, number one in 2017, this new journal replaces the loss of emphasis on librarianship apparent in the current pages of *Information & Culture*, thus Penn State and the editors, Bernadette Lear and Eric Charles Novotny, have given new reality to the dreams of the founders and editors of the *Journal of Library History* and *Libraries & Culture*.

While we rejoice in the emergence of a flagship journal, we remain committed to wider dialogue with scholars in related disciplines and subdisciplines. Library historians have, for example, made library-related presentations at regional, national, and international historical and literary conferences, and the occasional LIS scholar has earned a joint appointment with another academic department. Moreover, the library as a subject for scholarly inquiry, seems to be growing in popularity among non–LIS scholars. Three edited collections illustrate the point. *The Library as an Agency of Culture*, edited by Thomas Augst and Wayne A. Wiegand, appeared as *American Studies* (42:3, Fall 2001) and, in addition to LIS, contributors represented American studies, art history, communication, English, and history. A similar mix of authors contributed to *Institutions of Reading: The Social Life of Libraries in the United States*, edited by Thomas Augst and Kenneth Carpenter (Amherst, Massachusetts: University of Massachusetts Press, 2007) and *The Meaning of the Library: A Cultural History*, edited by Alice Crawford (Princeton, New Jersey: Princeton University Press, 2015). The bulk of this scholarship is devoted to the public library, but the research library has designated space and, when it attracts scholarly attention beyond LIS as well as from luminaries like Robert Darnton and Alberto Manguel, we become better equipped for telling our story in robust, interdisciplinary platforms for research and writing.

A wide range of conceptual alliances become apparent; American studies may be the most obvious, embracing reading tastes and civic spaces. Areas of study like analytical bibliography, cultural history, intellectual history, the history of books and reading, the history of higher education, printing and publishing, and social and religious history hold great promise and can provide needed context. Anne Buchanan and Jean-Pierre V.M. Hérubel regard LIS as open to import from various disciplines among them computer science, economics, and sociology.[2] In our final selection, Hérubel considers various options for the future that could move library history into wider intellectual terrain, promoting alliances with cultural studies or cultural history as holding the most promise for telling the academic research library story to a wider audience and preserving it for future generations.

Notes

1. Wayne Bivens-Tatum, *Libraries and the Enlightenment* (Los Angeles: Library Juice Press, 2012), 186.
2. Anne L. Buchanan and Jean-Pierre V.M. Hérubel, "Subject and Historiographic Characteristics of Library History," *Journal of Scholarly Publishing* 42:4 (July 2011), 516.

Historiographical Futures for Library History

Conceptual Observations for Future Historians

JEAN-PIERRE V.M. HÉRUBEL

Abstract: Where is library history going? Where has it been and how should it establish itself as a specialization within Clio's pantheon of historical specializations and discrete fields? As library history has nearly disappeared from LIS graduate curricula in the United States, where is library history or the library historian to go for support, education, and scholarship? Should this specialty be ensconced within American Studies, or should it find intellectual sanctuary within the larger historical community, where mainstream interests may or may not nurture library history? Should library history move beyond the library as an institution and the librarian's profession to encompass interdisciplinary as well as, multidisciplinary ventures? Should library history join forces with book history per se or print culture history as larger cultural issues assume greater relevance to historical research or, as evidenced by the increasing amount of scholarly interest being taken in the history of information, in the broadest sense of the term? These and other questions require to be aired if library history is to remain historiographically and methodologically alive. Therefore, in line with these conceptual and historiographical concerns, a discussion of the possible futures and solutions should open new paths in the field of library history.

Historiographical Futures for Library History

Within the discipline of historical research and scholarship, there exist many topics worth studying; this is especially true in the field of academic history. As a discipline, however, history may be regarded as an open continent occupied by competing tribes and territorial prerogatives.[1] As with any academic discipline, history is open to specialization, which has often resulted in honed interests focusing on a period, a movement, a geographical region, or social, political, military, or economic topic of interest.[2] Academic history can be described as a mansion consisting of many rooms and antechambers which have yet to be fully explored.[3] As specialization generates new disciplines and sub-disciplines, specific methodologies, techniques, perspectives, and even subjects of research and changes of emphasis come into existence. Scholarly societies can be usefully documented, along with the specialized journals focusing on their interests, such as the history of science, technology, exploration, medicine, pharmacy, or military development. Academic history has generally been broadly segmented under economic, social, political, military, diplomatic headings, etc., before being further broken down into narrower foci, such as the history of astronomy or the history of libraries. Like science, academic historians have always attempted to generate new knowledge and insights using highly refined approaches to elucidate the past in all its various aspects. In the context of academic history, library history has evolved and established itself betwixt and between the various historical topics and fields investigated.

Historical Amnesia and Librarianship

The following are some of the most crucial questions which arise in this context: what occurs when a subject is too specialized or too amorphous to constitute an appropriate subject of research? Are there any subjects of research that escape definition? Or do there exist some phenomena that need to be defined epistemologically in order to be worthy of research? What is the status of library history? Is it beyond the pale, or is it a subject relating to a single profession or a set of vocational activities that is grudgingly accepted as a topic worthy of historical scholarship or relegated to the hands of amateurs.[4] A *de visu* perusal of library school courses shows the marginal status of library history in first professional degree education. It is certainly possible to specialize at masters' and Ph.D. level in library history, but professional necessity often wins the day over historical academic pursuits.

Library and information science (LIS) professionals carry out their work in a way similar to other professionals. Practitioners of engineering, law, medicine or science, etc., do not generally become historians of their respective professions.[5] Indeed, one would be hard pressed to find a critical mass of practitioners pursuing the historical aspects of their professions apart from the occasional celebratory, institutional, or sponsored history: very few historiographically-driven analytical scholarly efforts have been made on these lines. All too often, these occasional forays have been devoid of historical and historiographical contextualization. Although the primary sources have often been consulted, and the chronological order of events accurately presented, they often lack the veracity and careful analysis required to meet the standards of mainstream academic historians. Various library historians have spoken about library historians' non-historical approach to learning and knowledge, emphasizing the *presentism* which can be observed in the curricula and publications in the field of LIS, and the fact that a social science approach has often been adopted to the detriment of the more historical perspective associated with the humanities.[6] In addition, it is significant that there exist few openings for library historians on LIS programs, where few members of the faculty are specialists in library history.[7] Although library history is still a going enterprise, complete with an official organization, the Library History Round Table, which organizes periodic seminars,[8] it continues to occupy a very marginal position within the academic space inhabited by LIS professional concerns and educational prerogatives.[9]

The Graduate Incubator and Library History

Graduate education demands specialization and requires graduate students to undergo a process of disciplinary and professional acculturation in a specific disciplinary field.[10] Nowhere is this requirement more demanding than for graduate students engaged in doctoral programs, where they have to undergo rites of passage in terms of disciplinary traditions, protocols, scholarly ethos, and other disciplinary specificities. In short, historians, whether they are medievalists, or American Studies scholars, become practitioners of their disciplines after undergoing a process of acculturation in these disciplines. Doctoral studies are a form of liminal experience which have profound effects on those who pursue this path. After navigating the first year of doctoral studies and courses, learning to use appropriate research tools and participate in seminars and mastering the dissertation process, graduate students learn to meet the demands of their chosen discipline.[11] Since interdisciplinary and multidisciplinary approaches are being used increasingly in many fields, it has become necessary to define the various disciplinary cultures involved and their characteristics in order to draw up an overall conceptual topography of disciplines and sub-disciplines. What are the differences and similarities between library history programs and those available in the fields of history, education, and journalism, etc., per se? And what if library history courses are ensconced within LIS programs where they are only one of many options available? What possible options exist for those pursuing historical specializations in disciplines where history as such does not constitute the primary focus?[12] What possible differences may exist between studies on the history of journalism, library history in journalism, and library science programs, for example, where historians are not trained at a department of history? The process of acculturation and the scholarly perspectives acquired will not necessarily be the same in all these cases. To what extent will the knowledge dispensed be affected by disciplinary specificities? In other words, how do academic publications reflect disciplinary configurations from the conceptual point of view? These questions have a direct bearing on the question as to where library history is going, and how it should it be set up in the future.

Similar sub-disciplinary conditions prevail across historical fields in the case of professional programs, where acculturation for professional practice is and remains paramount. Education history, journalism history, and library history have all been marginalized: including historical studies in the curricula of future practitioners is certainly a problematic issue, and difficult to justify rationally.[13] Unlike those pursuing mainstream studies in history, which involve long-term specialization in a major and two or three optional subjects, library, education, and journalism historians undergoing doctoral studies have to undergo previous studies in specific fields.[14] The dissertations and the occasional master's thesis they produce are only incidental, but not a fully-fledged experience in academic history.[15] Four or more years after obtaining a master's degree in history, the novitiate historian eventually graduates at doctoral level by producing a thesis. Throughout their doctoral studies, students are systemically exposed to and trained in historiography, its methods, the theoretical background involved, and acquire a thorough knowledge of history in general, as well as having their historical knowledge in two or three specific fields and in their main field of specialization tested by sitting examinations. Mainstream doctoral studies in history are completely immersive, contrary to what LIS historians experience during their training.

Library History's Past and Future Intellectual and Academic Space

The library as an agency or place has been one of the main themes in library history, and, the library has been described as a social nexus in many library history studies.[16]

Generally speaking, library historians have focused on a constellation of topics such as: collections, administration, cataloging, preservation, readers' services, and reference services.[17] The types of libraries studied have included university and college libraries, public libraries, and special libraries such as museum and corporate libraries, private libraries (although to a lesser extent), and subscription libraries, as well as technical services such as cataloging, preservation of materials, etc.[18] Other studies have dealt with professional organizations such as local, state and national associations. Here librarians' penchant for process history has resulted in large numbers of papers on how things were done, often without referring to larger societal concerns or influences—administrative history being the main focus.[19] Interestingly, complementing studies on these lines, many biographical studies have focused on key figures in librarianship, whose leadership was carried out at specific times and places under conditions not liable to be encountered elsewhere. From the strictly historiographical perspective, however, very little attention has been paid so far in studies in the field of library history to the *raison d'être* of historiography or questions of methodological validity.[20] The need for reflexive soul-searching may lead to a more sophisticated understanding of historical methods and the theoretical framing of historical findings, which should improve both the selection of research topics and the process of research itself, as well as placing studies in the overall context of the historiographical body of knowledge available.[21]

The expansive, if not protean, nature of information history is characterized mainly by its essential elasticity: it is not fixed spatially or centered, and includes a wide and fluid range of research topics. This field of study has arrived somewhat recently on the historical scene and promises to generate a methodological storm capable of sweeping away the cobwebs from Clio's view. Stating this does not mean belittling the fundamental spadework accomplished by the first library historians, nor does it question the veracity or validity of the scholarly contributions made by library historians (See Diagram 1).

Diagram 1. Spheres of Future Historical Research

Library History	Information History
• circumscribed subject ecology • phenomena filtered via libraries as places & processes • pronounced narrative structure • biographical • less open to other disciplines	• flexible subject ecology • phenomena filtered via nodes, flows, conditions • more analytical • less biographical • open to other disciplines

However, it is worth noting how these two seemingly separate spheres merge within the historical procedural enterprise, as generally understood by professional historians. As shown in the model below, both library and information historians adhere to the procedures long established by the members of the historical profession (See Diagram 2).

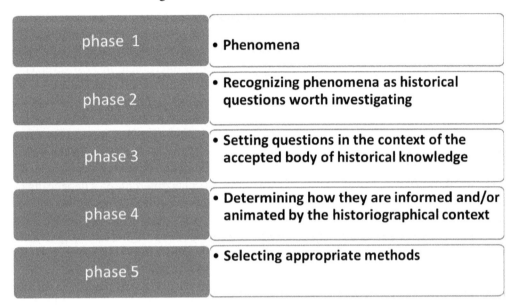

Diagram 2. Historical Research Process

Kin to scientific methods, the sequential phases followed by historians, especially academic historians carrying out their research, determine how they will pursue their research objectives. Adhering to these phases provides a verifiable and reproducible method that can be adapted as required, depending on the methods used, and the choice of tools can be informed by theoretical perspectives and models. Regardless of the school of thought, historiographical context, or methods used, historians have generally subscribed to this model whether they have adopted an *internalist* or *externalist* approach.[22]

Internalist versus Externalist Imperatives

Although there exists some dynamic tension between the *internalist* and *externalist* schools of historical research, from which library history has not been immune, library history can be said to have been more of an *internalist* enterprise than otherwise, since libraries and their various aspects have often been treated as though they were intellectually and culturally apart from economic, political and social considerations. In the main, library history has been institutional history privileging libraries' institutional characteristics such as space, process, and administration. Library history has been admittedly largely written by library practitioners, who have greatly enriched the body of literature available, but only within the confines of an intellectual ecosystem that seems to be cut off from the outside historical environment. Far from being purely antiquarian, many library historians have traced the history of their institutions, or written celebratory pamphlets praising the achievements of the pioneers and leading figures in the field or reporting how librarians' training programs developed, while others have dealt with finer details on which further research would be worth conducting. Although library historians' publications have effectively created a specialized branch of historical research, it still remains to be seen whether this special branch will manage to enlarge its scope and thus gain a stronger foothold in the mainstream field of historical research.

Much of library history is of the *internalist* kind, although the authors of many sound, effective discrete studies have started to work on more externalist lines. The insights and methodologies of mainstream historians would be worth using to take a new look at previous knowledge and findings, generating new interpretations. However, contradictory this may seem, externalist historical scholarship is not diametrically opposed to the *internalist* perspective, but is simply much more highly contextualized. Events are never regarded as being isolated phenomena but embedded within larger frames of reference. The history of libraries cannot be studied without taking into account the many factors and actors involved, their cultural background, and as their place in the web of society. *Externalist* approaches, for example, can re-frame the library as a cultural, societal, intellectual, or political filter; individual libraries play different roles depending on the context: regarding the library as an institutional membrane can open new ways of approaching library history, especially as society strongly determines library budgets, personnel, collections and public service policies far beyond the hermetically defined institutional context. Library history can be revisited by regarding the libraries as a place of confluence and interactions, which it would be of great interest to investigate.

If library history continues to focus on isolated libraries, it is liable to continue to be a marginalized intellectual pursuit cut off from the evolving currents which are shaping mainstream historical research, as well as the historiographically rich discussions and theory it has generated.[23] *Internalist* preoccupations are not necessarily pedestrian, but they focus on topics that can be circumscribed and explored with less concern for wider contexts. For example, it is all very well to study how microforms were introduced, implemented, and used at libraries by patrons and researchers in the 1940s; however, the broader issue of how technology informs or deforms users' attitudes towards their needs raises questions about the purpose of preserving and disseminating books, etc. Likewise, describing collections and acquisitions without weighing up the influence of factors such as value, inclusion, exclusion, censorship, and gatekeeping, which often depend on external forces and principles (such as utilitarianism) and ideologies makes this form of antiquarian activity methodologically sterile. Without their context, the phenomena under investigation become intellectually and historiographically isolated and suspended, and hence arcane.

The Promising Contribution of Information History to Library History

The advent of information history has now been recognized as relating to library history and worthy of sharing the prerogatives previously held by this branch. Although the controversy about this matter has subsided by now, the constellation of topics required to feature on the curricula of each of these specialties still remains to be defined.[24] Whether, as Donald Davis and John Aho have suggested, the concerns of academic historians, library history, and institution-based history should be incorporated into library history studies, or whether Jonathan Rose's suggestion that library history and book studies could be effectively merged rather than including on the curricula more antiquarian subjects, which can be intellectually ossifying and marginalizing, especially if they are nested in the context of historical studies.[25] Alistair Black's challenge to traditional library history and historians was not necessarily hostile: it was intended as an appeal to enlarge the spectrum of historical studies on libraries' activities.[26] Information is ubiquitous, and humans tend to depend upon some forms of information, which are liable to be loosely construed as knowledge, to carry out their activities. It is necessary to understand how human beings have generated, packaged, disseminated, and used information, whether it was inscribed on clay tablets, papyri, monastic accounts, military charts, maps, eighteenth century ships' logs, train station timetables, mortality tables, etc. There is a great deal of material available for information history to explore.

How can library history and historians do other than attempt to redefine library history as institutional history in the context of information history? Consider the history of museums: this too is institutional history, resplendent with scholarly contributions on architecture, administration, collections, celebratory narratives, and biographical studies. Yet here too, a perusal of its literature shows that larger issues are being discussed, which has enlarged the scope of historical research in museum studies by incorporating ethnographic, historical-sociological and economic approaches, as well as cultural historical analyses emphasizing that museums play a social and symbolic role in society. Of course, alongside these studies, one can also find many *internalist* studies focusing on acquisitions, the key actors in museums' activities, including the patrons and benefactors, as well as general histories of curatorship and administration. Some mainstream historians, anthropologists, art historians, and others not professionally involved in museology, recently produced studies which have put an end to the insular approach to the history of museums.[27] These studies based partly on social and political history, often informed by art history and concepts borrowed from anthropology and ethnology, contain historically oriented cultural critiques exploring the importance of power, cultural hegemony, and gender, as well as curatorial aims and the art of display in the context of museums and the societies for which they cater. One of the most crucial questions which arises is how information is used for the conveyance of ideas, for display purposes, for social control or enlightenment, and how knowledge is acquired in these environments. As museums are being increasingly regarded as physical contexts and loci, less research is based these days on an *internalist* approach.

In line with museum history and studies, library history could be approached via a spectrum of subjects, which could be addressed from the point of view of libraries, but not necessarily as institutions; libraries are just one sphere of activity involving information and knowledge, after all. The same can be said about archives, the history of which can be both institutionally based or give rise to more important questions pertaining to the flow of knowledge and information. There is certainly a need for a history of institutions, especially one which is critically grounded in academic historical methods. Dispensing with hagiographies and celebratory narratives can only strengthen institutional histories. In addition, there exists a recurrent problem for all these historical approaches, namely the need to take a more critical look at studies lacking analytically driven methods and theoretical perspectives, sound and historiographically

240 Historiographical Futures

informed research and framing, in which no attempt has been made to re-frame the history of libraries, museums, or archives, let alone information history.

The Siren Call of Multidisciplinarity

Firstly, before discussing multidisciplinarity, it is essential to define and understand the fundamental characteristics of the academic disciplines in question in the context of the arenas in which they exist and function (See Diagrams 3 and 4).[28]

Diagram 3: Disciplinary Morphology and Typology

Disciplinarity	Subdisciplinarity	Interdisciplinarity	Multidisciplinarity
• A highly defined and honed approach with focused objectives, and specific methodological and technical characteristics. Specialized nomenclature and consensus-driven protocols and procedures are adhered to and maintained. • *Examples*—History, Philosophy	• A highly specialized approach within a disciplinary framework concentrating on specific objectives, utilizing unique methodologies and techniques. Often, a particularistic area of interest is considered within the greater spectrum of a discipline. • *Examples*—Environmental History, Philosophy of History	• Two or more disciplines come together to examine a topic or set of topics and meld into a permanent relationship. • *Examples*—Historical Sociology, Political Communication.	• Two or more disciplines involved, providing their unique perspectives without actually melding. Disciplines come together to explore phenomena and work on stated objectives, while retaining their singular characteristics. • *Examples*—Latin American Studies, American Studies

Diagram 4: Disciplinary Configurations

Disciplines	*Subdisciplines*	*Multidisciplines*	*Interdisciplines*
• History • Art History • Philosophy • Musicology	• Economic History • Architectural History • Aesthetics • EthnoMusicology	• American Studies • Medieval Studies • Renaissance Studies • Canadian Studies	• Environmental History • Architectural Philosophy • Bioethics • Historical Musicological Theory

Two particularly attractive options for multidisciplinary studies are American Studies and Popular Studies, each of which has its own learned society, official journal, and annual conference.[29] Whether these possibilities are viable options for library history depends on whether or not it seems to be necessary for library historians to adopt a broader intellectual and subject landscape.[30] According to Wayne Wiegand, American Studies is a natural setting for those interested in libraries as institutions, as they are embedded with communities, especially in the case of public libraries.[31] Studies could break new ground by investigating topics such as libraries' interactions with reading culture, libraries and economic conditions, libraries and political influences, as well as libraries as aesthetic objects, including the history of their construction and the architectural use they make of space. Sociological and anthropological approaches and qualitative and quantitative methods could be used to complement archival studies, providing historians with a wider range of methods. Previous studies could even be revisited, using the latest techniques and models developed in the fields of social science. Multidisciplinary approaches would be worth applying to library history: approaches borrowed from mainstream history and its various sub-disciplines as well as other humanities and social sciences would certainly yield innovative and substantive insights. In addition, American Studies and Popular Studies are congenitally predisposed to experimentation and epistemological fermentation.[32] Studies on topics such as the publishing trade, high and lowbrow literature, intersections with the history of education, the distribution of information, and studies on the canonization of literature, music, and other cultural products would create a broader intellectual landscape. How did libraries deal with these issues and conflicts and the improvement of cultural norms? In short, multi-disciplinarity would release more hide-bound methods, approaches, and perspectives from their shackles. In historically oriented American and Popular Studies, evidence-based findings do not rest solely on printed material, but can include other media, e.g., photographs, films, posters, advertisements, literary works, etc., all of which enrich the analysis. However, multidisciplinary ventures have to be handled with care and due critical analysis: animated models and techniques may produce interesting results but may lack relevance to the historical or historiographic tradition.[33] For any academic historical study to be critically reviewed and vetted, it must be contextualized on the basis of rigorous scholarship.

Sociological studies on group dynamics and group formation processes can also raise questions about library patronage and administration, or even how the environments provided by buildings influence librarianship as a profession or libraries as places of societal confluence. Studies on the process of professionalization can serve to identify the conditions which shape librarianship as a profession, librarians' education and acculturation, and where librarianship stands within the system of professions. As a profession and a body of knowledge constantly exposed to technological developments, its evolution could be better understood historically if salient findings and models were borrowed from the fields of sociology and anthropology and used not only to elucidate the complex aims and motivations inherent to human behavior, but applied to libraries, the profession itself, the users and the various reasons underlying their motivation to make use of libraries and the opportunities for reading, learning, and recreation they provide. However, studies on the library as a social agency and an institutional structure still need to go beyond the current institutional historical fundamentals by embracing issues relating to information, knowledge, and society: in this way celebratory and institutional contributions to history would be completed and strengthened epistemologically.

Information history, which has sometimes been perceived as the exact opposite of library history, is perforce multidisciplinary in nature, and capable of casting a wider net for suitable topics of research as well as using a more sophisticated methodological toolbox.[34] It can potentially marshal a whole array of social science tools, including those developed in the fields of cliometrics, bibliometrics, historical demography, historical anthropology and sociology, as well as those of economic, cultural, intellectual, and social history. Virtually any information or source can be tapped to explain how information and knowledge flow in time and space. Various methods and techniques developed in the field of social science can be used to throw light on the hidden relationships involved in common usage, publication trends, the circulation of ideas, popular notions, consumer behavior, attendance at cultural events, etc. In addition, methods such as content analysis, if they are applied judiciously, can be used to find links between the history of collections, the history of reading, and the history of publishing, forming a continuum. Content studies on magazines, books, and other cultural products can provide information about the circulation of ideas as well as the collective consumption of knowledge and information. Nothing is a truly isolated occurrence because information is ubiquitous, and open to a multitude of possible uses by the actors in any given social field. Information history therefore creates wider scope for research on the social historical context.[35] Any interaction with information provides an opportunity for investigating human behavior and locating, ascertaining, and selecting topics worth examining more closely. The hidden structures underlying societies can indeed be illuminated by performing broader historical analyses. Library history must engage with other multidisciplinary historical studies, to the mutual benefit of both library history and information history.

The Promise Held by Other Sub-disciplines

A. Historical Studies on Books and Periodicals

Library historians could benefit from extending their range of interests to sub-disciplines which would present them with a challenge. Among the various topics which come to mind is the field of print culture, periodicals loom large. Not only are they ubiquitous, but they are also generally regarded as mirrors of society, to such an extent that they have often been used to perform content analyses, historical analyses, studies in various branches of the humanities and social science research. Popular periodicals, as well as more scholarly and scientific periodicals, can be investigated bibliometrically in terms of their contents or mined for characteristics influenced by their readers or *vice-versa*.[36] Broader social historical issues can also be elucidated by historians by examining periodicals of all kinds for their archeologically layered primary sources. Libraries and archives constitute privileged loci for studies on interactions with reading publics. In addition, both hardcopy and electronic periodicals lend themselves to studies on the latest trends in information history. These journals' circulation statistics, publication processes, and economics provide further grist for research. This naturally requires redefining what constitutes acceptable topics for library historians. If we stretch book history a little, including it within print culture history, topics such as book production, subject analysis, reading cultures, etc., can endow library history with much greater flexibility than it has enjoyed in the past.[37]

A larger, fairly elastic definition for categories such as library history, book history, studies on books and periodicals and publishing studies, would do away with the need for an all-inclusive definition by covering various methods and techniques, as well as theoretical models originating from the fields of social science and the humanities, including sociology, geography, literary history, and mainstream history.[38] Approaches such as GIS (geographical information systems), the cartographic mapping of evidence, political economy modeling, and ethnographic analysis can all shed light on questions not previously understood or even broached.[39] Large data analyses, both longitudinal and current, have brought to light patterns of interactions in library usage, patron/institutional interactions, as well as defining reading cultures and modeling publications and their distribution statistically. Information history is clearly carving out a niche for itself in this terra incognita—but library historians could also begin to explore these areas. Geographical dispersion studies could easily be made to focus on libraries and their services, while circulation studies could be mapped to account for previous findings. Beyond the purely definitional concerns, even studies on the history of media may be too narrow to include library history if they privilege mass communication systems such as television, radio, etc.

B. Studies on the History of Science and Technology

History of science and history of technology are additional fruitful fields for studying the history of libraries and information, since they open the possibility of making exciting permutations with findings on knowledge generation, storage, and dissemination.[40] Both of the latter sub-disciplines have their own professional associations, official disciplinary organs, and hold annual conferences; in addition, they are potentially rich sources of data on institutions, the circulation of information, the vetting of knowledge, etc. Scientists and technologists, especially those working in higher education and governmental institutions, conduct basic and applied research, publish their results, and interact at meetings and conferences. Their publications are worth examining for historical information about the approaches and methods traditionally used in the history of science and technology. These same primary materials can also be a boon to library and information historians; but the history of libraries and information may then require to be given a broader definition, of course. Although historians of science and technology have developed their respective specializations, concerted historical studies on how information is used, or how it is transmitted via communication systems, have yet to be systematically pursued. Nor should we neglect the library history angle, the locus where the discovery and dissemination of knowledge is institutionally anchored, which still requires to be firmly established in social history or contextualized studies.

From research laboratories to museums of science and technology, specialized departments in higher educational institutions and private facilities, scientific and technological research produces massive amounts of data and publications. These materials constitute a fecund matrix which can be used in many studies to map the contours of how knowledge is produced, disseminated, and used. Close historical examination of these materials can provide library and information historians with another set of subjects to pursue. Borrowing from the history of science and technology, establishing an intellectual foothold within these sub-disciplines, or broadening the purview of library and information historians can indeed open many opportunities for exciting research. It would be interesting to study how communication functions by examining research notes to determine how studies are accounted for and how findings are disseminated at laboratories, to the scientific community at large via informal channels and publications. Historical studies on research and academic communication systems have been previously conducted in numerous disciplines, especially the social sciences. Combining *historical bibliometrics* with studies on academic communication would also be a useful approach to scientific and technological history studies.

The Promise Held by the Historiographical Imperative

Invigorating a field of research brings both intellectual rewards and possibly also some negatives, depending upon how one's perspective is affected. For contemporary historians, the wave of new and compelling methods and techniques borrowed from other branches of the humanities and social sciences has expanded the horizon and spawned new areas and subjects worth addressing.[41] Historiography can be regarded as occupying two spheres, which are separate but capable of influencing each other. The one is purely theoretical, privileging the examination of the *raison d'être* of historical thinking and methodologies, and often concerned with veracity, the weighing of evidence, causation and logic, philosophical, epistemological concerns, etc., while the other is concerned with various schools of historical analysis. In the latter sphere, various approaches are used to re-examine accepted interpretations and schools of interpretations and how they fit the body of historical knowledge (See Diagram 5).

Diagram 5. Historiographical Processes

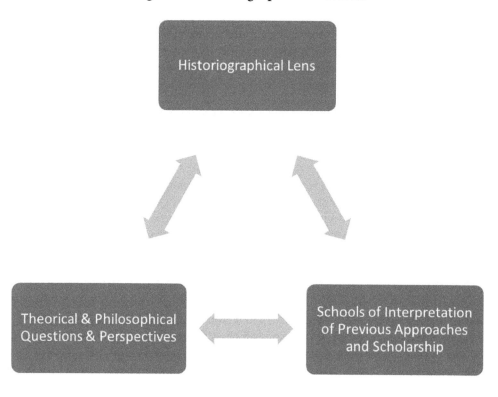

When the scope of historiographical research is broadened by importing other disciplinary insights, methods and techniques and perspectives, historiography is so greatly enriched that library and even information history is re-configured. Interdisciplinary borrowing also influences historians by introducing an epistemological lens that casts a different light on previous findings or can even lead to re-conceptualizing the subject under investigation. Studies on libraries and how they function and the history of information which are informed by interdisciplinary or sub-disciplinary approaches of this kind can be classified under different headings, depending on the methods, tools, and theories applied. When several borrowings are made, then the subjects, evidence, and/or previously vetted historiographic findings are liable to undergo a complete re-examination, bringing new facts to light (See Diagram 6).

Diagram 6. Possible Disciplinary Configurations Informing Historiographical Perspectives

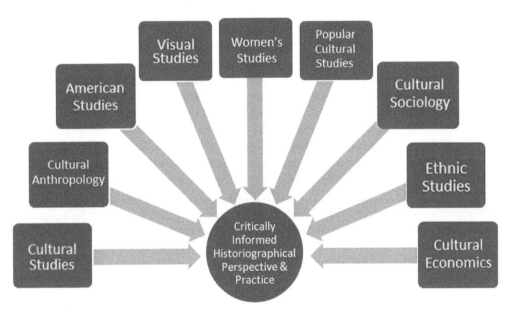

A re-invigorated library history must be re-set in the field of library science at the confluence between the generation and dissemination of knowledge in the social sciences and humanities. Classification of knowledge has been one of the hallmarks of serious intellectual pursuits at libraries, as well as providing users with the material they require to carry out their work. Among the questions worth addressing are how did libraries function temporally, spatially, and intellectually in various societies? Might studies on the larger questions as to how information and knowledge are discovered, acquired, disseminated, and used yield insights into the recently emerging historiographically-rich questions as to how libraries and library-related activities mesh with other societal institutions, such as other libraries, archives, museums, etc.? What makes these architecturally defined spaces instrumental to human activity? Why have a physical entity and the corresponding processes been established by societies, and why has a system of classification been used? Why has the library become a symbol, or a seat of ideology, or à la Foucault or Bourdieu, a place where power is institutionalized? What

246 Historiographical Futures

or who benefit from libraries? And how do libraries differ from each other in their aims and missions? These and other questions open a whole range of fascinating new topics worth pursuing by library historians.

Cultural History as an Interpretative Lens

Based on the critically reflexive points addressed in this discussion, it is possible to construct a historiographical prism through which various perspectives and techniques merge to form this newly emerging field of investigation. This new dynamic field encompasses more than its definition suggests because it promises to evolve continuously with time. The advent of cultural history as a field of research opens new possibilities for intellectual and methodological progress; in addition, it promises to re-vitalize, if not to re-configure the existing historiographical and methodological approaches not only to library history, but to information history as well. First, contrary to what has occurred with library history, cultural history has evolved in European history research circles starting with innovative work published in France and Great Britain. It has been gaining ground since the creation of the *International Society for Cultural History*, an official journal, and the organization of an annual conference.[42] Cultural history is an eminently multidisciplinary field as it seeks to integrate approaches and theories developed in the humanities and social sciences. As a special branch of history, cultural history has developed its own tools for investigating cultural institutions (in the fields of music, art, the performing arts, etc.), educational institutions, research communication and culture, mass communication, press practices, flows of news, book and magazine publishing, and topics of all kinds which come under the heading of cultural life. Cultural history includes both "high-brow" and popular culture, as well as encompassing *cultural practices* and questions such as artistic taste, musical and theatrical performances, and public reading preferences which tend to depend on publication trends. Cultural history is a suitable field for systematically examining crucial issues such as educational systems, learning conditions, class differentiation, and higher educational institutions and their disciplinary characteristics.

By providing library historians with a highly textured approach to historical topics, cultural history has refined the intellectual content of historical research but setting the topics under investigation in context of nineteenth and twentieth century research. However, cultural historians have been studying various popular and elite cultures since the middle ages. Cultural history has much to offer American library historians in terms of re-setting the institutional focus within a dynamic anthropologically and sociologically documented field.[43] Historical studies on subjects such as the perception of reality, *mentalité*, or how symbols are created and mediated, publications as the expression of societally contextualized human interests, how humans negotiate their needs for information and data, and how high and lowbrow cultural requirements, methods, techniques, and theoretical perspectives can re-vitalize the outlook for research on library history (See Diagram 7).

A few examples of what I have been talking about may suffice. Intellectual history is not isolated from society: ideas and knowledge are not born ex nihilo, nor do they lead a rarified, ethereal existence of their own.[44] The transmission of ideas, thoughts, recognized knowledge and emerging ideas, no matter how unfounded, or partially conceived, or poorly understood by readers and laymen they may be, exert pressure on libraries and archives. Collections and acquisitions whether they are based on traditional reading materials or on the latest media, electronic devices or print, the intellectual history of libraries and their interactions with societal conditions of learning and ideational transmission constitute a rich vein worth studying. Historical and geographical analyses and spatial dispersion analyses can bring to light hitherto unknown relationships between libraries, archives, and collections. Bibliometric historical studies may also show the existence of patterns of publication, diffusion, and usage possibly reflecting the existence of further connections between the influences at work in a given geographical place or reading public.

Diagram 7. Cultural History Lenses

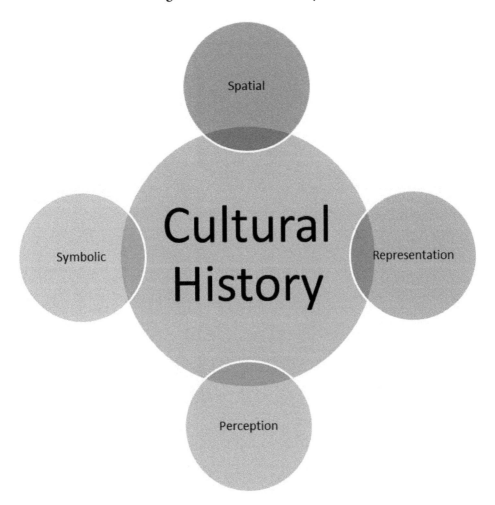

Another example is the possibility of using historical sociological findings to discern societal structure and cultural currents. Studies on educational attainment, prosopographical studies, and/or studies in which historiographically contextualized data are combined with group dynamics theories can result in discoveries about how patrons used information and knowledge obtained from libraries, archives, or other sources of information. Granular studies may also show what use library users made of their interactions, especially their perception of libraries, especially public libraries, as a good, or a necessary institutional place of negotiation or mediation. Another approach could consist of mapping the circulation of materials, or examining whether libraries, archives, and other places are symbolic *reflections* of society in terms of its composition, and its possible evolution. Studies on the various layers of population and patronage could help to reach a critically informed understanding of library or archival services, as well as to elucidate the factors underlying patronage and the history of print culture, reading, and publishing.

What would the cultural history model look like, however, if it was adopted by library and information science historians? Would it lead to revisiting other disciplines as well as benefiting from their approaches, concepts and tools? An example of a reinvigorated approach is presented below (Diagram 8):

Diagram 8. A possible new combined configuration

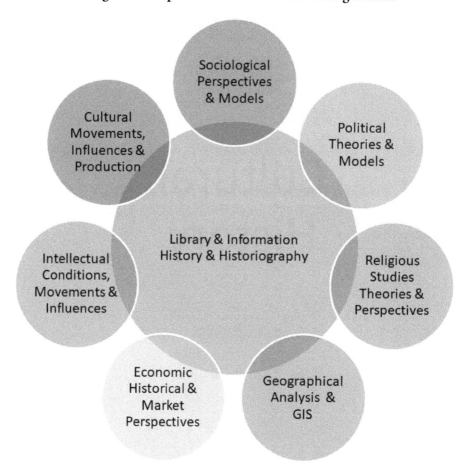

These possible combinations of disciplinary tools can yield interesting results; the examples of disciplines and topics presented here do not all have to be combined simultaneously, of course. Other permutations are possible, whenever historians need to enhance, expand, or extend the scope of their research and their methodological tools.

As library and information history is gradually enriched via cultural history's propensity to borrow from other disciplines, innovative approaches can also re-visit long-held facts and findings and historiographical perspectives. For example, the historical cultural economics approach focuses on the interplay between cultural products, markets, and the uptake of products such as books, magazines, art, theatre, etc., in the economic arena.[45] The cultural products available at libraries and museums provide particularly intriguing possibilities for historical research. Applying models and techniques imported from economic history or economics per se can re-cast the layout of ideas; studies on cultural products as investments can also show whether social segmentation privileges knowledge or information about the market conditions. When statistical approaches are combined with historical methods, discoveries can be made that can potentially re-frame library history and especially information history.

Another fruitful field of research is the complex ecology of higher learning and research.[46] Not only are colleges, institutes, and universities themselves cross-roads of knowledge and information, but they are also mirrored in academic libraries' intellectual structures. Apart from serving as reference material, collections and their relationships with the evolution of disciplines and disciplinary cultures and practices would be worth studying in order to map past intellectual mutations in disciplines and how those disciplines reflected either a single or multi-institutional environment. By combining retrospective analyses on collections with data on departmental, college, institute, or specialized centers' libraries, historians could determine how knowledge is formed and disseminated in the context of disciplinary developments. Assessing the strengths and weaknesses of collections in terms of their disciplinary relationships with research and higher education, mapping the existence of translations of works, etc., would provide library and information historians with a richer intellectual background for their research.[47] These micro and macro approaches give rise to questions about libraries' interactions with the professionalizing goals of some disciplines, their intellectual depth, and the methods of communication used.

An important caveat is needed here to further situate library history within the wider context of professional academic historical scholarship—especially historiography. The traditional approach to historical research adopted in the English speaking countries, has been based on the rationalistic belief that the past can be judiciously interpreted, which involves the assumption that historical analyses make it possible to reconstruct past conditions, events, sensibilities, mores, etc.[48] The more historians discover new evidence, the more accurate the picture of the past is likely to become, until it approximates a near Rankian level of certainty.[49] Most library history fits this approach, which is in line with the historical method of reliance on primary source documents, careful checking of the validity of primary sources, and setting the results obtained in the context of the accepted historiographic picture. Although this reliance on the primary source document as the gold standard in historical research is often necessary, slavish adherence to this rule precludes other possible innovative insights, or makes new theoretical perspectives and methods seem null and void or intellectually suspect. This is not necessarily the case, however.

Library and information history need not shun other approaches in order to ensure historiographical veracity; the many possible conceptual approaches inherent to cultural history can yield accurate information on topics such as reading and the perception of reality, the psychological effects of libraries, information and data, and/or the feeling of alienation, etc. These and other such fascinating historical topics can enlarge the scope of both library and information history. An additional feature of cultural history is its reflexive nature, since the responsibility for historical research is cast back onto the historian, and the entire historical approach is challenged.[50] History as a problematic or questionable enterprise can bring to light hidden assumptions and perspectives adopted by historians, influencing not only the subject under investigation, but the entire point of what it means to undertake historical studies on the past. By providing a more elastic frame of reference and a greater awareness of the historical enterprise, a meta-critical lens can produce new insights, as well as providing a necessary corrective to the ideological belief that historians are bound to be able to re-constitute the past accurately.

Concluding Comments: A Future Imperfect, but Possible

The door is now open to library history as an invigorated pursuit, addressing historiographically contextualized questions about what it means for history to be institutionally oriented, and regarding institutions as a prism through which knowledge, learning, and societal forces mingle and resist or mediate layers of cultural meaning. Information history need not necessarily challenge institutional history: it can simply be said to cover a larger territory, corresponding to that in which information is generated and transmitted, in whatever form, and for whatever purpose. Information history can be used to complement institutional history or provide it with a larger lens. Rather than competing with each other, the co-existence between the two approaches should yield fruitful rewards once institutional history has started to embrace a larger spectrum of topics and epistemological insights from other disciplines. If this is not the case, it will simply become a narrowly confined and highly honed subfield occupying a small ecological niche. The approach suggested here should enable researchers to make the most of both library and information history, making them interpenetrate and merge, and to bring the latest tools and epistemological concepts to bear on newly emerging subjects and configurations transcending the frontiers between the two domains (See Diagram 9).

Diagram 9. New Model for Historical Research in Library and Information History

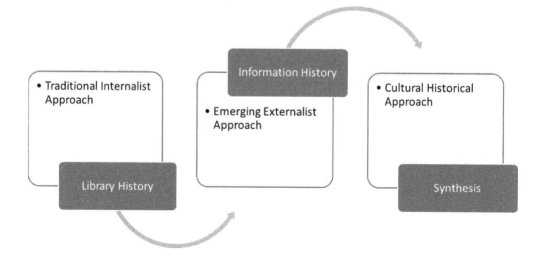

It should be possible for library history and information history to jointly develop common lines of inquiry, while still honoring their respective traditions. The broadly-based, yet historiographically and epistemologically nimble cultural history approach is re-conceptualizing both domains in meaningful ways, making use of both scholarly approaches as well as generating fruitful new subjects bridging both libraries and larger information culture issues. The cultural history approach invites historians to think beyond the borders and intellectual frontiers. It is worth noting of course that future historical specializations will each create their own separate research procedures, systems of vetting and legitimizing knowledge, standards of professionalization, and/or identifying and promoting consensus-driven methodologies and theories. Without detracting from the accomplishments of traditional library history or deterring the strides being made in the nascent field of history of information, it seems to be advisable to affiliate both approaches to the field of cultural history. Even if this is not done, enabling library history to benefit from the powerful advances made by information history thanks to what it has learned from cultural history will necessarily place library historians within the precincts of a larger historical research community.

Reconceptualizing library history, which has always embraced print culture, publishing, and reading studies, through the critical historiographical lens of cultural history, will put an end to the process of marginalization currently undergone by library history and library historians. Library history must harness its core characteristics, while showing its ability to broaden its scope by borrowing from other fields, including information history. Both endeavors can occupy their own intellectual spaces yet inform each other, while importing vital insights and approaches from cultural history. This modest proposal and the examples I have presented here do not preclude the continued use of traditional approaches; what I wanted to suggest in this discussion is that library history in the main needs to find its place within the wider expanse of professional historical practice in order to boost its vitality. Library history and library historians would do well to move beyond their comfortable ecological niche to embrace not a brave new world perhaps, but to move toward an exciting new horizon.[51] It is to be hoped that this suggestion, which is by no means prescriptive, will provide food for thought, which may be theoretical at first, but will become increasingly necessary as library history attempts to re-define itself and its *raison d'être* both within and outside the realm of library and information science.

Notes

1. For further discussion about this phenomenon, see Tony Becher and Paul Trowler, *Academic Tribes and Territories: Intellectual Enquiry and the Culture of Disciplines* (Buckingham; Philadelphia: Society for Research into Higher Education & Open University Press, 2001); Tony Becher and Sharon Parry, "The Endurance of the Disciplines," in Ivar Bleiklie and Mary Henkel, *Governing Knowledge: A Study of Continuity and Change in Higher Education; A Festschrift in Honour of Maurice Kogan* (Dordrecht: Springer, 2005): 133–44.

2. For a discussion of specialization in historical scholarship and disciplinary alignments, see Edward A. Goedeken and Jean-Pierre V.M. Hérubel, "Periodical Dispersion in American History: Observations on Article Bibliographies from the *Journal of American History*," *The Serials Librarian* 27 (1995): 59–74; Jean-Pierre V.M. Hérubel, "Historical Scholarship, Periodization, Themes, and Specialization: Implications for Research and Publication," *Journal of Scholarly Publishing* 39 (2008): 144–55; Anne L. Buchanan and Jean-Pierre V.M. Hérubel, "Taking Clio's Pulse ... or, Examining Characteristics of Monographic Publications Reviewed by *American Historical Review*," *Journal of Scholarly Publishing* 42 (January 2011): 160–81.

3. Jean-Pierre V.M. Hérubel, "Situating Clio's Influence in Humanities and Social Science Monographs: Disciplinary Affiliations and Historical Scholarship," *Journal of Scholarly Publishing* 41 (October 2009): 56–66.

4. For this discussion, it is critical to note that library U.S. historical scholarship and its attendant practice of community can be observed to constitute both spheres of amateur and professional academic historical and scholarly endeavor—see, Jean-Pierre V.M. Hérubel, "Clio's Dream, or Has the Muse Departed from the Temple? Implications for Library History," *Libraries & Culture* 39 (Fall 2004): 429–45. Central to this discussion is the focus on professional library history and library-focused historians, especially within the academy, whether they should be ensconced in other disciplinary communities and cultures, or with LIS academic culture.

5. For informative reading, consult Susan E. Lederer, Jonathan Zimmerman, James L. Baughman, Catherine Brekus, Mary L. Dudziak and Nancy F. Koehn, "Interchange: History in the Professional Schools," *The Journal of American History*, Vol. 92, No. 2 (September 2005), pp. 553–76; and, for an analogous illustration see John L. Rury, "The Curious Status of the History of Education: A Parallel Perspective," *History of Education Quarterly*, Vol. 46, No. 4 (Winter 2006), pp. 571–98.

6. For sound discussions on the problem of the ahistorical in professional library education as well as penetrating comments in support of the historical approach and appreciation for history, see R.C. Alston, "Library History: A Place in the Education of Librarians?" *Library History* 9 (1991): 37–51; James V. Carmichael, "A Historicity and the Library Profession: Perceptions of Biographical Researchers in LIS Concerning Research Problems, Practices, and Barriers," *Journal of Education for Library and Information Science* 31 (Spring 1991): 329–56; Donald G. Davis, Jr., "Ebla to the Electronic Dream: The Role of Historical Perspectives in Professional Education," *Journal of Education for Library and Information Science* 39 (Summer 1998): 228–35; and emphasizing the historical perspective is proffered in Lee Shifflett, "Sense-Making and Library History," *Journal of Education for Library and Information Science* 41 (Summer 2000): 254–59. For a compelling earlier piece worthy of considering, see Michael Harris and Stanley Hannah, "Why Do We Study the History of Libraries? A Meditation on the Perils of Ahistoricism in the Information Era," *Library & Information Science Research* 14 (April–June 1992): 123–30. These arguments against ahistorical approaches to knowledge or at least to library history have not lessened the concerted drive toward ahistoricity. Recently, the advocacy for inclusion of historical consciousness and awareness was proffered in Christine Pawley, "History in the Library and Information Science Curriculum: Outline of a Debate," *Libraries & Culture* 40 (Summer 2005): 223–38. Regarding book and library history within the curriculum, outside the U.S. context, see Pierre Delsaerdt, "From Légère Teinture to Central Place: A Revaluation of Book and Library History Within Library and Information Science Programmes," *Library History* 24 (June 2008): 143–51.

7. Interestingly, and critical to this discussion is the relatively recent addition of Dr. Alistair Black, to the Graduate School of Library and Information Science (GSLIS), University of Illinois, who specializes in information history. It should be noted that relatively few stand-alone courses focused on library history per se, exist in graduate library and information science programs. For the masters' degree, history or historical subjects or historically oriented modules may complement the professionally oriented vocational skills programming. Masters students may produce a historical paper, or thesis, but such may be voluntary. At some doctoral level programs, book arts, or print culture may be pursued in seminars, or for dissertations.

8. For an appreciation of the prerogatives and intellectual orientations, as well as the nature of past and contemporary library historical interests, for American library history in the main, consult Michael H. Harris, *A Guide to Research in American Library History* (Metuchen, N.J.: Scarecrow Press, 1968). Michael H. Harris, *A Guide to Research in American Library History*, 2nd ed. (Metuchen, N.J.: Scarecrow Press, 1974); Michael H. Harris and Donald G. Davis, Jr., *American Library History: A Bibliography* (Austin: University of Texas Press, 1978); Donald G. Davis, Jr., and John Mark Tucker, *American Library History: A Comprehensive Guide to the Literature* (Santa Barbara, Calif.: ABC-CLIO, 1989); for an appreciation of the evolution and significance of the former flagship journal of LHRT, *Libraries & Culture*, see Jean-Pierre V.M. Hérubel, "Authorship, Gender, and Institutional Affiliation in Library History: The Case of *Libraries & Culture*," *Behavioral & Social Sciences Librarian* 11 (1991): 49–54; Jon Arvid Aho and Donald G. Davis, Jr., "Advancing the Scholarship of Library History: The Role of the *Journal of Library History* and *Libraries & Culture*," *Libraries & Culture* 35, no. 1 (Winter 2000): 173–91; Edward A. Goedeken, "What We Wrote About and Who We Were: Historical Writings in *JLH/L&C*, 1966–2000," *Libraries & Culture* 38, no. 3 (Summer 2003): 250–65; for an insightful longitudinal survey and examination of LHRT-sponsored research, see Edward A. Goedeken, "The Library Historian's Field of Dreams: A Profile of the First Nine Seminars." *Libraries & Culture* 35 (2000): 161–72. For a global perspective on library history, consult these consummate compilations and analyses, Wayne A. Wiegand and Donald G. Davis, Jr., eds., *Encyclopedia of Library History* (New York: Garland Publishing, 1994); George S. Bobinski, Jesse Hawk Sheria, and Bohdan S. Wynar, eds., *Dictionary of American Library Biography* (Littleton, Colo.: Libraries Unlimited, 1978); Wayne A. Wiegand, ed., *Supplement to the Dictionary of American Library Biography* (Littleton, Colo.: Libraries Unlimited, 1990); Donald G. Davis, Jr., ed., *Dictionary of American Library Biography, Second Supplement*

(Westport, Conn.: Libraries Unlimited, 2003). Informed by and utilizing critical insights from Bourdieu's theoretical approaches, Maria Elena Gonzalez has investigated the evolution of the primary North American journal in library history in Maria Elena Gonzalez, "Crises in Scholarly Communications: Insights from Forty Years of the *Journal of Library History*, 1966–2005" (Ph.D. diss., University of Texas at Austin, 2008).

9. As far as this writer knows, the situation has not appreciably changed since his *cri de coeur*; see Jean-Pierre V.M. Hérubel, "Historiographic Turn: A Proposal for the Tenth Library History Seminar," *Library History Roundtable Newsletter* n.s. 1 (Spring 1994): 7–9. For a brief introduction to the literature appearing in other disciplinary journals, see Jean-Pierre V.M. Hérubel and Edward A. Goedeken, "Journals Publishing American Library History: A Research Note," *Libraries & Culture* 29 (Spring 1994): 205–09.

10. Importantly, the professionalization inherent to master's degree studies in library and information science programs means that students are not provided with the in-depth foundations necessary for successful historical education, nor with knowledge of the various approaches necessary to engage in academic historical research.

11. For a general account of doctoral studies, see Anne L. Buchanan and Jean-Pierre V.M. Hérubel, *The Doctor of Philosophy Degree: A Selective, Annotated Bibliography* (Westport, Conn.: Greenwood Press, 1995).

12. It is paramount to understand that many professional programs outside of academic disciplines and their respective acculturations do not necessarily emphasize nor give credence to historical specializations, as so often, professionalization demands perforce acculturation toward practice and the development of the practitioner in a respective profession, e.g., journalism, law, or medicine, including library science. An interesting discussion regarding library science and professionalization, is Jean L. Preer, "'Louder Please': Using Historical Research to Foster Professional Identity in LIS Students," *Libraries & the Cultural Record* 41 (Fall 2006): 487–96. For further insight into the crisis in journalism history and its place within professional education and scholarship, consult "Report of the AJHA Task Force on History in the Curriculum," September 2007, http://ajhaonline.org/, and Tim Vos, "Beyond our Subfield: Media History's Place in JMC Scholarship," *Clio Among the Media, Newsletter of the History Division of the Association for Education in Journalism and Mass Communication* 46 (Autumn 2011): 1, 3. For history of medicine, see Olga Amsterdamska and Anja Hiddinga, Chapter 11. "Trading Zones or Citadels? Professionalization and Intellectual Change in the History of Medicine," in *Locating Medical History: The Stories and Their Meanings* (Baltimore: Johns Hopkins University Press, 2004): 237–61. Instructively, from 1960 to 2001, Ph.D.s in the history of medicine, or similar disciplinary non-medical fields, i.e., history of science, or social studies of science, have dominated the history of medicine; library history could very well become the province of historians trained in programs other than in library science, where some history option may be programmatically present.

13. For instructive and informative readings of the phenomenon, see Rubén Donato and Marvin Lazerson, "New Directions in American Educational History: Problems and Prospects," *Educational Researcher* 28 (November 2000): 1–15; and, critically, Jack Dougherty, "Are Historians of Education 'Bowling Alone'? Response to Donato and Lazerson," *Educational Researcher* 28 (November 2000): 16–17.

14. A de visu examination of compilations of dissertations in library science primarily focused on historical subjects revealed a discernible pattern, indicating that historical dissertation subjects were not a major interest among library science dissertators. This pattern is in contrast to theses that have focused on historical subjects for masters' degrees. See Gail A. Schlachter and Dennis Thomison, *Library Science Dissertations, 1925–1972: An Annotated Bibliography* (Littleton, Colo.: Libraries Unlimited, 1974); Gail A. Schlachter and Dennis Thomison, *Library Science Dissertations, 1973–1987: An Annotated Bibliography* (Littleton: Libraries Unlimited, 1982); Gail A. Schlachter, "Abstracts of Library Science Dissertations," in Bohdan S. Wynar and Heather Cameron, eds., *Library Science Annual*, vol. 1 (Littleton: Libraries Unlimited, 1985); Gail A. Schlachter, "Abstracts of Library Science Dissertations," in Bohdan S. Wynar and Heather Cameron, eds., *Library Science Annual*, vol. 2 (Littleton: Libraries Unlimited, 1986); Gail A. Schlachter, "Abstracts of Library Science Dissertations," in Bohdan S. Wynar and Ann E. Prentice, eds., *Library and Information Science Annual*, vol. 3 (Littleton: Libraries Unlimited, 1987); Ken Haycock and Ann Curry, "Doctoral Dissertations in Library and Information Studies: Identification and Documentation, 1988–1996," in Bohdan S. Wynar et al., eds., *Library and Information Science Annual*, vol. 6 (Littleton: Libraries Unlimited, 1998); Ken Haycock and Ann Curry, "Doctoral Dissertations in Library and Information Studies: Identification and Documentation, 1997–1998," in Bohdan S. Wynar et al., eds., *Library and Information Science Annual*, vol. 7 (Littleton: Libraries Unlimited, 1999). For this period, the following combined data revealed:

Table 1 Dissertations in Historical Studies

Years	1925–29	1930–39	1940–49	1950–59	1960–69	1970–72	1973–81
% of total Dissertations	66.37	25.6	23.32	48.15	33.7	14.26	15

Sources: Schlachter and Thomison, *Library Science Dissertations 1925–1972* and *Library Science Dissertations, 1973–1981*.

Table 2 Dissertations in Historical Studies

Years	1983	1984	1985	1988–96	1997
% of total dissertations	12	7	6	9	10.4

Sources: Schlachter, *Abstracts of Library Science Dissertations*, vols. 1, 2, and 3; Haycock and Curry, "Doctoral Dissertations Library and Information Studies: Identification and Documentation, 1988–1996"

Table 3 Total Types of Degree Dissertations in Percent

Years	1925–72	1973–81	1983	1984	1985	1988–96	1997
Ph.D.	76.95	77.8	70	83	83	81.8	100
Ed.D.	13.2	12.3	20	14	14	12.9	
D.L.S.	8.55	4.8	6	3	3	4.1	
D.A., others		2.8	4			1	

Sources: Schlachter and Thomison, *Library Science Dissertations, 1925–1972* and *Library of Science Dissertations, 1973–1981*; Schlachter, *Abstracts of Library Science Dissertations*, vols. 1, 2, and 3; Haycock and Curry, "Doctoral Dissertations in Library and Information Studies: Identification and Documentation, 1988–1996."

Further decline in historically focused library science dissertations can be observed in Edward A. Goedeken's serialized bibliography, *Bibliography of Library History*, http://www.ala.org/lhrt/popularresources/libhistorybib/libraryhistory.

For additional discussion and data, see David H. Eyman, *Doctoral Dissertations in Library Science: Titles Accepted by Accredited Library Schools, 1930–1972* (Ann Arbor: Xerox University Microfilms, 1973) and Heather A. Thompson, "The Significance and Use of Historical Method in Library and Information Science Dissertations, 1984–1999," (M.L.I.S. paper, Kent State University, 2000). An important caveat is that with both Geodeken and Thompson's compilations and/or analyses, not all entries in library history were produced in library science programs—further pointing to other disciplinary orientations and contributions to library history not originating with library science programs.

15. Examining past and recent scholarship, appearing as theses, dissertations, books, or articles, one can see the contours of library history per se—see, again, and especially, the corpus of theses and dissertations in American library history, in Donald G. Davis, Jr., and John Mark Tucker, *American Library History: A Comprehensive Guide to the Literature* (Santa Barbara: ABC-CLIO, 1989), which builds upon and extends the efforts of Michael H. Harris and Donald G. Davis, Jr., *American Library History: A Bibliography* (Austin: University of Texas Press, 1978). Revealingly, Davis and Tucker point out that "in addition to dissertations and master's theses, the present bibliography also includes less formal master's and research papers accessible primarily, though not exclusively, at schools of library and information science. Such material has proven valuable by focusing on otherwise little-known people and institutions and by providing a depth of initial detail." However, "parenthetically, we regret the loss to ongoing basic library research due to the demise of sustained research assignments at the master's level in schools of library and information

science" (xiii). See Arthur P. Young, *American Library History: A Bibliography of Dissertations and Theses, 3rd rev. ed.* (Metuchen: Scarecrow Press, 1988). Young identified 964 master's theses and doctoral dissertations, including 210 research papers and reports for master's degrees. These grey literature studies broached many readily identifiable topics ranging from the traditional library as place-oriented studies to biographical or by type of library. Importantly, a selection of capstone research papers originating with masters' programs was included.

16. Consult these useful representative works: George Bobinski, *Libraries and Librarianship: Sixty Years of Challenge and Change, 1945-2005* (Lanham, Md.: Scarecrow Press, 2007); Andrew B. Wertheimer and Donald G. Davis, Jr., eds., *Library History Research in America: Essays Commemorating the Fiftieth Anniversary of the Library History Round Table* (Washington, D.C.: Library of Congress, Center for the Book, 2000).

17. Contemporary library historical scholarship is judiciously collected by Edward A. Goedeken on the website for the Library History Round Table (LHRT), the official library history venue for the scholarly pursuit of library history in the United States at http://www.ala.org/ala/mgrps/rts/lhrt/popularresources/libhistorybib/libraryhistory.cfm. Recently, a title change for the bibliography occurred in Spring, 2005 "Bibliography of Writings on the History of Libraries, Librarianship, and Book Culture," from the original entitled "Cumulative Bibliography of Library History." Moreover, for serious soundings and appreciations of where American library history is appearing and what may be its contours, see Edward A. Goedeken "The Literature of American Library History, 1999-2000," *Libraries & Culture* 37 (2002): 138-74; Edward A. Goedeken, "The Literature of American Library History, 2003-2005," *Libraries & the Cultural Record*, 43 (2008): 440-80. Michael H. Harris, "The Year's Work in American Library History, 1967," *Journal of Library History* 3 (October 1968): 342-52. Additionally, a very good snapshot of general trends may be ascertained by reading Edward A. Goedeken, "Assessing What We Wrote: A Review of the *Libraries & Culture* Literature Reviews, 1967-2002," *Libraries & Culture* 40 (2005): 251-66. *Libraries & Culture/Libraries & The Cultural Record*/and now *Information & Culture* in its different titular manifestation, has published soundings pertaining to recent scholarship in library history. Interestingly, Goedeken has broadened the scope to include print culture and various topics, as publishing, and reading history—harkening back to an earlier sense of library history encompassing contiguous topics pertinent to library historical research.

18. Illustrative studies include, but are not exclusive of, studies focused on such topics, Kasia Solon, "Present in Its Absence: Law Librarians and Technology at the Founding of AALL," *Law Library Journal* 98 (Summer 2006): 515-30; Erik P. Rau, "Managing the Machine in the Stacks: Operations Research, Bibliographic Control and Library Computerization, 1950-2000," *Library History* 23 (June 2007): 151-68; Juris Dilevko, "An Alternative Vision of Librarianship: James Danky and the Sociocultural Politics of Collection Development," *Library Trends* 56 (Winter 2008): 678-704; Kent A. Smith, "Laws, Leaders, and Legends of the Modern National Library of Medicine," *Journal of the Medical Library Association* 96 (April 2008): 121-33; Douglas A. Galbi, "Book Circulation Per U.S. Public Library User Since 1856," *Public Library Quarterly* 27 (2008): 351-71. Steven A. Knowlton, "Criticism of Cataloging Code Reform, as Seen in the Pages of *Library Resources and Technical Services* (1957-66)," *Library Resources & Technical Services* 53 (January 2009): 15-24.

19. See Wayne A. Wiegand, *The Politics of an Emerging Profession: The American Library Association, 1876-1917* (Westport, Conn.: Greenwood Press, 1986); Wayne A. Wiegand, "The Development of Librarianship in the United States," *Libraries & Culture* 24 (Winter 1989): 99-109; as examples for specialized library associations exemplified in art and law, see J. Margaret Shaw, "Twenty-Five Years of International Art Library Cooperation: The IFLA Art Libraries Section," *Art Libraries Journal* 32, no. 3 (2007): 4-10; Dennis Thomison, *A History of the American Library Association, 1876-1972* (Chicago: American Library Association, 1978); Frank G. Houdek, "AALL History through the Eyes of Its Presidents," *Law Library Journal* 98 (Spring 2006): 299-347.

20. It is paramount to acknowledge that library history is undergoing change, both as subject and as a specialization that is sensitive to its place within the contextualized academic disciplinary alignment of disciplines. For a discussion of library history's need to consider these possibilities, and for more expansive suggestions for where library history should venture epistemologically and subject-wise, see Edward A. Goedeken, "Our Historiographical Enterprise: Shifting Emphases and Directions," *Libraries & the Cultural Record* 45 (2010): 350-58; Anne L. Buchanan and Jean-Pierre V.M. Hérubel, "Subject and Historiographic Characteristics of Library History," *Journal of Scholarly Publishing* 42 (July 2011): 514-33. Goedeken is more supportive of the former library history historiography while Buchanan and Hérubel favor a more epistemologically open investigatory horizon for library historians.

21. For challenging discussions, see a standard work: Richard Krzys, "Library Historiography," in Miriam A. Drake, ed. *Encyclopedia of Library and Information Science* 2nd ed. (New York: Marcel Dekker, Inc., 2003): 3:1621-41; Lawrence J. McCrank, "Historical Information Science: History in Information Science; Information Science in History," in Carlos Barros and Lawrence J. McCrank, eds. *History Under Debate: International Reflection on the Discipline* (Binghamton, NY: Haworth Press, Inc., 2004), 177-98; Jean-Pierre V.M. Hérubel, "Historiography's Horizon and Imperative: The Legacy of Febvrian Annales and Library

History as Cultural History," *Libraries & Culture* 39 (Summer 2004): 293–312; Jean-Pierre V.M. Hérubel, "Historical Scholarship, Periodization, Themes, and Specialization: Implications for Research and Publication," *Journal of Scholarly Publishing* 39 (January 2008): 144–55.

22. Regarding insightful observations and remarks, see Michael H. Harris, "Externalist or Internalist Frameworks for the Interpretation of American Library History—The Continuing Debate," *Journal of Library History* 10 (April 1975): 106 –10. To the present, academic historians are still balanced on the fulcrum presented by the internalist/externalist debate. This is especially so in such specializations as history of medicine, science, or technology, but could very well be applied to library history and even to be sure, history of information, see Steven Shapin, "Discipline and Bounding: The History and Sociology of Science as Seen Through the Externalism-Internalism Debate," *History of Science* 30 (1992): 333–69; Steven Shapin, "History of Science and Its Sociological Reconstructions," *History of Science* 20 (1982): 157–211.

23. John M. Budd, *Knowledge and Knowing in Library and Information Science: A Philosophical Framework* (Lanham, MD: Scarecrow Press, 2001); John M. Budd, "The Library, Praxis, and Symbolic Power," *Library Quarterly* 73 (January 2003): 19–32; Gary P. Radford, "Trapped in Our Own Discursive Formations: Toward an Archaeology of Library and Information Science," *Library Quarterly* 73 (January 2003): 1–18; Douglas Raber, "Librarians as Organic Intellectuals: A Gramscian Approach to Blind Spots and Tunnel Vision," *Library Quarterly* 73 (January 2003): 33–53. Such theoretical orientations and questioning of the historical scholarly enterprise, situates the necessity of placing historical work within a historiographically rich environment where the historian can be free to experiment with subject matter and methodological innovation. Additionally, using philosophical or other unique approaches to historical scholarship can illuminate heretofore insights not otherwise easily obtained, see Thomas Clay Templeton, "Placing the Library: An Argument for the Phenomenological and Constructivist Approach to the Human Geography of the Library," *Library Quarterly* 78 (April 2008): 195–209.

24. Donald G. Davis, Jr., and Jon Arvid Aho, "Whither Library History? A Critical Essay on Black's Model for the Future of Library History, with Some Additional Options," *Library History* 17 (March 2001): 21–37.

25. Jonathan Rose, "Alternative Futures for Library History," *Libraries & Culture* 38 (Winter 2003): 50–60. Rose is judicious in maintaining an expanded view of the library as focus, while privileging the opportunity to creatively expand possible and foreseeable subjects within the purview of a more elastic library history.

26. This challenge to traditional library history in the wake of expanding information studies is proffered in Alistair Black, "Information and Modernity: The History of Information and the Eclipse of Library History," *Library History* 14 (May 1998): 39–45. It should be noted that Davis and Aho do support the library as nexus with reasoned points that can be supported historically, but the possibility of strengthening library history per se within the academic historical disciplines at large may rest with Black's enlarged visions which encompass the library as place and locus. For a reasonable response to this reaffirmed challenge, see Alistair Black, "A Response to 'Whither Library History?'" *Library History* 17 (March 2001): 37–39.

27. Within museum studies per se, especially, in material cultural museums, e.g., anthropology or history museums, various approaches to understanding how museums create and disseminate perceptions, hegemonies, or hierarchies of knowledge and learning are part and parcel of museum studies, especially when theoretical and historical conditions reveal the complexities of developing and maintaining museum environments within the larger societal phenomena. For some exploratory reading, see Flora S. Kaplan, *Museums and the Making of "Ourselves": The Role of Objects in National Identity* (London, New York: Leicester University Press, 1994); Susan A Crane, *Museums and Memory* (Stanford, Calif.: Stanford University Press, 2000); Victoria Cain, "Attraction, Attention, and Desire": Consumer Culture as Pedagogical Paradigm in Museums in the United States, 1900-1930," *Paedagogica Historica* 48 (October 2012): 745–69; William Gaudelli and Amy Mungur, "Presencing Culture: Ethnology Museums, Objects, and Spaces," *Review of Education, Pedagogy & Cultural Studies* 36 (January-March 2014): 40–54; Alaka Wali, "Collecting Contemporary Urban Culture: An Emerging Framework for the Field Museum," *Museum Anthropology* 37 (April 2014): 66–74. Among historians interested in the larger issues of museums and societal interconnections, consult Steven Conn, *Museums and American Intellectual Life, 1876-1926* (Chicago: University of Chicago Press, 1998); Steven Conn, *Do Museums Still Need Objects?* (Philadelphia: University of Pennsylvania Press, 2010); for an instrumental entrée to museum studies in the main, consult Sharon Macdonald, *A Companion to Museum Studies* (Malden, MA; Oxford: Blackwell, 2006) and Edward Porter Alexander and Mary Alexander, *Museums in Motion: An Introduction to the History and Functions of Museums* (Toronto: AltaMira Press, 2008).

28. For an accessible entrée into definitional concerns and conditions animating disciplines and disciplinarities, consult Jean-Pierre V.M. Hérubel, "Being Undisciplined; or, Traversing Disciplinary Configurations in Social Science and Humanities Databases: Conceptual Considerations for Interdisciplinarity and Multidisciplinarity," in Steven W. Witt and Lynne M. Rudasill, eds. *Social Science Libraries: Interdisciplinary Collections, Services, Networks* (Berlin: De Gruyter Saur, IFLA Publications, c2010): 25–39; Jean-Pierre V.M. Hérubel, "Disciplinary Morphologies, Interdisciplinarities: Conceptualizations and Implications for

Academic Libraries," in Daniel C. Mack and Craig Gibson eds., *Interdisciplinarity and Academic Libraries*, ACRL Publications in Librarianship No. 66 (Chicago: ACRL, 2012): 17–53.

29. Revealing is the operative definition of popular culture as evidenced in the association's official organs, "The *Journal of Popular Culture* is a peer-reviewed journal and the official publication of the Popular Culture Association. The popular culture movement was founded on the principle that the perspectives and experiences of common folk offer compelling insights into the social world. The fabric of human social life is not merely the art deemed worthy to hang in museums, the books that have won literary prizes or been named "classics," or the religious and social ceremonies carried out by societies' elite. The *Journal of Popular Culture* continues to break down the barriers between so-called "low" and "high" culture and focuses on filling in the gaps a neglect of popular culture has left in our understanding of the workings of society"; and, "Multidisciplinary in focus, The *Journal of American Culture* combines studies of American literature, history, and the arts, with studies of the popular, the taken-for-granted, and the ordinary pieces of American life, to produce analyses of American culture with a breadth and holism lacking in traditional American studies," http://pcaaca.org/.

30. Per the American Studies Association, the disciplinary composition "represent(s) many fields of inquiry, such as history, literature, religion, art and architecture, philosophy, music, science, folklore, ethnic studies, anthropology, material culture, museum studies, sociology, government, communications, education, library science, gender studies, popular culture, and others." Moreover, its official organ, *American Quarterly*, is defined broadly: "all members receive *AQ* four times a year—in March, June, September, and December. It is available online to ASA members and through Project Muse and JSTOR. *American Quarterly* "represents innovative interdisciplinary scholarship that engages with key issues in American studies. The journal publishes essays that examine American societies and cultures, past and present, in global and local contexts, offering work that contributes to our understanding of the United States in its diversity, its relations with its hemispheric neighbors, and its impact on world politics and culture. Through the publication of reviews of books, exhibitions, and diverse media, the journal seeks to make available the broad range of emergent approaches to American studies." http://www.theasa.net/.

31. Wiegand's position emphasized the naturally occurring and perhaps synergistic nature of American Studies for enriching various approaches to library history, see Wayne Wiegand, "Tunnel Vision and Blind Spots: What the Past Tells Us about the Present; Reflections on the Twentieth-Century History of American Librarianship," *Library Quarterly* 69 (January 1999): 1–32; Wayne A. Wiegand, "To Reposition a Research Agenda: What American Studies Can Teach the LIS Community about the Library in the Life of the User," *Library Quarterly* 73, no. 4 (October 2003): 369–82. It is necessary to invigorate the field via theoretical insights, and theoretical pursuits can be seen in the following works and discrete studies, in Phyllis Dain, "Women's Studies in American History: Some Critical Reflections," *Journal of Library History* 18 (Fall 1983): 450–63; Wayne A. Wiegand, "Introduction: Theoretical Foundations for Analyzing Print Culture as Agency and Practice in a Diverse Modern America," in James P. Danky and Wayne A. Wiegand, eds., *Print Culture in a Diverse America* (Urbana: University of Illinois Press, 1998): 1–13; Birger Hjorland, "Library and Information Science: Practice, Theory, and Philosophical Basis," *Information Processing and Management* 36 (May 2000): 501–31; Wayne Wiegand, "American Library History Literature: Theoretical Perspectives?" *Libraries & Culture* 35, no. 1 (Winter 2000): 4–34; Samuel E. Trosow, "Standpoint Epistemology as an Alternative Methodology for Library and Information Science," *Library Quarterly* (July 2001): 360–82; John Buschman, "The Integrity and Obstinacy of Intellectual Creations: Jürgen Habermas and Librarianship's Theoretical Literature," *Library Quarterly* 76 (July 2006): 270–99; Jack Andersen and Laura Skouvig, "Knowledge Organization: A Sociohistorical Analysis and Critique," *Library Quarterly* 76 (July 2006): 300–22; John Buschman, "Transgression or Statis? Challenging Foucault in LIS Theory," *Library Quarterly* 77 (January 2007): 21–44.

32. For an illustrative example of such research, see Thomas Augst, "The Business of Reading in Nineteenth-Century America: The New York Mercantile Library," *American Quarterly* 50 (June 1998): 267–305.

33. For discrete studies specifically focusing on disciplinary formation and function, see Jean-Pierre V.M. Hérubel and Anne L. Buchanan, "Disciplinary, Interdisciplinary, and Sub-disciplinary Linkages in Historical Studies Journals," *Science and Science of Science* 3 (1994): 15–24; Anne L. Buchanan and Jean-Pierre V.M. Hérubel, "Inter-disciplinarity in Historical Studies: Citation Analysis of the *Journal of Interdisciplinary History*," *LIBRIS: Library and Information Science Research Electronic Journal* 4 (1994): 1–13.

34. Alistair Black, "New Methodologies in Library History: A Manifesto for the 'New' Library History," *Library History* 11 (1996): 76–85; Alistair Black, "Information and Modernity: The History of Information and the Eclipse of Library History," *Library History* 14 (May 1998): 37–43. For a very well-honed introduction to information history per se, consult Alistair Black, "Information History," in *Annual Review of Information Science and Technology* 40 (2006): 441–73. Here, one can discern the breadth and depth of information history, which encompasses many layers of possible studies reviewed, throwing light on a rapidly evolving field where a multitude of approaches can benefit the expanded historical examination of libraries and information.

35. The practice of information history has already produced strong indicators that this field is

258 Historiographical Futures

accelerating and will open up a cornucopia of subjects and accompanying approaches yet to be fully realized. See Toni Weller, *Information History in the Modern World: Histories of the Information Age* (New York: Palgrave, 2011), and her earlier study, *Information History—An Introduction: Exploring an Emerging Field* (New York: Neal-Schuman Publishers, 2008). For an insightful account of the make-up of information history and its possibilities, see James W. Cortada, "Shaping Information History as an Intellectual Discipline," *Information & Culture* 47 (2012): 119–44. It is critical to understand that information history has effectively established itself with official organs for its perspectives which do include library history per se but privilege the innovative approaches inherent in the former's greater latitude offered by expanding the spectrum of subjects under study. For *Information and Culture: A Journal of History*, "The journal honors its (45+ year) heritage by continuing to publish in the areas of library, archival, museum, conservation, and information science history. However, the journal's scope has been broadened significantly beyond these areas to include the historical study of any topic that would fall under the purview of any of the modern interdisciplinary schools of information…" http://www.infoculturejournal.org/. This parallels the changes that have occurred with the British journal; "*Library & Information History* is a fully-refereed, quarterly journal publishing articles of a high academic standard from international authors on all subjects and all periods relating to the history of libraries and librarianship and to the history of information, in its broadest sense. Issues include substantial articles as well as book reviews, occasional surveys of recent publications, and guides to relevant sources. *Library & Information History* is a journal for anyone interested in the social, cultural and intellectual history of libraries and of information." http://www.maneyonline.com/loi/lih.

36. Periodicals, whether popular or scholarly, can be subjected to bibliometric examination, utilizing content analysis, etc., to ascertain trends, or emphases critical to understanding societal interests, perceptions, or artistic, cultural, popular pastime activities, or intellectual activity. Using publications to measure the pulse of societal interests and conditions permits a deeper understanding of what constitutes preoccupations and orientations otherwise not always accessible to social, media, and intellectual, cultural as well as library historians. For an introductory appreciation, see Jean-Pierre V. M Hérubel, "Historical Bibliometrics: Its Purpose and Significance to the History of Disciplines," *Libraries & Culture* 34 (Fall 1999): 380–88.

37. Various studies already point to new possibilities, see Thomas Augst and Kenneth Carpenter, eds., *Institutions of Reading: The Social Life of Libraries in the United States* (Amherst: University of Massachusetts Press, 2007); Juris Dilevko and Candice F.C. Magowan, *Readers' Advisory Service in North American Public Libraries, 1870–2005* (Jefferson, N.C.: McFarland, 2007); David S. Miall, "Empirical Approaches to Studying Literary Readers: The State of the Discipline," *Book History* 9 (2006): 291–311; Christine Pawley, "Retrieving Readers: Library Experiences," *Library Quarterly* 76 (October 2006): 379–87. Studies of reading and library as place and intersection are especially fruitful for innovative approaches and methodological insights for publishing. See Marvin Mondlin and Roy Meador, *Book Row: An Anecdotal and Pictorial History of the Antiquarian Book Trade* (New York: Carroll & Graf Publishers, 2005); Timothy Jacobson, George David Smith, and Robert E. Wright, *Knowledge for Generations: Wiley and the Global Publishing Industry, 1807–2007* (Hoboken, N.J.: John Wiley & Sons, 2007); Louise S. Robbins, "Publishing American Values: The Franklin Book Programs as Cold War Cultural Diplomacy," *Library Trends* 55 (Winter 2007): 638–50.

38. Book history represents a multidisciplinary approach to this specialization, see Paul Raabe, "Library History and the History of Books: Two Fields of Research for Librarians," *Journal of Library History* 19 (Spring 1984): 282–97; Scott E. Casper, Joanne D. Chaison, and Jeffrey D. Groves, eds., *Perspectives on American Book History: Artifacts and Commentary* (Amherst: University of Massachusetts Press, 2002); Jared Jenisch, "The History of the Book: Introduction, Overview, and Apologia," *portal: Libraries and the Academy* 3 (April 2003): 229–39; Joan Shelley Rubin, "What Is the History of the History of Books?" *Journal of American History* (2003): 555–75; David Finkelstein and Alistair McCleery, eds., *The Book History Reader*, 2nd ed. (London: Routledge, 2006); Leslie Howsam, *Old Books & New Histories: An Orientation to Studies in Book and Print Culture* (Toronto: University of Toronto Press, 2006); Simon Eliot and Jonathan Rose, eds., *A Companion to the History of the Book* (Malden, Mass.: Blackwell Publishing Ltd., 2007); Michael F. Suarez and H.R. Woudhuysen, eds., *The Oxford Companion to the Book* (Oxford: Oxford University Press, 2010). Moreover, reading studies, and print culture in the main, are thriving via such societies as SHARP (Society for the History of Authorship, Reading and Publishing), with its journal *Book History*, and in the U.K. the journal *Library History*, now *Library & Information History* represents masterful journals devoted to a widening subject spectrum, including the history of data, etc.

39. See Fiona A. Black, Bertrum H. MacDonald, and J. Malcolm W. Black, "Geographic Information Systems: A New Research Method for Book History," *Book History* 1 (1998): 11–31. Since this article, there have been growing attempts to implement GIS to discover and measure various cultural products, e.g., books and book production, cultural institutional locations, movements of ideas, and artistic productions, as well as attempting to locate networks and patterns of dissemination of ideas, etc. For examples, see Artl@s, http://artlas.ens.fr/?lang=fr, which is devoted to the spatial mapping of art and cultural production, etc. Additionally, the large-scale mapping of literary production may open up innovative approaches devoted to the spatial mapping of art and cultural production, etc. See Franco Moretti, *Atlas of the European Novel*,

1800–1900 (London; New York: Verso, 1998); Franco Moretti, *Graphs, Maps, Trees: Abstract Models for a Literary History* (London and New York: Verso, 2005). Another venue for innovative approaches to historical research is the quantification of phenomena, animated by humanities inspired prerogatives as entertained in *International Journal of Humanities and Arts Computing*, http://www.euppublishing.com/journal/ijhac.

40. Interesting examples are Thomas Broman, "Criticism and the Circulation of News: The Scholarly Press in the Late Seventeenth Century," *History of Science* 51 (June 2013): 125–50; and Adrian Johns, "The Uses of Print in the History of Science," *Papers of the Bibliographical Society of America* 107 (December 2013): 393–420.

41. For instrumental entrees to this bourgeoning field of activity, see the contents of a well-established journal, such as *History & Theory*, which continues to offer new insights into the historical enterprise. Especially informative for library and information historians, it "publishes articles, review essays, and summaries of books principally in these areas: critical philosophy of history; speculative philosophy of history; historiography; history of historiography; historical methodology; critical theory; time and culture; and history and related disciplines." http://www.historyandtheory.org/. Another far-reaching and innovative journal which offers historians thought provoking approaches to historical research, *Rethinking History*, "… allows historians in a broad range of specialties to experiment with new ways of presenting and interpreting history. *Rethinking History* challenges the accepted ways of doing history and rethinks the traditional paradigms, providing a unique forum in which practitioners and theorists can debate and expand the boundaries of the discipline." http://www.tandfonline.com/action/journalInformation?show=aimsScope&journalCode=rrhi20.

42. Cultural history has gained legitimate ground, with an established society, *International Society for Cultural History*, http://www.culthist.org/ an official organ, "*Cultural History* promotes the work and aims of the International Society for Cultural History, which was founded in 2008. It generates discussion and debate on the nature of cultural history and current trends and advances theoretical and methodological issues relating to the field. *Cultural History* promotes new and innovative questions about the past and invites contributions from both advanced and junior scholars. The intellectual shifts of recent decades have moved 'culture' to the forefront of academic attention while expanding the practice of 'history' beyond the boundaries of traditional disciplines. *Cultural History*, the peer-reviewed journal of the International Society for Cultural History (ISCH), engages fully with these developments. The only journal in the world that takes cultural history in general as its chief concern, *Cultural History* welcomes high quality submissions from any discipline that brings contemporary cultural theories and methodologies to bear on the study of the past, regardless of historical or geographical focus. The journal also invites articles that reflect on the ways in which more practical environments such as museums and the heritage industry engage with current debates in cultural history." For a series of how cultural history has evolved and for its nuanced potential for innovation, see Jean-Pierre V.M. Hérubel, "Historiography's Horizon and Imperative: The Legacy of Febvrian Annales and Library History as Cultural History," *Libraries & Culture* 39 (Summer 2004): 293–312; Jean-Pierre V.M. Hérubel, "Phoenix Ascendant: French Higher Education and Its Significance for Research and Learning for Library, Book, Print, and Media Culture History," *Libraries & Culture* 40 (2005): 156–75; Jean-Pierre V.M. Hérubel, "Observations on an Emergent Specialization: Contemporary French Cultural History-Significance for Scholarship," *Journal of Scholarly Publishing* 41 (January 2010): 216–40.

43. As a field, cultural history exercises methodological flexibility, incorporating many different social science and humanities disciplinary perspectives, capable of informed deployment of such borrowings–for examples of these approaches, consult Gerard Delanty and Engin F. Isin, *Handbook of Historical Sociology* (London, Thousand Oaks, Calif.: Sage, 2003); Nancy Partner and Sarah Foot, eds. *SAGE Handbook of Historical Theory* (London; Thousand Oaks, Calif.: Sage, 2013).

44. Intellectual history occupies a highly fluid position within historical studies, Jean-Pierre V.M Hérubel and Edward A. Goedeken, "Identifying the Intellectual Contours of a Historical Specialty: Geographical, Temporal, and Subject Emphases of the *Journal of the History of Ideas*," *Serials Librarian* 55 (2008): 276–95. Intellectual history's purview integrates actors and ideas, or thoughts within time and space, that is, within the social context.

45. Such studies can be found in *Journal of Cultural Economics*, http://culturaleconomics.org/index.html. Although at times highly quantitative and model oriented, the examination of cultural objects within the market, can be useful for historians.

46. See these examples of studies illuminating higher education's linkage's with both learning and research cultures: Karen Antell and Debra Engel, "Stimulating Space, Serendipitous Space: Library as Place in the Life of the Scholar,"163–76; and Thomas Mann, "The Research Library as Place: On the Essential Importance of Collections of Books Shelved in Subject-Classified Arrangements,"191–206 in John E. Buschman and Gloria J. Leckie, *The Library as Place: History, Community, and Culture* (Westport, Conn.: Libraries Unlimited, 2007).

47. Thomas S. Popkewitz, Barry M. Franklin, and Miguel A. Pereyra, *Cultural History and Education: Critical Essays on Knowledge and Schooling* (New York: Routledge Falmer, 2001). For a very sound introduction to cultural history vis-à-vis curricular history, relations of power and educational theory, etc., see

Thomas S. Popkewitz, Miguel A. Pereyra, and Barry M. Franklin, "History, the Problem of Knowledge, and the New Cultural History of Schooling: An Introduction," 3–42.

48. See Peter Novick, *That Noble Dream: The "Objectivity Question" and the American Historical Profession* (Cambridge: Cambridge University Press, 1988). In the past three decades, historical practice has been affected by innovations originating with social science and humanities perspectives, and techniques, e.g., quantification/Cliometrics, social theories, literary theories, ethnic/gender studies, and philosophical insights, etc., effectively informing and enriching historical scholarship.

49. It should be acknowledged that theoretical or theoretically informed historical research can pose problematic concerns for library or information historians, whether engaged in a broader spectrum of epistemological activity, where theory may possibly enhance discovery or may hinder the veracity of approach pursued by the historian. Rarely has the library or information historian employed theories originating from other disciplines, in historical analyses—rather, such approaches are more generally applied to library and information science in non-historically framed hypotheses and objectives. For such theories and examples, see M.H. Harris, "State, Class, and Cultural Reproduction: Toward a Theory of Library Service in the United States," *Advances in Librarianship*, 14 (1986): 211–52; J. Garrett, "Missing Eco: Reading The Name of the Rose as Library Criticism," *Library Quarterly*, 61(1991): 373–88; J. Zwadlo, "We Don`t Need a Philosophy of Library and Information Science. We're Confused Enough Already," *Library Quarterly* 67(1997): 103–21; Gary P. Radford, "Flaubert, Foucault, and the Bibliotheque Fantastique: Toward a Postmodern Epistemology for Library Science," *Library Trends* 46 (Spring 1998): 616–34. For approaches to non-historically oriented research, consult John M. Budd, "Academic Libraries and Knowledge: A Social Epistemology Framework," *Journal of Academic Librarianship* 30 (September 2004): 361–67; John M. Budd, *Knowledge and Knowing in Library and Information Science: A Philosophical Framework* (Lanham, Md.: Scarecrow Press, 2001); John M. Budd, "Meaning, Truth, and Information: Prolegomena to a Theory," *Journal of Documentation* 67 (2011): 56–74; John M. Budd, "Phenomenological Critical Realism: A Practical Method for LIS," *Journal of Education for Library & Information Science 53* (Winter 2012): 69–80.

50. Often, the historian is necessarily aware of the methodological effects upon the subject under investigation, adding to the complex epistemological challenges inherent to the analysis. This is especially true for the methodologically-driven historian while composing his/her scholarly narrative. Moreover, as historical research has embraced over the last forty years, various perspectives, from quantification, to literary theory, to critical theory, to postmodernism, to postcolonial and global historical perspectives and techniques, and other theories imported into library and information science research, could be historicized for cultural historical practice. See Gloria J. Leckie, Lisa M. Given, and John Buschman, *Critical Theory for Library and Information Science: Exploring the Social from Across the Disciplines* (Santa Barbara, Calif.: Libraries Unlimited, 2010).

51. Central to this discussion has been the underlying assumption that library history per se would actually remain as a singular endeavor; albeit one that requires a grounded home within the library and information science domain. Another, perhaps, more controversial option would be to situate library and/or information history within the mainstream academic history profession. This would necessarily change the intellectual condition of library history proper by informing it through the broader historiographical and professional concerns animating and driving the academic history profession. As mainstream historians practice their respective fields, whether highly specialized or not, library history would need to insinuate itself within these concerns and adapt to the professional training within history graduate programs. A major consideration here is whether mainstream academic historians would welcome such participation and would make allowance for a highly honed subject, essentially derived from a professional practice. The case of history of science has been an object lesson, as it has struggled to find its place within the historical profession at large—the externalist perspective is critical to such immersion. For library history, it may or may not be a matter of joining the larger historical profession—rather it may be wiser to continue until a concerted foothold is made, without losing one's subject identity by adhering to professional protocols that may deform library history or information history through larger professional exigencies. The American Historical Association and its continuous monitoring of the health of the profession within academia may leave more to be gained, if library/information history remains within the library and information science domain. Moreover, it may be prudent to enrich itself historiographically thereby carving out a respectable presence within American or Popular Studies, or actually, gain a recognizable profile within the information studies as conceived through the rebranding of library and information science programs. However, it is constituted, the fact remains that library history does need to revitalize itself within a larger, but more epistemologically rich intellectual environment—doing so within cultural history may be a viable option.

Further Reading

The Academic Library in the United States: Selected Historical Readings

JEAN-PIERRE V.M. HÉRUBEL, MARK L. MCCALLON, *and* JOHN MARK TUCKER

The more extensive and representative publications are cited in the introduction, "From the Bequest of John Harvard to the Dream of Alexandria." That section explores literature broadly construed: scholarship that has an overview perspective, that considers the whole or selected time-periods of academic library history, or that demonstrates commonly used methods of historical narrative. Of practical necessity, we have not discussed histories of individual libraries or biographies of individual librarians.

For "Selected Historical Readings," we cite publications that, with some exceptions, were not discussed in the opening essay. Here we include (1) foundational sources and selected specialized studies devoted to library practice (for example, public services, technical services, administration, automation, and other topics) still with emphasis on academic library history, along with articles especially well-written that we did not have the space to reprint. We include (2) a choice selection of sources on library history generally (continuous narratives, collected readings, reference sources), and (3) publications on conceptual and theoretical matters pertaining to library historiography. These appear most often, though not exclusively, as part of the continuous stream of periodical literature in venues such as *Library Quarterly, Library Trends, Library & Information History, Library & Information Science Research, Journal of Education for Library and Information Science, Journal of Library History* and its successor titles (*Libraries & Culture, Libraries & the Cultural Record, Information & Culture: A Journal of History*), and *Libraries: Culture, History, and Society*. We also (4) identify key sources on the history of American higher education.

Early Contributions

Brough, Kenneth J. "Evolving Conceptions of Library Service in Four American Universities: Chicago, Columbia, Harvard, and Yale, 1876–1946." Ph.D. diss., Stanford University, 1949. ProQuest (AAT 0177 629).

Cannons, H.G.T. *Bibliography of Library Economy: A Classified Index to the Professional Periodical Literature in the English Language Relating to Library Economy, Printing, Methods of Publishing, Copyright, etc., from 1876 to 1920.* Chicago, Illinois: American Library Association, 1927.

Carlton, W.N.C. "College Libraries in the Mid-Nineteenth Century." *Library Journal* 32 (1907): 479–86.

Eddy, Jr., Edward Danforth. *Colleges for Our Land and Time: The Land-Grant Idea in American Education.* Westport, Connecticut: Greenwood Press, 1957.

Evans, Luther H. "Research Libraries in the War Period, 1939–45." *Library Quarterly* 17 (1947): 241–62.

Gilchrist, Donald B. "The Evolution of College and University Libraries." *Bulletin of the American Library Association* 20 (1926): 293–99.
Irwin, Raymond. "Does Library History Matter?" *Library Review* 16 (1958): 510–13.
McMullen, Haynes. "Ralph Waldo Emerson and Libraries." *Library Quarterly* 25 (1955): 152–62.
Powell, Benjamin E. "The Development of Libraries in Southern State Universities to 1920." Ph.D. diss., University of Chicago, 1946. ProQuest (AAT T-00008).
Predeek, Albert. *A History of Libraries in Great Britain and North America.* Translated by Lawrence S. Thompson. Chicago, Illinois: American Library Association, 1947.
Rothstein, Samuel. *The Development of Reference Services through Academic Traditions, Public Library Service and Special Librarianship.* Chicago, Illinois: ACRL Monograph No. 14, 1955. Reprint. Boston, Massachusetts: Gregg Press, 1972.
Schmidt, George P. *The Liberal Arts College: A Chapter in American Cultural History.* New Brunswick, New Jersey: Rutgers University Press, 1957.
Shores, Louis. "Origins of the American College Library, 1638–1800." Ph.D. diss., George Peabody College for Teachers, 1934. ProQuest (AAT 0120507).
Stewart, Nathaniel. "Sources for the Study of American College Library History, 1800–1876." *Library Quarterly* 13 (1943): 227–31.
Strauss, Lovell H. "The Liberal Arts College Library, 1929–1940: A Comparative Interpretation of Financial Statistics of Sixty-Eight Representative and Twenty Selected Liberal Arts College Libraries." Master's thesis, University of Chicago, 1942.
Thompson, Lawrence S. "The Historical Background of Departmental and Collegiate Libraries." *Library Quarterly* 12 (1942): 49–74.
Thurber, Evangeline. "The Library of the Land-Grant College, 1862–1900: A Preliminary Study." Master's thesis, Columbia University, 1928.
Warren, S.R., and S.N. Clark. "College Libraries." In *Public Libraries in the United States of America: Their History, Condition, and Management; Special Report, Part I*, 60–126. Washington, D.C.: United States Government Printing Office, 1876.
Yenawine, Wayne S. "The Influence of Scholars on Research Library Development at the University of Illinois." Ph.D. diss., University of Illinois, 1955. ProQuest (AAT 0011551).

1960s

Boll, John J. "Library Architecture 1800–1875: A Comparison of Theory and Buildings with Emphasis on New England College Libraries." Ph.D. diss., University of Illinois, 1961. ProQuest (AAT 6104263).
Cutcliffe, M.R. "The Value of Library History." *Library Review* 21 (1967): 193–96.
Gelfand, Morris A. "A Historical Study of the Evaluation of Libraries in Higher Institutions by the Middle States Association of Colleges and Secondary Schools." Ph.D. diss., New York University, 1960. ProQuest (AAT 6100324).
Herbst, Jurgen. *The German Historical School in American Scholarship: A Study in the Transfer of Culture.* Ithaca, New York: Cornell University Press, 1965.
Marshall, John David, ed. *An American Library History Reader.* Hamden, Connecticut: Shoe String Press, 1961.
Rouse, Roscoe. "The Libraries of Nineteenth-Century College Societies." In *Books in America's Past: Essays Honoring Rudolph H. Gjelness*, edited by David Kaser, 26–42. Charlottesville: University of Virginia Press, 1966.
Rudolph, Frederick. *The American College and University: A History.* New York: Vintage Books, 1962. Reprinted with introductory essay and supplemental bibliography by John R. Thelin. Athens: University of Georgia Press, 1991.
Smith, Jessie C. "Patterns of Growth in Library Resources in Certain Land-Grant Universities." Ph.D. diss., University of Illinois, 1964. ProQuest (AAT 6500917).
Veysey, Laurence R. *The Emergence of the American University.* Chicago: University of Chicago Press, 1965.

1970s

Braden, Irene A. *The Undergraduate Library.* ACRL Monograph No. 31. Chicago, Illinois: American Library Association, 1970.
Cole, John Y. "Storehouses and Workshops: American Libraries and the Uses of Knowledge." In *The Organization of Knowledge in Modern America, 1860–1920*, edited by Alexandra Olsson and John Voss, 364–85. Baltimore, Maryland: Johns Hopkins University Press, 1979.
Edelman, Hendrik, and G. Marvin Tatum, Jr. "The Development of Collections in American University Libraries." In *Libraries for Teaching, Libraries for Research: Essays for a Century*, edited by Richard D. Johnson, 34–57. Chicago, Illinois: American Library Association, 1977.

Ellsworth, Diane J., and Norman D. Stevens, eds. *Landmarks of Library Literature, 1876-1976*. Metuchen, New Jersey: Scarecrow Press, 1976.
Harris, Michael H., ed. *Reader in American Library History*. Washington, D.C.: NCR Microcard Editions, 1971.
Harwell, Richard. "College Libraries." In *Encyclopedia of Library and Information Science*. Vol. 5, 269-81. New York: Marcel Dekker, 1971.
Heim, Kathleen M., and Kathleen Weibel, eds. *The Role of Women in Librarianship 1876-1976: The Entry, Advancement, and Struggle for Equalization in One Profession*. With assistance from Diane J. Ellsworth. Phoenix, Arizona: Oryx Press, 1979.
Holley, Edward G. "Academic Libraries in 1876." In *Libraries for Teaching, Libraries for Research: Essays for a Century*, edited by Richard D. Johnson, 1-33. Chicago, Illinois: American Library Association, 1977.
Holley, Edward G. "The Emerging University Library: Lessons from the Sixties." SUNY-Stony Brook, *Occasional Papers*, 1. Stony Brook, New York: SUNY-Stony Brook, 1975.
Holley, Edward G. *The Land-Grant Movement and the Development of Academic Libraries: Some Tentative Explorations*. Texas A & M University Miscellaneous Publications, 15. College Station, Texas: Texas A & M University Libraries, 1977.
Jackson, Sidney L. *Libraries and Librarianship in the West*. New York: McGraw-Hill, 1974.
Johnson, Edward R. "Subject-Divisional Organization in American University Libraries, 1939-1974." *Library Quarterly* 47 (1977): 23-42.
Jordan, Anne Harwell, and Melbourne Jordan, eds. *Cannons' Bibliography of Library Economy, 1876-1920: An Author Index with Citations*. Metuchen, New Jersey: Scarecrow Press, 1976.
Kaser, David. "Advances in American Library History." *Advances in Librarianship* 8 (1978): 181-99.
Kaser, David. "The Effect of the Revolution of 1969-1970 on University Library Administration." In *Academic Libraries by the Year 2000: Essays Honoring Jerrold Orne*, edited by Herbert Poole, 64-75. New York: R.R. Bowker, 1977.
McElderry, Stanley. "Readers and Resources: Public Services in Academic and Research Libraries, 1876-1976." *College & Research Libraries* 37 (1976): 408-420.
McGowan, Frank M. "The Association of Research Libraries, 1932-1962." Ph.D. diss., University of Pittsburgh, 1972. ProQuest (AAT 7312360).
McMullen, Haynes. "The State of the Art of Writing Library History." *Journal of Library History* 13 (1978): 432-40.
Radford, Neil A. "Academic Library Surveys Prior to 1930." *Journal of Library History* 8 (1973): 150-58.
Radford, Neil A. "The Carnegie Corporation and the Development of American College Libraries, 1928-1941." Ph.D. diss., University of Chicago, 1972. ProQuest (AAT T-23979).
Rothstein, Samuel. "From Reaction to Interaction: The Development of the North American University Library." *Canadian Library Journal* 29 (1972): 111-15.
Rothstein, Samuel. "Service to Academia." In *A Century of Service: Librarianship in the United States and Canada*, edited by Sidney L. Jackson, Eleanor B. Herling, and E.J. Josey, 79-109. Chicago, Illinois: American Library Association, 1976.
Rudolph, Frederick. *Curriculum: A History of the American Undergraduate Course of Study Since 1636*. San Francisco, California: Jossey-Bass, 1978.
Shiflett, Orvin L. "The Origins of American Academic Librarianship." Ph.D. diss., Florida State University, 1979. ProQuest (AAT 7926818).
Stevens, Rolland E., ed. *Research Methods in Librarianship: Historical and Bibliographical Methods in Library Research*. Conference on Historical and Bibliographical Methods in Library Research. Urbana, Illinois: University of Illinois, Graduate School of Library Science, 1971.
Stieg, Lewis F. "The Library and American Education: The Search for Theory in Academic Librarianship." *Library Trends* 27 (1979): 353-65.
Stone, Elizabeth W., ed. *American Library Development, 1600-1899*. New York: H.W. Wilson, 1977.
Thompson, James. *A History of the Principles of Librarianship*. London: Clive Bingley; and Hamden, Connecticut: Linnet Books, 1977.
Veit, Fritz. "Library Service to College Students." *Library Trends* 25 (1976): 361-78.
Veysey, Laurence R. "Stability and Experiment in the American Undergraduate Curriculum." In *Content and Context: Essays on College Education*, edited by Carl Kaysen, 1-63. New York: McGraw-Hill, 1973.
Weber, David C. "A Century of Cooperative Programs among Academic Libraries." In *Libraries for Teaching, Libraries for Research: Essays for a Century*, edited by Richard D. Johnson, 185-201. Chicago, Illinois: American Library Association, 1977.
Yueh, Norma N. "The Development of Library Collections at Former State Teacher Education Institutions: 1920-1970, with Special Consideration of Six New Jersey State Colleges." Ph.D. diss., Columbia University, 1974. ProQuest (AAT 7630171).
Zubatsky, David S. "The History of American Colleges and their Libraries in the Seventeenth and Eighteenth Centuries: A Bibliographical Essay." University of Illinois, *Occasional Papers*, 140. Urbana, Illinois: University of Illinois, Graduate School of Library Science, 1979.

1980s

Bailey, Joanne P. "'The Rule Rather than the Exception': Midwest Women as Academic Librarians, 1875–1900." *Journal of Library History* 21 (1986): 673–92.
Barr, Larry J., Haynes McMullen, and Steven G. Leach. *Libraries in American Periodicals Before 1876: A Bibliography with Abstracts and an Index*, edited by Haynes McMullen. Jefferson, North Carolina: McFarland, 1983.
Danton, J. Periam. "University Library Book Budgets—1860, 1910, and 1960: Introduction to an Inquiry." *Library Quarterly* 53 (1983): 384–93.
Davis, Donald G., Jr., and John Mark Tucker. "Academic Libraries." In *American Library History: A Comprehensive Guide to the Literature*, 127–63. Santa Barbara, California: ABC-CLIO, 1989.
Davis, Donald G., Jr., and John Mark Tucker. "'The Past Before Us': The Historiography of Academic Librarianship, Past and Future." In *Building on the First Century: Proceedings of the Fifth National Conference of College and Research Libraries Cincinnati, Ohio, April 5–8, 1989*, edited by Janice C. Fennell, 66–70. Chicago: Association of College and Research Libraries, 1989.
Geiger, Roger L. *To Advance Knowledge: The Growth of American Research Universities, 1900–1940*. New York: Oxford University Press, 1986.
Grotzinger, Laurel A. "Ten Years Work in Library History: The Monograph from 1975 to 1985." *Library Science Annual* 2 (1986): 56–69.
Hale, Charles E. "The College Library Section: 1889–1923: Predecessor to the Association of College and Research Libraries." In *Academic Librarianship Past, Present, and Future: A Festschrift in Honor of David Kaser*, edited by John Richardson, Jr., and Jinnie Y. Davis, 81–96. Englewood, Colorado: Libraries Unlimited, 1989.
Hamlin, Arthur T. *The University Library in the United States: Its Origins and Development*. University of Pennsylvania Press, 1981.
Hanson, Eugene R. "College Libraries: The Colonial Period to the Twentieth Century." *Advances in Library Administration and Organization* 8 (1989): 171–99.
Hardesty, Larry L., John P. Schmitt, and John Mark Tucker, comps. *User Instruction in Academic Libraries: A Century of Selected Readings*. Metuchen, New Jersey: Scarecrow Press, 1986.
Harris, Michael H. "State, Class, and Cultural Reproduction: Toward a Theory of Library Service in the United States." *Advances in Librarianship* 14 (1986): 211–52.
Holley, Edward G. "ACRL's Fiftieth Anniversary: For Reflection, Celebration, and for Anticipation." *College & Research Libraries* 50 (1989): 11–24.
Horowitz, Helen Lefkowitz. *Alma Mater: Design and Experience in the Women's Colleges from Their Nineteenth-Century Beginnings to the 1930s*. New York: Alfred A. Knopf, 1984.
Horowitz, Helen Lefkowitz. *Campus Life: Undergraduate Cultures from the End of the Eighteenth Century to the Present*. Chicago, Illinois: University of Chicago Press, 1987.
Jones, Plummer Alston, Jr. "The History and Development of Libraries in American Higher Education." *College & Research Libraries News* 50 (1989): 561–64.
Kaplan, Louis. "On the Road to Participative Management, the American Academic Library, 1934–1970." *Libri* 38 (1988): 314–20.
Kaser, David. "Collection Building in American Universities." In *University Library History: An International Review*, edited by James Thompson, 33–55. New York: K.G. Saur, 1980.
Levine, David O. *The American College and the Culture of Aspiration, 1915–1940*. Ithaca, New York: Cornell University Press, 1986.
Miksa, Francis L. "Machlup's Categories of Knowledge as a Framework for Viewing Library and Information Science History." *Journal of Library History* 20 (1985): 157–72.
Miksa, Francis L. *The Subject in the Dictionary Catalog from Cutter to the Present*. Chicago, Illinois: American Library Association, 1983.
Orne, Jerrold. "The Evolution of Academic Library Staff in the United States." In *University Library History: An International Review*, edited by James Thompson, 77–91. New York: K.G. Sauer, 1980.
Person, Roland Conrad. *A New Path: Undergraduate Libraries at United States and Canadian Universities, 1949–1987*. Westport, Connecticut: Greenwood Press, 1988.
Shiflett, Orvin Lee. *Origins of American Academic Librarianship*. Norwood, New Jersey: Ablex, 1981.
Waldo, Michael J. "A Comparative Analysis of Nineteenth-Century Academic and Literary Society Library Collections in the Midwest." Ph.D. diss., Indiana University, 1985. ProQuest (AAT 8527040).
Wiegand, Wayne A. *Leaders in American Academic Librarianship, 1925–1975*. Pittsburgh, Pennsylvania: Beta Phi Mu, 1983.
Williams, Robert V. "Theoretical Issues and Constructs Underlying the Study of Library Development." *Libri* 34 (1984): 1–16.
Young, Arthur P. "College and University Libraries." In *American Library History: A Bibliography of Dissertations and Theses*, 151–216, 399–400. Metuchen, New Jersey: Scarecrow Press, 1988.
Young, Arthur P. *Higher Education in American Life: 1636–1986: A Bibliography of Dissertations and Theses*. New York: Greenwood Press, 1988.

1990s

"Academic Libraries." In *World Encyclopedia of Library and Information Services*. 3rd Ed., 5–29. Chicago, Illinois: American Library Association, 1993.

Brubacher, John S., and Willis Rudy. *Higher Education in Transition: A History of American Colleges and Universities*. 4th Ed. New Brunswick, New Jersey: Transaction Publishers, 1997.

Carmichael, James V., Jr., ed. *Daring to Find Our Names: The Search for Lesbigay Library History*. Westport, Connecticut: Greenwood Press, 1998.

Carmichael, James V., Jr. "Library History without Walls." *Journal of Education for Library and Information Science* 36 (1995): 309–18.

Dain, Phyllis. "Scholarship, Higher Education, and Libraries in the United States: Historical Questions and Quests." In *Libraries and Scholarly Communication in the United States: The Historical Dimension*, edited by Phyllis Dain and John Y. Cole. New York: Greenwood Press, 1990.

Dain, Phyllis, and John Y. Cole, eds. *Libraries and Scholarly Communication in the United States: The Historical Dimension*. New York: Greenwood Press, 1990.

Davis, Donald G., Jr., and John Mark Tucker. "Before the Waters Parted: Minority Leadership in Academic and Research Libraries." In *Academic Libraries: Achieving Excellence in Higher Education: Proceedings of the Sixth National Conference of the Association of College and Research Libraries, Salt Lake City, Utah, April 12–14, 1992*, edited by Thomas Kirk, 48–53. Chicago, Illinois: Association of College and Research Libraries, 1992.

Davis, Donald G., Jr., and John Mark Tucker. "Change and Tradition in Land-Grant University Libraries." In *For the Good of the Order: Essays in Honor of Edward G. Holley*, edited by Delmus E. Williams, et al, 135–60. Greenwich, Connecticut: JAI Press, 1994.

Davis, Donald G., Jr., and Wayne A. Wiegand, eds. *Encyclopedia of Library History*. New York: Garland, 1994.

Ernest, Douglas J. "Historiography and the Land-Grant University Library." *Advances in Librarianship* 22 (1998): 155–81.

Graham, Hugh Davis, and Nancy Diamond. *The Rise of American Research Universities: Elites and Challengers in the Postwar Era*. Baltimore, Maryland: Johns Hopkins University Press, 1997.

Harris, Michael H., and Stanley Hannah. "Why Do We Study the History of Libraries? A Meditation on the Perils of Ahistoricism in the Information Era." *Library & Information Science Research* 14 (1992): 123–30.

Higley, Georgia M. "College, Community, and Librarianship: Women Librarians at the Western Land-Grant Colleges." In *Reclaiming the American Library Past: Writing the Women In*, edited by Suzanne Hildenbrand, 53–98. Norwood, New Jersey: Ablex, 1996.

Hildenbrand, Suzanne, ed. *Reclaiming the American Library Past: Writing the Women In*. Norwood, New Jersey: Ablex, 1996.

Kaser, David. "Andrew Carnegie and the Black College Libraries." In *For the Good of the Order: Essays in Honor of Edward G. Holley*, edited by Delmus E. Williams, et al., 119–33. Greenwich, Connecticut: JAI Press, 1994.

Leslie, W. Bruce. *Gentlemen and Scholars: College and Community in the "Age of the University," 1865–1917*. University Park, Pennsylvania: Pennsylvania State University Press, 1992.

Lucas, Christopher J. *American Higher Education: A History*. New York: St. Martin's, 1994.

Marsden, George M. *The Soul of the American University: From Protestant Establishment to Established Nonbelief*. New York: Oxford University Press, 1994.

McMullen, Haynes. "The Founding of Libraries in American Colleges and Professional Schools Before 1876." In *For the Good of the Order: Essays in Honor of Edward G. Holley*, edited by Delmus E. Williams, et al, 37–54. Greenwich, Connecticut: JAI Press, 1994.

Musmann, Klaus. *Technological Innovation in Libraries 1860–1960: An Anecdotal History*. Westport, Connecticut: Greenwood Press, 1993.

Shiflett, O. Lee. "Academic Libraries." In *Encyclopedia of Library History*, edited by Wayne A. Wiegand and Donald G. Davis, Jr., 5–14. New York: Garland, 1994.

Sinnette, Elinor Des Verney, W. Paul Coates, and Thomas C. Battle, eds. *Black Bibliophiles and Collectors: Preservers of Black History*. Washington, D.C.: Howard University Press, 1990.

Smith, Jessie Carney. "The Four Cultures: Twenty Years Later." In *The Black Librarian in America Revisited*, edited by E.J. Josey, 143–51. Metuchen, New Jersey: Scarecrow Press, 1994.

Smith, K. Wayne. *OCLC, 1967–1997: Thirty Years of Furthering Access to the World's Information*. New York: Haworth Press, 1998.

Stevens, Norman. "Research Libraries: Past, Present, and Future." *Advances in Librarianship* 17 (1993): 79–109.

Stieg, Margaret F. "The Dangers of Ahistoricism." *Journal of Library and Information Science Education* 34 (1993): 275–78.

Terry, James L. "Automated Library Systems: A History of Constraints and Opportunities." *Advances in Librarianship* 22 (1998): 21–38.

Tucker, John Mark, ed. *Untold Stories: Civil Rights, Libraries, and Black Librarianship.* Champaign, Illinois: University of Illinois, Graduate School of Library and Information Science, 1998.

Wiegand, Wayne A. "Research Libraries, the Ideology of Reading, and Scholarly Communication, 1876–1900." In *Libraries and Scholarly Communication in the United States: The Historical Dimension,* edited by Phyllis Dain and John Y. Cole, 71–87. New York: Greenwood Press, 1990.

2000s

Battles, Matthew. *The Library: An Unquiet History.* New York: W.W. Norton, 2003.

Bostick, Sharon. "The History and Development of Academic Library Consortia in the United States." *Journal of Academic Librarianship* 27 (2001): 128–30.

Burke, Colin. "The Ford Foundation's Search for an American Library Laboratory." *IEEE Annals of the History of Computing* 24 (2002): 56–74.

Davis, Donald G., Jr., and Andrew Wertheimer, eds. *Library History Research in America: Essays Commemorating the Fiftieth Anniversary of the Library History Round Table. American Library Association.* Washington, D.C.: Library of Congress, Center for the Book, 2000. Also published as *Libraries & Culture* 35:1 (Winter 2000).

DeLoach, Marva L., and E.J. Josey, eds. *Handbook of Black Librarianship.* Lanham, Maryland: Scarecrow Press, 2000.

Gyure, Dale Allen. "The Heart of the University: A History of the Library as an Architectural Symbol of American Higher Education." *Winterthur Portfolio* 42 (2008): 107–32.

Hessel, Alfred, Reuben Peiss, and Don Henrich Tolzman. *The Memory of Mankind: The Story of Libraries Since the Dawn of History.* New Castle, Delaware: Oak Knoll Press, 2001.

Kirk, Thomas G., Jr. "College Libraries." *Encyclopedia of Library and Information Science.* 2nd Ed. Vol. 1: 591–601. New York: Marcel Dekker, 2003.

Lerner, Fred. *The Story of Libraries: From the Invention of Writing to the Computer Age.* 2nd Ed. New York: Continuum, 2009.

McMullen, Haynes. *American Libraries Before 1876.* Westport, Connecticut: Greenwood Press, 2000.

Malone, Cheryl Knott. "African American Libraries." In *International Dictionary of Library Histories, Volume I,* edited by David H. Stam, 3–5. Chicago, Illinois: Fitzroy Dearborn, 2001.

Manquel, Alberto. *The Library at Night.* New Haven, Connecticut: Yale University Press, 2006.

Murray, Stuart A.P. *The Library: An Illustrated History.* Introduction by Donald G. Davis, Jr. Foreword by Nicholas A. Basbanes. New York: Skyhorse Publishing and Chicago, Illinois: American Library Association, 2009.

Owens, Irene. "Stories Told but Not Yet Unfinished: Challenges Facing African-American Libraries and Special Collections in Historically Black Colleges and Universities." In *Diversity Now: People, Collections, and Services in Academic Libraries: Selected Papers from the Big 12 Plus Libraries Consortium Diversity Conference,* edited by Teresa Y. Neely and Kuang-Hwei (Janet) Lee-Smeltzer, 165–82. New York: Haworth Press, 2002. Co-published as *Journal of Library Administration* 33, Nos. 1/2 and 3/4 (2001).

Rau, Erik P. "Managing the Machine in the Stacks: Operations Research, Bibliographic Control, and Library Computerization, 1950–2000." *Library History* 23 (2007): 151–68.

Schlup, Leonard C., and Stephen H. Paschen, eds. *Librarianship in Gilded Age America: An Anthology of Writings, 1868–1901.* Jefferson, North Carolina: McFarland, 2009.

Stam, David H., ed. *International Dictionary of Library Histories,* 2 vols. Chicago, Illinois: Fitzroy Dearborn, 2001.

Stam, Deirdre E. "Women's Libraries." In *International Dictionary of Library Histories, Volume I,* edited by David H. Stam, 175–79. Chicago, Illinois: Fitzroy Dearborn, 2001.

Tucker, John Mark. "Land-Grant University Libraries." In *International Dictionary of Library Histories, Volume I,* edited by David H. Stam, 88–90. Chicago, Illinois: Fitzroy Dearborn, 2001.

Valentine, Patrick M. "Small Select Library or Miserable Excuse: Antebellum College Libraries in the American Southeast." *Southeastern Librarian* 54 (2006): 7–11.

Wagner, Ralph Dinsmore. "A History of the Farmington Plan." Ph.D. diss., University of Illinois at Urbana-Champaign, 2000. ProQuest (AAT 9990178).

Weiner, Sharon Gray. "The History of Academic Libraries in the United States: A Review of the Literature." *Library Philosophy and Practice* 7 (2005): 1–12.

Young, Arthur P. "Aftermath of a Prediction: F.W. Lancaster and the Paperless Society." *Library Trends* 56 (2008): 843–58.

2010s

Axtell, James. *Wisdom's Workshop: The Rise of the Modern University.* Princeton, New Jersey: Princeton University Press, 2016.

Bivins-Tatum, Wayne. *Libraries and the Enlightenment*. Los Angeles, California: Library Juice Press, 2011.
Geiger, Roger L. *The History of American Higher Education: Learning and Culture from the Founding to World War II*. Princeton, New Jersey: Princeton University Press, 2014.
Goedeken, Edward A., and John Mark Tucker. "History of Libraries." *Encyclopedia of Library and Information Sciences*. 3d Ed. Vol. 3, 2080–95. Boca Raton, Florida: CRC Press, 2010.
Labaree, David F. *A Perfect Mess: The Unlikely Ascendancy of American Higher Education*. Chicago, Illinois: University of Chicago Press, 2017.
Richards, Pamela Spence, Wayne A. Wiegand, and Marija Dalbello, eds. *A History of Modern Librarianship: Constructing the Heritage of Western Cultures*. Santa Barbara, California: Libraries Unlimited, 2015.
Thelin, John R. *A History of American Higher Education*. 3rd Ed. Baltimore, Maryland: Johns Hopkins University Press, 2019.
Valentine, Patrick M. *A Social History of Books and Libraries from Cuneiform to Bytes*. Lanham, Maryland: Scarecrow Press, 2012.
Virgil, Candance L. "An Analysis of the Academic Library and the Changing Role of the Academic Librarian in Higher Education: 1975–2012." Ed.D. diss., Lindenwood University, 2013. ProQuest (AAT 3601227).

About the Contributors

Arthur E. **Bestor,** Jr. (1890–1994) taught at Columbia, Wisconsin, Stanford, Illinois, and the University of Washington. He earned Ph.B. and Ph.D. degrees from Yale, and published *Backwoods Utopias: The Sectarian and Owenite Phases of Communitarian Socialism in America: 1663–1829* (1950), winner of the Arthur J. Beveridge Award from the American Historical Association for the Best English Language Book in American History. Later research interests included public education and constitutional history.

Fay M. **Blake** (1920–2011) was a senior lecturer in the School of Library and Information Studies, University of California. She held a B.A. from Hunter College, an M.S. in L.S. from the University of Southern California, and M.A. and Ph.D. degrees from UCLA. She had served in the libraries at California Polytechnic and UCLA, and researched topics of information access in a post-industrial society.

John M. **Budd** is a professor emeritus at the School of Information Science and Learning Technologies, University of Missouri. He holds a B.A. and an M.L.S. from LSU, an M.A. from Texas, and a Ph.D. from North Carolina. He is a national leader on the topics of scholarly communication, education for librarianship, and academic libraries. His publications include *Six Issues Facing Libraries Today: Critical Perspectives* (2017), and his classic, *The Changing Academic Library: Operations, Culture, Environments* (3rd. ed., 2018) issued by ACRL.

John **Caldwell** served as the Director of the Library and a professor of history at Augustana College. He earned a B.A. from St. Vincent College, an M.A. from Pennsylvania, and an M.L.S. from Drexel. He also served in libraries at Drew University, California Lutheran, and California State–Stanislaus. He is interested in American history and biography, and his publications include *A History of American Colleges and Universities: A Bibliography* (1977).

Kenneth **Carpenter** was the Assistant Director for Research Resources for Harvard University Library. He earned an A.B. from Bowdoin and an M.S. in L.S. from Simmons. He published *The First 350 Years of the Harvard University Library: Description of an Exhibition* (1986) and *Readers and Libraries: Toward a History of Libraries and Culture in America* (1996); he also served as editor of the *Harvard Library Bulletin*.

Howard **Clayton** (1929–2009) taught in the School of Library Science (Library and Information Studies) at the University of Oklahoma. He had earned degrees in education from Emporia State in Kansas, music from the University of Chicago, and a Ph.D. from Oklahoma. He served in libraries at Kansas State, Southwestern College, State University College (New York) in Brockport, and Western Illinois, and he co-founded and edited the *Library College-Journal*.

Eric **Glasgow** (1925–2005) tutored in modern history at the Open University and taught history and English in the external B.A. degree program at the University of London. He held M.A. and Ph.D. degrees, having graduated from St. John's College, Cambridge, and Manchester University. He was interested in the history of publishing, public libraries, and local history, and his publications included *Some Early Greek Scholars in England* (1981).

272   About the Contributors

Michael H. **Harris** (1941–2017) was a professor emeritus at the School of Library and Information Science at the University of Kentucky. He earned a B.S.at North Dakota, an M.S.L.S. from Illinois, and a Ph.D. from Indiana. He compiled *Reader in American Library History* (1971) and he authored or co-authored several editions of *History of Libraries in the Western World* (1976–1999). He is well-remembered for analyzing the motivations of library founders, thus redirecting, and expanding public library historiography.

Jean-Pierre V.M. **Hérubel** is a professor at Purdue University Libraries and School of Information Studies. He earned a B.A. and MA from Penn State and an M.L.S. and Ph.D. from Kent State. His interests include print culture, aesthetics, the historiography of librarianship, and the history and sociology of scholarly communication. His publications include *Annales Historiography and Theory: A Selective and Annotated Bibliography* (1994).

Edward G. **Holley** (1927–2010) was the Dean of the School of Information and Library Science at the University of North Carolina at Chapel Hill and William Rand Kenan, Jr. Professor. He held a B.A. from Lipscomb, an M.A. in L.S. from Peabody (Vanderbilt), and a Ph.D. from Illinois. He served in libraries at Lipscomb, Illinois, and Houston where he was the Dean of Libraries. An award-winning historian and biographer, he was also President of ALA and Chair of the Board of Trustees of OCLC.

James E. **Hooper** served as the Director of Information Technology at the Baylor School, an academy in Chattanooga, Tennessee. He earned a B.A. from Southwestern (Rhodes College), an M.L.S. from North Carolina, and an M.A. from Illinois where he was mentored by James D. Anderson, a leading authority on the education of African Americans. His interests include the early American republic, twentieth-century American history, and the history of libraries.

Elmer D. **Johnson** (1915–2009) was a librarian and a professor of history at Radford College. He earned an A.B., a Certificate in Library Science, also A.M. and Ph.D. degrees, all from North Carolina. He served in libraries at North Carolina and Southwestern Louisiana (University of Louisiana at Lafayette). An accomplished historian and bibliographer, he published two editions of *History of Libraries in the Western World* (1965, 1970), and a third edition with Michael H. Harris (1976).

Philip D. **Leighton** is an Architectural Planner Emeritus, Stanford University Libraries. For nearly twenty-four years, he directed new construction and remodeling projects, eventually consulting with library and archive facilities worldwide, and emerging as a specialist in disaster preparedness. He edited, with David C. Weber, *Planning Academic and Research Library Buildings* (3rd ed., 1999).

Beverly P. **Lynch** (1935–2020) served as the Dean of the School of Library and Information Science at UCLA, as Executive Secretary of ACRL, and President of ALA. She earned a B.S. from North Dakota State, an M.S. from Illinois, and a Ph.D. from Wisconsin. She held library positions at Marquette and Yale, and the University of Illinois Chicago Circle (Illinois at Chicago) where she was University Librarian. Her research interests included evaluation of library services, and the structure of complex organizations.

Mark L. **McCallon** is a professor and the Associate Dean for Library Information Services at ACU. He holds a B.S. from LeTourneau University, an M.L.S. from TWU, and an Ed.D. from Baylor. His interests include learning commons installations in higher education, electronic resources management, the history and biography of reading and librarianship, and the freedom to read. His conference papers and publications on these topics include an edited issue of *Library Trends*, "New Perspectives on Intellectual Freedom."

Rikk **Mulligan** is a Digital Scholarship Specialist for Carnegie Mellon University Libraries. He holds B.A. and M.A. degrees from George Mason University and a Ph.D. from Michigan State. He has served as consultant, web designer, or lecturer for Longwood University, University of Mary Washington, and Virginia Commonwealth. He also served as Program Officer at the Association for Research Libraries. His interests include digital tools for the humanities, American studies, and popular culture.

John Mark **Tucker** is a professor emeritus of library science at Purdue University; he also served as the Dean of Library and Information Resources at ACU. He earned a B.A. from Lipscomb, M.L.S. and Ed.S. degrees from Peabody (Vanderbilt), and a Ph.D. from Illinois. He is interested in the history of academic libraries, particularly the period of the late nineteenth and early twentieth centuries. His publications include *Untold Stories: Civil Rights, Libraries, and Black Librarianship* (1998).

David C. **Weber** is the Director Emeritus, Stanford University, and past president of two ALA divisions. He holds a B.A. from Colby, a library degree from Columbia, and an M.A. from Harvard, and he directed the Stanford University Libraries from 1969 to 1990. His interests include university library administration and facilities management. He wrote *Practical Lessons in Library Management: Case Studies from the Workplace* (2017), and he edited, with Philip D. Leighton, *Planning Academic and Research Library Buildings* (3rd ed., 1999).

Wayne A. **Wiegand** is the F. William Summers Professor Emeritus of Library and Information Studies and a professor of American studies from Florida State. He holds a B.A. from the University of Wisconsin–Oshkosh, an M.A. from the University of Wisconsin–Milwaukee, M.L.S. from Western Michigan, and a Ph.D. from Southern Illinois. He has integrated library historiography into the wider intellectual terrain of print culture, cultural studies, and American studies. His books about ALA, Melvil Dewey, and the American public library have become definitive resources.

Index

Academic and Research Libraries Personnel Study 211
Adams, Herbert Baxter 110, 115
Adams, John 85
Aesop 76
African Methodist Episcopal Church 139
Agassiz, Louis 49, 107
Agilent Technologies 218
Agricultural Adjustment Administration 157
Aho, John 238
Aiken, Gertrude 142
Alabama A&M University 24, 137
Alabama State University 142
Albion College 61, 62, 63, 65
Alcorn State University 143
Alighieri, Dante 119
Alire, Camila A. 31, 32
Allen, Nancy 14
America Online 225
American Anthropological Society 121
American Antiquarian Society 34
American Association of Teachers Colleges 140
American Association of University Professors 148
American Association of University Women 66
American Baptist Home Mission Board 138
American Chemical Society 111
American Council of Learned Societies 22, 132, 148, 152, 154, 156, 157, 158,
American Documentation Institute 7
American Economic Association 111, 121
American Federation of Teachers 192
American Historical Association 53, 111, 114, 118, 121, 158; Historical Manuscripts Commission 114
American Library Association 3, 22, 53, 113, 114, 140, 141, 143, 152, 160, 190, 192, 195, 201, 202, 203, 204, 205, 206, 207, 209, 210, 211, 212, 213, 214; Association of College and Reference Libraries 204, 205; Association of College and Research Libraries 140, 190, 195, 197, 201, 202, 203, 204, 205, 206, 207, 208, 209, 210, 211, 212, 213, 214; College and Reference Section 54, 202, 204; College Library Advisory Board 204; College Library Section 13, 202; Library History Round Table (LHRT) 3, 230, 234; Rare Books and Manuscripts Section 220, 224
American Mathematical Association 121
American Missionary Association 138, 139
American Museum of Natural History 152
American Philosophical Society 106, 158
American Society for Information Science 7
American Sociological Society 121
American Statistical Association 121
Amherst College 19, 24, 48
Anderson, Anne Rucker 142
Anderson, Barbara 191

Anderson, Greg 14
Angell, James B. 32, 51, 107
Antioch College 32, 61
Apprentices' Library Company 106
Aquinas, St. Thomas 75
Aristotle 76
Armitage, David 4, 5
ARPANET 225
Arthur, T. S. 118
Association of American Universities 54
Association of Research Libraries 31, 55, 189, 204, 205, 206, 209, 220, 226; Administrators Round Table 204
Astor, John Jacob 89
Astor Library 91
Atkins, Stephen E. 16, 29, 30
Atlanta University (Clark Atlanta) 24, 25, 138, 140, 144; School of Library Service 143
Attebury, Ramirose 19
Atwood, Rufus B. 142
Augst, Thomas 230
Augustana College 61, 64, 65
Augustine 75
Avram, Henriette D. 211

Bacon, Francis 76, 119
Bailey, George 207
Baker and Taylor & Co. 211
Baldridge, J. Victor 205
Ball State University 16
Bancroft, George 93, 105
Barnard, Henry 96
Barr, Larry J. 8
Barringer, Sallie H. 14
Bate, W. Jackson 10
Battles, Matthew 33
Bechtel, Elizabeth 63
Beittle, A.B. 140
Belcher, Jonathan 79
Beloit College 62, 64
Bell, Steven 14
Bennett, Scott 222
Berkeley, George 79
Berlin Wall 217, 218
Berrigan, Daniel 192
Berrigan, Philip 192
Bertram, James 28
Bestor, Arthur E., Jr. 2, 101, 103
Beza, Theodore 75
Bibliothèque Nationale 149
Billings, Harold W. 180
Binkley, Robert C. 132, 133, 147, 148, 152, 153, 155, 156, 157, 158, 159, 160, 161, 162

276　Index

Bishop, William Warner 28, 52, 53, 202, 204
Bivens-Tatum, Wayne 33, 230
Black, Alistair 239
Blair, James 78, 79
Blake, Fay M. 2, 190, 191, 193, 198
Bluefield State College 140
Bobinski, George S. 7, 29
Boisse, Joseph W. 206
Boll, John 19
Bonta, Bruce D. 179
Boorstin, Daniel J. 81
Borden, Fanny 204
Boston Athenaeum 105, 202
Boston Public Library 202
Bourdieu, Pierre 245
Bowdoin College 86
Bowman, Martha A. 213
Boyd, Julian 31
Boydell, John 86
Boyle, Robert 46
Branscomb, B. Harvie 132
Branscomb, Lewis 54, 195
Bristowe, Reverend Dr. 79
British Historical Manuscripts Commission 114
British Museum 160
Brodhead, Richard 123, 125, 126, 127
Brookings Institution 149
Brooklyn College 14
Brooklyn Collegiate and Polytechnic Institute 90
Brough, Kenneth J. 12, 16, 18, 34
Brown, Charles Harvey 27, 203, 204, 205, 207, 213
Brown, Helen 207
Brown, Martha 142
Brown, Ollie Lee 142
Brown University 4, 18, 19, 24, 32, 46 48, 71, 79
Browne, Daniel 46
Brundin, Robert 19
Bryce, Herrington 31
Bryn Mawr College 20
Buchanan, Anne L. 17, 231
Buck, Solon J. 152
Buckland, Michael 225, 226
Bucknell University 192
Budd, John M. 1, 31, 32, 220, 221, 223
Bureau of Rolls 114
Burns, Robert 94, 119
Burton, Ernest 51
Bush, Vannevar 33, 51, 161
Butler, Nicholas Murray 32, 51
Butler, Pierce 6
Butlin, Iva M. 62

Caldwell, John 43, 44
California Library Association 197
California State College Librarians Round Table 197
Calvin, John 75
Carleton College 19
Carmichael, James V., Jr. 14, 15
Carnegie, Andrew 28
Carnegie Corporation 22, 28, 29, 53, 143, 144, 149, 152, 158, 203, 204, 229
Carnegie Endowment for International Peace 149
Carnegie Foundation for the Advancement of Teaching 131
Carnegie Institution of Washington 114, 115
Carpenter, Frederic Ives 154
Carpenter, Kenneth E. 14, 132, 147, 230
Carpenter, Olie Atkins 142
Carroll College 61
Carthage College 61, 65
Case Western Reserve University 7, 24, 139, 141, 152; Adelbert College 141; Center for Documentation and Communications Research 7
Center for Research Libraries (CRL) 28
Channing, Edward 114
Chapman, George 76
Chase, Sophia May 61
Cheyney University 24
Chrysostom 75
Cicero 4
Cincinnati College 90
Cisco Systems 218
Citadel (Military College of South Carolina) 82
City University of New York (CUNY) 55
Clap, Thomas 79
Clark, S.N. (Selden Noyes) 229
Clark Atlanta University 140, 144; see also Atlanta University
Clark University 51, 115
Clayton, Howard 82, 85
Clemons, Harry 18
Clift, David 205, 207
Cline, Gloria S. 206, 208
Cogswell, Joseph 91, 92
Colby College 16, 24
College of New Jersey 79, 86
College of Physicians 106
College of William and Mary 18, 45, 46, 47, 71, 78, 88
College of Wooster 62, 64, 65
Colson, John Calvin 9, 10, 15
Columbia University 16, 18, 20, 25, 27, 32, 45, 51, 52, 54, 71, 79, 119, 121, 122, 155, 172, 176, 177; School of Library Service 11
Committee on Medical Research 167
CompuServe 225
Conat, Mabel L. 206
Coolidge, Calvin 135
Cooper, James 94
Cooper, Peter 89
Cooper Union 90
Cornell, Robert F. 62
Cornell University 9, 16, 20, 21, 24, 25, 27, 50, 51, 52, 54, 107, 115, 175, 179, 180
Coughlin, Carolyn M. 32, 33
Council on Library and Information Resources 7, 22, 209, 222
Crawford, Alice 230
Cresap, Mark W., Jr. 205
Cummings, Martin 225
Cummings, Hilliard and Co. 88
Curtis, Florence Rising 140, 141, 142, 143
Cutler, Phyllis 180
Cutter, Charles Ammi 113, 202

Dahlman, Fredrich G. 114
Dain, Phyllis 10, 11
Dalton, Margaret Stieg see Stieg, Margaret
Dana, John Cotton 206
Danton, J. Periam 12, 16, 20, 21, 23, 26, 29
Darnton, Robert 34, 230
DARPA 225
Dartmouth College 18, 20, 24, 45, 71, 80, 89
Darwin, Charles 120, 121
Davenport, F. Garvin 61
Davidson College 24
Davis, Donald G., Jr. 3, 13, 14, 18, 238

Davis, Raymond C. 119
Davis, T.K. (Thomas Kirby) 64
Dawe, Grosvenor 229
Dawson, John 54
Day, Jeremiah 90
DeMott, H.C. 62
Dempsey, Lorcan 14
DePauw University 61, 62, 63, 64, 65
Descartes, René 76
Detroit Public Library 206
DeVinney, Gemma 14
Dewey, John 132
Dewey, Melvil 9, 11, 26, 51, 63, 113, 119, 229
Dickens, Charles 119
Dickenson, Joseph R. 62
Dickinson, Emily 126
Dickinson College 24
Diderot, Denis 33
Dillard University 25, 139, 144
Dix, William S. 27
Dougherty, Richard M. 27, 208
Douglas, Boyd 192
Downs, Robert B. 13, 27, 31, 55, 61, 195, 208, 210, 211
Draper, Lyman 121
Drexel University 179
Dryden, John 94
DSpace 220
Duke University 13, 54; Woman's College 27
Dummer, Jeremiah 46
Dunbar, Ralph McNeal 137
Dunlap, Connie R. 13

E*Trade 218
Earlham College 19, 24, 61, 62, 65
Eastern New Mexico State University 16
Eaton, Andrew 54
eBay 218
Ebeling, Christoph Daniel 91
Edmonds, Anne C. 207
Edwards, Morgan 79
Edwards Brothers, Inc. 156, 160
Eliot, Charles W. 32, 49, 51, 100, 107, 108
Ellsworth, Ralph E. 27, 54, 205, 208, 213
Emerson, Oliver Farrar 122
Emerson, Ralph Waldo 99, 118, 119
Emory University 27, 32
Environmental Sciences Service Administration 10
Erickson, Ernst 19
Eringhouse, J.C.B. 137
Eureka College 16, 61
Evans, Charles 86, 141
Evans, G. Edward 31, 32
Evans, Luther H. 158
Everett, Edward 91

Fairchild Semiconductor 218
Farmington Plan 12, 21, 22, 31, 160
Fay, Sidney B. 155
Fayetteville State University 137
Feng, Y.T. 177
Fields, James 123
First World Congress of Libraries and Bibliography 153
Fisk University 16, 24, 25, 135, 137, 138, 140, 141, 142, 144
Fister, Barbara 14
Florida State University 11, 16; School of Library and Information Studies 27

Force, Peter 121
Foster, William 119
Foucault, Michel 245
Franklin, Benjamin 70, 79
Freedman's [aka Freedmen's] Bureau 136
Freeman, Michael Stuart 20
Fullerton Junior College 19
Fussler, Herman 54

Gardner, Richard 209
Gates, Jean Key 23
General Education Board 131, 136, 140, 143, 144, 149
Geodetic Survey 92
Geological Society of America 121
George Peabody College for Teachers 16, 18
Gertzog, Alice 32, 33
GI Bill (Servicemen's Readjustment Act) 54, 224
Gibbon, Edward 93
Gibbs, Margaret Jane 63
Giles, Louise 207
Gilman, Daniel Coit 32, 51, 121
Gilmer, Francis Walker 88
Glasgow, Eric 71, 73
Goedeken, Edward A. 3, 14
Göethe, Johann Wolfgang von 119
Goldschmidt, Robert 154
Goodrich, Francis L.D. 28
Google 33, 34, 218
Gormley, Mark 207
Graff, Gerald 125, 127
Gras, N.S.B. 152, 159
Greenwood Press 8
Gregorian, Vartan 32
Griggs, Lillian Baker 27
Guldi, Jo 4, 5
Gutenberg, Johannes 172

Hale, Charles E. 208, 214
Hamerow, Theodore S. 127
Hamilton College 24
Hamlin, Arthur T. 5, 16, 26, 27, 34, 207
Hampton University 25, 137, 138, 140, 143; Library School 141, 142, 143
Hardin, Willie 19
Harding, Thomas S. 12, 16, 23, 24, 34
Haro, Robert P. 196
Harper, William Rainey 32, 51
Harris, Michael H. 2, 13, 27, 70, 71, 78, 82
Harris, William T. 92
Harrison, Frederick 118
Harrisse, Henry 160
Hart, Albert Bushnell 114
Harter, Michael D. 114
Harvard, John 3, 45, 70, 71, 73, 74, 75, 76, 78, 263
Harvard University 4, 14, 16, 18, 19, 24, 25, 27, 29, 31, 32, 34, 45, 46, 47, 48, 49, 52, 53, 55, 70, 71, 73, 74, 75, 76, 78, 80, 89, 91, 92, 93, 94, 99, 100, 105, 107, 108, 112, 113, 122, 150, 152, 154, 155, 159, 172, 173, 177, 202, 203
Harvard, Robert 73
Harwell, Richard B. 207, 208
Hassen, Marjorie 20
Hatch Act of 1877 224
Haverford College 20
Hawthorne, Nathaniel 119
Heathcote, Denis 176
Hemmes, Mrs. L.J. 62
Henrico Indian College 78
Herskovits, Melville J. 52

278 Index

Hérubel, Jean-Pierre V.M. 2, 17, 222, 231, 233
Hewlett, William 218
Hewlett Foundation 220
Hewlett-Packard 218
Higginbotham, Barbra Buckner 14
Higher Education Act of 1965 53, 54, 55
Highsmith, John Henry 140
Hilliard, William 88
Hinchcliff, Bill 198
Hintz, Carl 54
Hirshberg, Herbert S. 139
Historical Society of Pennsylvania 106
Holland, Philemon 76
Holley, Edward G. 2, 4, 13, 20, 27, 190, 201
Holmes, Oliver Wendell 119
Homer 76, 119
Hooper, James E. 132, 135
Hoover, Herbert 135, 155
Hope College 61, 63
Hopkins, Mark 86
Horn, Zoia 192
Houghton Mifflin 123
Howard University 24, 25, 135, 136, 137, 138, 139, 141, 144, 207
Howells, William Dean 123
Hulbert, James 142
Humboldt University of Berlin 107
Huntington Library 157
Huston-Tillotson University 139
Hutchins, Robert Maynard 132

Illinois College 24, 61, 65
Illinois Historical Survey 115
Illinois Wesleyan College 62, 65
Indiana University 8, 13, 16, 19, 20, 21, 54, 214
Institut international de Bibliographie 154
International Society for Cultural History 246
Intuit 218
Iowa State University 3, 19, 27, 204
Ithaka Harbors 218
Ivy, Horace Macauley 140

Jack, Theodore Henley 140
Jackson, Wallace Van 140, 143
Jameson, J. Franklin 5, 6, 132
Jaquess, James F. 61
Jeanes, Anna T. 136
Jefferson, Thomas 48, 88
Jewett, Charles Coffin 49, 87
Johns Hopkins University 9, 20, 25, 32, 51, 99, 107, 108, 110, 113, 115, 121, 122, 124, 176, 203, 222
Johnson, Elmer D. 71, 78
Johnson, Richard D. 13, 208, 214
Johnson, Samuel 10, 46
Joint Committee on Materials for Research 132, 147, 148, 152, 155, 156, 157, 158, 159
Jones, Faustina 142
Jones, Thomas Jesse 136, 140
Jones, Virginia Lacy 143
Josey, E.J. 198
JSTOR 218, 219
Juvenal 76

Kalamazoo College 62, 64, 65
Kaser, David 13, 16, 27, 30, 189, 201, 208
Kaufman, Paula 176
Kentucky Academy 90
Kentucky State University 142

Kenyon College 62, 63, 66
Keppel, Frederick P. 28, 158, 203
Kerr, Clark 195
Kilgour, Frederick G. 211
King Charles XV 65
King's College 79
Kingsley, James L. 90
Klein, Arthur J. 132, 136, 137, 138, 139, 140, 142
Knight, Edgar W. 142
Knox College 24, 27
Knoxville College 24, 141
Kraus, Joe 18, 46, 208
Kroth, Michael 19
Kuhlman, A. Frederick 201, 203, 207

Land Grant Act of 1890 120
Larned, Josephus Nelson 114
Laud, William 74
Laura Spelman Rockefeller Memorial 150
Law Association Library 106
Leach, Steven G. 8
Lear, Bernadette A. 230
Leighton, Philip D. 168, 169, 171
Leland, Waldo G. 152, 158
Lester, Mrs. A.E. 62
Lester, Robert M. 28
Lewis, David 225
Lewis, Emma 142
Lewis, Willard 204
Librarians Association of the University of California (LAUC) 196, 197
Library Company of Philadelphia 106
Library of Congress 14, 31, 95, 112, 113, 114, 121, 150, 154, 157, 160, 168; Division of Manuscripts 114
Licklider, J.C.R. 225
Lincoln University (Pennsylvania) 25, 135
LinkedIn 218
Locke, John 46
Logan, James 70
Logsdon, Richard 54
Long Beach City College 19
Longfellow, Henry Wadsworth 91, 93, 105
Los Angeles City College 19
Louisiana State University 11, 16, 18, 27, 32
Louisville Free Public Library: Colored Branch 142
Lowell, John 89, 93, 105
Luther, Martin 75
Lydenberg, Harry Miller 152, 153, 159
Lyells, Ruby Stutts 143
Lyle, Guy R. 27, 28, 32, 33
Lynch, Beverly P. 2, 27, 28, 32, 43, 206, 207, 221
Lynch, Clifford 57
Lynch, Mary Jo 11

MacLeish, Archibald 31, 160
MacMurray College 61, 64, 65
Macomb County Community College 207
Madison, James 89
Manguel, Alberto 33, 230
Mann, Horace 92, 90, 148
Marian College 19
Marietta College 61, 65
Martell, Charles 208
Martin, Susan K. 172, 176
Martin Luther University of Halle-Wittenberg 107
Massachusetts Bay Colony 74
Massachusetts Board of Education 90
Massachusetts Historical Society 111

Index   279

Massachusetts Institute of Technology (MIT)   25, 161, 220, 225
Mather, Cotton   70, 73
Mathews, William   119
McAllister, Elizabeth   192
McAnally, Arthur   54, 55
McCarthy, Stephen   9, 27, 54
McCormick, Willard Francis   205
McCrum, Blanche Prichard   27, 204, 205, 207, 213
McCuistion, Fred   140
McDiarmid, Errett   54
McDonald, David   175
McFarland & Co., Inc., Publishers   8
McKendree College   61
McMullen, Haynes   8, 82
McNeal, Archie   54
Meharry Medical College   142, 144
Meiklejohn, Alexander   132
Melanchthon, Philip   75
Mellon Foundation   218, 220, 225, 226
Mercantile Library   106
Metcalf, Keyes D.   27, 31, 34, 153, 160, 208, 211
Methodist Episcopal Church   139; Board of Education 138
Miami University   7, 24, 90
Michigan State University   19
Middle States Association of Colleges and Schools   139
Midway, Walter (Sir Walter)   74
Milam, Carl   201, 207
Miller, Richard E. Jr.   19
Miller, Robert   54
Mills College   178, 180
Milton, John   21, 46, 94, 119
Milwaukee Public Library   10
Minnesota Historical Society   152
Miranda, Francisco de   90
Missouri Valley College   16
Mitchell, Breon   21
Mitchell, Elisha   88
Modern Language Association   105, 111, 154
Modesto Junior College   19
Mohrhardt, Foster E.   28, 204, 209
Monmouth College   61, 64
Morehouse College   135, 140
Morgan College   138
Morison, Samuel Eliot   75
Morrill, Justin Smith   101, 120, 224
Morrill Federal Land Grant Act   19, 50, 92, 101, 108, 120, 136, 139, 142, 143, 203, 224
Mosaic (web browser)   225
Motley, John Lothrop   91, 93, 105
Mount Holyoke College   81, 207
Mudge, Isadore G.   111
Muhlenberg College   24
Muller, Robert   208
Mulligan, Rikk   221, 223
Murray, Joseph   79
Murray-Rust, Catherine   175

National Academy of Sciences   149
National Archives and Records Administration   115
National Association of Book Publishers   157
National Defense Research Committee   167
National Education Association   10
National Institutes of Health   168
National Recovery Administration   157
National Research Council   149, 151, 152

National Science Foundation   54, 55, 168
National Union Catalog   168
National Youth Administration   137
Naudé, Gabriel   33
Netflix   218
Netscape Navigator   225
New York Public Library   31, 32, 150, 152, 153, 157, 160, 172
New York Society Library   70
New York State Library   23
New York University   153, 155
Newberry Library   6, 115, 154
Newman, John Henry   119
Newton, Isaac   46
Nix, Athelma   142
North, Thomas   76
North Central Association of Colleges and Schools   139
North Central College   62, 63, 64, 65
Northern Illinois University   10, 16
Northwestern University   16, 52
Norton, Charles B.   49
Norton, W.W.   157
Nott, Eliphalet   86
Novotny, Eric Charles   231

Oberlin College   24, 81, 82, 94, 207
Oberly, Eunice Rockwood   211
OCLC (Online Computer Library Center)   168, 172, 173, 176, 201
Office of Strategic Research and Development   168
Ohio Library Association   141
Ohio State University   195
Ohio University   19, 24, 54, 67, 90
Ohio Wesleyan University   63, 64, 65
Olbrich, William Jr.   20
Olivet College   61, 62, 64
Orne, Jerrold   27, 40
O'Rourke, James R.   142
Osburn, Charles   16, 25, 26, 29, 34
Otlet, Paul   154

Packard, David   218
Paget, Richard M.   205
Pandolfo, Steven   180
Pargellis, Stanley   6
Parkman, Francis   93, 105
Pasadena City College   19
Pascal, Blaise   171
Passet, Joanne   14, 15
Peabody Education Fund   136
Peckham, Howard H.   92
Pelikan, Jaroslav   18
Penn State University   25, 179, 204, 230
Pennsylvania German Society   106
Perry, Bliss   123
Perseus   76
Person, Roland C.   16, 29, 34
Phelps-Stokes Survey of 1916   135, 136
Philadelphia Academy of Natural Sciences   106, 111
Philbrick, Francis S.   158
Plato   119
Plautus   76
Pliny the Elder   76
Plutarch   76, 119
Pollack, Luella   173
Poole, William Frederick   202
Powell, Benjamin   18, 54

Powell, Lawrence Clark 27
Power, Eugene B. 160
Prairie View A&M University 144
Prescott, William Hickling 93, 105
Preussische Staatsbibliothek 157
Princeton University 8, 13, 18, 20, 27, 31, 34, 35, 45, 46, 71, 79, 86, 122, 218
Providence Athenaeum 119
Providence Library Company 79
PSInet 225
Public Works Administration 137
Purdue University 14, 19, 222

Queens College 80
Quinn, Arthur H. 152, 159

Radford, Neil A. 16, 28, 29, 34, 204
Randall, William M. 18
Randolph-Macon College 24
Rayward, W. Boyd 11, 14
Reason, Joseph H. 207
Reed College 172, 173, 178, 180
Reese, Ernest J. 203
Reichel, Mary L. 14
Reichmann, Felix 8, 9
Rensselaer Polytechnic Institute 48, 90, 100, 107
Research Libraries Group (RLG) 172
Research Libraries Information Network 168, 173, 176
Reynolds, Margaret 142
Rhode Island College 79
Ricci, David 118, 125, 127
Rice, Stuart 161
Riggs, Donald E. 140
Robb, Mabel Grace 141
Roberts, Anne F. 14
Rockefeller, John D., Jr. 131, 135, 138
Rockefeller Foundation 22, 138, 149, 160
Rockefeller Institute for Medical Research 149
Rockford College 61, 62, 63, 66
Rom, Pat 192
Roosevelt, Eleanor 136
Roosevelt, Franklin Delano 136, 158
Rose, Jonathan 239
Rosenwald, Julius 135, 136, 142, 143
Rothacker, J. Michael 19
Royal Society of London 70, 149, 223
Rudolph, Frederick 12
Ruml, Beardsley 150
Rush, N. Orwin 207
Rutgers University 18, 24, 27, 45, 71, 80, 85

Sadler, Anne 74
Sadler, John 74
St. Mary's College 62, 66
San Francisco State University 16, 191; Black Student Union 191–92
Santayana, George 1
Savage, James 73
Savannah State University 135
Schellenberg, T.R. 157, 158
Schmidt, C. James 208
Schock, Kate 62
Scholarly Publishing and Academic Resources Coalition (SPARC) 220
Scott, Sir Walter 119
Seabrook, J. Ward 137
Segal, JoAn 207
Shade, Camille Stivers 142

Shakespeare, William 119
Shank, Russell 174, 180
Shaw, Charles B. 28, 156, 204, 209
Shaw, Ralph 27, 28, 42, 208
Shelley, Percy Bysshe 62
Shera, Jesse H. 6–8, 27, 34
Shiflett, Lee 5, 11, 12, 15, 16, 17, 26, 27, 30, 34, 100
Shipton, Clifford K. 34
Shores, Louis 16, 18, 31, 44, 51, 132, 141, 142
Showalter, Elaine 126, 127
Sibley, John Langdon 22, 34, 48, 49
Silliman, Benjamin 107
Simpson, Lowell 19
Slater, John F. 135, 136
Smith, Jessie Carney 16, 19, 24, 25, 35
Smith, Samuel Leonard 143
Smith College 155
Smith-Lever Act of 1914 224
Smithsonian Institution 49, 88, 92, 105
Social Science Research Council 132, 133, 148, 149, 150, 151, 152, 156
Society for the Promotion of Theological and Collegiate Education 65
Society of American Archivists 155
South Carolina State University 137, 139
Southern Association of Colleges and Secondary Schools 139, 140; Highsmith Committee 140; Southern Association Committee 140
Southern Illinois University 16, 29
Southern University 19, 142, 144
Southey, Robert 94
Southwark Grammar School 73
Southworth, Mrs. E.D.E.N. 126
Special Libraries Association 204, 205, 212
Spelman College 140
Spofford, Ainsworth Rand 119, 121, 127
Spotswood, Alexander 79
Stanford University 16, 18, 25, 115, 168, 173, 176, 178, 180, 218; Hoover Library on War, Revolution, and Peace 155
State Historical Society of Wisconsin 10
Steffens, Dorothy 202
Steiner, Fred R. 138
Stern, Fritz 10
Stieg, Margaret 10, 12
Stoddard, Solomon 48
Straight College 146
Stubley, Peter 178
Student Army Training Corps 64
Sullivan, M. Connor 51
Sun Microsystems 218
SUNY (State University of New York system) 55; Albany 14, 141; Buffalo 14, 16
Swarthmore College 20
Sweet, William W. 63
Syracuse University 24

Talladega College 135
Tappan, Henry Philip 48
Tauber, Maurice F. 27, 208
Taylor, Onilda 142
Telford, Frederick 203
Temple of Science 121, 125
Temple University 16
Tennessee State University 19, 142
Tennessee Valley Authority 137
Tennyson, Alfred Lord 119
Terence 76

Terman, Frederick 218
Texas A&M University 16
Texas Southern University 25
Thackeray, William Makepeace 119
Thelin, John R. 81
Thomas, J. Donald 207
Thomison, Dennis 202
Thompson, E.P. (Edward Palmer) 126
Thompson, Lawrence S. 208
Thorndike, Israel 91
Thornton, Eileen 207
Thwaites, Reuben Gold 121, 202
TIAA-CREF 131
Tiananmen Square Massacre 217
Ticknor, George 48, 89, 91, 92, 93, 105
Transylvania College 90
Treyz, Joseph H. 209
Trinity College (Connecticut) 19
Trinity College (N.C.) 24
Trinity University (San Antonio, Texas) 14
Tucker, John Mark 3, 14
Turner, Jonathan B. 108
Tuskegee University 24, 25, 138
Tuttle, Helen W. 13
Tyler, John 81

Union College (N.Y.) 86
United Negro College Fund 188
U.S. Bureau of Education 65, 92, 136, 142, 203
U.S. Civil Service Commission 10
U.S. Department of Education 137, 229
U.S. Department of State 114
U.S. Federal Bureau of Investigation (FBI) 192
U.S. Government Printing Office 154
U.S. House of Representatives 115
U.S. Military Academy 48, 82, 90, 92, 100
U.S. Naval Academy 92
U.S. Office of Strategic Services 7
U.S. Superintendent of Documents 10
University Federation of Teachers AFL-CIO 195
University Microfilms International 28, 160
University of Alabama 11, 16, 18, 188
University of Arizona 18
University of Arkansas, Pine Bluff 19
University of California (system) 18, 55, 120, 122, 188, 196, 198, 209
University of California, Berkeley 16, 18, 21, 25, 52, 120, 122, 174, 175, 188, 194, 195
University of California, Los Angeles (UCLA) 13, 16, 20, 21, 25, 27, 174, 180, 192, 197
University of California, San Diego 25
University of California, Santa Barbara 206
University of Cambridge 69, 73, 91; Emmanuel College 73, 74, 75
University of Chicago 18, 20, 25, 27, 28, 42, 44, 48, 51, 52, 53, 54, 109, 112, 115, 122, 132, 203, 204, 206, 229; Graduate Library School 6–10, 28
University of Chicago Press 6, 7
University of Cincinnati 16
University of Colorado 27, 54
University of Delaware 54
University of Evansville 16
University of Georgia 14, 18, 24, 85, 188
University of Göttingen 20, 91, 107
University of Houston 4
University of Illinois 13, 16, 18, 19, 20, 25, 27, 31, 51, 52, 54, 115, 120, 195, 214; Graduate School of Library and Information Science 8

University of Iowa 16, 19, 27, 29
University of Kansas 20, 27
University of Kentucky 16
University of Maryland 10
University of Miami 24, 54
University of Michigan 18, 19, 21, 24, 25, 27, 28, 32, 52, 99, 107, 119, 175, 180, 204; Department of Library Science 28
University of Minnesota 206
University of Mississippi 188
University of Nebraska 23
University of North Carolina 4, 8, 13, 16, 18, 20, 24, 27, 28, 71, 82, 87, 88, 92, 94
University of North Carolina, Greensboro 11, 16, 32; Library and Information Studies Department 11
University of Oklahoma 54, 55
University of Oregon 24, 54
University of Oxford 69
University of Pennsylvania 24, 45, 79, 106, 112, 121, 152, 158, 207
University of South Carolina 18, 24. 30
University of Southern California 25
University of Sydney (Australia) 16, 28
University of Tennessee 18
University of Texas at Austin 14, 172, 180, 230
University of Toronto Library Automation Systems 168
University of Vienna 12
University of Virginia 18, 24, 48, 86, 88
University of Washington 25
University of Wisconsin 16, 18, 21, 24, 120
University of Wisconsin, La Crosse 12
Urbana College 16
UUNet 225

Valparaiso University 64
Vanderbilt University 16 (see also George Peabody College for Teachers)
Vassar College 204
Vatican Library 28
Veaner, Allen B. 211
Ver Nooy, Winifred 206
Veysey, Laurence R. 132
Vincennes University 90
Virginia Military Institute 82
Virginia Negro Education Association 140
Virginia Union University 135, 138
Virgo, Julie 207
Voigt, Melvin J. 209
Vosper, Robert 13, 20, 21, 27, 30

Wabash College 19, 24, 62, 63, 65
Wagner, Ralph D. 12, 16, 31, 46
Waitz, Georg 114
Wake Forest University 24
Waldo, Michael 19, 24
Walter, Frank K. 205, 206
Waples, Douglas 9, 18
Warren, S.R. (Samuel R.) 229
Washburn University 16
Washington & Lee University 27, 204
Washington, Booker T. 138, 140
Washington Library Network 168
Washington State University 178
Washington University in St. Louis 16, 25, 27, 54
Wasserman, Paul 193
Watters, Mary 65
Wayland, Francis 48

282   Index

Weber, David C. 168, 169
Wedding, Harry Stringham 68
Weiner, Sharon G. 15–17, 34, 230
Wellesley College 27, 207
Wells, H.G. 33
Wesleyan University 19, 209
Western Illinois University 16
Western Reserve University *see* Case Western University
Westfield State University 16
Wheaton, Henry 93
Wheelock, Eleazar 80
White, Andrew D. 50, 51, 107
White, Carl M. 208
Wiegand, Wayne A. 2, 14, 16, 17, 27, 101, 118, 202, 229, 230, 241
Wilberforce University 24, 135, 139
William and Mary *see* College of William and Mary
Williams, Edward Christopher 141
Williams College 16, 19, 180
Williamson, C.C. 53
Wilson, Betsy 14
Wilson, Louis Round 18, 27, 41, 143, 144, 202, 204
Wilson, Woodrow 115, 123
Winship, George Parker 154

Winsor, Justin 34, 53, 54, 114, 202
Winthrop, James 47
Winthrop, John 70, 78
Winthrop, John, Jr. 70
Wissler, Clark 152
Witherspoon, John 79
Wittenberg College 61
Wooster College 61, 64, 65
Works, George Alan 203
Works Progress Administration 132, 148, 158, 160
World Wide Web 225
Wright, R.R. 139
Wyer, James I., Jr. 23
Wynar, Bohdan S. 7

Xavier University of Louisiana 141, 144; Sister Bernadette 141

Yahoo 218
Yale, Elihu 46, 79
Yale University 18, 19, 20, 24, 25, 45, 46, 47, 48, 51, 52, 70, 71, 79, 86, 90, 91, 99, 100, 107, 108, 113, 122, 150, 157, 161, 172, 222
Yocom, Frances L. 141
Yueh, Norma N. 19

Milton Keynes UK
Ingram Content Group UK Ltd.
UKHW051832170524
442876UK00016B/556